Political Psychology
A Social Psychological
Approach

BPS Textbooks in Psychology

BPS Wiley presents a comprehensive and authoritative series covering everything a student needs in order to complete an undergraduate degree in psychology. Refreshingly written to consider more than North American research, this series is the first to give a truly international perspective. Written by the very best names in the field, the series offers an extensive range of titles from introductory level through to final year optional modules, and every text fully complies with the BPS syllabus in the topic. No other series bears the BPS seal of approval!

Many of the books are supported by a companion website, featuring additional resource materials for both instructors and students, designed to encourage critical thinking, and providing for all your course lecturing and testing needs.

For other titles in this series, please go to http://psychsource.bps.org.uk

Political Psychology
A Social Psychological Approach

EDITED BY
CHRISTOPHER J. HEWER
& EVANTHIA LYONS

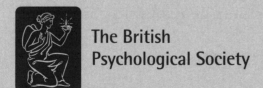

The British
Psychological Society

WILEY

Registered Offices
John Wiley & Sons, Inc., 111 River Street, Hoboken, NJ 07030, USA
John Wiley & Sons Ltd, The Atrium, Southern Gate, Chichester, West Sussex, PO19 8SQ, UK

Editorial Office
John Wiley & Sons, Inc., 90 Eglinton Ave. E., Suite 300, Toronto, Ontario M4P 2Y3, Canada

For details of our global editorial offices, customer services, and more information about Wiley products visit us at www.wiley.com.

Wiley also publishes its books in a variety of electronic formats and by print-on-demand. Some content that appears in standard print versions of this book may not be available in other formats.

Library of Congress Cataloging-in-Publication Data

Names: Hewer, Chris, 1957– editor. | Lyons, Evanthia, editor.
Title: Political psychology / edited by Christopher J. Hewer and Evanthia Lyons.
Description: Hoboken, NJ : John Wiley & Sons, 2018. | Series: BPS textbooks in psychology | Includes index. |
Identifiers: LCCN 2018013085 (print) | LCCN 2018029389 (ebook) | ISBN 9781118982389 (pdf) | ISBN 9781118982372 (epub) | ISBN 9781118982396 (cloth) | ISBN 9781118929339 (pbk.)
Subjects: LCSH: Political psychology.
Classification: LCC JA74.5 (ebook) | LCC JA74.5 .P633 2018 (print) | DDC 320.01/9–dc23
LC record available at https://lccn.loc.gov/2018013085

Cover image: The Leningrad (later Neptune) Cinema Mosaic: Gdansk, Poland by Anna Fiszer, 1957
Cover design by Wiley

Set in 11.5/13.5pt Dante by SPi Global, Pondicherry, India
Printed in Singapore by C.O.S. Printers Pte Ltd

10 9 8 7 6 5 4 3 2 1

Contents

Xenia Chryssochoou obtained her Ph.D. from the University Rene Descartes-Paris V and taught at different universities in France, Switzerland, and the United Kingdom before returning to Greece where she is currently Professor of Social and Political Psychology at the University of Panteion in Athens. She is interested in the social psychological aspects of identity and its construction in liberal societies in relation to conflict, political participation, and questions of cultural diversity.

J. Christopher Cohrs is Professor of Psychology at Jacobs University, Bremen, Germany. After receiving his doctoral degree (Dr. Phil) in 2004 from the University of Bielefeld, Germany, he was Lecturer in Psychology at Queens University, Belfast, Northern Ireland. His research focuses on ideology, political attitudes, prejudice, and representations of intergroup conflict. He is cofounder and coeditor of the international open-access *Journal of Social and Political Psychology*.

Stephen Gibson is a social psychologist based at York St. John University, UK. His research interests are in the areas of dis/obedience, citizenship, and national identity, and representations of peace and conflict. His most recent work has examined the archived audio recordings of Stanley Milgram's obedience experiments in order to develop a perspective on these studies as rhetorical encounters. He is the coeditor of *Representations of Peace and Conflict* (with Simon Mollan, 2012), and *Doing Your Qualitative Psychology Project* (with Cath Sullivan and Sarah Riley, 2012).

Artemis M. Griva received her Ph.D. in social psychology in 2014. She is currently a researcher at the University of Crete, Greece, and her research focuses on the social psychology of identity, globalization, and the sociocultural aspects of government policy. She has worked on research projects funded by the European Union (EU) and is author of scholarly and policy-oriented publications.

Christopher J. Hewer is Senior Lecturer in Social and Political Psychology at Kingston University, London where he teaches critical social psychology and the psychology of art and film. His research interests focus on collective memory, shifting memorialization, and forgetting in cultural discourse. Recent projects have addressed issues arising from contemporary memory in Britain for the Allied bombing of Germany and the Falklands conflict. Other work has explored the social construction of terrorism, national identity in Kosovo, and attitudes to the North Atlantic Treaty Organisation (NATO) in Republika Srpska.

Caroline Howarth is Associate Professor in the Department of Social Psychology at the London School of Economics and Political Science. She is committed to a form of social psychology that intersects with current social and political concerns—particularly those that lead to programs for social change. Living in multicultural communities in Kenya, South Africa, Papua New Guinea, and Fiji has influenced her approach to social psychology, directing her interests towards the political interconnections between community, identity, representation, and resistance. She is coeditor of *Political Psychology*, editor of *Papers on Social Representations*, and she publishes widely across social, community, and political psychology.

Sarah Jay is Lecturer in Psychology at the University of Limerick, Ireland. Her research integrates social psychology with sociological theory, and explores social class as a system of inequality. The objective of her research is to promote social justice and to use social psychology to examine and expose taken for granted systems that advantage the powerful.

Jack S. Levy is Board of Governors' Professor of Political Science at Rutgers University, and an Affiliate of the Saltzman Institute of War and Peace Studies at Columbia University. He is past-president of the International Studies Association and of the Peace Science Society. His primary research interests focus on the causes of interstate war, foreign policy decision-making, political psychology, and qualitative methodology. He is author of *War in the Modern Great Power System, 1495–1975* (1983); coauthor (with William R. Thompson) of *Causes of War* (2010) and of *The Arc of War: Origins, Escalation, and Transformation* (2011); and co-editor of *Explaining War and Peace: Case Studies and Necessary Condition Counterfactuals* (with Gary Goertz, 2007), *The Oxford Handbook of Political Psychology*, 2nd ed. (with Leonie Huddy and David O. Sears, 2013), and *The Outbreak of the First World War: Structure, Politics, and Decision-Making* (with John A. Vasquez, 2014).

Simon Locke was formerly Senior Lecturer in Sociology at Kingston University, UK. His research interests focus on rhetoric, conspiracy discourse, and the intersection between comic books and the public understanding of science. He is author of *Re-Crafting Rationalisation: Enchanted Science and Mundane Mysteries* (2011).

Evanthia Lyons is Professor of Social and Political Psychology at Kingston University, London, UK. Her research focuses on people's understanding of political processes and the factors that influence their engagement in conventional and unconventional political actions. She has recently completed an EU funded, multinational project looking at the processes that influence political participation among young people from different ethnic backgrounds. More recent work has focused on the way that people manage multiple group memberships; particularly, how different patterns of identification with ethnic, national, religious categories relate to prejudice, social stereotyping, political trust, and political violence. She is coeditor of *Changing European Identities: Social Psychological Analyses of Social Change* (with Glynis Breakwell, 1996) and *Analysing Qualitative Data in Psychology* 2nd ed. (with Adrian Coyle, 2016).

Shelley McKeown is Lecturer in Psychology in the Graduate School of Education at the University of Bristol. She received her Ph.D. in social psychology from the University of Ulster, Northern Ireland in 2012 where she was part of the Peace and Conflict Psychology Research Group. Her research focuses on understanding social identity processes and how best to reduce prejudice in diversity and conflict settings.

Orla Muldoon is Professor of Psychology, based in the Department of Psychology and Centre for Social Issues Research at the University of Limerick. Her broad research interests concern the impact of structural disadvantage on social identities and health and well-being.

Fergus G. Neville is Research Fellow at the School of Psychology and Neuroscience at the University of St. Andrews. He is currently employed on an ESRC-funded project examining the process and limits of behavioral spread in crowds. His work broadly concerns the relationship between social identities, norms, and group behavior, with a particular focus on crowd action, and experience. Dr. Neville also publishes research on violence prevention, and the social determinants and outcomes of child and adolescent health. He is currently an Editorial Consultant for the *British Journal of Social Psychology*.

Spyridoula Ntani received her Ph.D. in social psychology from the University of Surrey, and she is currently a researcher at Panteion University, Greece. Her research focuses on the development of extreme ideologies and political participation in times of crisis. She has taught social psychology at undergraduate level at different universities in Greece and has participated in funded research projects on fundamental rights protection, health care inequalities, and gender issues.

Emma O'Dwyer is Senior Lecturer in Political Psychology at Kingston University, London. Her research broadly focuses on the ways in which individuals and groups understand and relate to foreign policy, wars, and military intervention. She has explored these issues in relation to Irish foreign policy and its link to national identity, lay understandings of armed drones, and peace activism.

Stephen D. Reicher, Wardlaw Professor, School of Psychology and Neuroscience, University of St. Andrews is a Fellow of the British Academy, a Fellow of the Royal Society of Edinburgh, and a Fellow of the Academy for Social Sciences. He is also former Chief Editor of the *British Journal of Social Psychology* and is a Scientific Consultant to Scientific American Mind. Professor Reicher's work concerns the relationship between social identities and collective practices. In approaching 300 publications, he has studied such issues as mass rhetoric and leadership, nationalism and national identities, social exclusion and intergroup hatred, and the psychology of obedience and tyranny. Throughout his career, he has been interested in crowd psychology and his work has transformed both our theoretical understanding of this field and also public order practices in Europe, North America, and beyond.

Ron Roberts is a Chartered Psychologist and Associate Fellow of the British Psychological Society. He was formerly Senior Lecturer in Psychology at Kingston University and he previously held posts at the Institute of Psychiatry, University of Westminster, King's College Medical School, University College London, St. Bartholomew's Medical School, Queen Mary College, and the Tavistock Institute. He is the author of numerous research articles and books, including *Parapsychology: The Science of Unusual Experience*. 2nd ed. (with David Groome, 2017), *Just War: Psychology and Terrorism* (2007), *Psychology and Capitalism* (2015), and *The Off-Modern: Psychology Estranged* (2017).

Brian Schiff is Professor and Chair of the Department of Psychology, and Director of the George and Irina Schaeffer Centre for the Study of Genocide, Human Rights, and Conflict Prevention at the American University of Paris. Professor Schiff was guest editor of *New Directions for Child and Adolescent Development*'s *Rereading Personal Narrative and Life Course* (2014), coeditor (with A. Elizabeth McKim and Sylvie Patron) of *Life and Narrative: The Risks and Responsibilities of Storying Experience* (2017), and author of *A New Narrative for Psychology* (2017). He was the recipient of a research grant from the Harry S. Truman Institute for the Advancement of Peace (2014–2016) to conduct longitudinal interviews on the identity stories of Palestinian students at the Hebrew University of Jerusalem. In 2016, he received the Theodore Sarbin Award from the American Psychological Association's Division 24: Society for Theoretical and Philosophical Psychology.

Johanna R. Vollhardt is Associate Professor of Psychology at Clark University, USA and she is affiliated with the Strassler Center for Holocaust and Genocide Studies. Her research interests include psychological processes in the aftermath of ethnic conflict and genocide and, in particular, collective victimhood and acknowledgement of mass atrocities. She is cofounder and coeditor of the international open-access *Journal of Social and Political Psychology*.

Preface

This book has been compiled as a teaching and learning aid for students who wish to take political psychology as part of an undergraduate program. The text is designed to inform through empirical research and critical argument, and the approach taken in this volume is quite different to other books on political psychology, not least because it includes alternative approaches to psychological enquiry that challenge our "taken-for-granted" assumptions about the world. In places, the reader may encounter unsettling critique, or positions that are unfamiliar or alien. Indeed, what has often been missing in political psychology is a meaningful exchange of ideas with critical social psychology, sociology, history, media studies, and philosophy. Often, when academics schooled in different disciplines, epistemologies, and methodologies get together to discuss political psychology, they often find themselves talking at cross purposes because their vision of the world and their view of psychology are quite different. It is our hope that this text will lead to a broader understanding of the different intellectual positions that academics may take toward political psychology. To create a sense of mutual exchange and exploration in the classroom, there are questions for group debate and discussion at the end of each chapter. After many years of working in higher education, we take the view that transformative education does not take place so much through learning about research findings, but more through the questions that these studies raise and the discussions that follow. We hope you find the book interesting and useful.

Christopher J. Hewer and Evanthia Lyons

Political Psychology
A Social Psychological Approach

1 Some Historical and Philosophical Considerations

CHRISTOPHER J. HEWER

CHAPTER OUTLINE

WHEN PEOPLE COME TOGETHER

Life is a social encounter and when people come together as individuals, families, or groups, it soon becomes apparent that everyone has a different idea about how matters should be organized. Some will argue that everyone should do what is best for the majority while others simply want what is best for themselves or those close to them. Others may be less guided by relationships and instead seek the most efficient, systematic, and fair approach to decision-making. As time goes by, other questions come to the fore. Who has access to resources, how much, and how often? Who has the authority to say what can and cannot be done, and what gives a person the right to dictate to others? These questions reflect the political nature of our existence and such questions arise in the home, office, local neighborhood, or, indeed, between peoples and nations.

Then there is the question of how we should understand the world and our position within it. For thousands of years, human culture has ventured beyond the material and observable aspects of our existence to explore and embrace supernatural concepts in the form of God, gods, demons, or other unseen forces. Indeed, today, the world is ideologically divided between those who claim that there exists a nonphysical life-world beyond our senses and those who maintain that there is no such world. There are also many who are unable to decide. Given these circumstances, and the additional difficulties created by differences in language, history, and culture, there is huge potential for disagreement and division between individuals, groups, nations, and peoples.

We might conclude then that each **polity** has its own way of looking at the world and its own way of doing things. In psychology, the term "polity" is seldom mentioned, but it is important because it refers to people living under a particular regime (Gr. *polītiteiā*). Its root gives us two related Greek words—*polītikos*—from which we get *politics*—actions that proceed from a motive to enact policy, and *polītēs*—a citizen of a state. When we consider people grouped together, their motives to organize matters, and issues of belonging, the psychological implications become clear. Because we do not live in a political vacuum, every system—whether capitalistic, democratic, theocratic, or totalitarian—affects, influences, and perhaps even determines, the psychological state of the people. Therefore, if we wish to understand people, we need to take a closer look at the social, economic, and political systems that govern their lives. This analysis reflects one of the broader concerns of political

Political Psychology: A Social Psychological Approach, First Edition.
Edited by Christopher J. Hewer and Evanthia Lyons.
© 2018 John Wiley & Sons Ltd. Published 2018 by John Wiley & Sons Ltd.

psychology—"the behavior of individuals within a specific political system" (Huddy, Sears, & Levy, 2013a, p. 3). However, there is also a more general objective within political psychology; that is, to apply "what is known about human psychology to the study of politics" (Huddy et al., 2013a, p. 1).

SOCIAL PSYCHOLOGY

Social psychology has something to say about both areas of enquiry and featured in this textbook are psychological insights gained from research into topics such as intergroup conflict, prejudice and discrimination, migration, obedience to authority, crowds, militarism, political decision-making, and peace psychology. Indeed, a lot of work in political psychology *is* social psychology, which broadly speaking, fosters an attempt to understand the social and psychological processes involved in social relations. However, social psychology takes many forms and in this textbook the emphasis is on language, social interaction, the person (not to be confused with personality), identity, and the social construction of reality. What is more, many of the chapters raise questions and challenge "taken for granted" knowledge about psychology, politics, and human nature. Indeed, the material encourages a discussion of **epistemology** and **ontology**.

Epistemology is the branch of philosophy concerned with the theory of knowledge. It addresses two main questions: *how* can we know the world (by what method?) and *what* can we know about the world (what are the limits and scope of knowledge?). Ontology refers to the assumptions we make about the nature of being (what we are), our existence (what makes us who we are), and reality (what we believe the world/universe to be). Different epistemologies and ontological beliefs will inevitably produce different ways of explaining human behavior and different ways of explaining the political world. Only through a full consideration of these issues (which includes our own assumptions and beliefs), can we produce sound academic analysis. For this specific purpose, there are questions for class discussion at the end of each chapter.

At this point, we might ask two questions: what can social psychology tell us about the social and political world? And can its insights shed light on and provide solutions to human problems? These questions direct our attention to some key issues in the history of humanity, and identity, governance, and conflict are at the forefront. First, let us consider some key developments in the history of humankind that continue to play an important role in contemporary politics: the development of religious identities.

THE DEVELOPMENT OF RELIGIOUS IDENTITIES

The history of humanity shows that in the earliest forms of civilization, the worship of an unseen God or gods has been at the heart of culture. The remains of ancient temples located in various parts of the world are testimony to the worship of the many gods that dominated common thinking and practice. Ashtoreth, Baal, Molech, Artemis, Hermes, and Zeus are just a few of the many thousands of gods who had to be appeased. In the twenty-first century, a large number of religions including Hinduism, Buddhism, Taoism, Confucianism, Shinto, Judaism, Christianity, and Islam continue to influence the worldview of billions of people and we might add that Atheism, with its fervent rejection of the existence of God or gods, is the preferred alternative for many. In terms of their influence on world politics, Judaism, Christianity, and Islam have been particularly significant and all three traditions trace their ancestry back to Abraham who lived around 2000 BCE.[1]

INTERSECTING HISTORIES: JUDAISM, CHRISTIANITY, AND ISLAM

The history of Abraham and the Jews is contained in *the Torah*—the first five books of the Bible—Genesis, Exodus, Leviticus, Numbers, and Deuteronomy—also known as the Pentateuch.[2] The Genesis account outlines the founding of ancient Israel, identifying Abraham's son Isaac, and his son Jacob (whose name was changed to Israel—see Genesis 32 v 28) as the progenitors of the nation. Chapters 37–46 of Genesis describe the circumstances under which Jacob (Israel), his 12 sons, and their extended family eventually came to settle in Egypt. In time, this Hebrew speaking family grew into what we might call today "a large ethnic group," and a new regime in Egypt oppressed them and treated them as slaves. The book of Exodus provides an account of their enslavement and release from captivity in Egypt in 1513 BCE under the leadership of Moses. Once liberated, a **theocracy**

---

[1] Before Our Common Era.

[2] Another source is *The Antiquities of the Jews* written by historian Flavius Josephus in the first century CE, translated by William Whiston, and published in 1895 (*Whiston's Josephus: The excelsior edition*. London: W. P. Nimmo).

emerged—an administration with God as sovereign. Israel accepted a new divine law—the Ten Commandments with some 600 additional laws to govern all aspects of life—as well as a prescribed set of religious practices. After wandering in the wilderness for 40 years, Israel eventually conquered the land of Canaan to take hold of "the promised land." The territory of this new nation would, however, be under constant threat for the next 15 centuries from a variety of tribes and nations, including Moab, Edom, Amalek, Midian, Philistia, Persia, Assyria, Babylon, and Rome. By the first century CE,[3] the Jewish religious system became known as Judaism, although it was no longer solely based on the *Torah*.

Judaism's relationship with Christianity is significant. For many centuries, prophets in Israel such as Isaiah, Zechariah, Malachi, Hosea, Micah, Jeremiah, Daniel, and various writers of the Psalms had provided the means for identifying a Messiah (Shiloh) who would liberate Israel. Although Jesus' arrival in 29 CE fulfilled prohecy, he was nonetheless rejected by the Jews. The first five books of the New Testament of the Bible—Matthew, Mark, Luke, John, and the Acts of the Apostles provide an historical account of this new 'way' that was set to replace Judaism. The death of Jesus (the Christ or Messiah as identified by Christians) at the hands of the Romans, and the evangelical nature of this new message, ensured that Christian ideas spread very quickly across the known world. Most significantly for the Jewish nation, the destruction of Jerusalem in 70 CE by the Roman armies under General Titus resulted in the loss of their homeland, and those whose who survived were scattered into exile across the globe. Within a century, Jerusalem was rebuilt by Roman Emperor Hadrian and renamed *Aelia Capitolina*.

By 325 CE, the Council of Nicaea had established that the Christian faith was to be based on the worship of a triune god (a trinity) and this proved to be significant. Some three centuries later between 610 and 632 CE, Islam emerged with a new sacred text (the Qu'ran) and a mandate to worship a *singular* deity; Arab adherents also claimed ancestry to Abraham through his son Ishmael. Eventually, Jerusalem became a center of Islamic culture and, in the centuries that followed, Islam developed under the authority of the Ottoman Empire. However, between the eleventh and fifteenth centuries, Jerusalem became a battleground for Christians and Muslims as the Crusaders of Christendom bearing the sign of the cross, *(French: croisade, Latin: crux)* sought to regain the "Holy Land" from the Muslim Turks.

By the nineteenth century, French and British colonial powers had come to dominate the Middle East, and the First World War 1914–1918 brought Britain and its allies into conflict with the Ottoman Empire because it was an ally of

---

[3] In our Common Era.

Germany. In November 1917, British Foreign Secretary Arthur Balfour made an official declaration on behalf of the British government that it was their intent to secure Palestine as a permanent homeland for the Jews—a policy that was arguably influenced by Christian Zionism (Lewis, 2010)—the belief that the Second Coming of Jesus Christ would be established in Jerusalem through a restored Israel. This declaration, however, contradicted previous assurances from official British sources that independence for the Arab territories would be reward for helping the allies defeat the Turks.[4] A month later, in December 1917, the British defeated the Turks and took control of Jerusalem. After the League of Nations was formed in 1919, Britain was given a mandate to govern Palestine until 14 May 1948.

During World War II (1939–1945), the Nazi occupation of Europe claimed the lives of six million Jews, and after the war, many of those who had survived sought refuge in Palestine, their historic homeland, the place from which their forebears had been exiled over 18 centuries earlier. Although a new administration in Britain opposed the mass immigration of Jews to Palestine, once the UN mandate expired, the British withdrew, and the political situation became the responsibility of the United Nations. On the day the British left, David Ben-Gurion announced the establishment of the modern State of Israel and conflict between the Israelis and the Arab states ensued.

What significance do these identities and events have for the modern political world? Osama Bin Laden (2001), for example, described the occupation of Palestine by the West since 1917 as "80 years of humiliation" and further claimed that the US has been "occupying the lands of Islam," that is Lebanon, Saudi Arabia, and now Iraq—"plundering its riches, dictating to its rulers, humiliating its people, terrorizing its neighbors and turning its bases in the peninsula into a spearhead through which to fight the neighboring Muslim peoples" (Bin Laden, 1998). According to Bin Laden, Christendom was again manifesting itself as an Anglo–American crusade—part of a joint venture with Israel to regain the Holy Land from Islam—and this was now justification for global **jihad**. Here, we see a view of the ancient past resurfacing in the present.

We also see that historical divisions within Christendom have created identities of political significance. The social and political consequences of the Reformation in the sixteenth century that brought about a division between Roman Catholics and Protestants can still be seen in many parts of the world. Indeed, religious identities and the events that have endorsed and intensified them continue to shape the modern world.

---

[4] The Hussein–McMahon correspondence—Letters from Sir Henry McMahon, British High Commissioner to Egypt to Hussein bin Ali, Sharif of Mecca written in the period from July 1915 to January 1916.

THE ISSUE OF GOVERNANCE

The history of humanity can also be told in terms of its approach to governance. Among the many systems of rule that have been tried, monarchy—the anointing of kings and queens—has been the preferred system throughout history. In the Christian world, a belief in the **divine right of kings** provided the basis for absolute monarchy. Monarchs were deemed appointed by God, and therefore anyone who opposed the monarch opposed God (see Romans 13 v 1, 2). However, after many centuries, this form of rule was challenged by the people; rebellions and revolutions such as the English Civil War (1642–1649), the French Revolution (1789), and the American War of Independence (1776) all paved the way for the development of **democracy**: government for the people by the people.

There were also important cultural developments at this time. From the middle of the seventeenth century to the beginning of the eighteenth century, Europe entered the **Age of the Enlightenment**, which saw a movement away from religious explanation of natural and social phenomena toward more rational or reasoned explanations of the world. These developments along with further constitutional reform eventually led to a separation of "Church and state," which would allow political authority to function independently— without interference from religious institutions. This arrangement is broadly characteristic of modern democratic states although the precise nature of the relationship between "Church and state" varies within each country.

We might note that the historical developments in Europe provide an important contrast between the politics of the West and the Islamic world. Because the Islamic world has never been subject to the same or similar secularizing influences, there is still broad acceptance of theocracy—a divinely ordained and prescribed political order. Indeed, Islamic religious law provides a comprehensive system for regulating individual, social, and political life, which means that, for many Muslims, political consciousness, and religious identity are inseparable.

TRANSFORMATIONS IN THE TWENTIETH CENTURY

By the beginning of the twentieth century, the map of Europe had been redrawn by the creation of larger and more powerful states such as Italy in 1870, and Germany in 1871. The Balkan wars in 1912 and 1913 and the First World War 1914–1918 had a profound effect on world politics and cast a long shadow over human affairs. In 1917, a revolution in Russia established **communism,** a totalitarian political system and ideology to replace the monarchy, and after three long years of trench warfare on the western front, the stalemate between Britain's imperial forces (e.g., India, Canada, Australia, and New Zealand) and Germany ended when the United States entered the war as an ally to Britain in 1917. The huge resources of the Anglo-American alliance eventually brought about the surrender of Germany and an end to the war in 1918.

The postwar political settlement—the Treaty of Versailles—imposed harsh financial reparations upon Germany and this, combined with the world's financial collapse in 1929, brought unemployment and poverty to millions. Between 1919 and 1933 Germany tried to make democracy work; in 1932, over half the German people had expressed support for the democratic Republic by rejecting the political extremes of the left and the right (the Nazis received 36.8 % of the vote). However, in what were very complex political circumstances (see Shirer, 1960), Hitler wrestled power away from the people and parliament to create a one party state. Within a year of the democratic elections held in 1932, Adolf Hitler was dictator of the new German Reich.

Hitler's desire to expand Germany's territories toward the east resulted in the annexation of the Sudetenland and Austria in 1938. In 1939, Germany invaded Poland, and Britain and France declared war on Germany. In December 1941, Japan's attack on the United States brought America into a war with Japan and an alliance with Britain, which meant that US forces were again deployed in Europe to fight against Germany. Earlier in 1941, Germany invaded the Soviet Union, and the war in Europe was settled when the Soviet army successfully repelled the German invasion and advanced into Berlin. With the Allied advance in the west, the Germans surrendered in May 1945. In the Far East, two atomic bombs dropped on Hiroshima and Nagasaki by the United States brought an end to the war with Japan in August 1945.

After 1945, there were revolutions, counter-revolutions, invasions, and wars in South America, Africa, and the Middle East and new forces for independence emerged. Although victory in Europe and the Far East had secured Britain's imperial interests, there was now a clamor for independence and self-determination among people living under colonial rule. This eventually led to the dismantling of the British Empire; political freedom would now be achieved through "the will of the people." In the decades that followed, many British colonies gained independence and the British colonial system was transformed into a Commonwealth of Nations. European colonialism, which had nurtured a belief in the superiority of European peoples, was to end and democracy and self-determination was to govern future political developments.

At the end of World War II, a new ideological divide between "the free democratic world" and "totalitarian communism" came to the fore. In order to prevent the spread of communism, the United States embarked on wars in

Korea (1950–1953) and Vietnam (1955–1975) and as tensions between the Soviet Union and the West increased, the world entered a Cold War and a nuclear arms race. In 1962, after the United States had placed nuclear missiles in Turkey, the USSR[5] placed nuclear warheads in Cuba, close to the American mainland. The two superpowers were engaged in a tense confrontation, and given the stockpile of conventional and nuclear warheads on both sides, a full-scale war would have guaranteed mutually assured destruction (MAD). The Soviet authorities relented and the missiles were withdrawn.

THE SOCIAL AND MORAL ORDER

The twentieth century was also dominated by rapid social change. The industrial revolution of the nineteenth century in Britain brought about mechanization (largely through steam power), mass production, and new forms of transportation; for example, rail travel. However, these developments also made wealthy elites more prosperous, which increased social inequality and intensified class divisions. The early twentieth century also saw the rise of the women's movement—the fight for the rights of women to vote in government elections (see Hannam, 2012)—which inspired a feminist ideology that would emerge in the 1960s to challenge patriarchal values and practices.

After two world wars, the newly formed United Nations (1948) reflected on the catastrophic human consequences of Nazism and other totalitarian regimes, and it thus sought to establish human values that would protect individuals from powerful governments. Nazism had required the subordination of the individual to the state or nation and communism required similar state allegiance. The Universal Declaration of Human Rights in 1948 and the European Convention on Human Rights, which came into force in 1953, signaled the beginning of a new morality. Very slowly, the world started to embrace the idea of individual human rights.

The postwar period also brought about a shift in sexual mores. In Britain, the availability of the contraceptive pill (1961), and the legalization of abortion (1967) and homosexuality (1967) liberalized sexual attitudes. An emerging popular culture working in tandem with a new consumer culture would promote the "new morality" of a "permissive society" that, over the next 50 years, would change social values in many parts of the world. Since that time, the idea of "individual rights" has filtered down to counter traditional ideas of "what is right." Cultural commentator, Clifford Longley (2014) identifies the Universal Declaration of Human Rights and the European Convention on

---

[5] Union of Soviet Socialist Republics.

Human Rights as having moved the culture away from a "sin-based morality" (largely determined by Judeo–Christian teachings)—to a "justice based morality." The transition would also grant greater personal freedoms in relation to the construction and presentation of the self. Indeed, a new form of moral discourse has since emerged in which people of all persuasions, sexualities, and alignments publicly unite to indict discrimination and injustice as the most serious offense in the new moral hierarchy. Any counterclaim from the "sin-based" repertoire is seen as intolerant. For many people with conservative values, these changes have been confusing and have led to some apparent contradictions in the political sphere; for example, the legalization of gay marriage in the UK by a Conservative Prime Minister.

We also have to remember that the coming and going of generations also contributes to social change. As one generation passes off the scene, their values very often disappear with them and new values assimilated by a new generation are accepted as the norm. In a rapidly changing technological world, a rights-based morality has constructed new ways of thinking, living, and being. The world has also changed in other ways. Modern living is no longer a localized experience. Jet travel, communications, migration, and transnational corporations have transformed the physical and psychological world into a globalized experience, in which time and distance take on new meanings (Bauman, 2000). Indeed, if the enchanted world of God, saints, spirits, angels, or gods acting as agents in the everyday lives of people has largely disappeared (Taylor, 2007), we now live in a psychologized world where scientific understanding of individual human thoughts, motivations, and actions has become an alternative search for self-understanding.

THE SEARCH FOR SCIENTIFIC UNDERSTANDING

The emergence of psychology and sociology in the late nineteenth century was a product of Enlightenment thinking—an institutionalized attempt to understand and improve our existence through rational scientific means. In the nineteenth century, Karl Marx (1818–1883), Charles Darwin (1809–1882), and Sigmund Freud (1856–1939) presented new ideas that would influence these new disciplines, and that would change western intellectual thought. Marx had argued for a proletarian revolution that would bring an end to capitalism and social inequality, while Darwin had proposed that evolution through natural selection rather than God was responsible for life on earth; and Freud through his therapeutic encounters, maintained that the presence of internal, inaccessible sexualized sources of conflict within the individual was at the root of all human behavior. What effect did these ideas have on the political landscape? The history of the twentieth century shows that ideas have the power of material forces. Marx inspired a communist revolution in Russia, while Darwin's work brought about a "secular revolution" that sought to undermine all forms of religious explanation and religious authority. And in the 1960s—as if internalized sexual conflict was emerging from its repressed state within society—Freud's emphasis on sexuality was used in some quarters to justify the sexual revolution.

What is perhaps less well known is that Darwin's evolutionary ideas brought science and politics into an unholy alliance. Darwin's cousin, Francis Galton (1822–1911) used evolutionary arguments to advance the science of **eugenics**, which was intent on finding ways to improve the physical quality of the human population (Fanchner, 1979). Galton originally proposed state-sponsored arranged marriage of the highly intelligent as a strategy to produce better quality offspring (Fanchner, 1985), but by the 1930s, other methods such as the sterilization of criminals and "mental defectives" had become common practice in places such as the United States. Eugenic ideas spread across the world, and what started in nineteenth century Britain as a class-based social engineering project, eventually developed into a racial theory that placed certain social and ethnic groups at the bottom of the evolutionary scale—an argument that was used in Nazi Germany to justify the systematic destruction of the disabled and the genocide of six million Jews (Hothersall, 2004). We might ask ourselves, are there any scientific ideologies operating today (inside or outside of psychology) that make certain groups vulnerable? Indeed, we should be wary about anything that looks like "political ideology dressed up as science," and when reading scientific findings, we would do well to ask: who gains from this perspective? Whose interests are being served? Where is this research taking us? What are the implications? Are there political motivations behind the research? Who is funding it and for what purpose? To understand the political nature of psychology (and science) is perhaps as important as understanding the psychological nature of politics.

PSYCHOLOGY: A NEW WAY OF SEEING THE WORLD

Psychology had proposed a new way of looking at human existence and its content and focus eventually came to mirror the needs of the culture. In the postwar period, subdisciplines within psychology started to form to meet the particular needs of the military and the broader capitalist enterprise (see

Wexler, 1983; also Richards, 2002). These included industrial, consumer, occupational, vocational, and military psychology and the psychology of advertising. There were also developments in economic psychology, ergonomics, sport, and health psychology; and many studies in social psychology, directly or indirectly, set out to explain the Holocaust (e.g., Adorno, Frenkel-Brunswik, Levinson, & Sanford, 1950; Asch, 1951, 1952; Milgram, 1963; Tajfel, 1974; Zimbardo, 1969). Political psychology was no different; indeed, one of its tenets is that research should be "responsive to and relevant to societal problems" (Hermann, 1986, p. 2). Overall, the approach of political psychology has reflected the traditions and shifting positions in the parent discipline, although its origins may be traced back to different times and events in different countries (see Monroe, 2002; Stone & Schaffner, 1988). From the 1940s to the 1960s, the main focus was on relations between personality and politics, which was largely informed by psychoanalytic psychology, and as social psychologists started to explore attitude theory and change in the 1950s, political psychologists looked at voting patterns and beliefs systems. By the early 1970s, behavioristic approaches had made way for a more cognitive approach to understanding political behavior (Rahn, Sullivan, & Rudolph, 2002).

Given these developments, we might ask: what is the nature of political psychology today? The first *Handbook of Political Psychology* (Sears, Huddy, & Jervis, 2003) acknowledged that *there is no one political psychology*—that everything from social cognition to discourse analysis to Freudian psychodynamics forms part of the fabric of the discipline. Political psychology thus offers a broad collection of approaches with no single set of assumptions. What is more, it is multidisciplinary—drawing upon insights from politics, psychology, social psychology, international relations, sociology, anthropology, economics, philosophy, media, journalism, and history. However, because each discipline has its own conceptual language and methodology, it can make theoretical conversations between disciplines difficult. Nonetheless, the importance of seeking dialog and *listening* to other disciplines cannot be overstated.

In political psychology, it is acknowledged that when studying political behavior, "context can make a difference" (Hermann, 1986, p. 2). We could expand this idea to think about people, not only in different contexts that permit or exclude certain actions, but also people's behavior in different cultures and across time. What is more, recognizing the context-specific nature of human behavior will help us guard against theoretical imperialism—the tendency to impose theory, concepts, or explanations derived from a politically and economically dominant culture onto other cultures. We therefore need to check that our assumptions, explanations, constructs, classifications, and theories are appropriate to other cultural settings. For example, even the broad linear classifications of liberal-conservative that dominate American politics take on different meanings in Europe and elsewhere in the world.

THE INFLUENCE OF POLITICAL PHILOSOPHY ON SOCIAL PSYCHOLOGY

Given the broad and eclectic approach of political psychology, we have to accept that different approaches can lead to very different conclusions. Indeed, our own political philosophies can influence our understanding or interpretation of the human condition. To illustrate, let us consider a proposition: *that the type of society we live in determines the type of explanation we give for human behavior.* For example, religious societies (where religious creeds have priority over science) will likely resort to religious beliefs and concepts to explain human behavior, such as "I have been blessed by God"; "Unbelievers behave like this because ...", and so on. Similarly, in societies where scientific findings take precedence over religious explanation, science will be used to explain human behavior—particularly those behaviors we do not like or understand. For example, we might draw upon genetics or the idea of faulty brain chemistry to explain some forms of criminal behavior. Having science as our principal source of knowledge, we likely believe that *our* approach to knowledge is rational, reasonable, and objective and that, above all, we seek evidence-based arguments. In so doing, we may come to see our own society as *ideologically neutral*. However, on closer inspection we may find that western culture is saturated with ideology that we have never considered before, and that this has implications for the way we explain events and outcomes.

Consider a key political philosophy that is foundational to the politics of the western world: **liberalism**. The liberal mind is thought to be rational and judicious, and it embraces the notion of rights, choice, and autonomy. Principally, the aims of a liberal society are to maximize individual freedoms. American society, for example, was founded on the notion of preserving individual autonomy and liberty (Farr, 1996). We are also aware that we live in a society dominated by **capitalism**, which has three principal characteristics: private ownership, the free market, and profit (see Bowles, 2012).

It is no coincidence that liberalism and capitalism have a common root—a shared subject—*the individual* and *the freedom of the individual.* Indeed, "Liberals are *formally* committed to individualism" (Vincent, 1992, p. 32), and **individualism** as a political philosophy posits the idea that "the individual is more real than, and prior to society" (p. 32). Critics, however, claim that individualism *as a philosophy on how to live,* that is, a life based on self-interest, self-determination, and self-reliance has arguably led to widespread greed, loss of community, a decline in political and religious participation, crime, fear of crime, disregard for the environment, depression, and suicide. Nonetheless, individualism continues to play a central role in the lives of people in the West. For example, we believe that people should be free to pursue their self-interests and that by so doing they benefit society and the economy. We also believe that justice is served when individuals are held responsible for their own crimes and misdemeanors, which are usually committed against other individuals or individual property—rather against a religious or state ideology, community, or nation. Individualism also embraces the idea of individual human rights.

LOCATING THE ROOT OF HUMAN BEHAVIOR

The question is: if we have been socialized in a society founded on liberalism and individualism in which the freedom of the individual is paramount, how are we likely to see the world? What type of social psychological explanation are we most likely to give when we observe human behavior? Where are we most likely to look for its cause—within the psychology of the individual or within the social and political circumstances? With our beliefs in individualism fully operational, how might we explain poverty, for example? In a highly competitive economic system, it is inevitable that some will do better than others. However, to understand the psychology of social inequality, it would be a very limited analysis simply to look at "the individual" and make assumptions about why someone is doing well—namely, through their hard work and mental application, or not so well, because of a lack of initiative, ambition, or physical, and mental application. *We have to interrogate the nature of the system in which the inequality took place. We have to ask to what extent is the system contributing to the behavior?* That is, the observed inequalities may be properties of systems not individuals.

We often see this issue played out in other contexts on the daily news. For example, identifying the root of behavior either within an individual or within the politics of the culture is brought to public attention every time a mass shooting in the United States takes place. Media commentators and politicians alike often say that something must be done about the "gun culture" in the US. However, because bearing arms in the United States is a constitutional right, the customary response from powerful groups such as the NRA (National Rifle Association) is that there is nothing wrong with guns, the problem lies within people—the individuals who use them. In this analysis, we have an important a choice to make. We can either see the political circumstances—in this case, the right to bear arms, as a mere context or environment—or as a factor that significantly shapes or determines behavior.

If it is indeed the case that the social and political system shapes human behavior, we might ask: what processes are involved? It is worth taking some time to reflect on this. Social philosopher, George Herbert Mead (1934) argued that our sense of self develops in relation to other selves, and that we are born into a social milieu in which other selves have already internalized the values of the culture. In this way, whether we are aware of it or not, the values of the social, economic, and political system impose themselves upon us. We might therefore reflect: to what extent is behavior in the West determined or shaped by the social, economic, and political system? We can perhaps understand how a totalitarian political system can affect the minds and behavior of its citizens, but we may not fully recognize the way that our own system affects us. During the Cold War, commentators in the West had little difficulty pointing to the oppressed look on the faces of people in the communist bloc and attributing their demoralized state to a lack of personal freedom, but there was little reflection on the way that social cohesion and traditional values in the West were being undermined by a new materialism and consumer ideology. Nor were comparable attempts made to explain our personal and social problems in terms of our systemic failings even though we saw *their* behavior as having a systemic cause.

Moreover, the proposition that human behavior is rooted in the social, economic, and political system also allows us to see our own behavior in a new light as we consider alternative explanations of mood, mental distress, violence, crime, discrimination, and terrorism. Individualism promotes the idea that everything we think, say and do emanates from within the individual, and all the while we look to individual personality for answers, we fail to interrogate the social and political circumstances. The starting point for discussion and debate about the origins of human behavior in a truly political psychology has to involve the social, economic, and political system before we can draw any meaningful conclusions about the role of individual personality or cognition. Historians of social psychology have consistently argued that individualism has shaped the development of North American social psychology (Farr, 1996; Graumann, 1986; Greenwood, 2004; Pepitone, 1981) and **methodological individualism**—the idea that explanations of social relations and processes *must begin with an account of individuals* because they are the building blocks of society, has been a fundamental part of this approach (see Allport, 1933).

How does individualism affect the way we approach and understand the social world? Imagine that we were asked to study "the army" and that we were asked to provide a theoretical account of how the army works, which would include some understanding of the way that individual soldiers think. In Britain, we might immediately think in terms of rank, which reflects the class structure of British society. Traditionally, officers are recruited from the middle and upper classes while the lower ranks come from families of ordinary working people—a difference that also reflects different levels of education. In this setting, the concept of "the army" is a mirror image of class relations existing in the outside world. This very specific understanding not only provides an account of the social dynamics within the institution, but it also accounts for an individual's understanding of status, position, authority, obedience, chain of command, and so forth. In Britain, rank and social class are therefore fundamental to our understanding of "the army."

For those who subscribe to methodological individualism, this analysis is far too sociological; what they require is an analysis of the army in terms of the physical and mental states and experiences of individuals since the army is made up of individuals. An example of this approach is found in the American soldier series carried out after World War II. Stouffer, Suchman, Devinney, Star, and Williams (1949) surveyed over half a million US soldiers stationed worldwide on their personal preferences and attitudes to an array of topics. In this study, a sketch of social reality was inferred from patterns in the data across the samples. This psychological research was "social" insofar that it sought information about the social world, but it was based on an aggregation of individual responses. Indeed, similar methods are adopted today for opinion polling and market research.

However, what this approach fails to access are *the meanings* created by social structure, in this instance, social class, which largely determines how people behave. To apply the "opinion polling" approach to the study of the British Army, would miss these important social and structural elements *that make the army comprehensible to the people in it*. Therefore, the behavior of a British soldier during World War I or World War II, for example, could not be fully explained by simply understanding "what was going on in his head"; there is a whole social and cultural context involving power relations existing in the wider culture that needs to be considered. These very different ways of looking at "the army" produce two very different accounts. The question is: which one more accurately reflects social reality?

SOCIAL COGNITION

A brief review of the most recent *Oxford Handbook of Political Psychology* (Huddy, Sears, & Levy, 2013b) reveals that there is a distinct American flavor to political psychology insofar as *the individual is center stage*. Indeed, most social psychological research carried out in political psychology falls within the domain of **social cognition,** which tends to locate the source of behavior within the individual whether in the form of an attitude, stereotype, personality factor, or attribution. Social cognition emerged in the 1960s as an approach to social psychology that was directly influenced by cognitive psychology and particularly information processing theory. It focuses on the role of individual faculties such as attention, perception, judgment, and memory in the study of social phenomena such as interpersonal, intrapersonal, intergroup, and intragroup relations (see Forgas, 1981; also Fiske & Taylor, 1984).

However, this approach leaves the social and political context largely ignored, unexplained, and untheorized. For more sociologically minded social psychologists, the explanatory framework is simply too "cognitive" and it is not feasible to explain the complexities of the political world in such terms. To psychologize explanations when there are structural, cultural, or social causes of behavior, is to endorse a process of mystification where the real cause is replaced by a false one (see Cherry, 1995 and her reinterpretation of bystander intervention). The idea that human behavior emanates from within a decontextualized individual overlooks the fact that what we think, believe and do is largely a product of **power relations** and **identity politics** tied up within the social order. Nonetheless, social cognition remains the dominant approach in social psychology.

A SOCIETAL APPROACH TO POLITICAL PSYCHOLOGY

What then should we conclude from this intellectual divide within social psychology? On the one hand, we cannot ignore or play down the role of social structure, culture, or other societal factors in our analyses but, on the other hand, experience tells us that neither can we ignore the role of the individual. Individuals perceive, make judgments, attribute cause, entertain prejudicial and discriminatory thoughts and—in the case of political elites— make decisions that affect millions of lives. Doise and Staerklé (2002) advocate a societal approach that considers both individual cognitive functioning and societal factors and they argue that a theoretical bridge between the individual and the social is provided by **social representations theory** (SRT) (Moscovici, 1961/1976). SRT focuses on the *organizing principles* that direct people's thinking, talking, interacting, and understanding—and of particular interest is their use of language and **constructs**. The theory is principally concerned with the way in which lay knowledge (the everyday expressions and understanding of ordinary people) is created in specific social settings. For example, when conflict occurs, all the parties involved have different political positions, cultural beliefs, and histories. We need to be able to explain *how* and *why* such differences are possible and *how* and *why* they have come about. SRT provides the concepts and processes to explain divergent cultural perspectives (see Duveen, 2001).

The existence of two very different approaches to social psychology is an important consideration for anyone wishing to study social and political psychology (see Farr, 1996; Markova, 2012; Moscovici, 1972; Tileagă, 2013). Table 1.1 outlines some of the philosophical assumptions and practical differences between an American and a European approach to social psychology.

Each approach also posits a different model of reality, the most common of which is **perceptual cognitivism**—the idea that reality is "out there" and that all we need to do is perceive, accurately measure, and describe what we have found. This is the standard model adopted in science, and language is assumed to be transparent, passive, or acting as a mirror.

Perceptual cognitivism   Reality → Perception → Discourse

An alternative view is provided by the discursive model, which positions events in the opposite direction. We are born and immersed into a language system with pre-existing historical and conceptual constructs, that is, names, words, expressions, and so on, and these provide reference and give meaning to the world. It is through these linguistic constructs that we observe, discuss, and make sense of our experience.

Discursive psychology   Discourse → Perception → Reality

In this context, **discourse** refers to a way of talking about a particular topic. Although we may think that we can say what we want about a topic, to a large extent, much of the thinking has already been done for us by others who have set the limits for what can and cannot be said or thought. In this respect, *discourses define reality* and the existence of different discourses raises the prospect of different realities—indeed, multiple realities (Burr, 2003).

SOCIAL CONSTRUCTIONISM

At the heart of the discursive approach is **social constructionism.** Social constructionism challenges "taken for granted knowledge," which includes some of the principal constructs in psychology such as intelligence, personality, and health and illness (see Burr, 2003). For example, most people talk about "personality" as though it has real substance even though no one knows what it is or where it is located. Personality, as a concept, is simply an inference based on our interpretation of the speech and behavior of others. In everyday conversation, we often draw upon existing constructs to conceptualize certain groups or their actions, and when social constructs appear "natural," obvious, and self-evident, they provide a basis for a shared reality. Everyone assumes that everyone else knows what we are talking about; the construct is seldom challenged

Table 1.1 *Different approaches to social psychology.*

The assumptions of an American approach (Social Cognition)	The assumptions of a European approach
"Human nature is localised within the person" (Allport, 1968, p. 4). Other disciplines start by considering the system in which they live, i.e., sociology anthropology, political science, and economics.	Human nature is determined by social and economic conditions—social and economic forces mold thinking, behavior, identity, and worldview (Marx, 1888).
North American social psychology is located within general psychology—it is a branch of general psychology (Allport, 1968, p. 4).	The main ideas of European social psychology can be traced back to sociology and social philosophy, e.g., the work of Durkheim, and Mead. Social psychology provides a bridge between cultural anthropology and sociology (Moscovici & Markova, 2006).
The individual is the *primary reality* of the social and political world—the fundamental building block. Individual emotions, memory, and personality are used to account for social action.	The individual cannot be understood in isolation—the individual is in society and society is in the individual (Mead, 1934).
The term "social" has no special relevance—it simply refers to the environment.	The social, cultural, and historic context of people's actions is central to the analysis—the "social" in social psychology plays a critical role in our understanding.
Society is conceptualized as the accumulation of individuals, i.e., Society = Individual 1 + Individual 2 + Individual 3 … + Individual *n*. This **reductionist** and atomistic approach is often used in consumer research and opinion polling.	What goes on *between* individuals (language and communication) determines the nature of group dynamics and the nature of society.
Individual cognitive processes are universal, i.e., theories apply to all cultures across history.	Cognitive processes cannot be assumed to be universal—they are likely to be subject to cultural and historical influence.
The self (and personality) are coherent, consistent, and measurable.	The self is largely determined by cultural and historic location (people are different in different places and at different times in history). Identity (the preferred term) is subject to forces within the social order—it is fluid and socially constructed (Gergen, 1999).

(Continued)

Table 1.1 (Continued)

The assumptions of an American approach (Social Cognition)	The assumptions of a European approach
Attitudes reflect the psychological reality of the group.	Attitudes are positions taken up within very specific social circumstances to fulfill a particular function. Attitudes and opinions do not necessarily reflect common psychosocial realities shared by the group (Potter & Wetherell, 1987).
Methods are **positivistic**—scientific objectivity is assumed—studies are often laboratory based—emphasis is placed on rigorous experimentation. The aim is to uncover laws of behavior—these laws or principles are assumed to be timeless and universal.	Methods are eclectic (qualitative and quantitative)—the aim is to uncover the meaning of social phenomena (*verstehen*)—findings are an interpretive process—**reflexivity** is encouraged.
The world is "out there" ready to be studied, measured, and analyzed. Language is simply the means by which we express our understanding of reality.	The world is not simply "out there"; it is constructed through meanings, which are the product of language, culture, and socialization.

and it takes on a life of its own. This inevitably affects how we understand the subject and how we deal with it.

Feminists have argued convincingly for decades that *language constructs reality* and that located within language are the dynamics of power. For example, the exclusive use of the male pronoun "he" in written text, arguably excludes and diminishes all female readers—they are ignored, invisible, dismissed, or, from the writer's perspective, they simply do not exist. What is more, this positioning is subconsciously transferred to the reader who may internalize the power dynamic without question. Indeed, when we understand the processes by which language, discourse, and social constructs create inequality and disempowerment, their political nature is clear to see.

How does the process work? How do language, discourse, and the manufacture of social constructs determine our sense of social reality? First, we have to recognize that we are born into a world of constructs, and we are encouraged to accept them without question. Second, powerful institutions and people in positions of power largely determine what is "real." Once politicians or journalists label an event or a type of behavior in a particular way, the mold is set. One example would be "road rage"—angry behavior on the road that can, in some circumstances, result in loss of life. Once the media coined the term, people used the same construct to describe the behavior. However, some years ago, official police sources in the UK publicly rejected the term "road rage" stating that any intentional violent act that leads to loss of life was murder, whatever the circumstances and wherever it takes place. The implication was that they would not entertain any notion of extenuating circumstances (that it was "a crime of passion") or any explanation with quasi-psychiatric overtones (I suffer from road rage). This straightforward approach to language and the interpretation of the law cut through any attempt to mystify the situation with a new construct.

Social constructionists further argue that since the social world is the product of social, cultural and linguistic processes, there is no pre-ordained way of being. In other words, if we had been born into a different language, culture, and time in history, we would be a different person. The idea that people have no pre-ordained nature means that they have no essence—they are not made up of a substance that makes them what they are as in the case of salt or sand. To reject **essentialism** is to say that there is no human nature—that beliefs, values, or attitudes are not part of our makeup and that they do not determine behavior. Instead, human nature, beliefs, values, and attitudes are simply convenient linguistic constructs that we have at our disposal to explain the behavior of self and others. This may run contrary to our beliefs that there are good and bad people in the world or that some people are evil, but this essentialist view is one that social constructionism rejects given that we have no access to the inner thoughts and motivations of people (we can only observe behavior and interpret language). We can, however, say that some people *do* things that are either good or evil, which is quite different.

THE SOCIAL CONSTRUCTION OF REALITY

The main focus of social constructionism is to uncover ways in which individuals and groups participate in the construction of their own social reality. It involves looking at the ways that constructs are created, maintained, institutionalized, and how they eventually become tradition. Bound up in the creation of constructs is the process of **reification**. To reify mean "to make solid," which refers to a process through which something abstract is turned into something that is assumed to be concrete and real. In psychology, reification is commonplace and the naming of all sorts of physical and psychological deficits is largely determined by social and political processes rather than science.

To illustrate, consider what would happen if we had to earn our living by dancing instead of activities that require literacy or numeracy skills. If we assume the egalitarian position that everyone should be able to dance well, the culture would have to invent *dysdancia* (the inability to dance) to explain any widespread deficit. *Dysdancia* would then flourish as a concept, and because there would be an opportunity to make money and build careers, a proliferation of publications, courses, and advice with explanations ranging from the biological to the social would emerge. Other possible conditions could include—*dysathletsia* (when a child always comes last in school sports), *dyscanteria* (the inability to sing well enough to be in the school choir), or *dyscalcula de change* (the inability to work out change without a cash register). While these categorizations reflect observable behavior, they are nonetheless *political* constructions that bear little relation to science. Of course, one may investigate them using the scientific method, but the rationale for their construction is political.

What has this got to do with political psychology? We have to recognize that the culture is flooded with political constructions, which are a product of the social, political, and economic system. The behavior is real, it is not imaginary, but the way it is construed is a product of culture. Take for example, "terrorism." During the French Revolution, the term "terrorism" was coined to describe the actions of the French state. Since then, political elites have used the term to describe the politically motivated violence of people or groups that they neither like, nor agree with. To the public, such violent behavior appears random, irrational, highly dangerous, and threatening and, because the underlying historical, social, and political issues are seldom understood, there is a tendency to use the construct as a form of explanation; that is, people plant bombs because they are terrorists. However, the construct performs an important rhetorical and political function. By describing the violence of others as terrorism, it denigrates, devalues, and dismisses the violence as non-legitimate; it is seen as the work of a barbarous minority. What is more, the use of the term provides no explanation or any detailed information about grievances, arguments, or the objectives of the dissident group. It thus provides a convenient line of demarcation between the non-legitimate politically motivated violence of a minority and the legitimized politically motivated violence of established states (Hewer & Taylor, 2007).

Other words such as "extremist" and "radicalization" have also entered our political vocabulary even though no one ventures to offer a definition when they use these terms. By inference, we conclude that these terms describe people who have views and objectives that are dangerous, alien, and threatening even if we are not sure what they are. In such instances, researchers need to proceed with caution when studying such topics and should avoid reifying constructs and endorsing them through academic research (see Hermann, 1986). In such cases, rather than shedding light on social reality, our research may simply endorse a mainstream construction or worldview.

In this chapter, we have discussed some historical and philosophical considerations that provide a backdrop to the political world and political psychology. Through **empirical** research and sound critical analysis, social psychology can tell us much about the social and political world and, in some instances, it may offer solutions to specific problems. The forthcoming chapters will outline the contribution of a social psychological approach to political psychology and running more or less throughout the text is a critical stance to knowledge. Unsettling as this may be, it may open our eyes to the political nature of social and political psychology.

SUMMARY

- Religious identities and the historical events associated with them play a significant role in our understanding of modern politics and international relations.
- Individualism in social psychology has influenced political psychology in that it tends to locate the root of human behavior within the individual.
- The idea that living under a particular type of governmental system affects and influences people's thoughts and actions brings psychology and politics together in a common purpose. That is: to understand people, their motivations and needs, and how we might improve matters.
- Social constructionism adopts a critical approach to "taken for granted" knowledge: it interrogates our use of language, discourse, and constructs.

GLOSSARY

Age of the Enlightenment refers to a European intellectual movement of the late seventeenth and early eighteenth centuries that emphasized reason and individualism. It was influenced by philosophers such as Descartes, Locke, and Newton, and prominent figures included Kant, Goethe, Voltaire, Rousseau, and Adam Smith.

capitalism an economic and political system based on private ownership, profit, and market forces.

constructs are ideas or conceptualizations arising from our interpretation of the social world.

communism is a system of social organization in which all property is owned by the state, and each person contributes and receives according to their ability and needs.

democracy is a system of government that requires people to choose their representatives by voting for them in elections.

discourse refers to ways of talking about a topic. It can also be used to describe verbal communication in a more general sense.

divine right of kings is a political and religious doctrine that asserts that a monarch is subject to no authority other than God, deriving the right to rule from God. A monarch is therefore not subject to the will of the people, the aristocracy, or any other authority such as the Church.

empiricism is the philosophical position that valid knowledge is acquired through the senses (in an experimental context this is usually through observation). Data collected as text in qualitative research is also empirical.

epistemology is the branch of philosophy concerned with the theory of knowledge—what is legitimate knowledge and how it may be obtained.

essentialism is the view that objects including people are what they are because of their substance or essence, that the substance makes the object what it is.

eugenics is a set of beliefs and scientific practices that aims at improving the physical quality of the human population through selective reproduction.

identity politics refers to political positioning and political struggles based on the identity interests, perspectives, and objectives of social groups. Identity politics may be shaped by race, class, gender, gender identity, ethnicity, nationality, sexual orientation, religion, culture, language, accent, or dialect.

individualism is the political and moral philosophy that emphasizes the individual. Individualism promotes the pursuit of personal goals and desires; it values independence and self-reliance and asserts that interests of the individual should have precedence over the state. It opposes external interference from society or social institutions or the government. Individualism is often defined in contrast to collectivism.

jihad is an Islamic term that refers to the act of striving, applying oneself, struggling, or persevering. It is often used in political discourse to represent a "holy war" against unbelievers.

liberalism is a political philosophy founded on ideas of liberty and equality. Liberalism emphasizes the freedom of the individual, freedom of speech, freedom of the press, freedom of religion, free markets, civil rights, democratic societies, and gender equality.

methodological individualism is the process through which causal accounts of social phenomena show how they result from the motivations and actions of individuals.

ontology is the philosophical study of the nature of being, becoming, existence, or reality. Ontology often addresses questions concerning what entities exist or may be said to exist.

polity refers to any political entity or group of people that are collectively united by a common identity. They normally have a capacity to mobilize resources and matters are organized under some form of institutionalized hierarchy.

positivism refers to the philosophical position that only information derived from sensory experience interpreted through reason and logic, can provide the basis for authoritative knowledge. Positivism is based on empiricism.

power relations refers to the operation of power between different parties, for example, individuals, groups, and institutions. Power dynamics are often set and maintained through language, constructs, and discourse.

reductionism is the philosophical position that claims that we can understand the natural world / social objects / people / institutions, and so on by reducing them to their component parts. The counterargument is that full understanding of social phenomena is only achieved by encountering them as a whole and complete entity.

reflexivity requires researchers to examine the filters and lenses through which they see the world. The process requires critical reflection—a self-exploration that seeks an understanding of what they bring to the research and their own position within it. Reflexivity also requires sensitivity to "different voices" that may exist within the data, for example, marginalized groups, the assumptions of organizations, and so on.

reification takes place when an abstract idea is made concrete or "real" through language. This means that ideas, perceptions, perspectives can be organized into constructs that are eventually believed to be real or having substance.

social constructionism or the social construction of reality is a theory of knowledge that examines the development of constructed understandings of the world and the basis for shared assumptions about reality. The main argument is that people create models of the social world and share and reify these models through language.

social representations theory is a theory of communication that focuses on the everyday knowledge and understanding of people (commonsense). The theory posits that shared values, ideas, metaphors, beliefs, and practices in groups and communities provide a basis for a shared reality.

theocracy is a government that recognizes God as sovereign. God's will for the nation or people is implemented by strict adherence to a divinely authored written code.

FURTHER READING

Baradat L. P. (2012). *Political ideologies: Their origins and their impact* (11th ed.). New York: Longman.

Bowles P. (2012). *Capitalism*. London: Pearson.

Burr, V. (2003). *Social constructionism* (2nd ed.). Hove: Routledge.

Collier G., Minton H. L., & Reynolds G. (1991). *Currents of thought in American social psychology*. Oxford, UK: Oxford University Press.

Hannam J. (2012). *Feminism*. Harlow, UK: Pearson.

Hermann M. G. (1986). What is political psychology? In M. G. Hermann (Ed.), *Political psychology* (pp. 1–10). London: Jossey-Bass.

Himmelweit H. T., & Gaskell G. (1990). *Societal psychology*. London: Sage.

Hothersall D. (2004). *The history of psychology* (4th ed.). New York: McGraw-Hill.

Sandle M. (2012). *Communism*. London: Pearson.

Tileagă C. (2013). *Political psychology: critical perspectives*. Cambridge, UK: Cambridge University Press.

QUESTIONS FOR GROUP DISCUSSION

- When considering religious identities, what role does the past play in the present?

- What are some of the advantages and disadvantages of democracy? Are there any suitable alternatives? What would be an ideal administration or system of governance?

- What is meant by the term "polity?" How does this concept bring sociology, history, psychology, anthropology, and political science together?

- How might some political ideologies influence the social psychological explanations we offer?

- Provide some examples to show the relationship between language and power relations.

2 A Critical History
of Research Methods

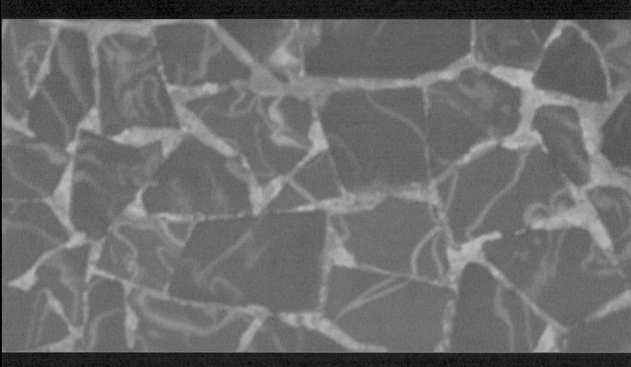

RON ROBERTS AND CHRISTOPHER J. HEWER

CHAPTER OUTLINE

In everyday conversation, people express their views about the state of the world and offer opinions, perspectives, and suggestions for improvement. This is the world of common sense. In contrast, professional psychologists claim to be specialist social or behavioral scientists who know about the human condition through scholarly study and scientific research. In this chapter, we review some of the issues in psychological research methods and discuss their problematic nature. To apply "what is known about human psychology to politics" (Huddy, Sears, & Levy, 2013a, p. 1) may seem straightforward enough, but the assumption that psychology is a pure and unadulterated science that sheds "natural light" on the political world is probably misplaced. Psychology is political and so are its methods.

WHAT DO WE WANT TO KNOW ABOUT THE WORLD AND WHY?

Let us start the discussion with a question: what precisely do we want to know about the world and for what purpose? Unlike other forms of specialized psychological research and practice, political psychology is rather vague about its aims. It may aspire to understand politics, or the relationship between politics and psychology, or interdependent relationships between individuals, groups, and social contexts, but this tells us very little about its human goals. In clinical psychology, for example, there is an assumption that its purpose is to assist people who experience a range of difficulties to live happier and more fruitful lives. In educational psychology, the goal is to help people to learn effectively and to progress through the system. The role of organizational or occupational psychology is to help organizations and the people in them work efficiently and productively. Is the aim of political psychology simply to understand how the world works in a psycho-political sense and to disseminate research findings to bureaucrats and politicians? Or are there implicit aims to advance democracy, to achieve full equality for women, to end racism, or to promote world peace? Do we have to be liberal and democratic in order to be a political psychologist? What is political psychology trying to achieve? And do we all agree with its objectives? Here, we are interrogating the political nature of political psychology.

In this respect, psychology (and particularly political psychology) occupies a controversial position between what *is* and what *ought* to be—a tension between what scientists discover and the policies that govern our lives. We should

Political Psychology: A Social Psychological Approach, First Edition.
Edited by Christopher J. Hewer and Evanthia Lyons.
© 2018 John Wiley & Sons Ltd. Published 2018 by John Wiley & Sons Ltd.

perhaps remind ourselves that not even natural laws tell us how to use them (Leahey, 2000) and psychological science (finding out what is) can easily shift toward moral discourse (a position on what ought to be). For example, does the discovery that smoking causes cancer mean that everyone should give up smoking? There may be economic arguments about the availability of health care to smokers or ethical issues about the treatment of one's own body, but science can only tell us "what is" not how we should live.

HOW CAN WE KNOW THE WORLD?

Let us now extend the question from what do we want to know about the world and why, to *how* can we know the world? To answer this question entails a discussion of the nature of knowledge. Knowledge from three principal sources—**rationalism**, empiricism, and **revelation**—have dominated human politics throughout history. Rationalism—the foundation of philosophy—refers to knowledge derived through argument and reason, while revelation—the foundation of theology—refers to knowledge obtained from the interpretation of sacred texts originating from a divine source. For centuries, philosophers and theologians argued their respective positions (see Hill, 2004) and when natural philosophy developed into modern science in the eighteenth century, experimentation and observation placed empiricism—knowledge apprehended through the senses—at the forefront of human endeavor. The three way debate between science, philosophy, and theology (e.g., see Gjertsen, 1992; Hill, 2004; Wolpert, 1992), became a power struggle between reason, empiricism, and faith in the divine word, and the outcome of this debate would have implications for modern psychology emerging in the late nineteenth century.

There is no simple linear history of psychology; psychological thought was the product of complex intellectual argument shaped by political conflict, philosophical doubt, and the scientific revolution of the seventeenth century (Leahey, 2000). And as philosophical doubt evolved into a crisis of skepticism in the eighteenth century, the advance of science presented a more confident model of a mechanized world that no longer required divine maintenance or divine intervention. The enchanted world where God was omnipresent and involved in all things was replaced by the idea that God had, so to speak (in modern terms), "constructed a perfect machine and left it running" (Leahey, 1980, p. 89). Scientific progress had indeed brought about a shift in theological thinking, which created tension between two epistemological positions: revelation as pronounced by God and empirical findings discovered by human endeavor. The debate intensified in the nineteenth century as the evolutionary ideas of Charles Darwin (as presented by Thomas Huxley—"Darwin's bulldog") came head to head with Bishop Wilberforce and other staunch advocates of the Biblical account of creation. The authority of religion that highlighted the need to submit to the superior knowledge of the divine was in decline, while the authority of science, which promised power over nature, was increasing.

It is in this historical context that psychology embraced empiricism— measurement and scientific analysis—as its preferred method for obtaining knowledge.[1] In the late nineteenth century, the political/intellectual campaign against myth, superstition, and faith continued, and therefore scientific credentials were of the utmost importance. Even the psychological complexities of the human mind proposed by Sigmund Freud in the early twentieth century were rejected by the psychological community for their lack of scientific credibility.

SEARCHING FOR UNIVERSAL LAWS OF BEHAVIOR

The primary objective of this new psychological science was to uncover laws of human behavior. By the beginning of the twentieth century, scientists had come to understand that the universe and all forms of life including the human body were governed by natural physical laws and systems. Early psychologists such as Watson (1913) took this model to assert that similar "natural" laws governed human behavior, and the task of psychological science was to reveal those laws. Psychologists believed that rigorous experimentation—the measurement, manipulation, and control of variables—would yield an understanding of causal factors in the social and psychological world. A century later, however, history shows that while scientists have been able to manipulate forces in the natural world—sending humans into space and controlling disease—there appears to be very little human behavior that conforms to strict scientific principles and therefore very little that can be predicted. This puts psychology and its relationship with the scientific method in a rather uncomfortable position. While the absence of universal laws of behavior does not necessarily undermine psychology as a scientific enterprise, it nonetheless calls into question the degree to which we can ascertain cause and effect relationships in the social world and therefore we must concede that such prediction is unlikely.[2]

The need to find cause and effect mechanisms is considered fundamental to scientific progress and using this approach to understand human behavior has inevitably brought **determinism** to the fore as an explanatory model of human

---

[1] Scientific psychology also sought to distinguish itself from its "occult doubles" (Leahey, 2000, p. 531), e.g., astrology, spiritism, and psychical research now referred to as parapsychology.
[2] Because psychology has sought to establish universal laws of behaviour, and has adopted the scientific method to do so, it has often been accused of **physics envy** (Leahey, 1980).

behavior. For example, in cognitive neuropsychology there is a tendency to explain all aspects of human existence, from art appreciation to mental "illness" to serial killing, in terms of biocognitive processes. There are important political implications here: to propose that behavior is the result of internal or external mechanisms poses a significant threat to the concept of free will. In most cultures—particularly those informed by a theological or humanistic model of human nature—it is assumed that humans are endowed with free will and are accountable for their actions. And despite the proselytizing advances of determinism in psychological science, most people retain this belief. This does not mean that freedom to act is absolute; our own experience tells us that behavior can be both shaped and constrained by hereditary factors, upbringing, experience, economics, culture, history, and language as well as the social, economic, and environmental pressures existing in everyday life. However, if we believe—broadly speaking—that people are free to act then we have to accept that this is incompatible with our assumptions about the computability of social reality.

These alternative stances are reflected in a Kantian analysis of mind. Prior to the emergence of modern psychology, philosopher, Immanuel Kant (1724–1804) acknowledged a distinction between these two psychological positions. "Pure reason," he argued, seeks causal explanation in a spatial and temporally bounded world, whereas "practical reason" starts from an assumed position of free will (see Scruton, 2001). To some degree, this distinction reflects the rationale underlying the two broad methodological camps (quantitative and qualitative) existing today. Both approaches have devised ways of dealing with different kinds of questions—those that seek to establish the role of impersonal causal processes (what is happening as a result of social, biological, and psychological forces?) and those that focus on localized meanings generated by human actors (how and why do people see the world in a particular way?). Neither has developed independently of the social and political environment; both come with their own histories.

THE COMPUTABILITY PROBLEM

The belief that complex, but predictable forces exist in the social world lies at the root of the computability problem. In the natural world, physical laws apply across time and place because of *the regularity of nature*. However, we can assume no such regularity or order in the social world. This raises a very difficult question for social and political psychologists: is social reality a computational problem? This question has received some attention within philosophy and the physical sciences but almost none in psychology. The central argument is that there is no functional quality to the universe other than its computational behavior (Penrose, 2013). Moreover, the idea that reality is computable means that it consists of rule governed physical processes—that the universe can be conceptualized as a vast computational device—the product of a deterministic or probabilistic computer program (Schmidhuber, 2013). We may not believe this to be the case when we look at the world, but many psychologists carry out their work as though it is. This algorithmic view of reality, which is both mechanistic and reductionist, holds that conscious experience, awareness, will, agency, intention, and understanding are illusions—**epiphenomena** of underlying physical algorithmic processes. What is more, this assumption underpins experimental psychology in all its various guises and provides a rationale for using mathematical and statistical methods. It is thus assumed that all observable phenomena in the world can be reduced to mathematics, and that mathematical patterns are the only "true" patterns of interest.

Although this debate is relevant for the whole of psychology including political psychology, it has been confined to discussions of the viability of artificial intelligence and the mystery of consciousness (Sheldrake, 2012). Many scholars have challenged the notion that rule based systems can explain the reality of consciousness and awareness (e.g., Hagen, 2012; Penrose, 1999; Searle, 1980), but social and political psychologists have yet to question whether the reality they grapple with—the world of political decision making, intergroup conflict, the dynamics of power, persuasion, and influence and their interaction in a changing social and material world, is amenable to precise quantification and rules. To look for mathematical patterns in a social system where none exist would be a pointless exercise.

However, the pressure of living in an evidence-based culture means that researchers are required to support their claims with data. Measurement is not only the hallmark of science, but also the activity from which we acquire a sense of reality about the world. We now live in an age of data where no government or commercial organization takes a decision without strategic or market research. We might say that knowing the environment in an empirical sense is to have a grasp on reality. What is more, the numerical data that results from measurement carries an assumed validity—we do not question the idea that numbers accurately reflect the world. In our everyday existence, numbers dominate the activity of buying and selling—they represent value in the monetary world and, in practical terms, counting and quantifying are actions that serve as a "reality check." Well-established branches of scientific enquiry have also demonstrated that numerical data converted into mathematical models give us control over the physical environment. Such models reliably inform building construction and engineering not only because they offer precise technical description, but because they allow us to make confident predictions about the environment. However, it is not the numbers in themselves that do this, but the laws and principles that govern the physical world. It just happens, rather conveniently, that these laws can be expressed mathematically.

Converting observable or detectable phenomena into numbers, quantities, and variables and manipulating them into mathematical models of reality is the standard scientific approach, and one that psychology has embraced with some enthusiasm. But whether this is the most appropriate method for understanding people, particularly in a changing social and political context, is a matter of debate. Political scientists may seek to gauge future behavior through opinion polling (often with limited success) or to report changing political circumstances using statistical data, but for psychologists seeking to establish more enduring principles about mind, behavior, and human nature, the situation is less satisfactory and not so promising.

THE HISTORIC NATURE OF RESEARCH FINDINGS

To establish a law or principle in any science requires replication over time in multiple settings. Without successful replications, we have to assume that patterns in psychological data are at best historical and not rule governed—this is something that would apply to both human behavior and the succession of historical events (Donagan, 1966). Most social psychological findings fall into this category: they are not laws as such but observations existing at a particular point in time (see Gergen, 1973). And because they are positioned in time (we might say metaphorically—in a time capsule), we may describe them as historical—relevant to the time and place in which they were derived. Social psychology thus explains what people did in social psychology experiments and why they did it at a particular time in history. What is more, because the fluid and dynamic nature of social reality stands in contrast to the largely static nature of measurement, data acquired through experiments, questionnaires, interviews or focus groups can only provide "snapshots" of reality at best.

If indeed there are no natural laws of behavior, and events cannot be predicted, and if research findings only provide a snapshot of reality, how might we study the socio-political world? This is the key question. What may assist us in the analysis is to appreciate that political events occur within a matrix of wider human, economic, and environmental events—and there may be patterns to these events, for example, we might conclude, for example, that illegal wars lead to unintended political consequences, or that bombing foreign infrastructure causes migration, and that migration creates issues of identity. The art of the historian or political scientist is to interpret past events and make sense of them. However, we have to bear in mind that the historical–political past is a world in perpetual construction with no final or uniquely true interpretation of historical processes and events (see Hewer & Roberts, 2012). The historical and political world is also emergent—not rule governed.

Social researchers also have to contend with a capricious human nature. While we might observe that people often broadly comply with what they are asked to do, we know from the studies of Asch and Milgram in the 1950s and 1960s that this is not always the case—people do not always conform or obey—some rebel or act in unusual ways, or behave in a manner that violates culture and convention; or they may exercise their will to harm others for reasons that we may not fully understand (Zimbardo, 1969). Human situations unfold in specific historical contexts, which is one reason why they are poorly understood. Indeed, psychological research often removes individual history from its analysis, and therefore conclusions are often incomplete, limited, or even flawed. In short, the dehistoricization of people is a problem. Roberts (2015, p. 6), for example, argues that:

> In reality, the enormous variety of possible situations coupled with the clash of people's unknown histories means that a prescriptive account of how people ought to be expected to behave based on prior probability cannot be known.

This proposition has serious implications for psychology. Marie Jahoda, in a foreword to Laing, Phillipson, and Lee's (1966) *Interpersonal Perception,* also argued that there are "no norms for interpersonal encounters" (1966, p. iv). In other words, what people say and do may not be governed by unseen psychological laws; speech and behavior may be subject to the forces of culture or context, but people are free to speak and act as they choose. If this is so, it creates enormous difficulties for an account of human behavior tied to statistical precepts. We might then ask why do psychologists use statistics? Psychology students will be familiar with the long lists of statistical tests and procedures together with the requisites of experimental design in their course syllabus. However, unlike the rest of the material they encounter in their degree courses, statistics is presented in an ahistorical form as if the prescribed analytic tools—statistical tests and the philosophical perspectives underlying them have either been self-evident truths since time immemorial or have been determined and universally agreed following painstaking scientific debate. Neither, however, is true. Although the debate about the appropriateness of a statistical approach to understanding the human condition is longstanding, it remains curiously absent from the psychology curriculum. So why do psychologists rely so much on statistical methods and how did this come about?

THE ORIGIN OF STATISTICS

It is only at the beginning of the industrial revolution that psychology gets its modern impetus. At this time, there are two significant social trends taking place that would profoundly influence the development of psychology and which would result in an alliance with statistics—a newly emerging discipline. The first concerns the physical sciences, which had already been successful in describing and predicting the world on the basis of mathematical laws—a process that came to be seen as an essential defining feature of scientific activity. The second concerns the emergence of mercantile capitalism, which brought large numbers of people flooding into the burgeoning towns and cities in search of work. It was now imperative for the state to gather information on the changing nature of social and economic life.

Thus, underlying the foundation of statistics as a discipline was a desire to collect demographic and economic data that would be useful to the state. In the English-speaking world, this was known as *Political Arithmetic,* but it later took its name from the German *Statistik,* first used by Gottfried Achenwall in 1749 when "compiling information about the state" (Davis, 1995, p. 26). We see in this period of early statistical work attempts to form crude life tables that enable the computation of probability estimates of life expectancy. One prominent use of statistical measures was to calculate the number of men of fighting age in London (Fienberg, 1992). Here then begins the political act of assigning people, and the social spaces they inhabit, to various boxes, categories, and packages.

It is important to stress that statistical science began, not to enhance human well-being or to promote a deeper understanding of the natural world, but to serve the needs of government and central administrative bodies. The commercial and scientific use of statistical information came much later. Indeed, one cannot fully appreciate psychology's preoccupation with coding, counting, and classifying people—that is, turning people and their characteristics, feelings, and activities into numbers—outside of a history of state surveillance and its relationship with capitalism. What is more, the status accorded empirical measurement, categorization, and countability not only explains the subsequent widespread use of statistical methods, but also the very nature of academic psychology—that it largely confines itself to the study of what is measurable.

By the nineteenth century, statistics as a discipline escapes from its political and administrative role to become a general theoretical method for the analysis and interpretation of data. Although it has made an enormous contribution to the development of analytic techniques in all the recognized sciences, it would be optimistic to assume that there would be no political interest or motive in a discipline that classified people and their behavior. Indeed, such imprints can be seen in psychometrics and behavior genetics, founded by Francis Galton and Karl Pearson and aided by Charles Spearman[3]—all of whom were committed to eugenics. We might say then that statistics was "bound up with eugenics" (Davis, 1995, p. 30) because eugenics needed statistics to demonstrate what was normal. However, the concept of the norm is inherently divisive, not least, because it sets standard and nonstandard subpopulations against each other.

THE CONSTRUCTION OF NORMS, NORMALITY, AND NORMALCY

What precisely do we mean by normal? And why do we need this information? Statistics often consist of descriptions of people and social groups along specific dimensions, for example, height, weight, family size, age, and so on from which an average or mean score is calculated. At the root of such statistical analyses is the bell curve, the normal distribution, which provides information about the distribution of human characteristics and performance within a population (see Figure 2.1). At the mid-point of the bell curve is the mean, which is a measure of

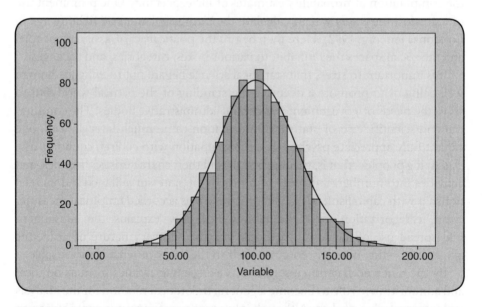

FIGURE 2.1 *The normal distribution (for a hypothetical variable with a mean of 100 and a standard deviation of 20, N = 1,000).*

---

[3] The statistical methods derived by Galton, Pearson, and Spearman (e.g., correlation, regression, factor analysis) form the backbone of many quantitative methods in psychology (see Fanchner, 1985).

what most people are like. This graph or distribution indicates that most people are average and that only a small percentage excel or are well below average.

Many characteristics such as height and weight fit the bell curve, but some aspects of human performance like the ability to eat, smile, or think do not because most people, if not all, can do these things so it is not possible to discriminate between people on these dimensions. Here, we have established the main purpose of the bell curve—to identify and describe the nature of individual differences within a given population. Without the concept of the "average man,"—the lynchpin of modern conceptions of normality first proposed by French statistician Adolphe Quetelet (1796–1847)—it would not be possible to engage in social comparison and classify people as either above or below average.

However, one of the problems with statistical norms is that they do not remain descriptive. They start as computational summaries of a set of data, but their function can shift almost imperceptibly toward prescription. This is because in a world of capitalist enterprise where individualism and knowledge of individual differences has economic value, they become the basis for saying how things *should be* rather than how things are. What is more, people have also developed the habit of wanting to assess themselves in relation to others—a form of competitive behavior that reflects the pressures of the social and political system. Indeed, statistics as a discipline may have contributed to a long history of state surveillance, but more crucially it has created a culture of self-surveillance with all its implications for mental and physical well-being. For example, when we establish an average height for a man, such information has the potential to diminish and demoralize 50% of the population because they are either average or below average. Consequently, some men will conclude that they are deficient and that they *should be* taller—a view that may come to be shared by women. The measure of "what is" now creates a social pressure for what is desirable, which is not a good psychological model for encouraging or accepting diversity in others or indeed ourselves.

This type of measurement fixation is also found in most areas of professional life particularly where finance or funding is involved. For example, in the UK, we see comparisons in the assessment of schools, colleges, and universities; and in recent years, league tables have been created to encourage competition and copious amounts of angst and self-criticism among those who work in education. The political argument is that without such knowledge, we cannot raise standards. The key question thus becomes: how are we doing in relation to everyone else? We must improve our performance. We must not be average or below average: we must excel! However, if we imagine a world where the concerted effort of students and teachers raises the mean educational outcome across the country to 95% so that everyone performs to an "excellent" standard, politicians will not conclude that teachers and students have worked hard or improved their performance, but that assessments must be getting easier and therefore standards are falling. Similar attributions take place every year in the UK when school examination results are released, and although we might describe these claims as attribution errors (see Heider, 1958; Ross, 1977), they are not mistakes—they are politically motivated attributions designed to undermine either the government, the examination boards, and/or the teaching profession.

USING STATISTICAL MEASURES AND MODELS FOR POLITICAL PURPOSES

The subtle shift from description to political prescription is also seen in the use of value-added models in education. These models reflect an expectation that people entering an education institution will have value added to their educational outcome due to the efforts of teachers and the resources provided by the institution. It is an "input–output" model that asserts that what goes in over a relatively short period of time must come out bigger and better and, as such, it is a perpetual growth model (most often seen in sales and marketing) that mirrors the expectations of capitalistic enterprise.[4] If no such value is added to a student or a student group (this is determined by measurable outcomes), then the teaching staff and/or the institution are judged to be performing badly.

Value-added modeling is based on regression analysis—a predictive technique founded on simple correlation, which was originally devised in the United States in the 1970s as a way to evaluate teacher performance in schools. Underpinning this type of modeling is the assumed mathematical relationship between an individual's test performance at a specific point in time and their subsequent performance, that is, the assumption that a child's test performance at age 9, for example, will reflect their performance at age 8. Any improvement beyond the average would indicate "value added" by the teacher. The statistical complexity and ingenuity of the modeling process is beyond question (see Kim & Lalacette, 2013 for a review of all types of value-added modeling), and attempts have been made to tease out socio-economic confounding variables as well as teaching practices, class sizes, and so on. It is important to note, however, that the technique was specifically designed for use in educational settings

---

[4]In the world of finance, investors are routinely warned that the instabilities of the market, caused by unpredictable events, may cause investments to go *down* as well as up. To investors, for whom profit is the only acceptable outcome, this cautionary advice often falls on deaf ears because they subscribe to the perpetual growth model—the idea that economic growth is linear and continuous rather than cyclical or curvilinear. Similar assumptions are made about individual student performance and outcomes in education.

where children would have one teacher over a period of time, and to ensure that sound comparisons could be made across classes, institutions, and states, **standardized tests** were required. Most importantly, the techniques are predicated on the assumption that *students are randomly assigned to teachers*.

In higher education, most of these conditions are not met; students are not randomly assigned to classes (students often attend in clusters of varied ability and with varying motivations), and many teachers are involved in the period between initial measurement (input) and final assessment (output). Nonetheless, the broad assumption is that someone entering higher education would be expected to leave with a class of degree commensurate with their entry qualifications, and having carried out a regression analysis, the pressure exerted on teachers and institutions is that they should always perform above the **regression line**. While this may seem quite reasonable on the surface, the way that statistics are used to promote and maintain this argument requires some examination.

If we know that a linear relationship exists between two variables (e.g., height and weight; i.e., as people get taller their weight increases), we can make an *approximate* prediction of a person's weight from their height. However, when dealing with human factors, it is not possible to predict *perfectly* the value of one variable from another as if all the data are perfectly linear. In the example of height and weight (see Figure 2.2), we know that many people are short but large in body mass or tall and thin. This is a natural variation among human beings; people neither present themselves, nor perform in a uniform manner.

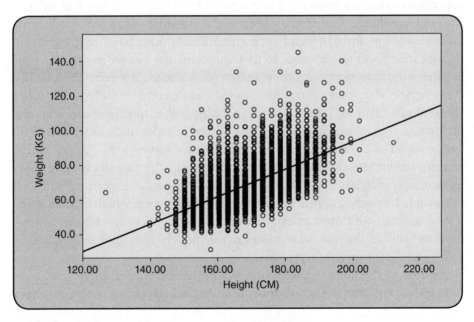

FIGURE 2.2 *The relationship between height and weight.*
(Source: Data from Health & Lifestyle Survey UK: Cox, 1987).

Nonetheless, it is possible to derive a mathematical model in the form of a straight-line equation ($y = mx + c$) from these data. In the equation, y is the variable along the vertical y axis, x is the variable along the x axis, m is the gradient or slope of the line, and c is the intercept, the numerical value at the point at which the line crosses the y axis. The regression line—the line of best fit—is the mathematically constructed mid-point of the data. *It is a descriptive measure that is imposed on the data*: it has no formal existence in the real world.

The regression line *describes* the general orientation (direction) and gradient (the degree of slope) of the data, and such models work well as an approximate technique for prediction, but a problem develops when it is used *to prescribe how reality should be*.

For example, if we had been involved in teaching some of the participants to live more healthily and to eat more nutritiously, we cannot be held responsible for any variability in the data unless we had been given complete control over their genetic constitution and their eating and exercise regime throughout their lives. What is more, the scores may be subject to random or uncontrolled developments; for example, individuals may eat too much or too little, and the data may be cohort dependent, that is the results are due to the particular nature of the people in that data set—therefore no generalization can be made about the teaching program.

In the context of educational outcomes, the assumption of a regression model is that educational development is linear, that is that someone entering education will perform in strict accordance with their entry qualifications. This is a curious assumption since the years from 18 to 21 are often stressful, disruptive, and emotionally turbulent, and economic pressures often make it difficult for students to perform to their full potential. On the other hand, many students do well and appear to add value to their performance, but we have to remember that *a position above the line only exists because others are below the line*. For every person with lower entry educational qualifications who has performed "beyond expectations," there is a person with higher qualifications who has performed "below expectations." Thus, in the broader analysis, the level of "value added" is always equal to the level of "value subtracted." "Value" in this context, is therefore a relative concept, and although the measure may be politically meaningful, it is scientifically meaningless. Indeed, the political utility of value-added modeling appears to outweigh its limitations, which include problems associated with nonrandom allocation of students to teachers or institutions as well as the risk that misspecified models[5] can lead to inaccurate value-added measures (Murphy, 2012).

Because of the linear assumptions of a regression model, there can be no "ups and downs" and the act of drawing a line through reality is nothing short

---

[5] This is when causal variables are omitted. Murphy (2012, p. 9) notes that "determining whether causative variables are omitted in practice is impossible."

of a political act that permits others to identify "apparent underperformance"—another example where description leads to prescription. Given the nature of regression, it is impossible for every data point to be above the line because, if the data move upwards, the line is adjusted—the mid-point divides the data—and the same relative claims will be made. We might conclude then that "apparent underperformance" is built into this technique. Moreover, with such an adjustment, lower entry grades now produce a better degree classification, which could lead to the political attribution that everything is getting easier and that academic standards are falling.

In a tight economic climate where institutional survival is paramount, these models perform a political function. They permit politicians, bureaucrats, and managers in education (under pseudo-scientific cover) to exert pressure upon the workforce. Despite their best efforts, 50% of schools or universities will always fall below the mathematical dividing line, and such data will continue to be used to accuse individual teaching professionals or whole departments of substandard performance. However, the description/prescription issue is only one of many issues for quantitative methods. In the next section, we will discuss the use of **null hypothesis significance testing** (NHST), the problem of replication, and the file drawer effect.

THE NULL HYPOTHESIS SIGNIFICANCE TEST

Although the computability problem appears to have been omitted from mainstream discussions about the nature of psychological and social reality, psychologists continue to use quantitative methods. And the cornerstone of the statistical world presented to psychology students and represented in countless publications as "the method for evaluating scientific hypotheses" (Haller & Kraus, 2002, p. 2), is the null hypothesis significance test (NHST), originally proposed by Fisher in 1935.[6] While mastering the formal procedure of conducting significance tests is fairly straightforward, there is considerably less mastery of what the results of these procedures actually mean.

Two major misconceptions are associated with their use—that smaller p-values denote stronger effects and that statistical significance is a measure of theoretical or practical significance (Gliner, Leech, & Morgan, 2002). These problems arise because fundamentally the procedure does not provide

---

[6] R. A. Fisher was also a eugenicist (Davis, 1995, p. 30).

the desired information. What the NHST tells us is the probability of obtaining the observed data in a random sample, *if the null hypothesis were true*, that is: the conditional probability p $(D|H_0)$, whereas what researchers really want to know is a different (conditional) probability, that is: the probability of the null hypothesis being true, given the data we have—p $(H_0|D)$ (Kirk, 1996). This is often the standard but erroneous interpretation offered by students. The situation is further compounded by the use of "critical" significance levels as arbitrary pass/fail decision hurdles to determine whether to reject or accept the null hypothesis. This problem also has its origins with Fisher. Note the following comments by Fisher (1926, p. 504) where rejection of the null hypothesis is tied in with acceptance of the experimental hypothesis:

> If one in twenty does not seem high enough, we may, if we prefer it, draw the line at one in fifty (2 per cent point), or one in one hundred (the 1 per cent point). Personally, the writer prefers to set a low standard of significance at the 5 per cent point, and ignore entirely all results which fail to reach this level. A scientific fact should be regarded as experimentally established only if a properly designed experiment rarely fails to give this level of significance.

Though Fisher did not maintain this faith in the utility of the 5% level—it has become enshrined in statistical folklore as the decisive threshold for accepting/rejecting hypotheses, though it is by no means universal. Particle physicists for example use the so-called **five-sigma threshold**—equivalent to five standard deviations from the mean—before giving credence to a result. Furthermore, there is the added problem that psychologists rarely use random samples and they gloss over the problem of making do with the highly biased samples that are routinely available to them—opportunity samples of young university students. For the appropriate statistical inferences to be drawn, most of the statistical procedures in common use are predicated on the observed data having being obtained from random samples. Filho et al. (2013, p. 33) remind us that, "it is pointless to estimate the p value for non-random samples." However, if this were rigidly applied, it would, at a stroke, nullify the findings of most psychological studies. This is because, as they also note (p. 40) the use of a non-random sample means that the "underlying assumptions of both the normal distribution and **central limit theorem** do not hold." Thus, without randomization there is no proper basis for statistical inference predicated on the NHST.

Most texts ignore the widespread dissatisfaction with the NHST (see Morrison & Henkel, 2006 for a review of existing criticisms) and present the topic as a (historical) debate free zone, a matter merely of technique. It is not surprising then that with discussion discouraged, there is much confusion. Ziliak and McCloskey (2011, p. 25) lament that it is "hard for scientists trained in Fisherian methods to see how bizarre the methods in fact are and increasingly harder the better trained in Fisherian methods they are." Carver (1993, p. 1) went further: "statistical significance testing is … being used in a manner which corrupts the scientific method."

By the mid-1990s, over 40 alternatives to the NHST had been suggested (Kirk, 1996). For many years, the favored alternative approach was Neyman–Pearson hypothesis testing. Rather than examining the data with respect to the null hypothesis, this method involved a direct comparison between pairs of distinct specified hypotheses. Predefined selection criteria based on a likelihood ratio of their respective probabilities could then be used to choose between them. This differs from Fisher's approach where rejection of the null hypothesis does not imply automatic acceptance of some alternative hypothesis H_1. This is because, in principle, an infinite number of alternative hypotheses ($H_1 \ldots H_n$) can account for the data.

The principal difference between these techniques is that Fisher's approach uses a **signal to noise ratio** to inform decision making (the weight of systematic to chance variation) to determine whether a detectable effect is present, whereas the Neyman–Pearson approach is geared toward improved experimental testing of specified hypotheses and deals with **effect sizes**. It was Neyman who, in developing the latter approach, first proposed the formulation of **confidence intervals** in data exploration (Neyman, 1937). What psychology students are taught today is really a mixture of these two approaches with no awareness that many statisticians consider them to be incompatible. These methods date back to the early twentieth century and their development has resulted in statistical methods becoming the common language of the academic psychology community. They have, however, created a preoccupation with statistical significance[7] at the expense of the social significance and the overall meaning of the data.

BAYESIAN METHODS

Currently the most popular alternative to the NHST in some quarters of the discipline is the Bayesian approach (Lecoutre, Lecoutre, & Poitevineau, 2001; Mason, 2016), which entails a very different philosophical position about the nature of probability. Probability, in this context, is a measure of how much information an observer has about the world rather than it being an intrinsic property of the world (Stone, 2013). Bayesian analysis is thus a method for

---

[7] An additional problem in psychological research is that because of small samples and between-subjects designs, statistical analysis often lacks **statistical power**—such that it is unable to detect an effect where one exists.

interpreting evidence *in the context of prior experience or knowledge* and it provides an "inference engine" that yields precise probability estimates for a number of alternative answers.

Bayes' rule is formalized as follows:

$$p(\text{hypothesis}|\text{data}) = \frac{p(\text{data}|\text{hypothesis}) \times p(\text{hypothesis})}{p(\text{data})} \quad (2.1)$$

Because the human brain is considered to be a Bayesian inference engine, the technique has been applied in risk analysis and decision science and in health, business, cognitive psychology, and artificial intelligence in particular. Applications in the broader historical and social sciences have been less successful and more problematic (see e.g., Jackman, 2004 for a discussion of Bayesian analysis in political science). Indeed, Gelman (2008) has argued the method has a number of important limitations and considers Bayesian methods to have been oversold as an all-purpose statistical solution to difficult problems. In some cases, it may even be considered as a class of methods in search of a problem (Gelman, 2011).

The main area of contention concerns the estimation of prior probabilities. This can be illustrated by reference to some questionable applications of Bayesian principles. On the historical front, attempts have been made to assess the veracity of Jesus as a historical figure based on estimated probabilities derived from incomplete historical sources (Carrier, 2014). While we may draw inferences from incomplete historical records, science has to deal with empirical evidence and incomplete historical manuscripts likely fall short of this definition. A similar issue occurs in cosmology where respective likelihoods have been computed to suggest that some version of string theory in particle physics is true, and that the multiverse exists—when there is no current physical evidence for either (Castelvecchi, 2015; Wolchover, 2015). What is more, had this reasoning been applied to the world of physics in the late nineteenth century, it would have led to the definitive conclusion that **the ether** exists.

However, even some proponents of Bayesian analysis have argued that deriving "truth" on the basis of non-empirical arguments would "open the floodgates to abandoning all scientific principles" (Wolchover, 2015). The dangers for psychologists are all too real. To what extent can our competing hypotheses about psychological or social reality reasonably be expressed as mathematical probability distributions? The dangers multiply when psychologists consider states of mind that, by definition, are subjective and nonempirical. This is not to dismiss Bayesian methods out of hand but to highlight the potential dangers of adding yet another form of mathematical rhetoric to the psychological toolbox in the absence of objective and replicable evidence.

THE ISSUE OF REPLICATION

In recent years, we have witnessed increased scrutiny of published psychological research findings and the apparent difficulties in replicating them. For example, the Open Science Collaboration (OSC) (2015) sought to reproduce the results from 100 studies published since 2008 in three major psychology journals (*Psychological Science, Journal of Personality and Social Psychology*, and the *Journal of Experimental Psychology: Learning, Memory, and Cognition*). The attempted replications, while adhering closely to the original designs and with comparable sample sizes, obtained statistically significant results in only 36% of the studies, with reported effect sizes much smaller than those originally obtained. For social psychology, the successful replication rate was only 25%. These troubling findings are not the first to emerge. Following an attempted replication by Chris French (2012), Richard Wiseman and Stuart Richie of an apparent demonstration of precognition by Bem (2011), French and his colleagues had considerable difficulty getting any journal to review their paper let alone publish it. In French's words:

> This whole saga raises important questions. Although we are always being told that "replication is the cornerstone of science" the truth is that the "top" journals are simply not interested in straight replications – especially failed replications. They only want to report findings that are new and positive.

Wider interest in the discipline was awakened only when French took his concerns to *The Guardian* newspaper, prompting a hastily summoned "stellar cast of contributors" (*The Psychologist*, 2012, p. 349) to comment. For Ritchie et al. (2012, p. 346) the affair raises questions about our "current statistical paradigm" and a preoccupation with novelty at the expense of consolidating knowledge. Also among the findings from the OSC group, was that results that were originally surprising are less easy to replicate. Novelty, it seems, makes interesting reading and may "sell" well, but it does not guarantee truth or practical worth, nor is it necessarily good science.

The situation may even be worse than this suggests: the OSC found replication rates for multivariate interaction effects were only 22%. In addition, Roberts (2005) points to the complete absence of any attempts to fully replicate structural equation models (SEMs). In Miles and Shevlin's (2003) introduction to the technique, they make no mention of replicability other than it being "a problem." Roberts (2015), however, argues that in cases where generalization is implied or where the data imply more than a momentary snapshot of reality, some evidence of attempted replication should be offered. In other words, has the same model been reproduced in an independent sample (splitting the original sample and testing the model in two smaller samples may be a first step). Has the replication been able to (a) explain the same degree of variance while (b) employing the same predictors with (c) the same specified pathways, and (d) the same explanatory power (effect size). Despite the lack of replication of SEMs, their presence in journal articles adds to their citation value. Indeed, their presence in journal articles is a positive predictive factor of citation frequency (Hegarty & Walton, 2012) and it is hard not to see this particular technique and multivariate statistics as a whole as functioning as a form of statistical rhetoric. Often, it is the weight of complexity in the data processing analysis that convinces others of its scientific worth, rather than the strength of evidence for the specific claims.

THE FILE DRAWER EFFECT

Closely related to the problems evident in replicating psychological research and the use of the NHST is the bias toward accepting articles for publication that produce statistically significant results. Those studies that do not produce statistically significant results are less likely to be submitted by authors because they are aware of the bias, that is, they know that such studies are more likely to be rejected by journal editors (Sterling, Rosenbaum, & Weinkam, 1995). The end result is known as the **file drawer effect** (Rosenthal, 1979), which has been highlighted by Kirtsch (2009) as exerting a huge effect in the erroneous interpretation of the results from trials of antidepressant drugs. While attempts are being made to reduce this—by setting up public databases that register clinical trials in advance—there is a long way to go before confidence in the integrity of published research can be restored. This problem, however, is not confined to psychology (e.g., Hopewell, Loudon, Clarke, Oxman, & Dickersin, 2009). Indeed, Ioannadis (2005) has persuasively argued that most published research findings are false.

To add to these problems, there is also an issue of false reporting and questionable practice. For example, John, Loewenstein, and Prelec (2012) found that a high proportion of their sample of 2000 psychologists admitted to engaging in dubious research practices. Prevalence estimates obtained for data falsification were 9%, for rounding down p-values—39%, for failing to report all conditions—42%, and for selectively reporting studies that "worked"—67%. Self-admission rates for questionable practices were highest for social psychologists, which means that the integrity, validity, and legitimacy of a good deal of psychological research findings cannot be taken for granted.

A CAUTIONARY NOTE ON THEORY

It is also worth making a cautionary point about theory. Often academics, journal editors and examiners will argue that empirical findings have to be understood in a theoretical context otherwise the data are meaningless. The tendency for social psychology to be preoccupied with theory, particularly its own theory, is an issue. Greenwald (2004), for example, challenges the view that "empirical research is valuable only to the extent that it advances theory" (p. 275) and he reminds us that neither the work of Asch or Milgram was theoretical, but we nonetheless conclude that their studies of conformity and obedience were important, thought provoking, and socially and politically significant. What is more, the demand that all work must proceed from within the bounds of existing theory assumes that all new observations can be adequately explained in terms of existing theoretical frameworks. Even in physics—the most successful of the natural sciences—not all data is immediately explainable in theoretical terms and, most importantly, the discipline considers all data to be important even if they are currently beyond theoretical explanation.

For example, a project that reveals that people in the UK know little or nothing about nuclear weapons or nuclear warfare could have considerable political significance, but there would no need to explain this finding theoretically any more than there would be a need to explain Britain's exit from the European Union (EU) in theoretical terms. Indeed, the broader question remains: should we presume that social psychological theory is more important than empirical findings? To further the argument that empirical statements must be explained theoretically, social psychologists often cite the Eurobarometer—a series of public opinion surveys that have been conducted regularly on behalf of the European Commission since 1973—as an example of theoretically meaningless statements. For example—"20% of Swedish nationals oppose membership of the European Union" (This is a fictitious example to illustrate the point). In what way and to whom are such statements meaningless? They may appear meaningless to social psychologists who are consumed with a need to advance theory, but to politicians and political psychologists not charged with having to produce social psychological explanations, the statement may indicate something of considerable interest or importance. What is lacking is detail, not theory.

If we were to probe more deeply and find that, for example, the respondents are migrants, we might consider whether they oppose membership of the EU because they wish to discourage the free movement of people, as it would undermine their own economic position. Further investigation would provide detail, but no formal theory is required. To insist that all findings have to be explained in terms of social psychological theory is a short step away from a branding policy—an identity project—designed to market the discipline and its practitioners. There may be pressures to advance theory in order to fulfill the demands of learning outcomes for MSc/PhD degrees, but these are the demands of institutions and professional bodies rather than the demands of science. Theory, when applied appropriately, is enlightening, but we need to get some perspective on the matter. For example, the **antirealist position** is that theories are neither true nor false but useful—like library catalogs—they help us find our way around (Poincarè, 1952), Indeed, when theory is not readily available, we may still be able to make good sense of the world and "find our way around" without it.

CONCLUSIONS

In many respects, an ahistorical approach to research methods reflects psychology's problem with its own history, and modeling the social sciences into a "deformed likenesses of physics" (Donagan, 1966, p. 157) is not likely to meet with success. The arcane procedures and specialist language of statistical methodology does little to encourage a natural curiosity in students, and the root of the problem may be that psychology has adopted "methods of proof" rather than "methods of discovery" (Markova, 2012, p. 113). Indeed, the problems associated with statistical significance and hypothesis testing should make us reflect, review, and reconsider the prominent role of quantitative methods in the established teaching curriculum. Statistical methods may be appropriate to establish certain *propositions* about the state of social reality, and inferences drawn from empirical data may add to an evidence-based argument, but these are always some distance away from absolute truth. What is more, we need to consider *all* evidence in our analysis including evidence to the contrary. There is no reason to assume that an in-depth understanding of human beings should emerge from a tradition that has sought prediction and control over its subject matter, or that understanding about such matters will naturally emerge from the language of numbers. Quantitative methods may have their place when used appropriately, but we need to be sure about what we are doing, why we are doing it and the nature of the claims we are making.

SUMMARY

- The search for laws of behavior has been fruitless because behavior is often capricious - it does not conform to laws and it is not predictable. Unlike the natural world, which is governed by the laws of nature, the social world is not computable. At present, no major political event of any importance has been predicted by psychological theory.

- The use of quantitative methods in the behavioral sciences originally arose in a context linked to state surveillance and their continued use raises issues of social power, that is: in psychological research, we need to know who is asking the questions and for what purpose.

- The employment of statistical methods—particularly the NHST—has been linked to serious problems of misinterpretation, failures of replication, publication bias, and fraud. These problems have been largely overlooked in a quest to present psychology as a science.

- A good deal of data, while not explicable in theoretical terms, may nonetheless advance our understanding of the political world.

GLOSSARY

ether or **aether** refers to a hypothetical transmission medium—a space-filling substance or field—that was once thought necessary for the propagation of electromagnetic or gravitational forces.

antirealism is a position that involves the denial of an objective reality. In mathematics, antirealists argue that the truth of a mathematical statement consists in our ability to prove it, whereas realists contend that the truth of a statement consists in its correspondence to objective reality.

central limit theorem states that the sampling distribution of the sampling means approaches a normal distribution as the sample size increases regardless of the shape of the underlying population distribution.

confidence intervals provide a sample estimate of the range of values of a parameter in a population likely to encompass the true value.

determinism is the philosophical position that claims that individual human behavior is caused by either internal or external forces beyond our control.

effect size is a way of quantifying the magnitude of a statistical relationship (whether difference, association, or correlation). This standardized score enables comparison across studies of a specific effect even when different measurement scales have been employed. It is frequently used in meta-analyses where results of several studies are combined to indicate a summary effect.

epiphenomena refer to the by-products of some hypothetical or actual causal process, that is: it occurs as an effect of a primary phenomenon and plays no causal role within it. For example, in the philosophy of mind, psychic states (mental phenomena) are held to be caused solely by physical phenomena.

file drawer effect refers to a bias in scientific publication whereby authors are more likely to submit statistically significant findings and/or editors are more likely to accept them for publication.

five-sigma threshold refers to results that are so infrequent that by chance they would not be found within five standard deviations of the mean.

The conventional level of statistical significance in psychology ($p = .05$, two-tailed) can be described as meeting the two-sigma threshold. This means that the magnitude of the observed results, if randomly sampled from a normal distribution, would not be found within two standard deviations of the mean.

is/ought controversy refers to the tension created when statements about "what is" are used to determine "what ought to be"—this is sometimes referred to as the "naturalistic fallacy."

null hypothesis significance test is a procedure for testing hypotheses in which one first determines the probability of obtaining results of the observed magnitude, given a population of randomly sampled events, and then judges this against a prior conditional hypothesis of no effect (H0).

physics envy is a term used to critique areas of academic research that employ jargon and complex mathematics in order to appear rigorous and credible. In particular, the term has also been applied to the search for universal laws of behavior in psychology.

rationalism is the philosophical position that claims that reason is both the principal source and main justification of knowledge. Rationalism asserts that truth is not sensory (therefore not empirical) but rather it is intellectual and can be ascertained through deductive reasoning.

revelation refers to knowledge derived from sacred texts said to be originating from a divine source.

signal-noise ratio is where the strength of a desired signal (observed effect) is compared to the background level of noise (magnitude of error).

standardized tests are devised, administered, scored, and interpreted in a consistent manner, which allows cross comparison with other samples.

statistical power refers to the ability of a statistical procedure to detect an effect where one really exists.

FURTHER READING

Greenwald, A. G. (2004). The resting parrot, the dessert stomach and other perfectly defensible theories. J. Jost, M. R. Banaji, & D. A. Prentice (Eds.), *The yin and yang of social cognition: Perspectives on the social psychology of thought systems* (pp. 275–285). Washington, DC: American Psychological Association.

Heather, N. (1976). *Radical perspectives in psychology.* London: Methuen.

Parker, I. (2007). *Revolution in psychology.* London: Pluto Press.

Roberts, R. (2015). *Psychology and capitalism.* Winchester, UK: Zero Books.

QUESTIONS FOR GROUP DISCUSSION

- What do statistics tell us about people? Why do we use statistics in psychology? What other methods are available and what may these be able to tell us?
- Why do we have to be careful when describing populations using measures of central tendency?
- What is the best way to do research in political psychology?
- In what way are questions about human behavior political questions?

3 From Alienation to Estrangement: Political Thought and Psychology

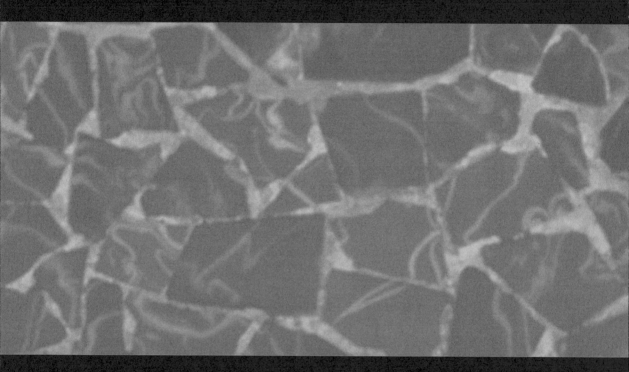

RON ROBERTS

CHAPTER OUTLINE

A neglected aspect of political psychology—and psychology, its parent discipline—concerns the nature of human experience in the world; how we as people, each of us, a unique living embodiment of our total life experience, engage with society and the overarching political system (see Itten & Roberts, 2014). In this chapter, we raise questions about the relationship between the personal and the sociocultural-political realm and ask whether existing theoretical models of psychological experience accommodate our sense of humanity or alienate us from it. In other words, we need to reflect on the type of political psychology we are promoting, our motives and objectives for doing so and an awareness of what the consequences might be. To do this, we review the work of Karl Marx, Michel Foucault, and Svetlana Boym—three approaches that deal with alienation, subjectivity, and estrangement respectively. Within this framework, we also consider the ideas of Erich Fromm, and R. D. Laing whose work also addresses the political nature of experience and the importance of context in a world that is social, cultural, and historical.

MECHANISTIC MODELS

At the root of most mainstream social research is an assumption that the social world functions like a machine—that when something goes wrong—there must be a reason and a cause. The task of the social scientist is to identify the root problem and suggest ways to improve matters. In tandem with this mechanistic model of the social world, psychology has advanced the view that people are little more than biological machines responding to needs, desires, and drives moderated by a schematic cognitive understanding of the world. In addition, some social psychologists have claimed that behavior is guided by scripts (see Abelson, 1981; Schank & Abelson, 1977) and, in some circumstances, potent social forces and relationships (Milgram, 1974). In this explanatory narrative, however, there appears to be no place for "the person"; moreover, events in this clockwork universe are never capricious, spontaneous, novel, or unpredictable. What is more, it is assumed that the broad spectrum of human behavior can be understood and explained in terms of the measurement and analysis of "component parts," which usually take the form of constructed or imagined variables of mind and behavior emanating from within the individual. Examples include "self-esteem," **"authoritarianism,"** or "beliefs in democracy," and measurement of these variables invariably seeks to establish relations of cause and effect, association, or correlation. Whether this approach is appropriate and whether mechanistic models tell us much about people, their behavior, or their potential is a matter of debate. Nonetheless, such models persist in all areas of contemporary psychology as the individual is theorized, objectified, and ultimately reduced to a set of cognitive and biological systems within the body—an approach that reduces, diminishes, and eventually eliminates "the person," their unique experience and sense of humanity. The purpose of this chapter is to rediscover and reincorporate "the person" into psychological theorizing and starting with the work of German philosopher Karl Marx (1818–1883), we consider some alternative approaches to understanding people, their behavior, and their subjective experience in a political context.

KARL MARX

Considerable confusion still surrounds Marx's place in the social sciences, which is largely due to an understanding of Marxism that is linked to the communist movements of the twentieth century. In the West, fear of the political content of Marx's ideas has led to its exclusion from mainstream psychological thought and therefore much of its value for understanding people in social and political settings has been neglected. Indeed, Marxism is more than a political philosophy; it is a method of enquiry for the study of social processes, a theory of economics, and a theory of historical change and development.

At the core of Marx's thesis is the concept of **historical materialism**, which was founded on an intellectual platform constructed by German philosopher Georg Hegel (1770–1831). Hegel had given an account of the gradual development of consciousness and knowledge but, based on his observations of the industrial world at the time, Marx argued that *material conditions* were responsible for determining human consciousness, and he proceeded to outline a "lawful" explanation of the historical development of the human condition in terms of a succession of antagonistic class-relations. In his analysis of nineteenth century England, the first industrial nation, Marx argued that history had passed through stages, that is, from primitive communism, slave society, feudalism to capitalism. According to Marx, the economic inequalities bound up within industrialization and capitalism would eventually lead to socialism and end in communism. The "end of history" would be the moment when all human beings acquire full self-awareness and become free. But, as we know capitalism did not collapse as Marx had predicted.

What concerns us here is the emphasis that Marx placed on the historical nature of human life and the quality of human experience under capitalism. Marx sought the improvement of humanity through the realignment of social and economic relations, and central to his entire political philosophy were concerns about the nature of human experience and the relationship between the individual and the social. Marx argued that psychological states are contingent on socioeconomic relations, which alerts us to the pervasive effect of economic factors on our way of thinking. To illustrate, consider the way that two people—one with limited resources and the other with considerable wealth— may react to a policy to lower taxes for the rich. The self-interests for these two individuals are quite different: one stands to benefit and the other likely perceives an injustice, and two very different emotional and behavioral responses to political authority may result. The wealthy individual may favor compliance, the other, resistance, resignation, or revolution. The point here is that thinking and behavior in this social context is not founded in "individual personality" but in economics.

However, oppressed or disadvantaged people do not always support the idea of revolution or change. Indeed, what puzzled Marx was that the harsh working conditions in nineteenth century England were not just the consequence of a malign source of power exercised from above, they were also the result of complicity on the part of the workers. For Marx, the key question was, "Why do workers participate in their own oppression?" The answer, he concluded, could be found in the concepts of **alienation** and **mystification**: forms of dislocation from an inherent human nature that would give rise to particular psychological states. According to Marx, human nature was not the property of any individual but a characteristic of the whole human species and attaining this true nature would only be possible (at a species level) through historically determined economic and political development, which would eventually free people from the oppression of economic slavery. As Hegel had sought to account for the perfection of ideas and spirit, Marx sought the perfection of humanity in the social and economic realm.

Alienation

Marx identifies alienation and mystification as characteristic forms of group psychology and inevitable features of life in a socially stratified society where the means of production lay disproportionately in the hands of one class—the capitalists. Although this would be primarily to the detriment of the majority of the working population, that is, those who provide their labor, both capitalist and worker would be alienated, which would be mediated, in part, through relationships with the material world of manufactured objects, the labor process, and one another—a set of mutually interlocking influences. Alienation from nature, work, self, and others was a feature of industrial society, and capitalist social relations ensured that "other people" were turned into things (see Fromm, 1942): instruments for advancing personal wealth.

Alienation would be further compounded by technology. Marx noted that industrial production was organized to suit the work of machines and within such a system, the human worker becomes ancillary to the machine—a cog in the clockwork manufacture of commodities for use and want, but not need. This develops into a situation where workers start to feel and act like machines so that they are no longer author of their own actions and are unable to determine the character of these actions. This affects their ability to define not only the nature of their relationship with work but also their relationship with other people. A modern-day example is the "call center" where the operative is required to respond to customer enquiries in a standardized and systematic manner, often repeating a well-prepared procedure or script.

From the Marxist perspective, however, it is not only individuals who are alienated, but also entire collectives; groups, families, cultures, societies, and nations—even the scientific community—may generate and experience alienation. Given these psychodynamic overtones, it is not surprising that Marx's conception of alienation (and mystification) can be found in some strands of psychoanalytic thought. Two theorists who have both explored the implications of Marxist humanism in their analysis of social relations are Erich Fromm and R. D. Laing.

ERICH FROMM

Erich Fromm (1900–1980) has probably been foremost among the psychoanalytic fraternity to make use of Marx's insights. Fromm argued that in Marx's early writings (The Economic and Philosophical Manuscripts; see Fromm, 2011) and in his later most famous work (Capital) there was a treasure trove of hopes and insights for students of the human character. Fromm saw Marx as a humanist who understood the potential of the human character and whose concept of alienation was fundamental for understanding the contemporary human malaise—perverting, as Fromm saw it, our understanding of life, love, and labor. Writing in the middle of the twentieth century, Fromm (1942, 1997) argued that personal, social, and gender relations had become enslaved to the operations of the market, producing a mentality that has shifted away from norms of solidarity, mutuality, and community toward those based on manipulation and instrumentality. In his analysis, he contrasts two modes of existence. The first, the "being mode," is concerned with love; it is conceived as an art and described as an "interpersonal creative capacity" (1957, p. 4). This state is not primarily about a relationship to a specific individual but it is "an attitude, an orientation of character which determines the relatedness of a person to the world as a whole." The alternative is the "having mode," a psychological state concerned with the acquisition of material possessions, money, and power, whose bedfellows are aggression, greed, envy, and violence. Fromm saw these psychological responses to material conditions as attempts to resolve fundamental issues of autonomy and separateness from others. The extent to which each of these modes are prevalent in society (as with other characterological and psychological propensities), Fromm believed could be understood by careful description and analysis of human behavior under prevailing social conditions.

Fromm also recognized that the conditions of our existence influence the kind of psychological knowledge we are likely to produce as well as the methods by which we believe this knowledge is most appropriately acquired. Indeed, the prevalence of capitalism confounds any attempt to understand human behavior from an objective standpoint. This stems not just from alienation but also from the range of epistemological products in the form of psychological constructs that have been consistently reified and internalized by contemporary western culture. Fromm further laments that "modern academic and experimental psychology" has become "a science dealing with alienated man, studied by alienated investigators with alienated and alienating methods." (1973, p. 69). Not only are we theorized and objectified under contemporary systems of scientific psychological representation to be nothing other than biological and biochemical machines (with human agency, will and intentionality given epiphenomenal status in the clockwork universe), but psychology, dominated by capitalist values (particularly in the US), has generated, endorsed, and promoted its own set of psychological constructs that fit perfectly within this cultural ideology. Psychological propensities such as the ability to act with good sense and judgment or benevolently toward others have taken on the characteristics of interiorized personal qualities: commodities that we are said to possess—IQ, personality, self-esteem, resilience, and so on.

Under capitalist social relations these "characteristics" acquire market value—something to be cultivated under market conditions and sold to "consumers" as the solution to alienation, unemployment, lack of achievement, and economic adversity. Psychology thus proposes, not the reorganization and restructuring of society in order to solve human problems, but a kind of psychological make-over to better prepare people for life's injustices and adversities, which are taken as immutable facts of the world. In this regard, the self-help and counseling industry may at times function alongside the pharmaceutical industry to re-engineer individuals as (biomedically) fit for purpose in an unchanging unjust world. The circular relationship between capitalism and psychology accordingly precludes the possibility of any genuine understanding of the human condition. The question is: how might we envisage a truly different way of thinking about people? What might we discover about ourselves if we were to pursue an alternative approach to psychological theorizing? Fromm does not give us any easy answers to this—but he does lay bare the problem and strongly suggests that a more hopeful vision of the world may emerge from a theoretical and practical sense rooted in "being" rather than "having." Fromm, however, was not alone in understanding the importance of Marx's ideas. R. D. Laing, a psychiatrist and psychoanalyst, also contributed to a truly critical variant of psychology and psychoanalysis by employing the concepts of alienation and mystification to explicate social relations and expose the micropolitics that lie behind attributions of mental disorder within the family.

R. D. LAING

R. D. Laing's use of alienation as an analytic tool to understand the social dynamics of the family was an approach that eventually challenged the validity and legitimacy of the mental health system. To understand the connection between work of Marx and Laing we have to appreciate that, from a Marxist perspective, capitalism has created a psychological divide (alienation) between personal needs and desires on the one hand, and actions on the other, particularly in the labor market. Fromm had earlier claimed that, "modern man believes himself to be motivated by self-interest and yet ... actually his life is devoted to aims which are not his own," (1942, p. 101). Although most people fail to recognize their "false consciousness," Laing raised an important question: what happens when someone acquires insight into their self-alienation? What psychological effects ensue when they come to understand the relationship between their social conditions or actions and the wider forces of power? How might this realization affect identity, behavior, or family interaction and with what social consequences? To illustrate, consider what might be our response to someone who claims to be a puppet responding mechanically and obediently to "alien" orders—or to a person who describes their body as an empty shell controlled by external alien powers? As their distress becomes more apparent, psychiatric intervention becomes more likely and they may find themselves designated as psychotic—out of touch with reality—and showing signs of "paranoid schizophrenia." However, Laing observed that many troubled patients were often subject to controls and disempowerment within the family, and at the time when Laing conducted his studies, the medical establishment failed to consider that such expressions might be accurate, metaphoric descriptions of the person's relationship to their world and the system of social and material relations. Laing's link between "insanity" and the social order placed power and the insistence of particular versions of reality center stage. Referring to the medical establishment, Laing (1971) observed, 'They think anyone who wakes up, or who, still asleep, realizes that what is taken to be real is a 'dream', is going crazy." (p. 74).

Mystification

Laing (1965) also employed Marx's concept of mystification in his analysis of the micropolitics of family life, which he described as:

> ... the substitution of false for true constructions of what is being experienced, being done (praxis), or going on (process), and the substitution of false issues for the actual issues ... If we detect mystification, we are alerted to the presence of a conflict of some kind that is being evaded. The mystified person ... is unable to see the authentic conflict... He may experience false peace, false calm, or inauthentic conflict and confusion over false issues (Laing, 1965, pp. 344–345).

In Laing's analysis (see Laing & Esterson, 1964), conflict often occurs in the family when individuals who are oppressed by more powerful members of the family, challenge the existing rules, roles, values, or traditions. In response, those who wish to maintain the status quo may employ "political" tactics, which include the manipulation and control of memory, denial, mystification, and the invalidation of experience of other potentially supportive members of the family—explicit attempts to undermine their perception of reality. For those enmeshed in such a system, the support and solidarity available from others *within the system* is crucial to psychological wellbeing. Without it, individuals are rendered alone, confused, and uncertain about what is real and what is not. What is likely to be of particular interest to political psychologists is that Laing's analysis of the family and his attempt to expose the debilitating effects of mystification arguably extends to other complex social systems, whether in the workplace or within a community of nations (Roberts & Hewer, 2015).

Marx's concepts of alienation and mystification impel us to conclude on a reflexive note—we need to reflect on the nature of psychological theory, specifically, whether current theory and practice contributes toward, or actively participates in, a process that reproduces these states in people. Currently within psychology, the dominance of neuroscience, and cognitive psychology as explanatory narratives, and the conceptualization of humans as complex biocomputational organisms embedded within deterministic accounts of evolutionary development and genetic inheritance, not only eliminate "the person," but also fail to account for free will and agency—the ability to shape and determine the conditions of our existence. This is an important political and moral question since the abolition of free will renders the world devoid of meaning. At issue here is whether our accounts of the human condition alienate us further and hinder the development of alternative possibilities for constructive personal and social change. Marx's humanism impels us to reflect, not only on the explanatory power of psychological theory, but also its effect on the world.

MICHEL FOUCAULT

The relationship between self and society is also examined by French social theorist, Michel Foucault (1926–1984). Foucault was primarily concerned with oppressed and deviant groups and his work comprised an historical and cultural critique on madness, illness, and criminality. His analysis spans the history of ideas, the nature of historical change, and the relationship between power and knowledge.

Discursive Regimes, Power, and Freedom

Foucault argues that we comprehend reality through an anonymous ensemble of concepts, devoid of singular consciousness, and located beyond individual reach. Through their own internal architecture and dynamic potential, these concepts generate *discourses of power and knowledge,* which direct human activity, shaping the practices of culture, arts, and science in unpredictable but coherent ways. In *The Archaeology of Knowledge,* Foucault (2002) examines the organizing principles that underpin the evolution and development of discursive regimes. In a similar way to Marx, he embraces a dialectic in which contradiction is the source of discursive change. In this thesis, he argues that **subjectivity**—the ways in which we construct and understand our "selves"—is also the product of discursive practices and power relations. Furthermore, Foucault insists that **power relations** always involve relations of domination; a position consistent with a view of history as the replacement of one form of tyranny by another. His conception of power, however, articulates a certain type of relation between individuals and is less concerned with top–down institutional or sovereign power.

Given the power of **discursive regimes**, we might wonder to what extent individuals are free to act. Foucault avoids the infinite regress of cause and effect relationships in a deterministic world, by talking about the "agency" of particular discursive regimes. In this world, the subject is not "free" in the sense of being able to choose from existing alternatives or to initiate new courses of action, and thus Foucault abolishes all interiority (Foucault, 2002, p. 232). However, the abolition of a thinking, feeling, and experiencing subject from the origin and maintenance of discursive regimes has moral implications. For example, if we were to trace the perpetration of evil to power located within particular discursive regimes, it would absolve all human actors of responsibility. The question is; to what extent do Foucault's ideas allow conceptual space for morality, intentionality, and self-directed initiatives that develop in the pursuit of emancipation, liberation, and freedom?

Disciplinary boundaries

Foucault also challenges the legitimacy of existing subject boundaries. To Foucault, disciplines such as psychology, history, or sociology are anything but neutral, not least because they promote social practices that produce certain types of discourse, and these affect our conceptions of subjectivity, that is, how a person may be positioned or understood. Even labels adopted by sub-disciplines have implications. For example, the term "political psychology" implies that all other psychology is nonpolitical—a position that may prevent students from discerning the political nature of all psychological research. And given psychology's historic association with eugenics, missile development, brainwashing, and interrogation techniques, this may inadvertently serve as a further act of mystification—one that allows the public to applaud a discipline that appears to help and care for people when it also contributes to their harm.

Foucault also argued that the objects of discourse themselves (e.g., madness, political economy, history) have no inherent objectivity, but are defined by a set of practices that seek to embed themselves as solid entities into the fields of discourse. Consequently, reality is socially constructed and can only be known through discourse. Foucault also challenges existing anthropological categorizations of events, for example, intentionality, the authorship of text, and the terms that we employ to denote modes of relatedness between events—whether discursive or otherwise. When Foucault questions the understanding behind such terms as influence, cause and effect, or correlation, he is arguing for a more fluid conception of the territory under investigation.

This is somewhat reminiscent of Kurt Lewin's field theory. In Lewin's (1951) formulation, a field denoted all modes of relatedness between individuals and their environment at a given moment of time and the influence of the field on its subsequent development includes current and future actions of various actors and objects contained within it. Lewin's framework of a self-propagating "social field" is similar to Foucault's notion of a "discursive field" that binds together language, social institutions, power, and forms of subjectivity across different times and places, and which defines "the possible positions of speaking subjects" (Foucault, 2002, p. 137). The connections between events, actors, and objects are inherently probabilistic and therefore the expression of simple chains of cause and effect do not adequately map or model these events.

Here, Foucault presents an alternative conception of the social world—one dominated by discourse. Foucault thus stands apart from the mechanistic and deterministic view of history favored by Marx and appeals to a more holistic hermeneutic (interpretative) framework—a temporally bound field of meaning. In this respect, the discursive nature of unchallengeable common sense shares something of the flavor of the common myths that feature in the theory of social representations (Moscovici, 1961/1976). However, despite the uncertainty inherent in the human arena, psychology has clung steadfastly to a mechanistic and deterministic philosophy that is more suited to nineteenth century physics and, in so doing, has eschewed the values implicit in a discursive qualitative account of human life.

Politics and governance of the self

Foucault's key works in the field of madness, sexuality, and punishment have opened up challenges to existing structures of power and has emboldened many to challenge medical power, sexual repression, and social control—all of which are regulated by the modern psychiatric system. The histories of madness, sexuality, and punishment can be traced back through three genealogical axes—truth, power, and ethics, which create the basis for a history of the subject, that is, the historical development and confluence of political and ethical practices concerned with the governance of the self. The self—in social constructionist terms—is an abstraction housed within the body. Hence the various means of "self-regulation" that come to be practiced involve various disciplinary practices on the body. In this "biopolitical" arena, the human body is the center of a political struggle: a struggle with ourselves and the exterior political authority. At the root of the struggle, Foucault identifies the practice of internalizing the gaze of the powerful other so that we become both perennial guard and prisoner of our selves. Ever mindful of policing our thoughts and actions in order to satisfy the imagined gaze of the other, provides endless possibilities for capitalist enterprise to sell us the antidote to the manufactured gap between self and perfection. What is more, this internalization of gaze creates a new set of practices that bolster the discursive regime.

Here, Foucault's analysis of surveillance represents the broader political nature of his work. Its explanatory power and prescient nature can be seen in acts of self-harm among the distressed and the current widespread preoccupation with cosmetic surgery. However, for social and political psychologists attracted to a Foucauldian account of the world there is a cautionary note. Foucault's insights, if applied to a research domain, also compel us to interrogate the legitimacy of that domain. This degree of reflexivity is logically consistent, but it can lead to radical conclusions. For example, Parker (as cited in Hepburn, 2003) claims that psychology, rather than being a natural science, is an "ideological system … and coercive apparatus for normalising and pathologising behaviour" (p. 47). Furthermore, he argues that psychology has assumed a political and functional role as a new form of **disciplinary regulation** (Parker, 2007).

It is perhaps ironic that Foucault's thesis, formulated in post-war democratic France, draws pessimistic conclusions about the possibility of freedom from contemporary enslavement of the self. For Foucault, it would seem that individual human freedom (or its absence) is, of necessity, inextricably bound up with conditions of the self from which it is difficult to escape. An alternative perspective on human freedom, however, is presented by Svetlana Boym who shares Hannah Arendt's view (see Arendt, 1978), that there is an ineradicable core of freedom at the heart of the human condition, within which lies hope of resistance and creativity. It is noteworthy that both lived under totalitarian regimes: Boym in the Soviet Union and Arendt in Nazi Germany.

SVETLANA BOYM

Boym's contribution to the debate comes from within a critical tradition of comparative literature, architecture, philosophy, and aesthetics. Her work embraces a range of disciplinary interests that critically engage with the modernist project, fashioning an innovative challenge to the way we "do" psychology; indeed, her work invites us to rethink the purpose of psychological enquiry. The term "modernity" originally referred to a critique of the new, fleeting rhythms of time and life in the burgeoning urban metropolis produced by French art critic, poet, and essayist Charles Baudelaire (1821–1867) (see Benjamin, 1999). Over time, however, the term "modernity" has been transformed from a *critical* position on contemporary life into a *"project* of modernity," which has come to describe the "progress" brought about by reductionist science, mechanization, and the drive to industrial modernization. Psychology and psychotherapy are products of the "project of modernity," which, in partnership with science and technology, have promoted a form of psychological theory and practice that has contributed to capitalist modernization. This type of theory and practice, however, is arguably divorced from the everyday concerns and experience of ordinary people (Itten & Roberts, 2014).

Estrangement

At the heart of Boym's thesis is a new way of looking at the social world, which reinvigorates modernity as a critical project. Starting from a position of dislocation, Boym's (2001, 2008, 2010) theorizing emphasizes the notion of **estrangement** *for* the world as opposed to estrangement *from* it. The Slavic roots of the word estrangement suggest both distancing and making strange, which implies a radical dislocation from one's usual point of view, a reframing and recontextualization of reality—one, moreover, that affords an entirely different set of possibilities—for perception, understanding, and action. While Marx's view of alienation and mystification convey a form of dislocation between people that is broadly negative, many examples of estrangement have positive consequences. Indeed, Boym sees estrangement as a position from which one can enact a range of creative and human possibilities that can enhance our existence. Estrangement *for* the world thus liberates—it breathes new life into the possibilities of being and resurrects the notion of "the ordinary marvellous" (Boym, 2005, p. 583). Originally, an artistic technique, estrangement morphed into an existential art and practice of freedom, which stresses the importance of renewal and new beginnings in life and underpins possibilities of resistance.

How might estrangement work in a political context and with what effect? Perhaps the most powerful example was the campaign to unseat Chilean dictator Augustus Pinochet after years of state-sponsored repression and violence. In Pablo Larrain's film *No* (Dreifuss, Larrain, & Larrain, 2012), we come to see that the regime was vulnerable to attack, not through arms, but through art. An alternative future—a vision of freedom from tyranny—was constructed from humor, music, and drama and exuberantly performed on the Chilean streets by ordinary people. This act of estrangement proved to be as powerful as any political program dedicated to ending the regime. Art and entertainment liberated the people from the dread of Pinochet and, eventually, his generals deserted him.

Humor, particularly—and its performative relation, comedy—have the power to estrange. Humor requires that an aspect of the world is made strange (defamiliarized) and later returned (familiarized but reformulated) in a punch line. Interestingly, irony and satire have long been recognized in psychotherapy and counseling as a legitimate means of speaking to power, and many of the techniques, practices, and strategies employed can be construed as estrangement in action, working upon pain to produce a "sea change into something rich and strange" (Shakespeare, 2004, p. 46). Facial expression, vocal intonation, verbal, physical, and emotional contradiction used to create zones of physical and psychological safety (see Kauffman & New, 2004 for further discussion), are arguably acts of "estrangement," which provide a new vantage point from which self and reality can be observed. During World War II, satire was used to undermine the image of Adolf Hitler. For example, Chaplin's (1940) comic depiction of *The Great Dictator* ridiculed the Nazis, and many similar works followed in the postwar years, such as the TV comedy series *Hogan's Heroes* (Feldman, 1965), the Hollywood musical spoof *The Producers* directed by Mel Brooks (Glazier & Brooks, 1968), and the British comedy 'Allo, 'Allo (Croft, 1982), which commanded an international audience in the 1980s. Comedy is indeed a subversive political activity and estrangement is the means by which creative opposition and resistance to power is achieved. The Russian punk band *Pussy Riot* provides another telling example. Their "gig" in Moscow's largest cathedral was a visual and musical spectacle exposing the relationship between the Orthodox Church and the increasingly authoritarian Russian State (see *Express Tribune*, 2012). Using irony and satire as a means of speaking to power, the action estranges because it is outrageous and considered beyond the boundaries of everyday action, that is, who would have the audacity to speak against the Church and State in this way? However, in the face of punishment and political sanction, its execution removes any debilitating paralysis brought about by fear.

Off-modern psychology

Despite the efforts of Hegel and Marx to provide a systematic and orderly account of history, it appears to be neither orderly nor governed by laws. In this vein, Boym questions established narratives of "progress" and assumptions of linear social time and her invocation of the **off-modern** brings to the social and political some of the paradoxical features of the quantum world—opening doors to "a superposition and co-existence of heterogenous times" (Boym, 2001, p. 30). In other words, the nature and pace of human social and cultural life takes on different forms in different parts of the world. For example, modernity as lived and experienced in the financial centers of London and New York is rather different to that found among the indigenous communities of Alaska.

Another element of Boym's thesis is the need to reconsider the past in terms of "what could have been." Boym describes an alternative intellectual history of modernity through an approach that "… doesn't follow the logic of crisis and progress but rather involves an exploration of the side alleys and lateral potentialities of the project of critical modernity" (Boym, 2008, p. 4). In this way, "unforeseen pasts and ventures" may be recovered. The world is the way it is, but its current form was not pre-ordained and events are not inevitable. What is more, life is lived in the shadows of possibilities that once inhabited the past and, therefore, to understand the present, we need to understand *the possibilities* of the past. Thus, we are left to ponder, for example; just how would world events have panned out had the Versailles Treaty not been so harsh on Germany after World War I or if Adolf Hitler had become an artist instead of a political activist? Although the clock cannot be turned back, these questions open up discussions about how the world might have been and thus how it could be in the future.

In her expansive elaborations of the off-modern, Boym repositions, and reinvents the psychological within a cultural phenomenology of political and everyday history, suffused with a fragile temporality encompassing people, places, language, memory, imagination, emotion, art, artifact, and home. Here we witness a seamless merging of the search for meaning, dignity, love, and freedom in individual life with a broader political canvas in which the ghosts of past actions and inactions inhabit the urban and domestic spaces of the real and the might have been. Within this markedly different approach to the psychological and the psychotherapeutic, it becomes possible to imagine psychology (or psychologies) less concerned with explaining the material workings of the human organism or with generating statistical commonalities, and more oriented toward addressing the complexities of life, which include reflective dimensions of *being* and *having been* in the world. These existential considerations also address the complexities of life imbued with an elusive and fragile sense of time passing—our appearance and disappearance from the world, which is felt more acutely with age.

Art and dissent

An "off-modern" psychology advocates a stance that is artistic, interpretative, and performative, at ease with changing and modifying the world, while attempting to know it. Its philosophical roots can be traced to the Soviet avante-garde—in particular the work of Soviet artist Viktor Shklovsky (1923/2005) who saw in estrangement the possibility of maintaining wonder and joy in living. For Shklovsky, art is central to a playful, dissenting but serious reworking of the world, capable of producing profound knowledge and pointing the way to a potentially very different "order of things." Writing in the 1920s, Shklovsky remarked that the Soviet artist of the day had two choices, "to write for the desk drawer or to write on state demand" (Boym, 2008, p. 20). Despite the absence of a third way, Shklovsky argued that this was "precisely the one that must be chosen" (Boym, 2008, pp. 20–21). This defiance of Aristotelian logic represents a rejection of everyday assumptions and the work of estrangement is often directed to intentionally undermining a taken for granted "truth."

Boym's and Shklovsky readings of estrangement are powerful reminders that there are political options other than surrender or defeat—and that resistance is not futile. In London, in 2015, an exhibition at the Victoria and Albert Museum entitled *Dissident Objects* examined the use of art by political movements intent on social change. The objects on display included banners, defaced currency, textiles bearing witness to political murders, designs for barricades and blockades as well as video games and inflatable balloons bearing political messages. The objects preserved a social memory of oppression and resistance and invited public participation to engage in the construction and dissemination of an alternative knowledge of the past with an implicit message that justice can never be served without full knowledge and memory of the past. Estrangement as resistance in a quest for freedom becomes the means by which we may rebuild and preserve a corner of the world from an oppressive reconfiguration of reality.

In this regard, Boym (2012) argues that we can always exercise the small amount of freedom available to us within the public sphere since knowledge, technique, and purpose can be combined into an "art of resistance." In the context of our daily lives, it then becomes possible to disrupt passive thinking and provide discomfort for those who have broadly accepted the injustice of others as a form of common sense. An off-modern psychology is therefore, in a sense, both a realist political philosophy and a rethinking on the nature of psychology in a political context. In the modern age, faced with global retreats into fundamentalist patterns of thought, and ecological and economic degradation, it emphasizes the possibility of renewal while rejecting any form of regime that seeks to damage others in the name of a Utopian, mechanical, reconstruction of the social, civil, and political order.

Indeed, an off-modern perspective offers a very different kind of psychology—one that resonates with Hannah Arendt's claim that "all aspects of the human condition are somehow related to politics" (1958/1998, p. 7). Imagination and reality exist side by side and knowledge of this relationship may be put to use to change the world. This approach also challenges the assumption that verbal discourse is the only appropriate performative strategy through which psychological knowledge may be reproduced and distributed. If a principal function of art is to disrupt the existing order (see Smoliarova, 2006), then art becomes central to politics, dissent, participation, and change. For political psychology, the emphasis moves away from the measurement of what is, or what purports to be, toward a study and practice in which people, their humanity, expression, needs, and desires are paramount—a psychology that estranges the status quo and challenges the dehumanizing automation of life.

SUMMARY

- We need to become aware of the wider horizons of psychological reality and the birth of psychological ideas and social change. For political psychology to move toward a more human science, it must address the precise (relational) content of human life as it is experienced.

- Political psychology needs to adopt an epistemology that is rooted in the everyday, in the world of people's experience of the world—of themselves, others, and the material landscape in which we move and continually create.

- Understanding politics is not merely to create narratives of victory and defeat or providing commentary on the unjust excesses of power.

- Psychological knowledge should reflect upon the human desire to live well and try to promote an aesthetic devoted to improvement and renewal.

- Boym reminds us that there is a virtual world of past and future possibilities, which help us to understand the actualities of the present and the avenues for change.

- Estrangement is a means of revitalizing human existence in the face of oppression and the mechanization and routinization of life.

- Psychology of resistance—the journey may be critical, intellectual, artistic, and practical and may encounter the many contextual complexities of reality. This may entail freeing psychological knowledge from formal professional methodology and theory.

GLOSSARY

alienation refers to the nature of existence, that is, the psychological state of an exploited class or individual.

disciplinary regulation refers to a form of self-imposed social control (usually of the body) maintained in response to cultural messages.

discursive regimes refer to the power dynamics of knowledge that pervade society. Power is constituted through accepted but shifting forms of knowledge, scientific understanding, and "truth."

estrangement refers to a process through which we may achieve new ways of looking at life, the world, our existence; to see things as not seen before so as to instill a sense of resistance and hope.

historical materialism is a theory of history and society proposed by Karl Marx, which involves an analysis of the organizing structure of the production of material goods.

mystification refers to a state of mind or existence in which power relations or the social dynamics of capitalism obscures social reality.

off-modern is a term that refers to a revived view of "modernity as a critique of contemporary life," which proposes a consideration of the world as "it could have been" under different historical circumstances.

power relations refers to the analysis of power dynamics existing between people or institutions in any social, cultural, or historical context.

subjectivity refers to a focus on actions and/or discourses that give rise to the self.

FURTHER READING

Boym S. (2001). *The future of nostalgia*. New York: Basic Books. Retrieved from http://www.svetlanaboym.com/offmodern.html.

Gutting G. (2005). *Foucault: A very short introduction*. Oxford: Oxford University Press.

Collier G., Minton H. L., & Reynolds G. (1991). *Currents of thought in American social psychology* (pp. 151–160). Oxford: Oxford University Press.

QUESTIONS FOR GROUP DISCUSSION

- How might we envisage political psychology without variables, measurement, hypotheses, or quantitative research methods? What would be its objectives, methods, theory, and approach?

- How might mystification and alienation be used to control people in organizations? Do all members of an organization share a similar "social reality"?
- Taking into consideration the work of Foucault and Boym; to what extent can we say that we live in a free society? What do we mean by freedom?
- What has R. D. Laing's work on the family contributed to our understanding of power, psychological states, and politics within the family? To what degree can these insights be applied to other social settings?
- Should works of art, buildings, and social spaces be part of our analysis when "doing" political psychology? What do these things tells us about contemporary life?

4 The Politics of Psychological Language: Discourse and Rhetoric

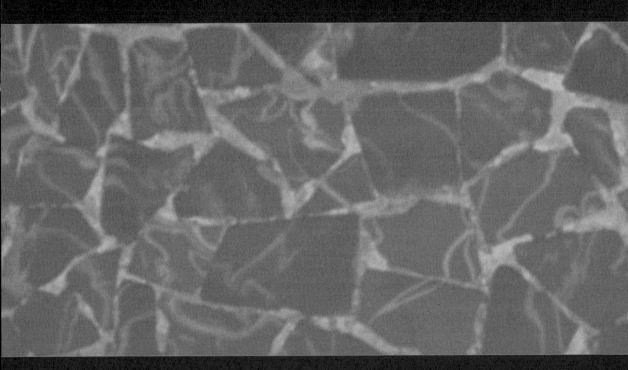

SIMON LOCKE

CHAPTER OUTLINE

Toward the end of the twentieth century, two psychological perspectives developed with language as their core concern. **Discursive psychology**, established by Edwards and Potter (1992), though building to some extent on Potter and Wetherell's (1987) "discourse analysis," drew on the broader "linguistic turn" emanating from mid-century developments in the humanities and social sciences that highlighted language as central to human existence and social interaction (Potter, 1996). **Rhetorical psychology**, established by Billig (1987) seems to have been an independent development, although it struck a chord with the "rhetoric of inquiry" that had begun in the United States in the 1970s (Billig, 1991; Nelson, Megill, & McCloskey, 1987; Simons, 1989). The major figures behind the two approaches worked in the same department at Loughborough University, UK in the 1980s, and there is evidence of mutual support in some of their writings (Billig, 1991, 1997; Potter, 1996, 2012) to the point where Billig (2009) has included his approach under the rubric "discursive psychology." On the other hand, there is also evidence of some disagreement, notably in Billig's criticisms of **conversation analysis (CA)**, upon which discursive psychology substantially draws (Billig, 1999a, 2013; Edwards, 2014). The aim of this chapter is to present an overview of these lines of agreement and disagreement, setting them in the context of other relevant perspectives, that is, **cognitive psychology (CP)** and **critical discourse analysis (CDA)**. This is done, not with a view to offering some kind of resolution, but simply to highlight that the politics of experience suffuses academic work, and involves the intertwined issues of **ideology**, **relativism**, and **reflexivity**.

DISCURSIVE PSYCHOLOGY, RHETORICAL PSYCHOLOGY, AND COGNITIVE PSYCHOLOGY

To outline the main ideas of discursive psychology and rhetorical psychology, it is helpful to set out their major differences from CP. Firstly, both reject the view that the study of psychological phenomena must involve attempting to excavate the internal mental states of individuals, or 'stuff' inside people's heads; "mental furniture" as Potter (1996) calls it. As Edwards and Potter (1992) see it, the problem with CP is that it assumes that there is "an ontologically given, and more or less correctly perceived external world" (p. 20), which is

Political Psychology: A Social Psychological Approach, First Edition.
Edited by Christopher J. Hewer and Evanthia Lyons.
© 2018 John Wiley & Sons Ltd. Published 2018 by John Wiley & Sons Ltd.

faithfully reflected in a more or less stable internal world consisting of things like "schemata." Individuals are understood to be walking around with constructions of reality inside their heads that they simply access according to the demands of the social setting. Discursive psychology questions these assumptions. In rhetorical psychology, Billig (1985); see also Billig, 1991, 1996a, 1996b, 2009, 2013) presents a similar critique using the metaphor of the "bureaucrat": the image of the individual as someone with a head filled with filing cabinets into which the phenomena of reality are placed so that everything is neatly categorized and filed away under labels such as "attitudes" or "opinions."

For both discursive and rhetorical psychology, this "technicized" view of people is drastically over-simplified. It fails to recognize what is readily apparent in everyday life: that the same person may characterize the same situation in different ways at different points in time; and different people may characterize the same situation in different ways at the same point in time. In other words, people routinely present *versions of reality*. Indeed, some settings, such as parliamentary and legal proceedings, exist as formally institutionalized orders of interaction precisely because we know that people present different versions of reality that somehow need to be sorted out.

THE SCIENTIFIC LABORATORY

Another such setting is the scientific laboratory, which was established at the start of the modern period in the late seventeenth century to provide a context of public "witnessing": an attempt to resolve prevailing theological disagreements about the existence and nature of a vacuum, a debate linked to the politics of the time (Shapin & Schaffer, 1985). Indeed, the primary purpose of scientific laboratories is to establish "matters of fact" in a manner that is supposed to be independent of political (or other social) interests. Whether this is the case is questionable, but for now it is sufficient to recognize that laboratory science, in its institutionalized form, is living testament to the continuing human tendency to produce differing versions of reality.

Indeed, according to contemporary psychological textbooks, one of the features of ordinary common sense is that it is marked by a wide diversity of views about, among other things, internal mental phenomena: a variation that justifies the need for psychological science to cut through the incoherent, error-filled babble of ordinary understandings and establish the truth of things, the matters of fact in respect of human psychology. This accords with the assumption of CP—that there is an "ontologically given and more or less correctly perceived external world," so that, from among the many different versions, there must be one that is true and correct. Accordingly, psychologists assign themselves both the "task of identifying" and "the right of deciding" which one it is, as well as proposing possible grounds (reasons and causes) as to why individuals advance versions that are incorrect, such as the so-called "fundamental attribution error" (Ross, 1977). The problem with this approach is that we assume that we can faithfully and adequately represent "ontologically given" reality, when this is precisely what is called into question by the presence of competing versions.

In political and legal debate, people advance their versions of reality because it is in their interests to do so, or as Edwards and Potter (1992) put it, because they hold some "stake" in the version. The question is: *on what grounds can it be said that psychologists have no stake in the version(s) of reality they advance?* The issue becomes more complex when we realize that offering a version as an "expert observer" inevitably involves us in the debate, so that we come to favor one side over another. Rather than resolving the matter, our version may become caught up in continuing controversy, with the added complication that our version carries scientific legitimacy. This raises tricky questions about who counts as a relevant "expert" and what justifies psychological scientists according themselves such status. Indeed, these questions highlight the politics of expertise, knowledge, and experience (Pollner, 1987; after Laing, 1967).

THE VALIDITY OF EXPERIMENTS AND SURVEYS

Laboratory-based experiments are an institutionalized device to provide legitimation to the claim that knowledge is evaluated in an independent manner. Their status in this respect, however, remains contested. Their credibility is often disputed on grounds of ecological validity: concerns over the extent to which behavior inside a laboratory corresponds to behavior outside. A similar validity issue concerns the use of social surveys to "measure" psychological phenomena such as "attitudes," "opinions," or "beliefs." The activity of filling out a survey may bear little relation to the real world situation it is assumed to be measuring (a recent, very public example was the failure of opinion pollsters to even come close to accurately forecasting the result of the UK General Election in May 2015). From the perspective of both discursive psychology and rhetorical psychology, these errors occur because the basic assumption informing surveys is flawed, that is, the notion that attitudes and opinions constitute stable forms of "mental furniture."

Whatever form the "stuff" inside our heads might take, we cannot simply assume that it is the same "stuff" we express when we talk and write. As Billig (2009, p. 9) puts it, "we think because we can talk, rather than we talk because we can think." Attitudes and opinions are not, then, isolated "things" that we "hold," but interpersonally constituted relations formulated through an understanding of contrasting viewpoints. Attitudes and opinions cannot exist unless there are contrasting positions available; they can only exist in competing opposition, not in isolation. To assume that people carry around one stable outlook, which is maintained throughout the diversity of daily social interactions, is to fail to recognize the extent to which our views are in perpetual motion; that we are all always considering, qualifying, and weighing up where we stand. To ask for an opinion from a set of pre-formulated responses on a questionnaire is to decide in advance for people just where and how they may stand. But people often object to the assumption that their views can simply be read off from pre-defined categories (Myers, 2004). Accordingly, they may want to argue with a social survey or, indeed, an experiment (see, e.g. Reicher, 2014 on Milgram's study of obedience).

It is, then, unsurprising that a frequent outcome of experimental studies is that psychological phenomena refuse to behave in accord with their assumed character of being categorical variables. Rather than resolving the incoherence of common sense, experimental studies often throw up a mess of inconsistent and incoherent findings (see, e.g. Billig, 1978 on studies of the so-called "authoritarian personality"; also Billig, 1996a, 1996b, chapter 4), and even where some consistency is found, the problem of generalization remains. In the case of the fundamental attribution error, for example, there may be some consistency in experimental set-ups where the researchers know the correct attribution (Byford, 2011, chapter 6), but in real world situations, this is exactly what we do not know. In real life, we never know whether we are *accurately* attributing behavior to internal personal characteristics or external situations. Here, the distinction between the laboratory and politics becomes extremely blurry indeed.

LANGUAGE, DISCOURSE, AND RHETORIC

The main argument of both discursive and rhetorical psychology is that, instead of trying to classify and rearrange *invisible* "mental furniture," psychologists should focus on the *publicly manifest* "mental furniture" that people construct in their versions of reality. Rather than trying to establish a definitive version of reality, we should instead treat the different versions as our focus of interest to see how they are put together, arranged in relation to each other, and designed to suit the interactive context of their presentation. The question is: what are people *doing* socially and interactively with their versions of reality. This requires a study of "language-in-use," the actual talk and texts people employ: in other words, their discourse.

The use of the term "discourse" in discursive psychology owes a good deal to the influence of research in the sociology of scientific knowledge. Gilbert and Mulkay's (1984) study of a group of biochemists in controversy compared interview data with the scientists' formal research reports. Gilbert and Mulkay identified two **"interpretative repertoires"** (linguistic registers or types of voice) that the scientists used to present contrasting accounts of their own beliefs and those of their opponents. When accounting for their own beliefs, both sides in the debate used the **empiricist repertoire**; and when accounting for their opponents' beliefs, both used the **contingent repertoire**. The empiricist repertoire involved referring to empirical data (natural causes), typically from laboratory research, which was presented in a manner that made them appear to be a direct, unmediated representation of reality. One technique was the use of the passive voice, for example. "it was found" rather than "we found," which Beer and Martins (1990, p. 171) describe as "the rhetoric of no rhetoric." The contingent repertoire, on the other hand, involved reference to a diverse range of psychological conditions (such as personal bias) and sociological interests (such as religious belief) that the scientists claimed were interfering with their opponents' view of empirical data and causing their mistaken views. Both sides in the controversy employed the same two repertoires and the same resources of explanation to account for their own beliefs and those of the other side.

Gilbert and Mulkay drew our attention to the conventions of scientific argumentation; they also argued that the explanatory accounts of social scientists should be subject to the same principles of analysis as the accounts they were studying, that is, they should apply the tenets of **symmetry** and reflexivity to their own accounts. Symmetry means treating all beliefs equivalently, whether taken to be "true" or "false," and reflexivity means applying the same principles of analysis to the explanations offered by social scientists as are applied to the explanations presented by natural scientists. To be fully symmetrical, rather than presenting their own social causal explanations, sociologists of scientific knowledge were required to study the *social* causal explanations given by natural scientists alongside their *natural* causal explanations. In other words, they needed to study the discourse of the scientists while being aware of their own rhetoric.

The study showed that laboratory-based scientists routinely confront alternative versions of reality and like politicians, legal practitioners, and ordinary people, they have discursive resources available to them to justify preferring one version over others and to account for what they present as the errors of the others. Among these resources are representations of psychological furniture. Scientists employ as much ordinary reasoning as the rest of us, making reference to all kinds of purported psychological furniture as part of their practical psychological reasoning (adapting Garfinkel, 1967). Discursive psychology simply argues that this practical psychological reasoning is what psychologists should be studying.

An example is Edwards' (2007) study of complaints in which he contrasts "object-side" and "subject-side" explanations. That is, complaints may either be accepted as referring to something external to the complainer about which they are justified to complain (hence, object-side); or they may be viewed as not justified and therefore the complaint is not external to the complainer, but a feature of their personal disposition as a "moaner" or "whinger" (subject-side). For discursive psychology, then, the focus of empirical study becomes *when and how complaints are treated in one way rather than the other*. The parallel with the conventions of scientific argument is apparent: the empiricist repertoire is used to present a version of reality as grounded in Nature and external (object-side); the contingent repertoire is used to present a version of reality as accountable by, among other things, psychological processes and so internal (subject-side). Contrastive object-side and subject-side accounts may be offered for any kind of factual or descriptive claim.

More broadly, the existence of different versions of reality confronts us with a fundamental dilemma regarding any given version: is it a fact or an artifact? Is it something that exists in the real world, or merely a human construction, an invention of the person presenting it? This dilemma is ever present and people have available a range of resources to manage it, to provide justifications for treating a version in a particular way. In modern times, one way of doing this is to present our preferred version as "scientific," although there is no guarantee that this will make it "accepted." The matter is always, at least potentially, open to debate or argument, as in disputes over global warming/climate change, and the continuing creation-evolution controversy.

To speak of argument is to speak of **rhetoric** and discursive psychology and rhetorical psychology are in agreement that discourse is always rhetorical, in the sense that whatever is said or written is a version presented in relation to other potential or actual competing versions. People use their versions of reality to counter competing versions; as Potter (2012) puts it, discourse is "rhetorically situated." For every object-side description, there is a subject-side alternative; and for any empirical claim, a contingency may be advanced in opposition. This is how people defend, justify, and legitimize one view, and reject, undermine, and delegitimize competing views. They employ argumentative reasoning, seeking to persuade others (or indeed themselves) to see things one way rather than another and to do this, they use what Aristotle (1946) called "the available means of persuasion;" that is, rhetoric.

ARGUING AND THINKING

Rhetoric, in modern times, is usually associated with politics rather than science, but there is now a substantial amount of work in science and technology studies, and the rhetoric of inquiry to argue otherwise. Moreover, the view presented by Billig (1996a) suggests that *science is only possible because of rhetoric*.

It is not simply that scientists are competent rhetoricians trying to persuade others to accept their version(s) of reality, but that without rhetoric, the thinking that informs scientific research and theoretical development would never have developed. For Billig, *we think because we can argue,* and we can argue because we are perpetually faced with different versions of reality and the associated dilemma over facts and artifacts among a range of others (see Billig et al., 1988). Indeed, experimental research in all the contemporary sciences is directed toward trying to resolve arguments, although invariably they give rise to further arguments, that is, that "more research is needed."

Arguments do not simply exist like objects hanging around for us to chance upon; they arise because people *make* them using the language our social world provides. Language enables us to represent reality in multiple ways; it is a repository of distilled arguments, expressed in such things as everyday sayings and proverbs that sum up contrasting views. In the English-speaking world, for example, we have the saying: "sticks and stones may break my bones, but words can never hurt me"; but then we also say: "the pen is mightier than the sword." These two expressions contrast the materialist and idealist views of reality. The first can be used to reject the view that words and the ideas they express can do any material harm, while the second insists that words can be harmful to social standing and thus to material position and power. The proverbs sum up the sides of the argument, but are not the argument themselves. Rather, they provide the seeds from which arguments may flower (Billig, 1996a) as we consider how they may apply to our own circumstances. These sayings are persuasive; they stimulate our thinking, which then feeds back into the social world from which it originates, restating the arguments as it strives to resolve them. A standard strategy to resolve the argument in contemporary times is to appeal to expertise, but this does not guarantee success. Rather, it leads to consideration of two interrelated issues over which discursive psychology and rhetorical psychology are less than fully united: relativism and ideology.

RELATIVISM AND IDEOLOGY—OR THE DP-CA/RP-CDA FANDANGO

The issue of relativism arises from the arguments of both discursive psychology and rhetorical psychology. For discursive psychology, the traditional role accorded science to resolve different versions of reality by establishing the truth of matters is put aside in favor of making the versions themselves the object of study, especially insofar as psychological furniture is employed in their construction. Thus, no versions are treated as erroneous and none simply true; all are viewed for the interactional, persuasive work being done with them relative to their immediate context of production. But discursive psychology also produces a version, which must also then be a discursive construction. So what is the difference between this and cognitive psychology, which is also just another version? The difference seems to be that *discursive psychology acknowledges its rhetorical constitution*, such as its use of the rhetoric of realism (Potter, 1998b) and embraces relativism on both epistemological and moral grounds (Edwards, Ashmore, & Potter, 1995).

Potter (1996), however, has argued that embracing relativism does not mean, as critics often assert, the effective abandonment of scientific study. Rather, *relativism is a methodological principle* that gives us a fuller understanding of psychological phenomena, because instead of trying to condemn some versions as merely "common sense" and elevate others as "scientifically legitimate," we view them all equally for the practical, interactional work being done with them. Furthermore, in acknowledging the discursive constitution of our own version, we draw attention to the means of persuasion we employ. We acknowledge our own rhetoric: that the views we present are not simply given by the world, but are constructed arguments that require defense and justification, and are always open to challenge.

Argumentation is also fundamental to rhetorical psychology, but its position on relativism is more ambivalent. Billig (1991, pp. 22–26) addresses the issue through the arguments of the great Sophist, Protagoras, whose dictum that "there are two sides to every question" and, more contentiously, *that an equally persuasive case can be made for either side,* is a major source of inspiration. The implication of this view is that there are no ultimate grounds—whether God-given or determined by Nature—for deciding between the sides in a debate. Rather, any grounds we offer are based on our ordinary concerns and interests, and for which we must accept responsibility. Such grounds are always open to challenge not least on the basis that they may reflect personal circumstance or be self-serving; or, as we might say, be subjective rather than objective.

We are free to participate in the debate, to make arguments for one side against the other, not because we can claim to have access to an ultimate truth, but precisely because we cannot. All we have are arguments and, because of our involvement in shared humanity, we can and perhaps should participate in the debate. However, we do not do so to hammer down the iron fist of absolutism—which would stop the argument; rather, we participate in order to sustain the debate, to keep the argument alive, extending always an open palm in ready acceptance of further negotiation. Thus, on the one hand, we are relativists, accepting that there are no ultimate truths, but only contrasting alternatives; but, on the other, we are not, because we have our own commitments and beliefs—not least our commitment to maintaining argumentation.

IDEOLOGY

On the matter of ideology, discursive, and rhetorical psychology are more divided; this became particularly apparent in a debate between conversation analysis (CA) and critical discourse analysis (CDA). CA is an important influence on discursive psychology, because of its stress on the interactional work being done during ordinary, everyday talk. The founder of CA, Sacks (1995), sees ordinary conversation as the primary phenomenon of social life, the basis of human communication through which we accomplish the practical work of constructing and sustaining a shared social world (Heritage, 2009). CA focuses on the sequential ordering of talk between participants in ordinary conversation, both the fact that talk comes in ordered turns and how the taking of turns in sequential order is managed as talk flows along. From studying the flow of **talk-in-interaction**, CA aims to build a description of the "machinery" used to accomplish this activity.

Discursive psychology takes from this both the general stress on the interactive "business" that is being done with this machinery and an interest in many of the specific features at work, especially the way they are used to construct and deploy psychological furniture (see, e.g. Edwards, 2000). In addition, discursive psychology advances a similar epistemological claim as CA: that its analyses are warranted by reference to the next turn in the sequence. In effect, this means that the analyses they present are not (just) an(other) interpretation of what is going on in the talk, but rather a description of *the sense being made of the talk by the participants themselves*, which through transcription is made available for other analysts to check (Potter, 1996).

This raises a crucial issue concerning context. For many conversation analysts, it is vital that analysis does not go beyond the talk to "gloss" its sense in any way outside of that discernible in the sequential order. Analysts should not impose additional senses by reference to wider sociological or psychological frames of understanding (Schegloff, 1997). To do so is to claim to have access to a surrounding context (whether external or internal) taken to be determining the talk, but which is not available to the participants doing the talking—for example, by interpreting the meaning of a statement or turn as expressing some hidden motivating force, whether psychological (e.g. repression) or sociological (e.g. ideology). All that is available is "the talk"; during their talk, participants present their understanding of what is being talked about and their sense of the relevant context. Therefore, this is the only context to which analysis should refer.

On this issue, discursive psychology and rhetorical psychology are somewhat divided, although in certain respects their positions are not entirely clear. For one thing, although discursive psychology is strongly influenced by CA, their views on relativism are rather different. While discursive psychology defends at least some form of relativism, CA appears committed to a form of **inductive empiricism** that treats descriptions of the "machinery" of talk as directly grounded in observable (or hearable) phenomena that occur naturalistically, that is, without any inducement by the analyst. The talk is out there in the world and all they are doing is describing how it works. This is a pretty stark form of realism and how discursive psychologists reconcile this with their relativistic stress on the discursive representation of reality is not obvious.

CRITICAL DISCOURSE ANALYSIS

CDA styles itself "critical" because it claims to expose the workings of ideology in everyday discourse, such as news media. Following the example set by critical linguistics (Fowler, 1991; Hodge & Kress, 1993), critical discourse analysts have sought to identify how a particular structure of social relations within society is maintained by being embedded in the taken for granted terms of ordinary language (e.g., Fairclough, 2001). Through close analysis of the linguistic features employed in texts such as daily newspapers, this approach seeks to show the intimate workings of *social power* regarding such matters as gender, class, and race relations. It shows how a wider structure of social relations informs ordinary language in ways that users of the language are unaware. Indeed, they may actively employ that language to further their own gender, class, or racial interests.

A key focus of this kind of work has been on linguistic transformations, such as "nominalization" and "passivization." Nominalization refers to the turning of verbs into nouns, such as (in the seminal example analyzed by Kress & Trew, 1978), turning "to picket" into "picketting." This leads to a loss of information about the actors involved since active verb forms require specifying who is doing the picketting ("so-and-so pickets"), whereas the noun appears simply as a thing that happens in itself ("picketting occurs"). Similarly, passivization refers to the turning of active into passive verb forms, such that "so-and-so pickets X" becomes "X was picketed," with again a loss of information about the actors. For critical discourse analysts, such linguistic transformations can serve ideological purposes because they invest social relations with a thing-like existence, reifying gender, and racial relationships to appear as necessities and inevitabilities, and turning malleable social constructs into immutable "facts" that serve the interests of powerful social groups.

In a significant debate in the pages of *Discourse and Society* about the merits of CA and CDA, Billig clearly aligns himself on the side of CDA (Billig, 1999a, 1999b; Schegloff, 1997, 1998, 1999a, 1999b; Wetherell, 1998). This debate centered on the issue of context: whether social analysts are justified in assuming the relevance of gender to social interaction even if there is no direct or explicit reference made to it by the people involved. In a strong response to Schegloff's defense of the position that analysts should not assume the relevance of any context not hearably "oriented to" by the "participants," Billig countered with the example of rape in which no direct reference to that activity can be heard, but which can be reasonably inferred. There is some tension between discursive psychology, rhetorical psychology, and CDA. Although discursive psychology is critical of the assumption of a wider ideological context invoked by CDA, Potter (1996) nonetheless identifies passivization and nominalization as important processes in "fact construction." Meanwhile, Billig shares with CDA a concern with the workings of ideology, which he sees as central to social psychology, but he is nonetheless critical of its technicized terminology.

THE POLITICS OF EXPERIENCE

The issues regarding relativism, ideology, and reflexivity emerge from the relationship between social science and ordinary thinking: these are "the politics of experience." This term originates with Laing (1967), but I take my sense from Pollner's (1987) discussion of how "reality disjunctures" are dealt with by mundane reasoning. "Mundane reasoning" refers not only to ordinary common sense ways of thinking but also to science, because it is based on a set of pregiven assumptions, or "mundane idealizations" that the world is "determinate, coherent and non-contradictory" (Pollner, 1987, p. 17). However, these assumptions are constantly threatened by "reality disjunctures" in the form of contrasting versions and mundane reasoning has a range of means available to neutralize the threat.

Among other things, we have developed institutional arrangements—parliamentary proceedings, courts of law, and scientific laboratories—to discount some versions and to justify acceptance of one definitive version. However, there is no guarantee that disjunctures will be resolved, because of an inherent uncertainty in the relation between individual empirical experience and its interactive reportage. As Pollner (1987, p. 77) puts it:

> equivocality is perpetuated by a mode of reasoning in which each of the disputants, treating [their] version as a given and thereby ironicizing competing experiences, finds the experiential claims of the other to be the product of an inadequate procedure for perceiving the world.

Much like the empiricist and contingent repertoires in scientists' discourse, reality disjunctures have the potential to be upheld indefinitely because of the mundane idealization that the world is determinate and coherent. These assumptions insist that the world is not merely knowable but knowable in common, that it is the same world for all of us and therefore our experiential descriptions should be in agreement. However, because different versions are possible and the same warrants and discountings are available to each of us, disjunctures can be maintained indefinitely. To avoid this, some sources are invested with superior validity, such as those offered by scientists. The politics of experience then involves a socially legitimized expert version of events being given superiority over the accounts of ordinary people as a matter of social convention. However, as the case of conspiracy discourse shows, this is not always uncontestable.

CONSPIRACY DISCOURSE

At this point, we may make a brief comparison between the approaches to **conspiracy discourse** employed by cognitive psychology and rhetorical psychology. I use the term "conspiracy discourse" rather than "conspiracy theory" to highlight my own discursive approach to social and cultural phenomena (Locke, 2011). However, I use the terms interchangeably to refer to what Barkun (2003, p. 6) calls "superconspiracy theories": the claim that the world is run in the interests of a single, powerful group, which acts covertly and toward malevolent ends, such that nothing happens by accident, everything is connected, and nothing is as it seems. Conspiracy discourse is routinely discounted by social scientists by reference to one form or another of psychological or sociological fallacy or pathology (typically "paranoia"; see Billig, 1978; Byford, 2011). Often, the credibility of conspiracy discourse is rendered invalid on the grounds of its "nonacademic" quality in contrast to proper scholarship, which is said to conform to a higher standard of evidence involving "falsificationism" (Popper, 2002) and "organized skepticism" (Merton, 1968). Byford (2011) also claims that academic historians revise their theories in the light of evidence, unlike conspiracy theorists who interpret evidence to fit the theory.

However, Kuhn (1970), a professional historian of science, argued persuasively that scientists do not try to falsify theories, but use the prevailing paradigm to design experiments and make sense of the findings. Following his lead, sociologists of scientific knowledge disputed Merton's norms of science as nothing more than "standardized verbal formulations" (Mulkay, 1993, p. 71) that scientists use to justify knowledge claims. In other words, academics employ rhetorical resources as demonstrated in a recent cognitive psychological study of conspiracy thinking.

A COGNITIVE APPROACH TO CONSPIRACY

Noting that psychological studies of belief in conspiracy theories show a tendency for those who accept one theory also to accept others, Wood, Douglas, and Sutton (2012) sought to find out whether this occurs when two such theories present contradictory views (i.e., there is a reality disjuncture between two conflicting versions). They suggest that this may occur because the contradiction is "overruled by [the theories'] coherence with a broader conspiracist worldview," which inclines believers to accept any theory that is compatible with the "higher-order belief ... that authorities are engaged in motivated deception of the public" (p. 768). They propose this on the basis of "explanatory coherence theory," which advances a model of cognition in which explanations and evidence are "represented by nodes in a connectionist network. Activation flows from evidence nodes and higher-order knowledge structures ... to the various explanations, which in turn excite or inhibit one another depending on whether they are mutually coherent or contradictory" (p. 768).

In the first of two studies, they administered a questionnaire to psychology undergraduates to establish their level of acceptance of different conspiracy theories that Wood et al. (2012, p. 769) describe as "mutually contradictory." These included the statements that: (a) "One or more rogue 'cells' in the British secret service constructed and carried out a plot to kill [Princess] Diana"; and (b) "Diana faked her own death so that she and Dodi [Fayed] could retreat into isolation." The results led them to claim that it is possible for believers to "simultaneously endorse several contradictory accounts" (p. 770) and in the second study they found that this could be explained by a belief that the authorities are involved in motivated deception. Wood et al. (2012, p. 772) argued that explanatory coherence theory might provide "insight into the processes underlying the development of conspiracist beliefs, and of other beliefs influenced by superordinate ideological considerations."

Of note here is their use of the term "ideology" and that they do not propose applying the disparaging connotations of ideology to psychological science. There is also an interesting irony, in that their notion of ideology (p. 771) draws on earlier work by Adorno, which attempted to explain "contradictory anti-Semitic beliefs." On this basis, Wood et al. draw a parallel between conspiracy thinking and "orthodox" Marxism as examples of "monological" beliefs. In a paradoxical manner, Wood et al. draw on a Marxist notion of ideology to describe Marxism as ideological in order to distinguish types of belief that can tolerate "contradictions." However, there is no sense that they would include their own psychological beliefs in this analysis. From their position, contradictions are only found in other kinds of beliefs called "monological" and the possibility that CP might also be "monological" does not enter the picture. Indeed, reflexivity is completely absent from their study.

REINSTATING THE THINKING PERSON

We might also ask whether cognitive psychologists think of their own cognitions in terms of the mechanistic processes described by the explanatory coherence model. In this mechanistic fabulation, "evidence nodes" simply "activate" when they come across "pieces of evidence" and set off "flows" to "higher-order knowledge structures." What exactly are these things? This description as a representation of living, interacting, and *thinking* human beings is quite bizarre! There is no sense whatsoever of *a person* actively thinking. We also need to ask what is meant by a "piece of evidence?" Does evidence simply exist waiting to be encountered by "evidence nodes" somewhere in the brain? Overall, the study fails to understand the nature of conspiracy discourse. First and foremost, conspiracy theorists *argue*; they do not simply encounter "pieces of evidence," but actively work to find (and/or manufacture: fact or artifact) material that they treat as evidence. In the same way that laboratory scientists construct statistical measures, conspiracy theorists are actively involved in thinking and arguing over what counts as evidence, defining what should and should not be considered and what is and is not a contradiction (Billig, 1991, pp. 115–120). One particular peculiarity about the approach of Wood et al. (2012, p. 768) is that they begin by asking how believers in conspiracy theories "reconcile the presence of … competing, mutually contradictory accounts" and yet they do not read what conspiracy theorists write to examine their arguments, nor talk to them to try to elicit their explanations. Instead, they ask students to respond to preformulated statements that the researchers take to be contradictory—and fail to check if the students also find them so.

In this respect, they fail to consider how conspiracy theorists actively *think*. Conspiracy theorists are extremely adept at accounting for things that might seem to others to be contradictory—just like scientists can account for anomalies in their data that might upset their favored theory. Consider the two statements given about Princess Diana's death that Wood et al. call "unambiguous contradictions." To a conspiracy theorist, there is every possibility they would be considered nothing of the sort, because there many ways of thinking about them to make them compatible. For example, it is not without the bounds of possibility that "rogue cells" within the British secret service did carry out a plot to kill the Princess, but as they were so doing, she was also faking her own death. After all, there is nothing in the first statement to say that the rogue cells were *successful* in their plot to kill her. Or, Diana herself may have arranged for the rogue cells to carry out such a plot as the means of faking her death and the person who was actually killed might have been a double or a clone. The point is that the notion of "contradiction" is not itself unambiguous. To see statements as contradictory is to interpret them in a particular way, to present a version of them. But this is not the only way to interpret them, because alternative versions are always possible.

As Protagoras might have said, there are two sides to every contradiction, one of which is that it is not a contradiction. Contrary to Aristotle's syllogistic logic in which A cannot be both A and not-A, in the social constructions of mundane rhetorical reasoning, A *can* be both A and not-A. The profound difficulty faced by established social science from conspiracy discourse is the skill with which believers are able to turn the tables by figuring out ways in which A might be not-A. Billig (2009) rejects this mechanistic way of thinking about thinking, where an imaginary cognitive mechanism that does the work of determining whether or not there are any contradictions is treated as an unobservable reality. In this model, the person, active thinking, and arguing do not exist, but this is not what happens in real life. When confronted by contrasting views within conspiracy discourse, mundane reasoning can make sense of them by ruling them out of the ordinary run of things and designating them as "abnormal." However, the problem now is that conspiracy discourse has become so widespread in popular culture that it is now the norm (Birchall, 2006; Knight, 2000; Latour, 2004; Parish & Parker, 2001).

Indeed, when conspiracy thinking was confined to a relative minority in western societies, it may have seemed acceptable to describe it as "bizarre" (see Billig, 1978, 1991) but for academics to simply declare what is normal and what is not with respect to the views of ordinary people merely accentuates the politics of experience. Of course, we might still wish to *argue* that there is good reason to dismiss conspiracy discourse especially when dealing with the anti-Semitism of the extreme right, but the idea that individuals are caught up in an ideological framework of which they are unaware is exactly what conspiracy theorists (including anti-Semitic ones) claim about everyone else. As both sides engage in an endless competition of claim and counter-claim about whose thinking is determined by covert powers and processes, there is little point in continuing the game. We need to think about conspiracy discourse in a different way. However objectionable we might find the views expressed, *we should attend to the way that conspiracy discourse is constructed* without attempting to discount or delegitimize it either in terms of mechanistic theories of cognitive processing or ideological determination. We should not simply dismiss conspiracy discourse; but this does not mean that we cannot argue against it. Conspiracy discourse needs to be treated as argument and, where we disagree with it, we need to argue against it. To do this means taking the thinking behind it seriously and not treating the cognitions of the people involved any differently from our own cognitions. It means recognizing and fully accepting that every-one employs mundane reasoning, that there is nothing special about academic thinking, beyond perhaps the fact that we are paid to do it. It means engaging with conspiracy theorists as thinking people, not as mechanistic robots; and, in so far as we disagree with them, it means making the effort to explain why. In so doing, we may not change their minds, but we may at least come to understand our own arguments, and ourselves, just a little better.

SUMMARY

- Discursive and rhetorical psychology reject the main assumptions of cognitive psychology arguing that we should study the linguistic representations of psychological phenomena rather than invisible "mental furniture."
- The central psychological issue is "the politics of experience," which involves issues of relativism, ideology, and reflexivity.
- Different versions of reality are always possible and each version is constructed in rhetorical contrast to other actual or potential versions.
- Laboratory-based psychology cannot establish a definitive version of reality because it is caught up in the politics of experience both inside and outside the laboratory.
- Rhetorical psychology claims that an equally persuasive case can be made for either side in an argument and that, because of this, we are free to argue a case for one side over another.
- Conspiracy discourse illustrates the politics of experience concerning the relation between experts' theories of ordinary people's stupidity and ordinary people's theories of experts' stupidity.

GLOSSARY

cognitive psychology is a branch of psychology that infers the existence of mental systems and structures (assumed to be inside people's heads) from experimental data.

conspiracy discourse refers to the language of conspiracy theories viewed symmetrically and reflexively as rhetorical constructions of versions of reality.

contingent repertoire refers to an interpretative or discursive repertoire employed by scientists in controversy to represent the descriptions of reality presented by opponents as erroneous and often attributable to psychological or sociological causes.

conversation analysis is the study of talk-in-interaction.

critical discourse analysis refers to an approach to the study of ordinary language that tries to identify ideological processes and power relations in linguistic categories and transformations.

discursive psychology is a form of social psychology that studies how people construct versions of psychological phenomena through talk and text in relation to the immediate contexts of social interaction.

empiricist repertoire refers to an interpretative or discursive repertoire employed by scientists to represent their knowledge claims as direct descriptions of reality.

ideology refers to widespread ideas and beliefs that inform common sense ways of thinking and interacting and sustain a particular order of social division and social relation.

inductive empiricism is a philosophy of science that sees knowledge as grounded in observations of particular phenomena from which statements of general relationship can be derived (induced).

interpretative (or discursive) repertoire refers to a way of speaking or writing; a linguistic register or type of voice that provides resources and techniques for interpreting and representing reality in one way or another.

relativism is the idea that views of the world cannot be divorced from social context; this includes the views of scientists (and this view).

reflexivity is the idea that scientific/academic beliefs, theories, and discourse should be subject to the same forms of analysis and explanation as scientists/academics apply to any other type of belief, theory, or discourse.

rhetoric is the art and study of using the available means of persuasion, that is, argumentation.

rhetorical psychology is a form of social psychology that treats psychological phenomena and processes as products of argumentation and studies them accordingly, with particular interest in ideological constructs.

symmetry refers to a tenet of the sociology of scientific knowledge that states that we should explain both true and false beliefs by reference to the same social causes or processes. More broadly, we should treat all beliefs and knowledge claims equivalently whatever their source or assumed validity.

talk-in-interaction is any kind of talk or conversational exchange occurring in any social setting, including both formal, institutional, and informal, noninstitutional varieties.

FURTHER READING

....

Billig, M. (1996). *Arguing and thinking: A rhetorical approach to social psychology* (2nd ed.). Cambridge: Cambridge University Press.

Edwards D., & Potter J. (1992). *Discursive psychology*. London: Sage.

A USEFUL FOLLOW UP THAT ADDRESSES ISSUES OF RELATIVISM AND REFLEXIVITY:

Pollner M. (1987). *Mundane reason: Reality in everyday and sociological discourse*. Cambridge: Cambridge University Press.

Potter J. (1996). *Representing reality: Discourse, rhetoric and social construction*. London: Sage.

FOR FURTHER DEBATE AND DISCUSSION OF THE DP-CA/RP-CDA FANDANGO:

Billig M. (2013). *Learn to write badly: How to succeed in the social sciences*. Cambridge: Cambridge University Press.

Wooffitt R. (2005). *Conversation analysis and discourse analysis: A comparative and critical introduction*. London: Sage.

QUESTIONS FOR GROUP DISCUSSION

- Are people like bureaucrats with heads filled with filing cabinets? What do we mean by "mental furniture?" Provide some examples from contemporary psychology.

- Why is the emphasis in discursive psychology on "versions of reality?"

- How does "the politics of experience" call into question the division between psychological experts and ordinary people?

- What is the relationship between thinking, talking, and arguing?

- Why do some reject relativism? Is it a lack of understanding or does it present a deep-rooted psychological threat to absolutist beliefs?

- What does the study of conspiracy discourse offer to political psychology?

5 Identity

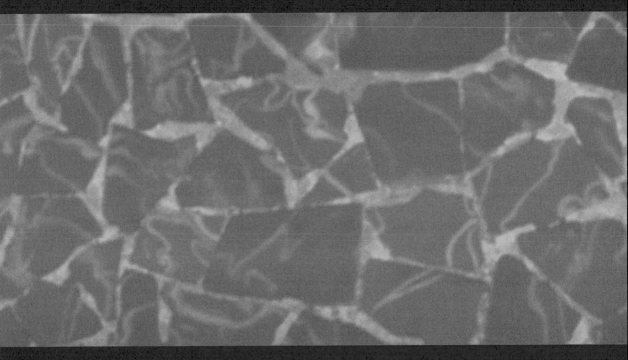

CHRISTOPHER J. HEWER AND EVANTHIA LYONS

CHAPTER OUTLINE

IDENTITY AND HUMAN RELATIONS

The variations between people, the way they look, act, and express themselves have the potential to entertain, fascinate, and enrich our lives, but regrettably, history is full of accounts of human catastrophes such as war, slavery, ethnic cleansing, and genocide that remind us that being a member of a particular group at a particular time has been a calamitous experience for many people. Our everyday observations of the world, and perhaps even our own experience, lead us to conclude that identity is a contentious issue that often underlies a power struggle over basic human rights and fair and equal access to the world's resources. Within political psychology, identity provides a conceptual base from which we can account for the meanings that people attach to political processes, institutions, phenomena, and actions. In this chapter, we address the role that identity plays in both generating a sense of belonging and in creating division, and the aim is to present some of the more important ideas, theories, and findings on self and identity that are relevant to political psychology.

CATEGORIZATION

Because we have the unique ability to reflect on who we are and the groups to which we belong, categorization appears to be an integral part of living in a social world, and it appears to satisfy two psychological needs—a sense of belonging *with* others and a sense of distinctiveness *from* others. A common identity allows us to be accepted as a legitimate member of a group. At the same time, we may seek to assert our individuality or distinctiveness within the group or in relation to other groups. For some, belonging may be more important than distinctiveness or vice versa, or it may be that these different needs come to the fore at different times and in different situations.

In any discussion about identity, there are two main considerations: (a) the way that other people see or categorize us (and how we may categorize others) and (b) how we choose to categorize or present ourselves to others. Many categorizations are beyond our control and stay with us throughout our lives. At birth, we are assigned as either male or female, we are given a name and

Political Psychology: A Social Psychological Approach, First Edition.
Edited by Christopher J. Hewer and Evanthia Lyons.

we soon learn that we belong to a family and live in a particular place, which is part of a larger country. We may be given a religious identity and we come to understand that there are people like us and not like us on a variety of dimensions, and that our sense of belonging or distinctiveness in relation to others carries both personal and political implications. Other categorizations, however, may be more malleable, transient, or subject to change. For example, we may gain or lose weight, get married or divorced, or go from employment to unemployment or retirement—these are nonetheless changes that have psychological consequences.

When considering identity, there is also the issue of **intersectionality**. For example, if someone describes themselves as middle class, French, female, and Catholic, these group memberships are interdependent—one does not exist without the other—they intersect. The salience of each identity, however, is likely to vary according to social circumstance. For example, when we travel abroad, we become aware that we are not part of the local community and thus become more aware of our own nationality or ethnicity. Other situations may make us more conscious of our gender, religion, or social class. What is more, the combination of these identities may affect their meaning and the way that specific identities are enacted. For example, to be a *French* Catholic or a *female* Catholic creates quite different subjective meanings compared to other members of the Catholic faith.

SELF AND SOCIETY

What do we understand by self and identity? Although self and identity are, at times, used interchangeably, they are widely seen as distinct concepts. Augoustinos, Walker, and Donaghue (2006) explain:

> *Self* is more often used to refer to people's beliefs about themselves, about their own ideas of who they are, and their personal characteristics, abilities, experiences, emotions and agendas. Our *identity* locates us in a world made up of groups of people and usually concerns the social groups and categories to which we do and do not belong. (p. 186)

Not everyone would necessarily agree with this line of demarcation. Some extend identity to include "emotions, beliefs, and attitudes" that motivate and direct action (e.g., Breakwell, 1986, p. 43), and social constructionists see identity as an alternative to personality because it avoids all the connotations of essentialism (Burr, 2003). In some instances then, identity may refer to our membership of a group; it may represent a label or category that has been imposed upon us; it may be a reflective term to represent the way we see ourselves, or the way that others see us. A variation in use or an occasional blurring of the distinction between self and identity should not overly concern us. To some degree, the conceptual distinction between self and identity reflects the different philosophical positions and historical developments within social psychology. In North American social psychology, the social cognition perspective conceptualizes the self as an individualized construct that is assumed to be self-contained and autonomous. This approach models the self as a body of knowledge focused on "content free" information processing within the head of the individual (Deaux, 1992). Although mental processing is involved in the formation of the self, there is nonetheless a broader question: what role does society play in this process?

Other perspectives may see the self as located within a collective or community, or as a product of social interaction. An approach that provides a foundation for this line of argument stems from the work of American social philosopher, George Herbert Mead (1863–1931). **Symbolic interactionism** posits that the mind, self-consciousness, and the self develop through social interaction (Mead, 1934). Mead argues that the self is both an object ("me") and a reflexive subject ("I"). The "I" refers to the agentic nature of the self while the "me" refers to the sense of self that is a product of social communication and adaptation processes. As a reflexive subject, the "I" reflects on the self as an object ("me") and adapts to the speech and actions of others to produce a desirable social response. In this process, language functions as a form of symbolic interchange that facilitates self-development over time, and people navigate their way through these dynamics in a variety of situations. In this conceptualization, the process of reciprocal exchange between self and society means that the self is not a self-contained unit; rather, it is embedded within a culture of relationships and a system of communication. The content and structure of the self is therefore a product of time, place, and culture (Gergen, 2009a; Stryker, 1987).

OCCUPATIONAL IDENTITY: ROLES AND PERFORMANCE

The formation of self and identity is particularly linked to the roles we perform, have performed, or aspire to perform. Of particular importance are occupational roles. In former times, people were defined by their trade or occupation, and the surnames of many families in the English-speaking world reflect this, for example, bowyer (bow maker), fletcher (arrow maker), butcher, baker, carver, tanner, farmer, and so on. Since the end of World War II, occupational certainty has largely disappeared; there are no longer "jobs for life" and work roles come and go to meet rapidly changing social, political, and economic demands. Jobs such as coal mining or shipbuilding have been replaced by service industry occupations. Many people are now employed in call centers or work as delivery drivers to meet the demands of Internet shopping; and the emergence of the "gig economy—non-permanent employment and uncertain "zero-hour" contracts—not only creates financial insecurity, but also inhibits the development of occupational identity. In a sense, we *are* what we do, or we become what we do. Occupational roles also illustrate the link between action and identity—that identities are performed, and that roles mobilize specific actions. In all social contexts, roles give an individual the authority to act in a way not permitted by others, for example, soldier, teacher, police officer, firefighter, and so on. We might say that, "action is the social expression of identity" (Breakwell, 1986, p. 43). Not only does identity facilitate action, but the mechanism also works in reverse: that when identity is in doubt, action is paralyzed.

In previous epochs, occupational roles were fixed and fully constrained within social hierarchies. The social system did not permit social mobility (once a blacksmith always a blacksmith): trades such as butcher, baker, and blacksmith were passed down through the generations. Although this kept people in their original social position, it nonetheless offered certainty in relation to identity—a sense of belonging and purpose in society (Fromm, 1942). When the message to a new generation today is that "you can be what you want to be," we have to ask, what does this mean for people in psychological terms? While the discourse of opportunity may be liberating, it also likely induces anxiety because it creates a quest for identity that may not be achieved. Once formal education has ended, social and economic realities often take hold, and limited opportunity within the economic system can impose identities upon people that do not fit. Workers may find themselves in jobs that are both unsuitable and unfulfilling. Their future appears uncertain and limited. Low pay further disempowers them because they cannot afford to leave their job: they are tied. Even for those who can afford to take the risk and embark on a midlife career change, the risks remain, and the stakes are high.

POLITICAL MOBILIZATION: NATIONAL IDENTITY AND NATIONALISM

The relationship between action and identity can also be seen in international relations. Two world wars, and numerous accounts of ethnic cleansing and genocide in the twentieth century illustrate the devastating consequences of arousing national or ethnic identity to action. Given the prominence of national identity in the twentieth century, we might ask: what is a nation? While we might think of nationhood in terms of language groups bonded by ancestry, culture, ethnic identity, or attachment to territory, scholars tend to think of nations as imagined communities (Anderson, 1983). Closer analysis reveals that nation-states are broadly self-defining. In other words, establishing consistent and universally defining criteria of a nation is difficult (see Reicher & Hopkins, 2001b). What *is* common among nations, however, is their selective view of the past, which is transmitted across generations through commemoration, national symbols, rituals, narratives, and history lessons in schools (Carretero, 2011). The past as an expression of identity is not only performed ceremonially, it is also found within the activities and expressions of everyday life.

Closely aligned to national identity is **nationalism**. There are many definitions of nationalism and most involve a conception of the nation as an organized political entity concerned with sovereignty over territory, and political and economic affairs. Nationalism in its more malign form, however, involves a sense of exaggerated and assertive superiority that promotes the interests of one nation over all others, which often translates into devaluation or even hatred of other nations or groups. Some scholars make a distinction between patriotism (a strong positive regard for one's country) and nationalism (a belief in the superiority, power, and dominance of one's own country in relation to other nations) (e.g., Feshbach, 1987, 1990; Kosterman & Feshbach, 1989), while others claim that nationalism is simply a more complex form of patriotism (e.g., Druckman, 1994). Kelman (1969) sees this distinction in terms of attachment. An instrumental attachment to nation, he argues, is based on rational considerations, and an analysis where benefits outweigh costs results in patriotism; whereas a sentimental attachment to nation is more emotional and involves an elevation of tradition, cultural achievements, and national symbols, and this likely leads to nationalism. However, despite scholarly attempts to intellectualize the distinction between patriotism and nationalism, the difference may be wafer thin.

There may be examples where patriotism involves no comparison with another country. For example, when Robert Mugabe resigned as leader of Zimbabwe in 2017, many people took to dancing in the streets, and some draped themselves in the national flag as if to say, "Now, we now have our country back." In such circumstances, however, the broader question becomes: what do people do with their patriotism? How is it used? And how quickly and under what circumstances might patriotism become nationalism?

Nationalism was at the root of conflict and human suffering in the twentieth century. Despite this, few challenge national identity as a political construct or wish to exchange it for a more inclusive pannational identity. Why is this? Why is national identity so powerful and pervasive? Some would claim that it is a fundamental bond between people. In practical terms, recent historical conflict and the threat of future conflict ensure the continuation of national identities. In some parts of the world, people live with daily hostilities or the threat of invasion, and therefore the salience and continuity of national identity is not surprising. Other nations have strong historical memories of war, conflict, invasion, and occupation, and because of this, national governments continue to maintain a military resource to defend the freedom and autonomy of the state and its citizens.

However, there is more to nationalism than simply a desire to defend territory and freedoms. Billig (1995) draws our attention to a form of **banal nationalism** that manifests itself in "the ideological habits, which enable the established nations of the West to be reproduced" (p. 6). In this context, banal does not mean benign or harmless because western nation-states are militarily powerful. Billig argues that nationalism is banal in the sense that "it seems to possess reassuring normality" (p. 7), and while "nationalism, as a condition is projected onto 'others'; 'ours' is overlooked, forgotten, even theoretically denied." (p. 17). Theorists, he claims, often treat their own national allegiance as something invisible, something that is assumed to be part of the human condition. National loyalties are thus presented as "'needs for identity', 'attachments to society' or 'primordial ties', which are theoretically posited to be universal psychological states, and not peculiar to the age of nation-states." (p. 17). In Billig's analysis, nationalism is what *other* nations do, while we simply embrace patriotism. Even in times of peace, international sports competitions such as the Olympic games endorse national identity as part of the natural order of things.

National groups are not only categories of history, but also categories of habit and convenience. We might talk about America, for example, as a political entity, and in so doing we may conflate the political entity (America) with the people (Americans), that is, we may talk about a nation and its people as though they are the same thing. However, even in democratic nations, the actions and disposition of the political entity do not always reflect the sentiments of the people—they do not necessarily support its political actions. For obvious reasons, this type of conflation often occurs in times of war, and usually continues in the decades that follow. In such cases, national categorizations are problematic in that they allow us to structure and represent the world without having to acknowledge historic changes within political institutions, shifts and differences in public opinion across generations, generational shift, individual differences, or a nuanced understanding of people. This raises an important question about national identity and the nature of national groups. *Is there really a basis for assuming a continuous national essence across time?*

It is true that a new generation builds upon previous generations. Overlapping lifespans ensure that a younger generation assimilates the accounts and explanations of a previous generation, which leads to some understanding of their collective existence. After the passing of many generations, however, we have to ask: to what degree is there continuity? Does anyone in modern Britain really identify with the colonial activities of Clive of India? Or is it that we now simply occupy the same territory, speak the same language, and share a common past that unites us to previous generations? Are we truly psychologically linked to previous generations or is our association merely circumstantial? To what extent do their beliefs and actions become ours through cultural inheritance? Or is it that traces of continuity have filtered down through the generations?

These questions come to the fore particularly when uncomfortable questions are raised about a nation's historic conduct, for example, war, colonialism, genocide. Often, it is assumed that nations have an enduring character or political essence despite changing their population over many generations. We may then think of nations and the people that comprise them in terms of national character (stereotypes), which may also be habits of thought—cognitive shortcuts designed to reduce complexity. Therefore, when we refer to a nation in a spirit of complaint, we have to be precise about our terms of reference. In such circumstances, it may not helpful to think in term of national essences, not only because it presents a barrier to good relations, but also because it suggests that political change is not possible.

When involved in discussion and debate, we have to be precise: are we referring to the nation as a *current* political entity or its historic equivalent? Is our complaint really about the people, the military decisions, the parliament, or the government? For example, the political institutions of modern Germany no longer resemble authoritarian Nazi Germany of the 1930s and 1940s—and the generation responsible for war crimes has now passed off the scene. Indeed, to hold subsequent generations responsible for the actions of their forebears may not align well with our sense of justice. In these difficult circumstances, the most pressing question may then be: how should a nation remember its past? When a nation has to live and work through a difficult political legacy, it inevitably constitutes a threat to identity, which may mean that national identity has to be reconstructed or reconfigured. This is usually achieved by acknowledging and addressing the past, and setting in motion political change to ensure that such injustices are not repeated.

IDENTITY THREATS

Another threat to national identity arises through **globalization** as industries close and communities of local people lose their livelihoods. This threat to identity is often compounded by migration, because of the belief that it increases competition for jobs, drains limited social resources (realistic threat) and will likely result in a dilution of cultural values (symbolic threat) (Stephan & Stephan, 2000). Some countries have also been sensitive to **cultural imperialism**. For example, the Americanization of culture, which has extended to Europe and beyond since 1945 means that we now take for granted the political, economic, and moral ideology contained within American entertainment as well as the consumption that accompanies it. In France, the use of English words in the French language has always caused concern,[1] and now the prominence of English in the world of information technology, which has resulted in the widespread use of English words in the work place, has now brought intervention from the French government.[2]

Threats to culture, economic interests, or identity may cause public and politicians alike to think along the lines of "Our country first!" and in order to persuade others, they may invoke a vision of a better past. They may even talk about making the country great again. However, as Boym (2007) observes, it is perhaps ironic that the twentieth century opened with thoughts of creating a Utopian society through the application of science to human problems, but ended with nostalgia—a harkening back to an imagined past—perhaps even returning to a place (in our imagination) that never truly existed.

IDENTITY POLITICS

Within nation-states, identity is closely related to issues of social inequality, exploitation, and marginalization. The term **identity politics** can be traced back the Civil Rights Movement in the US in the 1960s, and it is now used to refer to all forms of political positions resulting from the interests and perspectives of particular groups. These positions usually gain prominence because of disputes or perceived grievances in relation to access to resources, jobs, housing, and so on, and the objective of the oppressed or deprived group is usually to achieve equality or social recognition, or simply to receive humane and fair treatment.

Identity politics may also arise because we feel psychologically constrained. In our quest for identity, we may reflect upon and critical evaluate our group memberships and their implications for us. We may ask: What should I become? What am I able to become? How do I fit within this society? How should I behave? What am I supposed to believe? How am I to live my life? These questions may create a sense conflict between how we see ourselves and the way that our family, community, or society wants us to be. A sense of internal self-discrepancy between our *actual*, *ideal*, and *ought* self may result, and this tension may lead to a range of negative or difficult emotions (Higgins, Klein, & Strauman, 1985). The central issue here is power relations. Kitzinger (1989, p. 82)

---

[1] http://www.dailymail.co.uk/news/article-530403/France-protects-dreaded-English-language-banning-fast-food-podcasting.html.
[2] http://www.dailymail.co.uk/news/article-2268722/Zut-alors-The-French-banned-world-hashtag--email-blog-English-intrusions-beloved-language.html.

summarizes the position by quoting feminist Jill Johnston, "Identity is what you can say you are according to what they say you can be." When an individual's expression of identity is dependent on the permission of others, identity dynamics become linked to power relations, which raise the prospect for discrimination, social inequality, conflict, even persecution. Groups who see themselves as deprived or oppressed may eventually challenge the social order. Indeed, a sense of **relative deprivation** has been a strong motivational force for social change (Gurr, 1970; Runciman, 1966), particularly in democracies where groups have the right to protest and the right to vote in government elections.

In the decades after World War II, a new generation in the West asserted their democratic right to protest against all forms of perceived social injustices that were part of the social order at that time. The 1960s and 1970s saw the rise of the second wave of feminism, the Civil Rights Movement, and the Gay Liberation Movement. There were student protests in the US and Europe against the war in Vietnam, and in Germany, those who had grown up after the World War II, started to question and challenge the older generation and force them to account for their relationship to the National Socialist regime before and during World War II. There were even protests against Soviet authority in the communist bloc. In 1968, in Prague, Czechoslovakia (now the Czech Republic and Slovakia), a new leader of the Communist Party liberalized restrictions on the media, travel, and citizens' rights. Moscow's displeasure at these reforms eventually led to military occupation and 8 months of peaceful resistance.

What these events show is that as the relationship between self and society becomes more complex and diverse, new alliances, conflicts, and anxieties emerge giving rise to new identities and novel social and political behavior. At the forefront of current developments is sexual identity. LGBTQ+ now refers to people who profess to be lesbian, gay, bisexual, transgender, transsexual, two-spirited, queer, or questioning. To add to the complexity, and to illustrate the current dynamic, fluid, and fragmented nature of sexual identity, there are additional categories such as intersex, asexual, ally, pansexual, agender, gender queer, bigender, gender variant, and pangender. What has brought about these new identities? Within 50 years, shifts in public opinion, changes in legislation across the western world, the passing off the scene of previous generations, and strategic government lobbying have transformed homosexuality from an illegal practice requiring punishment or treatment to an available identity. The mass media, and in more recent times, the Internet and social media have had a central role in the advance of gender fluidity and the creation and evolution of new identities. The widespread social connection provided by the Internet and its "democratic" space has emboldened people to create new categories that fit a particular orientation or disposition, and once they are made available to others, people are free to explore, endorse, or reconfigure in accord with their own form of sexual self-identification.

IMAGE, IMAGES, AND APPEARANCE

We also see within our technologized culture, the self as a commodity in the marketplace—where appearance is sold for personal gain. The Internet, particularly, has made people acutely aware of their image and many people construct identity through image (a psychological conception of their own image and those of others) and images (visual representations of self and others). In the virtual world, we become what we are able to convince others to believe we are—a creation of our own self-image or fantasy. By tinkering with our lifestyle image on Facebook or Instagram, it is possible to create ideal or altered personas, or even pretend to be something or someone we are not. And because the tools of image construction and reconstruction are simple, immediate, and available to all, the Internet has ensured that appearance (rather than substance or action) is now the primary means by which most people assert identity. We therefore have to ask: what is the relationship between appearance and reality? Are we what we *are* or what we *claim* to be, or *appear* to be? How do people function in a world where appearance is so important? Will this new generation (and those to come) find it difficult in psychological terms to maintain a sense of identity without an Internet connection? And if the self is a product of internalized responses from others, to what extent is the Internet psychologically safe? For a younger generation, identity is now constructed in unison with the sound of the smartphone. As thousands of followers are acquired on-line, users are exposed to the whims of incessant, unsolicited commentary, and walk the tightrope of receiving either abuse or validation. This is a risky environment!

Nonetheless, the new technology has fitted well with the needs and desires that have been at the center of social and cultural developments over the last 50 years. Noting the changes that capitalism had brought to western society, French philosopher Guy Debord, (1967/2014) observed:

> The first stage of economy's dominion of social life brought about an evident degradation of *being* into *having* – human fulfilment was no longer equated with what one was, but with what one possessed. The present stage, in which social life has become completely occupied by the accumulated productions of the economy, is bringing about a general shift from *having* to *appearing* – all "having" must now derive its immediate prestige and its ultimate purpose from appearances. (p. 5)

Writer and broadcaster, John Berger made a similar observation in *Ways of Seeing* (1972), claiming that: "Men *act* while women *appear*. Men look at women while women watch themselves being looked at. This determines not only most relations between men and women but also the relation of women to themselves" (p. 47). The relationship between appearance and gaze in the lives of women also received attention in Susie Orbach's *Fat is a Feminist Issue* (1978), and 40 years on, the image of the body—its appearance—remains a prime site of identity construction. The stigma of aging or being overweight is magnified as high definition images of young, slim, and perfectly formed individuals dominate the media. Although many people now experience anxiety in relation to their body image, the consumption culture responsible for creating the anxiety, conveniently offers to sell the antidote through image enhancing products, for example, beauty regimes, weight loss programs, equipment for body toning, or psychotherapy. Whether discussions about weight, fitness, or appearance are situated among concerns about health, economics, or aesthetics, the body and face are center stage as never before. The Internet now feeds our preoccupation with appearance. Everyone can now appear in the public eye if they wish. We can now be seen, noticed, heard, known, recognized, appreciated, and understood, but the price is a loss of privacy, risk of surveillance and, at times, a degree of personal distress caused by unwanted intrusion and abuse.

Although the digital revolution is a new phenomenon, post-war culture in the West had been showing signs of what was to come. The construction of "celebrity" in the late twentieth century through visual image and sound was driven by new technologies—the gramophone, cinema, radio, television, the Internet, and, most recently, the smartphone. These technologies created a proliferation of sounds and images that would be made available to the public for sale. In an anthropological sense, what the culture was saying, doing, and thinking—the nature of historical social representations (Moscovici, 1961/1976)—can now be inferred from the artwork of the period, for example, literature, film, and popular music. Among the many examples to be found in popular culture, the film *La Dolce Vita* (Amato, Rizzoli & Fellini, 1960) poses many questions about life in the modern age; even photographer Paparazzo, a marginal character in the film, eventually became an archetype for all celebrity photographers to come. The period that followed also produced living works of identity construction such as Michael Jackson, David Bowie, and Madonna who morphed from one image of themselves to another—both confusing and astounding their audience.

Since the late 1920s when tobacco companies started to use propaganda techniques to manipulate the habits and opinions of the masses, we have been living in the "society of the spectacle" (Debord, 1967/2014), where the image has become of central importance to the culture. According to Debord, "The spectacle is not a collection of images; it is a social relation between people mediated by images" (p. 2), and the construction of social relations through images has, he argues, replaced genuine human interaction.[3] What is more, we see this process in the daily news media. When media outlets selectively report news, they inevitably involve themselves in identity construction. Whether news accounts

---

[3] This has also given rise to Baudrillard's (1981/1994) view that, caught as we are in this network of image mediated relationships, we are no longer living in the world but in a simulated reality.

are sensational, tragic, trivial, or contentious, whether strictly political or whether they feature sporting encounters or the lives of celebrities, they highlight salient identities by focusing on distinction, conflict, division, or disorder. In addition, they not only offer a position on issues such as international conflict and social inequality, they also endorse celebrity. Just as advertisers appeal to target groups to sell products for profit, media outlets take a position on world events, and in so doing they set out (or exclude) a range of political ideas and identities. Once we (the viewers) assume a particular stance on identity, we then position ourselves on issues such as migration, asylum, or the fate of refugees.

POLITICAL IDENTITIES

Most identities have political significance, and while some are directly related to membership of political parties, others may include social groupings such as nationality, class, ethnicity, or sexual orientation. In political analysis, **political cleavages**—the main lines of political division in a society—may correspond to significant identities within a society, and different countries likely have very different political cleavages. Some countries, for example, may be divided along the lines of Catholic, Protestant, Communist, or Social Democrat. There may also be intersecting cleavages. For example, in the UK, supporters of Labour, Liberal, and Conservative parties are now divided into two new cleavages after Britain's decision to leave the European Union—those who voted to *leave* and those who voted to *remain*.

Intersecting cleavages also emerge in relation to specific social concerns such as climate change (once referred to as global warming), and the acceleration of social change, and the multiple political issues arising from the complexity of modern life, means that new intersecting political cleavages make political outcomes difficult to predict. Moreover, the traditional political cleavages in domestic politics—for example, right, center, and left wing—may be undergoing realignment across the western world. How might social and political developments be understood in theoretical terms? How does social categorization influence intergroup relations? What role does identity threat play? What can social psychology offer in terms of theory?

SOCIAL IDENTITY THEORY

Following the genocide of European Jews in World War II, Henri Tajfel set up a number of experiments in an attempt to tease out the social and psychological factors involved in intergroup discrimination. His studies of social identities (group memberships) produced a theory of intergroup relations—**social identity theory** (SIT) (Tajfel, 1977, 1981b). The theory assumes a psychological Marxist view of the world that there first exists society and that "society comprises social categories which stand in power and status relations to one another" (Hogg & Abrams, 1988, p. 14).

In this set of experiments, Tajfel defined social identity as "that part of an individual's self-concept which derives from his knowledge of his membership of a social group (or groups) together with the value and emotional significance attached to that membership" (Tajfel, 1977, p. 63). Tajfel (1977) explains that the definition served practical empirical purposes—the need to be consistent throughout a number of studies—rather than being an attempt to present a dogma or to offer an absolute definition of identity. Tajfel (1977) recognized the limitations and limited context of his work, acknowledging that identity is far more complex both in content and in the way it is formed, derived, and constructed than social identity (as defined by his experiments) implies. The experiments nonetheless revealed some important findings.

In earlier studies, Tajfel had observed that people tend to perceive outgroup differences as greater than ingroup differences; they also consistently underestimated variations within each group while overestimating differences between groups (Tajfel, 1959; Tajfel & Wilkes, 1963). The minimal groups research (Tajfel et al., 1971) went a step further. In these experiments, participants in each group had no knowledge of the other group. There was no previous history of conflict, no social interaction, nor any particular reason for acting in self-interest. Nonetheless, it was possible for the researchers to create ingroup favoritism and outgroup discrimination on the basis of trivial criteria such as the toss of a coin. Tajfel (1978) concluded that social identity is the result of (a) social categorization and (b) social comparison. There was also a motivational principle—a desire for positive distinctiveness or positive self-esteem. What the minimal groups studies show is that we are prone to make group categorizations, which easily lead to negative evaluations of those who are not members of our own group.

Work on identity at this time was also influenced by Gergen's (1971) distinction between personal and social identity. Personal identity refers to self-descriptions involving personal attributes or references to self in relation to others, while social identities are those salient group memberships that feed into personal identity (Tajfel, 1981b; Tajfel & Turner, 1979, 1986). Turner (1982) argued that personal and social identity represent different levels of self-categorization. People categorize the self as either "I" (personal identity)—the lowest level—or "we" (a social identity) at a higher level. The highest level might be *we humans* where the out-group is aliens or animals. The importance of social context where social identity becomes the most salient means of distinguishing self from others is the essence of **self-categorization theory** (SCT) (Turner, Hogg, Oakes, Reicher, & Wetherell, 1987). The theory posits that as we encounter people from other groups, we position ourselves according to identity needs depending on the particular issue or agenda. The move toward a specific social identity away from personal identity results in *depersonalization*—a redefining of the self in terms of group membership where we adopt the norms, beliefs, and behavior of fellow group members. However, despite the broad acceptance of SIT and SCT within social psychology, political psychologists have not always embraced the social identity paradigm with enthusiasm despite its obvious application to the political sphere. Huddy (2001), for example, claims that the approach is limiting insofar as we need to consider *sources* of identity, which usually require a detailed understanding of history and culture as well as understanding the way that historic events are understood within the culture. She further argues that we need to take into consideration the subjective meanings of identities as well identity choice, stability, and strength.

IDENTITY PROCESS THEORY

Another important consideration in the formation of identity is motivation. As we contemplate who we are, who we want to be, and what we want to achieve, we likely reflect on how we feel about ourselves (self-esteem), how we engage with the world in order to achieve our goals—particularly, whether we feel in control of our lives (self-efficacy)—and the extent to which we need to distinguish ourselves from others (distinctiveness). These are arguably some of the main guiding principles involved in identity processes (Breakwell, 1986). In addition to self-esteem, self-efficacy, and distinctiveness, there may be other identity motives including continuity, meaning, and belonging (Vignoles, 2011). **Identity process theory** (Breakwell, 1986, 1992) is a theory of identity rather than a theory of group or intergroup processes. The main tenet of the theory is that the development of personal identity is a dynamic process where identity is seen as the outcome of an interaction between characteristics such as memory and consciousness, and the physical and societal structures and processes existing over time. Identity is articulated through thought, emotion, and action in a context of personal and social power relationships.

The theory proposes that an identity has two dimensions. The content dimension comprises information about the person that makes them unique, that is, attitudes and beliefs systems, behavioral styles, self-ascribed attributes, and group memberships, while the value dimension refers to the values attached to each element of identity. Identity is also conceptualized in terms of two processes. The assimilation–accommodation process refers to taking in new information and restructuring of existing identity structures to accommodate such information. The evaluation process assigns value to this new information. These identity processes are guided by four main principles that determine desirable end-states for the structure of identity, that is, self-esteem, continuity, distinctiveness, and self-efficacy. Self-esteem represents a desire to be evaluated positively; continuity, a desire to give a consistent account of oneself over time; distinctiveness, a desire to be unique; and self-efficacy, a striving to exercise control in determining outcomes. These guiding principles operate in a social and historical context.

One main element of the theory is to explain how people adopt different strategies for coping with threatened identities. An identity is threatened when the "processes of identity, assimilation–accommodation, and evaluation are, for some reason, unable to comply with the principles of continuity, distinctiveness, and self-esteem, which habitually guide their operation" (Breakwell, 1986, p. 47). A threat can originate externally from a change in circumstances, such as retirement or unemployment or internally from, for example, a person's attempt to change their social network. There are a number of intrapersonal, interpersonal, and intergroup strategies that can be adopted to cope with such identity threats, and, given the complexity of political allegiances and shifting identities, Identity Process Theory allows us to study the content, process, and context of individual and group identity over time.

DISCURSIVE APPROACHES TO IDENTITY

An alternative approach to the study of identity emerges from social constructionism, specifically from the claim that identity is constructed in and through discourse: that the self is made apparent through discursive positions taken up (or resisted) within social interaction. Discursive approaches assume that identities are constructed and therefore there is no attempt to seek out theoretical accounts of self or comprehensive explanations of identity that are consistent or continuous over time and place. The emphasis is on the way that the self is experienced—the way that the interior or private experience of self—*subjectivity*—is created by social situations. Gergen (1991) describes the **relational self** as a "manifestation of relationship" (p. 146), where various accounts of self are *situated* within a physical or social location or context. How does construction take place? There are two competing views (a) that construction moves progressively from existing social discourses to the domain of identity (These are known as "capital-D" social discourses) or (b) that construction starts with "small-d" discursive practices, which result in identities emerging in interaction (Bamberg, Fina, & Schiffrin, 2011).

Among the many discursive approaches available to researchers, **positioning theory** (Davies & Harré, 1990) has been used to resolve group conflict. The theory is particularly interested in the conventions of speech and action that are unstable, subject to change, or contestable. As Moghaddam, Harré, and Lee (2008) explain: "For the most part, positioning theory sees people as trapped within discourse conventions, ways of making sense of whatever is going on. Actions are identified by their then and there meaning for the people engaged in an episode." (p. 10).

In any social interaction, each party takes up a different subject position, which is particularly pronounced in roles such as doctor/patient or teacher/pupil. In both positions, the person is *constructed* through the role and the discourse surrounding it; for example, a doctor may ask personal medical questions and a patient may respond by disclosing them. Such encounters reveal a set of implicit beliefs about what is right and proper to say and do. Indeed, roles bring rules, constraints, and obligations to the setting that allow people to act, and scripted expressions, which are often integral to the role, for example "Please, take a seat. Tell what the problem is," become rhetorical acts that position others in relation to status and power. Unlike other approaches to identity, positioning theory is not concerned with motives or cause. When motives are expressed verbally, they are simply interpreted as social acts that make actions intelligible to others. In all social encounters, we may accept, reject, or attempt to renegotiate the positioning. For example, research into discourses of cancer (Willig, 2011) noted how the position of "cancer fighter" required the patient to combat their condition *actively* rather than accept it, and when this position was rejected, medical staff and others evaluated it negatively.

This approach to identity construction offers a method for exploring what is possible and what is permitted in any given social encounter. Attributed meanings will vary because different people will likely read a situation in different ways, and different meanings may be attributed to the same action. In some instances, there may be different—possibly conflicting—story lines. For example, in the 2016 American presidential election, Donald Trump positioned Hillary Clinton as "incompetent" and "crooked" based on the questions arising from her use of her email account while in office. When others attempted to position Trump as a misogynist after "sex talk" tapes came to light, Trump dismissed the recordings as "locker room" talk—the kind that every "every man" engages in. And in a strategy to align himself with "every man," he then went on to claim a sense of collective victimhood that allowed him to say, in effect, "Not only am I just like any other man—but they have refused to give you voice and I will be that voice." When analyzing positioning dynamics, the question is: who has the ability to position? Will the identity claim hold, and will the audience recognize and identify with the claim?

NARRATIVE IDENTITIES

Identity is also derived from the content and structural features of life stories. To answer the question, who am I? We likely draw upon a personal life narrative to bring purpose, unity, and a sense of continuity to our sense of self; we bring together the past, present, and future to give an account of who we are and where we are going (McAdams, 1985, 2011). The life story thus becomes a representation of identity where we become the story we choose to tell others about ourselves. Whether one is a political leader, a victim of trauma, or someone who has been involved in conflict, each has a life story within which they interpret and attribute meaning to life events. **Narrative psychology** may therefore reveal the complexities of identity construction, as well as cultural meanings and strategies for making sense of difficult situations or traumatic events. The range of narrative approaches, however, is complex and diverse, and each has its own set of aims, values, and assumptions (see Schiff, 2017 for a detailed review).

CONCLUSIONS

What should we conclude about identity and its role in human politics? Identity is a powerful source of political motivation and threats to identity usually result in political action. What role can social psychological research play in the future study of identity? After World War II, a considerable amount of social psychological research addressed questions that were raised by genocide and other war crimes. Since then, the success of identity politics has resulted in a fragmentation of identity and the creation of new identities. How should we understand these developments? While theories such as SIT and SCT are useful, they may require a more refined application to reflect the nuanced identity differentiation that is currently taking place. We therefore need to think critically about these developments and the questions they raise, as well as being open to theoretical approaches from other disciplines.

National identity still provides the major fault lines across the political landscape, and international conflict continues to create human suffering through displacement and migration. The mass migration of refugees that has resulted from these conflicts will no doubt create complex identity issues for migrants, the receiving communities, and the next generation. Research may need to look at the content, structure, and function of hybrid identities among the diaspora where narratives of place and homeland are central to identity construction. Research may focus on how these groups develop, maintain, and manage the content, process, and performance of their **diasporic identity** in exile. In other parts of the world, national identities, and allegiances are fragmenting as smaller nations and regions seek political independence. And within established nation-states, traditional conceptions of national and cultural identity that once carried people along may be shifting, fading, diminishing in strength, or they may simply no longer hold among a new multicultural generation. Around the world, identity remains a contentious issue, and we need to consider the best way to study its dynamics in a variety of political contexts.

SUMMARY

- Social identities are a source of social cohesion and a potential source of conflict.
- Action is the social expression of identity.
- Social identities are easily aroused and are potent sources of political mobilization especially in cases of identity threat.
- Identities are constructed through discourse and are often the result of positioning.
- The life course as a narrative plays an important part in the formation of an integrated and continuous identity.

GLOSSARY

banal nationalism is a form of nationalism that largely escapes our notice, but which nonetheless reinforces national identity through mundane activities.

cultural imperialism is a form of influence that seeks to establish a civilization's dominant cultural values in other lands. This is normally achieved through the dissemination of cultural products, for example, literature, film, music, entertainment, science, and so on.

diasporic identity refers to the unique sense of national identity developed by a group in exile, which is often different to the sense of national identity in the home country.

globalization is an economic process of integration between nations involving the flow and exchange of money, goods and services, ideas, culture, technology, and data.

intersectionality refers to the interconnected nature of social categories as they apply to individuals or groups.

identity politics refers to the positions, perspectives, interests, and actions of groups who share a common identity and experience, and who wish to maintain or advance their political interests.

identity process theory is a theory of identity that outlines an integrative framework for the collective examination of identity, social action, and social change.

narrative psychology is concerned with the storied nature of human experience, particularly how people deal with their own understanding of their life course.

nationalism refers to the attachment, pride, and loyalty derived from identification as a member of a nation. It can also refer to a political movement that seeks autonomy and political independence.

political cleavage is a term used in political science to refer to the lines of demarcation between blocs of voters.

positioning theory is a method of analysis developed within discursive psychology that examines how identities are produced and performed during social interaction.

social identity theory is a theory of intergroup relations based on the notion of salient group membership.

self-categorization theory claims that the salience of social identities (categorizations) shifts according to the (identity) needs of the situation, which reduces the salience of personal identity.

symbolic interactionism is a sociological approach to social interaction, which emphasizes self as both object and subject.

FURTHER READING

Billig M. (1995). *Banal nationalism*. London: Sage.
Breakwell G. M. (1986). *Coping with threatened identities*. London: Methuen.
Reicher S., & Hopkins N. (2001). *Self and nation*. London: Sage.

QUESTIONS FOR GROUP DISCUSSION

- Why is it that people do not forget the importance of their nationality?
- To what degree is modern technology affecting identity?
- What is the difference between national identification, nationalism, and patriotism?
- What cultural values may be exported to other parts of the world through entertainment? How might this present a threat to identity?
- Do nations have essences?

6 Narrating as Political Action

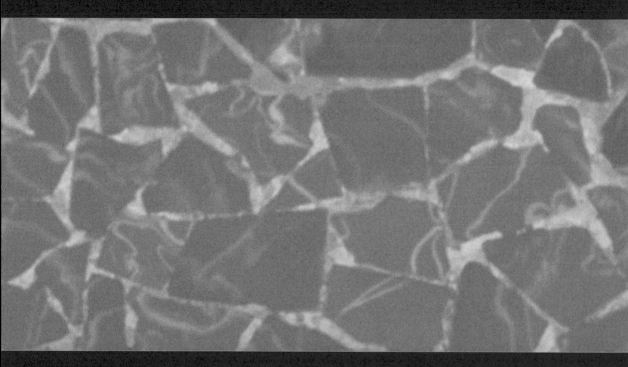

BRIAN SCHIFF

CHAPTER OUTLINE

What can a narrative perspective offer to political psychology? How can thinking about the personal and social process inherent in narrative interpretation help us to better understand the workings of political life? The purpose of this chapter is to describe the theoretical and practical utility of a narrative perspective for grappling with the problems of political psychology. Although, as I will argue, the benefits of thinking about political psychology as a narrative enterprise are enormous, the descriptive task is equally challenging. Indeed, "narrative" and "political psychology" are contested terms that are defined in multiple ways and have permeable boundaries. Perhaps this is the fate of all interdisciplinary concepts that travel from one discipline to another and are translated and transformed in the process (Hyvärinen, 2010).

Although the problem of framing political psychology narratively is complex, my intention is not to dismiss the difficulties inherent in the undertaking. Some precision of terms is necessary. A narrative perspective offers students of political psychology a complex and insightful understanding of the very nature of the political as integrated in the fabric of everyday life and entangled in social and cultural horizons of meaning making.

PSYCHOLOGY AND POLITICS

The interdisciplinary interest in psychology and politics has a longstanding tradition that is largely responsive to the changing fashions of dominant psychological theories of the time (psychoanalytic, behaviorist, cognitive, social) and research traditions (qualitative and quantitative) (McGuire, 1993; Sullivan, Rahn, & Rudolph, 2002). The domain seems to cover everything that touches political life, including, but not limited to psychobiographical exploration of political figures, political rhetoric and discourse, voting behavior, peace and reconciliation, and political identities. Definitions of political psychology are equally broad. Political psychology is the: "field of inquiry at the intersection of political science and psychology" (Iyengar, 1993, p. 3); "study of mental processes that underlie political judgments and decision making" (Kuklinski, 2002, p. 2); "application of what is known about human psychology to the study of politics" (Huddy, Sears, & Levy, 2013a, 2013b, p. 1). Where we throw the boundaries around the phenomenon is problematic. And, of course, problems do not neatly divide themselves along disciplinary lines (Iyengar, 1993).

However, it would be a mistake to cordon off the political as a type of human action and to impose limiting conditions upon what constitutes political

Political Psychology: A Social Psychological Approach, First Edition.
Edited by Christopher J. Hewer and Evanthia Lyons.
© 2018 John Wiley & Sons Ltd. Published 2018 by John Wiley & Sons Ltd.

psychology to phenomena considered *explicitly* political. In limiting our focus, we only narrowly capture the meaning of what politics means. In this spirit, Tileagă (2013) calls for an interpretive political psychology that "can attain a deeper level of understanding of political behaviour" (p. 1) and argues for the examination of "idiographic aspects of social existence" (p. 4). In order to arrive at a more useful, and realistic, portrayal of political actions we need to think more expansively about the intersection between politics and other aspects of life experience but also consider the intensive exchange between personal and social systems of meanings.

SPEECH AND POLITICAL ACTION

As Arendt (1958/1998) observed, "whenever the relevance of speech is at stake, matters become political by definition, for speech is what makes man a political being" (p. 3). As Arendt highlights, speech, what we will call narrating, in and through its social functions, is the vehicle for political action. Arguably, politics and narrative are present and operating in most, if not all, aspects of our day-to-day lives. Most everything is political most of the time; indeed, anytime that meaning is at stake. Although, for Arendt, "there may be truths beyond speech" separate from our "political being" (p. 4), such as abstract scientific or technological truths; these truths subvert our typical social orientation, to one another, in the plural. It is only in their active involvement with others and through narrative that humans come to set out meanings and make sense of self and world. "Men in the plural, that is, men in so far as they live and act in this world, can experience meaningfulness only because they can talk with and make sense to each other and to themselves" (p. 4).

THE PERSONAL AND POLITICAL NATURE OF NARRATIVE

We might think through the phenomenal relationship between politics and psychology by thinking about the problem differently—integrated in the lives, interactions, and words of persons who act to engage a world already constituted by meaning and to make these meanings present in the concrete here and now. As Andrews (2007) observes,

> I am convinced that there is a profound sense in which the personal is political, and the political is personal. It is through the minutiae of daily life that human beings access the political ripples, and tidal waves, of their times (p. 2).

First, we might argue that an *expansive* conception of the political, in which narratings of all stripes are viewed as political actions, is necessary and warranted. Persons, in concert with others, are engaged in the ongoing and, forever incomplete, process of fixing and unfixing interpretations of self and world. From this expansive stance, how persons make a world and how the world comes to make persons is, expressly and centrally, a political project. And, from this expansive stance, one could rightly ask: Can narrative ever really be outside or beyond the realm of politics? Or, can politics ever really be outside or beyond narrative? They seem to require and nurture one another. When we talk about politics and narratives, we are really discussing the creative process of mutually making up, a **poiesis**, of self and world (Freeman, 2010).

Second, narrating as political action requires a more *intensive* view of the relationship between persons and the social world. Narrating exists at the cusp between these two realms, neither wholly one or the other, but located in the intersection between both. A productive approach to the problems of political psychology should be able to capture the personal and social into a single theory that encompasses both.

EXPANSIVE POLITICAL NARRATIVES

An expansive stance on political psychology is a narrative one, integrated in the life and experience of persons, in constant interaction with social others, attempting to make sense of self, other, and the world. But, it is important to contextualize and clarify exactly what we mean by narrative. In the social sciences, the term narrative is used very loosely. Also, I take a distinct point of view on narrative psychology that orients researchers toward the *function* of narrative meaning making (Schiff, 2012). What is narrative psychology? How can narrative inform our understanding of political psychology?

One way of answering these questions is to say that psychologists have always done something like narrative. Or, at least, some psychologists have always done something that resembles narrative psychology—and have been doing so for a long time. Arguably, narrative psychology has its roots in the longstanding traditions of case study research in psychoanalysis, which investigated autobiographical and clinical materials for how persons create meaningful compromises and defenses to unwanted experiences and thoughts, and in the personological tradition of Henry Murray, Gordon Allport, and Robert White, which employed the in-depth study of personal documents to understand the development of personality.

PSYCHOANALYTIC AND PERSONOLOGICAL TRADITION

Not only do the psychoanalytic and personological traditions extend back to the early part of the twentieth century, but they have had a continuous, but mostly marginal, presence in the discipline. However, since the early 1980s, psychology has witnessed an explosion of theories and methods of study labeling themselves "narrative." Although their approaches differ substantially, for many, narrative represented a way to approach questions of sense and meaning free from the limitations imposed by reductive statistical methodologies and mechanistic theories of human nature. The turn to a narrative metaphor was a turn to the close analysis of the process of creating meanings in social and cultural context (Bruner, 1990; Cohler, 1982; Sarbin, 1986).

One of the key differences between the psychoanalytic and personological traditions, pre-1980s, and the current focus on narrative, post-1980s, is the prominence given to the active constitutive properties of narrative. Pre-1980s, "personal documents" are thought of as an alternative, and complementary, methodological orientation to quantitative approaches in which researchers pay close attention to life documents in order to understand aspects of individual development and personality (Allport, 1962; White, 1952/1966). Post-1980s, narrative is framed as the constructive process of forming identities and making realities. The difference is one between narrative as a methodology for investigating personality or psychological symptoms and narrative as the activity of developing interpretations of self and world.

NARRATIVE APPROACHES

Currently, narrative psychology is a diverse field of inquiry that is difficult to succinctly characterize. In a review of psychological and sociological perspectives on narrative, Smith and Sparkes (2008) argue that narrative approaches can be viewed along a continuum from those emphasizing "thick individuals" and "thin social relationships" to those emphasizing "thin individuals" and "thick social relationships." They describe five contrasting perspectives on narrative: psychosocial, intersubjective, storied resource, dialogic, and performative. Each of these perspectives has their own definition of what narrative is, the purpose of narrative, and how narrative functions to produce and sustain aspects of personal and social identity.

Another way of viewing the current state of narrative is fragmented along psychology's traditional perspectives and methodological commitments. However, across the fragments, there is agreement that narrative is intimately involved in the process of making self and making world. For example, cognitive approaches focus on the linguistic and mental processes underlying the construction of coherence over time (Habermas & Hatiboğlu, 2014). Personality psychologists view the life story as a level of personality above traits and personal concerns that contains characters, themes, imagos, and tone and provides the person with a sense of unity and purpose (McAdams, 2001). Social psychologists focus on the interactional processes by which persons working together with others construct coauthored stories of self and world (Bamberg, 2004; Georgakopoulou, 2007; Gergen, 2009b). In terms of methods of study, the narrative perspective is split between those adopting mainstream approaches that reduce narrative processes to counted data (László, 2008) and those that argue that narrative is best studied using rich qualitative data from interviews and conversations.

This simplified description only captures some of the complexity that we find among psychologists working with the narrative concept. However, if we rely on what psychologists are doing right now, we might say that there are almost as many different varieties of narrative psychology as there are narrative psychologists.

NARRATIVE HERMENEUTICS

The perspective that I take on narrative psychology puts front and center the dynamic interpretative process inherent in how persons, along with others, make sense of self and world. From the perspective of what Brockmeier and Meretoja (2014) call a **narrative hermeneutics**, "the stuff of narrative understanding appears as an ongoing flow of interpretive and self-interpretive acts: a stream of attempts to figure out what one's and others' experiences, intentions, emotions, beliefs, desires, and anxieties could possibly mean" (p. 11). A hermeneutic or interpretative perspective on narrative concentrates our scholarly efforts, rightly, on the active, but always tentative, striving for meaning. Interpretations come to mind, are tested out, offered to ourselves and others, break down, and are revised. The process is not contained in the split second snapshot but is a long term one that unfolds and evolves in dialog with others and in developmental and historical time.

NARRATIVE AND NARRATING

Narrative as an interpretative action places more weight on the process or function of narrative, what narrative does and can do, over and above the form or structure that constitutes a narrative. From this perspective, narrative is not a text type but the practice of engaging social and cultural resources (Hammack & Toolis, 2014) and making interpretations present and known (Schiff, 2012) in order to grapple with what things mean. Although the linguistic and formal properties of speech can be important clues to the meaning of a given telling, I concentrate on the details of how narrative interpretations are accomplished and to what end. Thus, my preference for the word "narrating" over "narrative," where narrating describes the activity of engaging and articulating interpretations.

The expansive move is to include "political actions" within the framework of "interpretative actions," arguing that there is no clear line that separates political actions from other varieties of interpretations that we make about the self, world, and others. Political action is part and parcel of how persons, in social and cultural space, make interpretations and is rooted in these everyday practices. A narrative perspective that is able to describe political actions in the context of everyday meaning making can better account for the intersecting routes and passageways that motivate choices, beliefs, and other endeavors that one might consider *explicitly* political. After all, meanings come from other meanings and the beliefs persons possess and actions that they carry out are clearly invested by other kinds of self-understandings encountered in our immediate social relationships and the larger cultural context. In order to understand political actions, we need to see them in a more holistic framework, which is exactly what a narrative perspective promises for political psychology.

INTENSIFYING PERSONS AND SOCIAL CONTEXT

The opposition between persons and social context remains a trenchant problem in social science theory and method. Partly, this problem is the result of a disciplinary division of labor between those disciplines traditionally concerned with collectivities and the eclectic set of psychological perspectives focused on individuals. But, it is more than a question of disciplinary boundaries. Even those interdisciplinary spaces, such as the study of memory, which should be the setting for discussions on the interplay between persons and social context, are mostly descriptive of the difficulties of bridging levels of analysis.

COLLECTIVE MEMORY

It is instructive to take a brief look at how the literature on collective memory deals with persons and the social world. As Olick (1999) argues, the foundations of the concept of collective memory, introduced in the work of Maurice

Halbwachs, left us with "an unresolved tension between individualist and collectivist strains" (p. 334), which leads to two incommensurable concepts of collective memory that "seem to be of radically distinct ontological orders" (p. 336). Olick frames the problem as grounded in two "radically different concepts of culture ... one that sees culture as a subjective category of meanings contained in people's minds versus one that sees culture as patterns of publically available symbols objectified in society" (p. 336). Based upon these differing conceptions of culture, Olick distinguishes between an individualist strain of social memory that he calls *collected* memory and a collectivist strain that he calls *collective* memory. Olick ends his argument by stating that his ultimate goal is to bring together these two strains, as he writes, "there is no individual memory without social experience nor is there any collective memory without individuals participating in communal life" (p. 346). However, he offers no concrete proposals and the division remains intact: how can we bring together these two "ontological orders" into conversation with one another and move beyond the idea that there is a disembodied social process distinct from thoughts in the head?

REPRESSION

The problem is that collectivities do not really have memories in the same sense as individuals do and the terminology transforms as we move from one level of analysis to the other. The muddled distinction between individual and collective memories becomes clear when we take a concrete example, such as repression or trauma, and apply it to the individual and collective realms. Following Kansteiner (2002), certainly, individuals forget or repress certain aspects of their past for reasons. In the classical Freudian formulation, repression is part of the person's individual psychological structure, which, through the use of psychological energy, forces thoughts that run counter to ideas of our ideal self or are socially unacceptable to the unconscious. Social groups may ban books or sanction, legally or through more subtle means, the public discussion and display of particular points of view or actions. But, there is no similar interplay between the conscious and unconscious mind because groups do not have minds. There is more than one kind of repression and we are using the word differently when we move from the individual to the collective. Although we may be completely justified to call both acts of repression, they are by no means equivalent but are only related metaphorically.

Although the term *repression* in individual repression and collective repression, like the term memory in individual memory and collective memory, has distinct meanings as it traverses levels of analysis from the person to the social world, the phenomena that they seek to describe are not wholly separable.

What persons experience and tell about serves as the basis for more genuinely collective understandings, and collectivities do provide the tools for persons to understand their experience. For example, a historical event might be omitted from secondary school textbooks or taught in the most superficial manner, *collective repression*, in part because the persons who experienced the events were so traumatized by the events that they lived through, *individual repression*, that they don't want to speak, or even, to think about them.

RELATIONAL CONTEXTS

Olick's "two cultures" problem, that underpins his ontological division, effectively dissolves with a more comprehensive, and updated, culture theory. Vygotskyian and Bakhtinian inspired theories of culture see no essential division between persons and social context but place both in a single process of mutual definition (Hammack & Toolis, 2014; Holland, Lachicotte, Skinner, & Cain, 1998). Contrary to Olick, there is no culture in the head and culture in the world. Meanings are not the exclusive property of cultures or persons, but share a common denominator, the same common stock of textual tools, or what Wertsch (2002) calls **semiotic means.** Persons engage meanings within a social context, in a specific time and space, typically in the frame of everyday social interactions, and persons make present meanings in their (re)articulation. As I have argued elsewhere, the relational aspect of our encounter with meanings is key (Schiff, 2002). Primarily, we find meanings through our contact with others and use them because they help us to make sense of self and world. But, we also encounter meanings through various media.

MEANINGS AND ACTION

Semiotic means are primarily linguistic, narratives that allow for a fluid transition of experience, between persons, as resources for understanding self and the world. Meanings travel through language—through spoken and written narratings. This is where the real action is and where we should be focused. Narrating provides a means for describing the "mnemonic transitivity" (Zerubavel, 2004), whereby meanings circulate between persons.

Still, the textual tools are only part of the picture. Textual tools are always articulated by, at least one, speaker and are addressed to, at least one, listener. In the action of telling, persons come to appropriate and use the textual tools of a given cultural community precisely because they have participated in situated dialogs where these specific meanings are discussed and enacted. Likewise, new textual tools are always in the offing with the potential to be taken up among the members of a social group. In other words, we need to pay attention to the way that collective remembering is both produced and consumed (Kansteiner, 2002; Wertsch, 2002).

PRODUCERS AND CONSUMERS OF MEMORY

Although this distinction between producers and consumers is helpful, when we consider our day-to-day lives, the roles are never completely clear. When we engage in a dialog with others we are, perhaps, discovering novel ways of understanding self and world and thus consumers but we are also active in animating sedimented meanings or combining them into new configurations. Consuming and producing are interactive, organic, dynamic, and circle back on one another. We consume as we produce and produce as we consume. The challenge is to think more descriptively and realistically about the lines that connect together persons and social meanings.

In my view, the interplay between the individual and the collective is better described by changing metaphors to a narrative one. And, there is a substantial gain in theoretical precision by framing matters narratively. Political narratives speak to the way that the social world becomes part and parcel of personal experience and understanding and the way that personal interpretations reach beyond the narrow concerns of the person in order to make an impact on others. There is no grand master or cultural narrative that is theoretically distinct from the smaller life story. Although sometimes we might be justified in separating out these elements to focus on one or the other, thinking through their complex pathways and interrelationships will advance our understanding of political psychology. This exchange is the essence of an intensive view of persons and the social world.

PALESTINIANS WITH ISRAELI CITIZENSHIP

Beginning in 2012–2013, I completed 24 interviews with Palestinians students holding Israeli citizenship at the Hebrew University of Jerusalem. The group included 19 women and five men and both Muslims and Christians. The interviews were designed as a dialog to investigate reflections and stories about identity—who they are now and how they arrived at these self-understandings.

I argue that in order to understand problems of political psychology, we need to employ a narrative perspective that (a) examines how political actions are embedded in other domains of meaning making (**the expansive hypothesis**) and (b) describes the passageways and routes bridging personal and cultural narratives (**the intensive hypothesis**).

I apply these two theses to the life stories of Hiba and Lana. Both Hiba and Lana come from villages in the North of Israel and are in their last year of studies. Hiba is Christian and Lana Muslim. The cases argue that political identity is an active and ongoing construction, integrated into a host of other meanings and that relationships serve to engage new ways of understanding self and others.

HIBA: THE REAL STORY

The interview with Hiba begins with a brief description of the complexities of her identity.

> It's a question I have been trying to figure out since like I remember my self. And I think since I came here to Jerusalem 4 years ago, it's more clear for me. I consider myself as a Palestinian Arab with an Israeli citizenship who lives in Israel. (…) It has not changed; just it got more clear to me. (…) Questions that passed 4 or 5 years ago. I got some answers to the questions like: "Where do I belong more?" "What side represents me more?" "Where I see myself?"

What is noteworthy is Hiba's claim to both consistency and change (Lieblich, 1993); she has become more of what she already was. There is a sense in which her identity is founded in other aspects of her life, particularly her strong identification with her family. But, this identity becomes more clear through social relationships when she "came to Jerusalem" and to the university.

Brian: But did you have a different idea of yourself before?

Hiba: (…) I wouldn't say a different idea, but it was very not clear, it's like questions all the time. You watch news, you get confused. You talk to people, you get more confused. If you see what happens around you, it just makes you wonder where you belong. Where is your place? Basically I come from a family. I live today in a village. It's in the North, but basically I'm a refugee. I belong to a family—I don't know if you heard about Iqrit? Iqrit Village? It was evacuated in 1948, but it's very special because up to now the case is still alive. Many villagers have been evacuated in 1948 and the case is just like there. And my family still lives the case at home. It's just the presence of what happened till today, like we sit together and talk together.

In the first few minutes of the interview, Hiba states that she experienced some confusion about her identity. Then, Hiba orients us to a history. She situates herself within her family, her family in a village, and the village in the history of 1948 and its consequences. Iqrit, the actual name of the village, is used with Hiba's permission.

As Hiba recounts, the case of her village is still in litigation; it was taken to Israel's Supreme Court who ruled in favor of the rights of the villagers to their lands. But, because the village is in a "strategic" area, close to the border with Lebanon, the military has not let villagers return.

For Hiba's family, and the "Iqritians," as she calls them, who are dispersed in different towns and villages, Iqrit and the history that befell the village are still present until today. She recounts various ways that as a family, community, and individual, she holds onto the past and the hope of returning to Iqrit. In the family, she listens to the reminiscences of her grandparents. Her grandfather still counts the days since he left the village. Even linguistically, the family reserves the word "home" to refer to Iqrit and not their current, post-1948 village. Every month, the family and other Iqritians go to the village church to pray. The community maintains the cemetery and has the legal right to bury their dead there. And, every summer, Iqritians gather in their village for 2 weeks, what she calls "camp" when:

> They tell the actual story of what happened, like a journey in the village. This is where the school was. This is where the church. This is where Atallah family house, for example. And they know everything even though they were young children.

The history of the village and its destruction is reenacted, repopulating the abandoned village landscape. Individually, Hiba has begun a project of filming and documenting the stories of her grandparents and the community.

> I'm working on a project now. I'm trying to do a documentary film about what really happened. I'm interviewing old people who have lived in 1948 whether they were young or children, to listen to the story because I believe quite of what's going to lead me to my place or to be O.K. with who I am and to try to understand who really I am is to understand what exactly happened to my grandfathers, to the people; what really happened. I want to hear the real story from people who lived what happened.

Hiba's current interest in documenting the history of Iqrit is a change of direction from her current course of study in social service. It is difficult to know if she will complete the project. But, clearly, this is a project about placing her identity in a grounded history. To know "the real story" is her attempt to "understand who I really am." Beyond the personal, there is also an attempt to make this reality public to keep alive the historical experience of her family's evacuation during the 1948 war and make known "what really happened," "the real story." In other words, Hiba's sense of herself as "Palestinian Arab with an Israeli citizenship who lives in Israel" is grounded in the meanings of her social experience in her family and as an Iqritian.

I want to suggest that the university played a consequential role in Hiba's understanding of self and history. Her relationship with Arab students at the university was pivotal in accentuating her sense of herself as "Palestinian" and coming to understand herself as "Iqritian."

> Brian: So that's still the same, but now you feel that you can invest more in that idea (Iqrit). Is that what you are saying?
>
> Hiba: Yes. The Iqrit Case is with me all the time and nothing has changed. Although now I know I should work and do something about it, not just hear the stories. For example, this documentary—I hope that someday when it is finished, I can use it to do something real with it (...) When I came here, I saw people working for their cases whether it's for the identity or not. And it provoked me to make it real, not just to feel pain inside and get angry at matters, not to keep everything inside of me just to do something about it.

Experiencing the story of her village through the stories of other students and their actions, inspires Hiba to see her own history in a new light. It inspired her to take some concrete action. Once again, "to make it real" and to "do something about it."

> On Independence Day I was here in Jerusalem. It's an example of what I did too. It was important for me to do something on this day. So I went with my friends to Lifta. Do you know Lifta? It's an abandoned village near Jerusalem also in 1948. We went there the whole day. We looked for the houses. These are important places. You feel you belong there because I am from Iqrit which has a similar story to Lifta. Now I see Iqrit and other places even near Jerusalem, not on the border with Lebanon, with people who are refugees like ourselves from Lifta (...) People I met here at the University—for them it was maybe clearer or they just understood the situation as I did.

Through her connection with Arab students at the university and witnessing their actions to keep alive the memories of Palestinian villages around Jerusalem, Hiba comes to see Iqrit as part of a larger picture, related to the struggles of other villages. They are stories that she can connect to. Through her participation in Arab groups, she is able to come to a revised understanding of what Iqrit is and what it means to be an Iqritian and, ultimately, use this energy for self-understanding.

LANA: TORN BETWEEN THE TWO

Like Hiba, Lana identifies as Palestinian and her experience coming to Jerusalem has clarified this identity. But, coming to Jerusalem has also accentuated a sense of affinity with Israeli culture and a particular alternative subculture of Israeli youth that she, perhaps sardonically, calls "hipsters." It has also led to increased social distance with Palestinian youth.

> This is very hard because the thing of identity has been occupying me since I got to Jerusalem. I grew up in a village in the North. Eighteen years I was only there. I did not move. I did not live like out of the village. (….) Then I came to Jerusalem and I started to feel the conflict more and I became more attached to my identity as an Arab person, as a Palestinian. That was on the national level. But on the social level I found that I might be an outcast for behaviors that I have. For, I don't know, ways of life that are not really norms in the Arab lives.

Coming to Jerusalem Lana becomes more attached to a Palestinian identity, which she calls her "national" identity in contrast to her "social" identity that is outside the accepted "norms in Arab lives." However, there is no clean separation between the national and the social. She feels an "outcast" from Arab society but yet doesn't fit completely into the Israeli Jewish world. Lana continues:

> I should have also mentioned that I don't have friends from my village. And even in high school I usually tried just to shut up when we were having discussions about all kinds of stuff because I knew that there would be a mark on me if I opened my mouth and said my honest opinion. (…) I remember once I was in 11th grade and I said that I have no problem to go home and to get a ride from a male mate of mine in his car. And someone said: "We are not living in Europe." And that was like the last time I. Since then I said. That's it. I just have to keep my mouth shut.

Lana highlights her distance from the people in the village—even before the university. It is a strange position, to feel like you belong to a group that you do not feel like you belong in—an outcast, in which heartfelt opinions and expressions are silenced. The turmoil in her identity has been intensifying. Once again, she continues:

> And I have been living in Jerusalem for 4 years. And I went through a lot of conflicts with myself as well regarding my identity, with the people I should hang out with. And again it's becoming harder and harder each year because. (…) I don't know. There is some, how do you say this? I'm kind of torn between the two. I have Jewish friends and I have Arab friends. I have more Jewish friends than I have Arab friends. And sometimes it's just on the surface that with Arab friends it's easier for

me to express myself language-wise, you know, same slang, same things we grew up on. But with my Jewish friends I'm more comfortable with. I don't know, drinking alcohol, smoking. It's more. If I'm hanging out with Jewish friends and I'm drinking, I'm not concerned about whether someone is going to say a word about me. But when it comes to Arabs, they are not really friends, you know—Arab people that I hang out with sometimes. It concerns me, but it is still there. And sometimes my Israeli friends make me feel that there are no blocks, there are no barriers between us, but sometimes it's still there on some levels.

Lana describes a superficial closeness with Arabs. She describes a feeling of being criticized by Arab students for behaviors that come with her alternative life style that Lana considers not only normal but an authentic part of herself. There is a problem of authenticity; as she says, Arabs are not "really" friends. She expresses a deeper and more natural, but incomplete, intimacy with Jewish friends.

But, Lana doesn't feel that she "belongs 100 %." There are experiences in her relationships with Israeli Jews, which hold her back from full belonging and assimilating. She labels them blocks or barriers. For instance, she breaks up with her Jewish boyfriend because she realizes that, "it's all only because it's cool to have an Arab girlfriend." Lana is concerned about being treated as a kind or type of person, a stereotype. In other words, she doesn't really belong.

Because Lana's relationship with Israeli Jews is so close, and she is able to blend so seamlessly, the barriers are subtle. Later in the interview, she says:

When I hang out with people that I love, these people, but I'm aware also of the fact that they were in the army. And it also tears me from the inside because this, I don't know, this lovely girl that I'm hanging out with. She used to be on. I don't know... a check point or something. Tormented. I may not be aware to this, but she maybe she tormented some. I don't know, some people that I belong with. And it's not about my national definition because I know what my definition is... But these daily experiences, this tiny stuff.

With all the complexities of her identity, the question is: can Lana authentically be her true self? Lana does not feel like she belongs completely to any world. Lana feels comfortable with her free thinking leftist Jewish friends and a desire to be part of their world. But, there are barriers. On the Palestinian side, Lana feels distant from Arab youth at the university. She questions their motives in their own roles/identities, even Arab hipsters. "Each of them is going to head back to his village, get married with a girl his mother picked for him." Their commitment to the free spirited lifestyle of a "hipster" is only temporary and artificial.

She has fashioned, what I call, a "Jerusalem" identity, which is largely associated with the hipster lifestyle and mostly in the company of Israeli Jews. But, it is difficult for Lana to maintain this Jerusalem identity in all situations—it is difficult to maintain who she is in Jerusalem when she is back in the village with her family.

This lack of consistency has emotional costs. Her mother calls her a "free spirit" and laments having a daughter like her. She knows that her parents are "not really satisfied with the way I choose to live my life." It "breaks [her] heart" that she cannot interact openly with her parents like her Jewish friends.

She tells one revealing story about getting her nose pierced and why she removed her nose-ring.

> Two months ago I had a piercing here. And it was only for one month because then I went home and it was a Holocaust when they saw the piercing. And my father just told me: "There are things that are not acceptable. In Jerusalem do whatever you want as long as it does not affect us. I never ask you what you do there. But if you are coming to visit or to live or whatever, you will have to respect this place and the rules of this place." And I tried to defend myself and I said that I feel that this year I have become more aware of things that I'm growing up and I'm studying more. So he said: "I know, I know all of this. But still there are things that aren't acceptable."

The use of the word "Holocaust" is shocking. I don't read the word as making a political statement but as attempting to describe the intensity of her parent's reaction. Although she does her best to keep the worlds of Jerusalem and the village separate, they do intrude on each other. Lana's Jerusalem identity is not as free as it seems but, is anchored, if only partially, by the village and her relationship with her family.

CONCLUSIONS

I have argued that narrating as political action provides a way of understanding political actions as interpretative practices integrated in the life experience of persons and in the context of social relationships and cultural world. Political actions are not limited in scope but bring into play an array of related ways of thinking about self and world. And, new constructions are encountered in the present, with the help of current social relationships, and read backward to fashion an identity.

Hiba's sense of herself as Palestinian and Iqritian is based in the system of values inherited from her childhood. But, relationships with politically active Arab youth at the Hebrew University provided new avenues for identity poetics as part of the larger project of preserving the reality of the past. There is an inversion of temporal perspective, she now sees the struggle of her family and her village through the eyes of her current social group and uses their insights to understand her own life circumstances and the need for action.

Lana's complex, and conflicted, sense of her identity is grounded in her search for an authentic and alternative way of being that is foreign to, and at odds with, her family of origin and the Muslim village where she grew up. Lana's incomplete closeness to Israeli Jewish youth and distance from Arabs entails a feeling of being "in between" Palestinian and Israeli worlds. Although Lana clearly is Palestinian, she is becoming more "normalized" (her word) into mainstream Israeli culture. Her assimilation is checked by subtle perceived rebukes by Israeli Jews, which seem to erect barriers to full belonging. Also, her relationship with her parents appears to provide a kind of anchor. Indeed, it is hard to imagine Lana giving up her Palestinian identity without completely giving up her parents.

In Hiba and Lana, we find two different ways of storying the challenges of being a Palestinian in Israel. However, in both life stories we see the way that political identity is both expansive, part of the larger life of the person, and intensive, cultural meanings are accessed and appropriated through direct social relationships.

SUMMARY

- Dissatisfied with the limitations of statistical methods of analysis and mechanistic theories, in the 1980s and the 1990s psychologists turned to narrative as a way of understanding meaning making in social and cultural context.
- Narrative theory and research on social and political action provides a rich and complex understanding of social processes.
- Currently, narrative psychology is a diverse, and fragmented, field of inquiry, largely, split along psychology's traditional encampments (personality, cognitive, social, clinical, etc.)
- We need to develop a theory of narrating as a political action, that engages sociocultural resources and makes present interpretations of self, other, and the world.
- Narrating is the primary form of political action. Narratings are always addressed to others in the context of a social encounter, a dialog, and with the effect of reworking sociocultural resources and, potentially, creating new systems of meaning for future use.
- An example of narrative research within political psychology would be "identity stories" of the Palestinian citizens of Israel.

GLOSSARY

expansive hypothesis refers to the thesis that political actions are a form of narrating and that there are no clear lines that separate political actions from other varieties of interpretation that persons make about the self, world, and others.

intensive hypothesis refers to the thesis that the person and the social world depend on each other and are always in constant interaction and exchange. A productive approach to political psychology should be able to capture the personal and social into a single theory that encompasses both.

narrative hermeneutics is a perspective on narrative that emphasizes the interpretative aspects of narrative as a project of understanding self, other, and the world.

poiesis is a term that encompasses the idea that narrative interpretation is a form of poetic activity in which persons make sense of experience and world in order to "make" life and "make" self.

semiotic means refers to resources, primarily linguistic, and narrative, that allow for a fluid transition of experience, between persons, as a vehicle for understanding self and the world.

FURTHER READING

Andrews, M. (2007). *Shaping history: Narratives of political change*. New York: Cambridge University Press.

Arendt, H. (1998). *The human condition* (2nd ed.). Chicago: The University of Chicago Press. (Original work published 1958)

Schiff, B. (2002). Talking about identity: Arab students at the Hebrew University. *Ethos, 30*(3), 273–304.

Schiff, B. (2017). *A new narrative for psychology*. New York: Oxford University Press. (This volume outlines the rational, history, theory and methods of narrative psychology).

Tileagă, C. (2013). *Political psychology: Critical perspectives*. Cambridge, UK: Cambridge University Press.

QUESTIONS FOR GROUP DISCUSSION

- How can it be said that Hiba's and Lana's accounts of their identity were truly "political?"

- What is the validity status of insights acquired through a narrative approach? How does it compare with quantitative methods that measure variables?

- If we are trying to understand people in a political context, why are researchers so attached to numbers, big data, and statistical tests? Why are numbers thought to be closer to reality than words, speech, or text?
- What does a narrative approach to political psychology offer social research?
- How might a narrative approach be used in other political contexts?

7 Connecting Social Exclusion and Agency: Social Class Matters

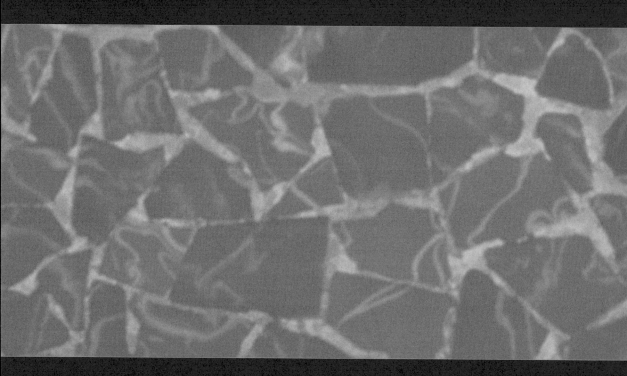

SARAH JAY, ORLA MULDOON, AND
CAROLINE HOWARTH

CHAPTER OUTLINE

This chapter discusses social exclusion as expressed through concrete class-based inequalities and experienced by the working classes on several dimensions including material consumption and resource accumulation, education, well paid work, and social engagement (Thompson, Russell, & Simmons, 2014). This is in contrast to much social psychological research exploring social exclusion that focuses on the psychological processes, mediating factors, and consequences of exclusion and isolation at an interpersonal level, when individuals experience exclusion from a particular group (e.g., Abrams, Hogg, & Marques, 2004). We will also explore the connection between social exclusion and agency using qualitative data to show how structural inequality and culture shapes the models of agency that are available and normative in different classed contexts (Stephens, Fryberg, & Markus, 2012). While the arguments and empirical data in this chapter are largely based on studies in the UK and Republic of Ireland, the principles likely apply to other social and cultural settings.

CLASS MATTERS

Often psychology presents agency as an individual attribute, for example in terms of **self-efficacy** beliefs, which can be seen as central to human agency (Bandura, 2006). Indeed, social and political psychologists have not focused as much research attention on the consequences of social class as other systems of inequality. In recognition of this gap, there have been several calls to action (Lott & Bullock, 2001; Ostrove & Cole, 2003; Williams, 2009) and the American Psychological Association recently set up a task force to explore the consequences of poverty and published a report on socioeconomic status (Saegert et al., 2007).

It would be inaccurate, however, to suggest that there has been no insightful psychological theorizing or research on social class or the consequences of economic advantage and disadvantage. For instance, cultural psychologists in the US suggest that a sociocultural perspective is needed to understand class. They demonstrate that *individualism* and *independence*, so valued in Western culture, are the product of middle class experience and resources (Markus & Kitayama, 2010; Stephens, Fryberg, et al., 2012; Stephens, Hamedani, & Destin, 2014). Similarly, "choice" varies in meaning depending on who has access to resources (Stephens, Markus, & Townsend, 2007). Social psychologists also show how

Political Psychology: A Social Psychological Approach, First Edition.
Edited by Christopher J. Hewer and Evanthia Lyons.

rank, resources and culture within middle and working classes create a different life experience in terms of sense of control, generosity, essentialism, and judgment of others (Kraus & Keltner, 2013; Kraus, Piff, & Keltner, 2009, 2011; Kraus, Tan, & Tannenbaum, 2013; Piff, Kraus, Côté, Cheng, & Keltner, 2010; Piff, Stancato, Côté, Mendoza-Denton, & Keltner, 2012). Additionally, there is some work on the impact of class in education in terms of belonging (Ostrove & Long, 2007), stereotype threat (Croizet & Claire, 1998; Croizet, Desert, Dutrevis, & Leyens, 2001; Spencer & Castano, 2007), social identity (Iyer, Jetten, Tsivrikos, Postmes, & Haslam, 2009), dispossession, and privilege (Fine & Ruglis, 2009). Lott (2002) explores classism and calls for an examination of the ways in which, by paying little attention to class, psychologists and psychology collude in the exclusion of the poor.

Issues related to class are pressing as recently it has been demonstrated that across the capitalist developed world, levels of income inequality are returning to those that existed a century ago (Piketty & Goldhammer, 2014). Since the 1980s, the income of the world's wealthiest 1% has grown at a much faster rate than for the rest of the population, the 99%. This means that wealth has once again become concentrated in the hands of a few while millions live in poverty, the majority of whom are working (Cribb, Hood, Joyce, & Phillips, 2013). At the same time, there has been a heated debate among social scientists and politicians about the relevance of social class when trying to understand and analyze current inequality (Pakulski & Waters, 1996). Indeed, popular discourse often assumes that societies have become "classless." With the increasing political emphasis placed on individual agency, the structural persistence of social class in important fields of opportunity such as education, is more or less denied even though the links between level of qualification, grades achieved, status of employment, and earning prospects have never been stronger (Smyth & McCoy, 2011). Indeed, post-secondary school qualifications are now considered essential for securing employment. However, the unequal distribution of wealth and income and associated cultural and social resources mean that class is more often reproduced rather than transcended within the education system (Reay, 2006; Whitty, 2001).

Importantly, the class structure is different from other systems of inequality such as gender, ethnicity, ability, or sexuality. People living on low incomes are not disadvantaged because their identity or culture is devalued or because they are stigmatized per se. They are disadvantaged because their low income and related resources restricts access to ways of living and being, to the practices and activities that they and others value (Sayer, 2005). However, poverty has always been stigmatized (Kerbo, 1976; Mickelson & Williams, 2008; Warr, 2005a, 2005b; Williams, 2009). If there were no shared understanding of the practices and ways of being that are valued and normative, there would be no class-based shame or anxiety about "respectability" (Sayer, 2005; Skeggs, 1997). Thoughts and feelings around failure, entitlement, guilt, envy, pity, superiority, and inferiority are internal responses linked to external social and structural processes. Respect and shame are social emotions experienced in response to expectations, reactions, and treatment by others. Moreover, shame can be seen as a mechanism of social control that produces conformity and sometimes resistance (Sayer, 2005). Reay (2005, p. 911) calls this the "psychic landscape of class" and argues that these emotions and cognitions should not be pushed into the realm of individual psychology. To do this, would be to blame individuals for the social exclusion they experience, which would make bringing about change to classed-based inequality even less likely.

These subjective microlevel aspects of class have been the focus of a revived interest in class in British sociology in the past decade (Le Roux, Rouanet, Savage, & Warde, 2008). In moving away from a purely macro-level analysis of class that places employment relations as the central driving force that structures inequality, cultural class theorists recognize the contributing role of identities, cultural activities, and tastes in the process of structuring class. This understanding draws upon Pierre Bourdieu's (1984) formulation of social class, which recognizes both the importance of economic capital, and way that "the economic" cannot be separated from social and cultural capital resources (Savage, Warde, & Devine, 2005). The benefit of this analysis is its attention to the accumulation and convertibility of capital over time that lead to systematic advantage for the better off in certain social, cultural, and institutional settings. This underpins the process of class reproduction.

CULTURAL CAPITAL

At the root of this process, is **cultural capital**, which refers to the knowledge, language, values, and tastes largely gained through third level education. This type of capital is initially accumulated in the home and then used by children in school. Eventually, it is converted into qualifications that allow for relatively secure, well paid employment. This illustrates an important point; rather than seeing inequality as static, this position points to the *cumulative nature of advantage and disadvantage*.

In order to substantiate the claim that cultural practices and tastes are inextricably linked to class, Le Roux et al. (2008) conducted Geometric Data Analysis and Multiple Correspondent Analysis on the detailed data of 1,529 UK individuals. They were interested in both cultural practices in the domains of music, literature, television, film, visual arts, sport, and eating out and tastes measured as likes and dislikes. They found a reasonable fit when mapping these practices and tastes onto three distinct classes. The professional (upper) middle class includes professionals, large managers, and employers (24% of the UK's workforce), an intermediate middle class includes business oriented lower managers (30%) and a large working class includes lower supervisors and technicians, routine, and semiroutine workers (46%). They found a clear association between UK cultural tastes and practices and class groups overall. In some cases, the relationship was strong; for example, television watching was strongly linked to class, but for other practices such as going to the pub, a looser relationship with class was evident.

THE PRECARIAT

This analysis is helpful because it identifies three distinct groupings of people, which may reflect a lay understanding of the class structure. A more recent and even more detailed analysis of the same question offers a much more fine grained and fragmented view of class structure (Savage et al., 2013). This research draws on a huge data set of over 12,000 UK participants gathered in conjunction with the BBC, and includes measures of economic, social, and cultural capitals and practices. Although impressive in its findings, and probably much closer to the fragmented "reality" in the UK at least, this analysis offers seven distinct sociological classed categories with labels not in common usage. Most importantly, they identify a relatively large group (15%) whom they label as **precariat**. This, the poorest class economically, has little social capital and low scores on cultural capital and engagement (see also, Hodgetts, Groot, Garden, & Chamberlain, 2017). This group experiences social exclusion through unemployment, under-employment and the most insecure types of contemporary employment (such as zero-hour contracts) to a greater extent than any other group, and are likely to have benefited least from capitalist restructuring in recent times. There is a stronger association between class of origin, education, and class destination for the most disadvantaged (Goldthorpe, 2003). Moreover, they are unlikely to have third level qualifications and are therefore unable to benefit from the social networks and cultural resources available to the more affluent as they try to secure employment.

In summary, social class matters in terms of cultural practices, social resources, and access to social networks. It can have very significant consequences for the under-privileged insofar that it imposes significant structural barriers to adolescent educational achievement and subsequent employment opportunities (Ball, 2003; Goldthorpe, 2003; McCoy, Smyth, Watson, & Darmody, 2014). For many, class is a chronic stressor and remains a persistent driving force for social exclusion, and inequality in health, housing, and well-being (Adler et al., 1994; Anderson, Kraus, Galinsky, & Keltner, 2012; Ball, 2003; Benzeval et al., 2014; Marmot, 2004; Wilkinson & Pickett, 2009).

CAPITALIST RESTRUCTURING AND POVERTY

Huge social and economic transformations have occurred since the New Right Agenda, led by British premier Margaret Thatcher and US president Ronald Reagan in the 1980s, intensified free market forces and subsequently increased inequality (Hedin, Clark, Lundholm, & Malmberg, 2012). Accordingly, capitalism has been restructured, moving from organized to disorganized and, as a result, economic growth is no longer guaranteed to trickle down to the benefit of all (Warr, 2005b). One of the consequences has been sociospatial divisions and polarization, reduced contact, and connection between the poor and nonpoor. This is particularly the case for the precariat. In Ireland, for example, poverty has become concentrated in residential areas, mostly rented local authority housing, which tends to be located on the margins of cities, built between the 1950s and 1970s to service the industry that is no longer there (Tate, 2008). A policy focus on home ownership meant that the number of rented local authority houses fell between 1987 and 1994, and those occupying the remaining housing stock are now the most disadvantaged (Hourigan, 2011; Nolan & Whelan, 1999). The most disadvantaged experience cumulative disadvantage, have manual class origins and have experienced childhood poverty. This has a strong impact on educational achievement (Humphreys, 2011) and the effect on those living in urban local authority housing has been a significant rise in unemployment, welfare dependence, and poverty.

Warr (2005b) notes how the poor and the non-poor are further divided by the privatization of public spaces. Shopping streets have become shopping centers, and social inclusion means engaging with the flow of money, information, and consumption largely paid for by employment. Participation is always possible for those who have the money to do so while those without the means are socially and economically excluded and made to feel unwelcome. Poverty thus leads to increasing discomfort in public spaces, immobility, and disconnection (Warr, 2005a). Furthermore, the restructuring of employment has been so uneven that the most vulnerable have experienced a dramatic decline in the availability of low and unskilled work. Despite a continued enthusiasm for work found within working classed communities in both the Mediterranean (Murad, 2002) and the UK (MacDonald, Shildrick, Webster, & Simpson, 2005), the opportunities available are mostly for "poor work," which is insecure, low paid, and sporadic. These large scale processes of social change underpin a context of changing social class relations (Nolan & Whelan, 1999), which is becoming apparent nationally and internationally.

STIGMA

The poor are also subject to pathological representations and negative stereotypes as detached, deviant, and disconnected from mainstream societal values and norms (Mickelson & Williams, 2008; Weis, 2013; Williams, 2009). Such representations often assume a distinctive underclass, a potentially criminal, and aggressive subculture among the poor. Nolan and Whelan (1999) found a highly significant relationship between risk of poverty and social class in Ireland, but found no evidence of an urban underclass. Rather, they suggest that the distinctiveness experienced by public housing tenants results from a sense of shared disadvantage in terms of employment opportunities, living standards, reduced psychological well-being, heightened fatalism, and lowered life satisfaction; all of which are intensified by stigmatization (Mickelson & Williams, 2008; Williams, 2009).

This stigma can damage relations between advantaged and disadvantaged communities leading to social isolation, early school leaving, and subsequently impacting on health and well-being for members of disadvantaged communities (Major & O'Brien, 2005). Recent research in Limerick city, Ireland, has shown that stigma is more than a negative stereotype of the poor, it is an active process that breaks down trust in the providers of services who are there to alleviate disadvantage (Stevenson, McNamara, & Muldoon, 2014). Furthermore, a study comparing implicit and explicit evaluations of residents from disadvantaged and advantaged areas in Limerick, found that the disadvantaged residents were devalued and excluded from attributes of citizenship (McNamara, Muldoon, Stevenson, & Slattery, 2011). These results were obtained from advantaged residents of the city as well as residents of the disadvantaged areas who had internalized these prejudices. A further study, however, found a positive relationship between community identity and psychological well-being mediated by feelings of collective efficacy, but this relationship did not promote collective action (McNamara, Stevenson, & Muldoon, 2013). Rather, stigmatization, perceived prejudice, and discrimination at an institutional level and divisions within the community, undermined the ability of community residents to work together to improve their situation (Bradshaw, Jay, McNamara, Stevenson, & Muldoon, 2015; McNamara et al., 2013).

COLLECTIVE IDENTITIES

Despite the important difference between class and other systems of inequality, it is worth considering the vital role that shared or collective identity plays in changing policies and challenging stigmatizing representations of oppressed groups. Under the right conditions, group memberships may play an important role as antecedents of collective action (Simon & Klandermans, 2001; Tajfel & Turner, 1979). Through collective action, the civil rights, feminist, and more recently, the lesbian, gay, bisexual, transgender, and queer plus rights and pride movements have challenged subordination, prejudice, discrimination, and inequality. Indeed, these movements and community projects increase awareness and debate about the structural and historical nature of inequality. Another example is the Occupy movement (see Pickerill & Krinsky, 2012). Interestingly, in contrast to shared identity leading to collective action, in this case, collective action, with the creation of at least 1,600 protest camps, led to the development of a shared identity as "the 99%" (Cornish, Montenegro, van Reisen, Zaka, & Sevitt, 2014). With support and encouragement, awareness, and cultural understanding can promote social creativity to challenge, resist, and reevaluate negative social representations among those whose identities are stigmatized (Howarth, 2002a, 2002b). As such, a collective challenge can increase an individual's positive identification with their group (Branscombe, Scmitt, & Harvey, 1999). Unlike other forms of inequality, however, class-based inequalities are seldom questioned, debated, or resisted; they seem "natural" and are "individualised out of our collective conscience" (Reay, 2005, p. 924). This inevitably limits social debate about class and makes social movements and social change less likely (Dixon, Levine, Reicher, & Durrheim, 2012).

THE INDIVIDUALIZATION OF CLASS

Under the neoliberal agenda, market logic has replaced the welfare state in determining not just the economy, but all aspects of contemporary living (Lynch, 2006). Citizens are no longer considered passive, but have been redefined as "privatized rational consumers," as active entrepreneurs of the self, willing and able to compete and make market-led choices (Walkerdine & Bansel, 2010). Individualist ideologies encourage the notion of individual responsibility and freedom of choice, but they mask the way that inequality radically shapes the ability to make important choices (Ichheiser, 1949; Le Grand, 2006; Reay, 1996), and even the cultural meaning of choice for class groups (Snibbe & Markus, 2005; Stephens, Fryberg, et al., 2012). Class is further individualized by the notion of **meritocracy**. Meritocratic ideologies promote the idea that success is an outcome of individual merit. Furthermore, hard work is presented as the route to opportunity and a view that "anybody can succeed if they work hard enough" prevails. Socio-economic background is deemed unimportant and these ideologies and discourses have become prevalent, dominant, and almost "common sense" in Western societies, which has dissolved any serious discussion of advantage, opportunity, or power relations in relation to social class.

Up until the late twentieth century, there was a large and visible working class, against which the middle classes compared and defined themselves; class was a visible marker of social differentiation (Bourdieu, 1984). Although many people still occupy working class jobs, deindustrialization, the demise of apprenticeships and the trade union movement has meant that the traditional industrial working class has become less visible and therefore can no longer be used as a reference point of cultural definition (Savage, 2003) or political mobilization. Additionally, "jobs for life" were replaced with insecurity and short term contracts, with an emphasis on "life-long learning" and self-reinvention. These shifts eroded traditional roles and community ties and an empty cultural space was thus created, which Savage (2003) claims has been colonized by the middle class. Although unnamed because of individualization rhetoric, middle class norms, and practices now define what is blandly assumed to be "right," valued and appropriate (Reay, 2005).

At the same time, huge increases in service sector work and expanding higher education access promotes not only the possibility but *the necessity of upward social mobility* (Walkerdine, 2003). Indeed, there is an implicit assumption that we all now have to be middle class. Therefore, anyone living up to middle class norms is considered "normal" and responsible while those whose cultural practices and aspirations do not meet middle class standards are viewed as failures. In this way, the individual is held responsible for their personal health, well-being (Lynch, 2006) and its regulation (Walkerdine, 2003). What becomes clear is that "class" is not only a persistent social structure, but also a psychological construct that positions people in terms of ethical, moral, and economic value. It remains a process underpinned by power relations, group processes, advantage, and disadvantage, despite being disguised as a highly individualized phenomenon (Jay & Muldoon, in press).

AGENCY AND SOCIAL CLASS

To understand how social class shapes models of agency, attention needs to be paid to the material, social, and cultural resources that are accessible in different class contexts. Walkerdine (2003) argues that the archetypal middle classed persona is an individualized (neoliberal) subject. Brought up in relatively affluent material and social conditions, middle class children tend to be socialized to believe they are unique and their opinion is valuable. They may choose what to eat, who to play with, what activities they like, for example. They are taught that the world is a safe place (Kusserow, 2012).

Given such opportunities, these children develop confidence, a sense that they have influence and control and can focus on their goals (Stephens, Fryberg, et al., 2012). This leads to the development of norms of independence, which fosters a sense of security, ownership, and entitlement to "pave your own path."

In contrast, growing up with restricted material resources with few financial safety nets and less predictable environments, working class children learn the value of compromise. They are socialized to understand that the world does not revolve around them. Parents focus on toughening their children because the world is potentially dangerous and uncertain (Kusserow, 2012). Because choices and influence are constrained by external factors, they must pay attention to the situation and the intentions and emotions of others to achieve their own goals (Kraus, Rheinschmidt, & Piff, 2012; Stephens, Markus, & Fryberg, 2012). For this reason, the working class are more likely to develop views that center on interdependence with others.

SOCIAL CAPITAL

To examine the arguments laid out thus far, we now present data collected by the first author through focus group interviews with young people from middle class and working class backgrounds in second level education in Limerick city in Ireland. This material has informed our ideas about education, agency, and social class (Jay, 2015). The positive resource potential of social relationships, often termed **social capital** (as outlined by Putnam, 1995), is available in both working and middle class contexts. However, the type of social capital available in working and middle class contexts tends to be quite different (Humphreys, 2011).

Bonding social capital refers to close connections between similar individuals and homogenous groups and is prevalent in working class contexts. As its name suggests, it acts like social glue enabling reciprocal helping and community embeddedness (Putnam, 1995). From our focus group data, some of the working class participants needed to move to an education center outside their neighborhood in order to progress in their education. They were aware of their parents' preference for them to stay close to home and they expressed fear of leaving their own areas because of the threat of "outsiders."

Bridging social capital, on the other hand, refers to loose connections and networks existing between diverse individuals and heterogeneous groups that bolster mobility and opportunity (Campbell & Jovchelovitch, 2000), more commonly found in middle classed contexts (Warr, 2005b). Such resources impact on how people are able to act, and how this understanding becomes valued, appropriate, and normative over time and part of class identity content.

For our middle class participants, their education was a priority and seen as a bridge toward "paving their own paths" toward a career, if necessary, away from family, community, and country.

Individual mobility is offered as an incentive for continuing commitment to education, but for working class students, this often means exiting their own cultural milieu and entering another governed by middle class values (Lehmann, 2009). In this transition, they may sense that they are relinquishing their bonding social capital, which may cause some internal discomfort and conflict for students and their parents (Thomson, Henderson, & Holland, 2003). Qualitative and ethnographic research consistently highlights the structural and objective financial, social, and cultural "capital disadvantages" experienced by first generation working class students in higher educational settings (Christie, Tett, Cree, Hounsell, & McCune, 2008; Lehmann, 2009; Reay, Crozier, & Clayton, 2009; Reay, Davies, David, & Ball, 2001).

CULTURAL INCOMPATIBILITY IN EDUCATION

This work also highlights pain and discomfort that working class students may feel, particularly in more elite institutions, as they leave their familiar class context. Quantitative longitudinal research indicates that middle class students feel a sense of identity compatibility with higher education before entering and once they progress into higher education (Jetten, Iyer, Tsivrikos, & Young, 2008). The more compatible prior class identity was with the higher education context, the more they identified as "a university student," and the greater their sense that university would advance their individual mobility. This type of compatibility, however, was not experienced by the working class students in our study. Their class background did not present "a good fit" to the higher education context before, on entry, and throughout their higher education experience. From the focus group data, there was a sense that universities are for the privileged, while institutes of technology are more compatible with working class identity. Although it is only 4.2 miles (6.76 km) from their home, the university was still "too far away." Another longitudinal study found that feelings of compatibility and multiple group memberships gained from extracurricular activities such as sports and after school clubs, were a source of protection during the stressful transition to higher education (Iyer et al., 2009). Indeed, middle class students who were more likely to take advantage of this resource, exhibited higher levels of psychological well-being (as indicated by the General Health Questionnaire)—a measure that is linked to self-efficacy—the ability to "make things happen."

THREATS TO IDENTITY

It would appear that the cultural orientation of higher education can create a sense of uneasiness for working class students, making them feel as though they "don't quite fit." This threat to identity (see Breakwell, 1996) is an uncomfortable psychological state that reduces the likelihood of them remaining at university. Indeed, they may seek to protect their identity by withdrawing physically or psychologically from education.

Different sociocultural contexts support different models of social capital, agency, and understanding of what is appropriate for self and others to do (Stephens, Fryberg, et al., 2012). Having choice, freedom, and control in the future were the central concerns of our middle classed participants and they saw education as the principal route for ensuring those concerns would be met. There were, however, parallels between the groups; both valued education and financial security and sought to avoid negative outcomes. But the contextual influence was very different for the two groups. The working classed participants live in a context of significant cumulative disadvantage, a situation that has been shown to generate strong feelings of fatalism (or lack of control) (Nolan & Whelan, 1999). Indeed, autonomy, control, freedom, and independence were less available to the working class psychological experience and therefore were not presented as immediate concerns.

THE TRANSMISSION OF CULTURAL CAPITAL

Cultural capital also appears to differ according to class context. Cultural capital refers to the experience, practices, and tastes, as well as academic ability and language skills (Lareau & Weininger, 2003) valued in the education context. Middle class parents transmit the cultural capital gained through their own education to their children, which influences their transition toward higher education. Despite their aspirations, working class parents are less able to influence the education trajectories of their children or intervene in their schooling because they have not had access to the same cultural capital mobilized by the middle classes (Bourdieu, 1986). It was common for the parents of our working class participants to have no first-hand experience of third level education to pass on to their children. This cultural capital is associated empirically with class differences in achievement outcomes (Scherger & Savage, 2010).

Among middle class participants an *independent* model of agency in which choice, independence and autonomy were highly valued was seen as a driving force to maximize their potential within the education system. However, most of the working class participants had much less access to choice, control, and independence and therefore the cultural orientation for these students was to adopt an *interdependent* model of agency.

IMPLICATIONS FOR A SOCIAL AND POLITICAL PSYCHOLOGY OF SOCIAL EXCLUSION

Despite many well-intentioned policies to tackle educational inequality and the attainment gap between classes, class remains a persistent structural force that shapes and predicts achievement outcomes. This is the position in the UK (Reay, 2006), USA (Sirin, 2005), Canada (Lehmann, 2009), and Republic of Ireland (RoI) (Williams et al., 2011). Recent national evidence in the RoI shows that, by the age of nine, a child's competence in reading and mathematics is related to their socioeconomic circumstances (Williams et al., 2011) and those who do not complete schooling are disproportionately working class (Byrne & Smyth, 2010).

Although the material conditions of social class contexts do not completely determine outcomes, they do influence action that is likely to become normative and appropriate (Stephens et al., 2007). Middle class experience and resources bring with them both tangible and hidden advantages. Tangible advantages such as financial, social, and cultural capital (Bourdieu, 1986; Savage et al., 2005) may promote hidden psychological advantages. This may encourage a sense of power, entitlement, control over situations and thus a sense of independence from social constraints (Kraus et al., 2012; Stephens, Fryberg, et al., 2012): essentially a sense of personal agency.

On the other hand, resources and opportunities available in working class contexts tend not to promote social separation but interconnection and reliance upon others (Bakouri & Staerklé, 2015). Stephens and colleagues (Stephens, Fryberg, et al., 2012) propose that the working classes tend to operate through an *interdependent model of agency*, where it is normative and appropriate to respond to the expectations and influence of others and the context and to adjust and fit it, rather than do what best suits your personal situation at a given point in time. In contrast, the middle classes behave in terms of an *independent model of agency*, separate from context, where preferences and goals are freely chosen, with a focus on influencing and standing out from others (Snibbe & Markus, 2005). Neither is more effective, natural, or normal than the other (Markus & Kitayama, 2010) and neither is inherent in individual psychology.

Rather, these are two sociocultural orientations shaped by available resources and experiences within two sociocultural contexts (Stephens, Markus, et al., 2012). However, as a neoliberal individualizing agenda continues to dominate society and our institutions (Lynch, 2006), independent agency is the presumed standard for all. This independent model of agency is valued and rewarded at work and in educational settings. We routinely celebrate *individual* academic success rather than collaborative endeavors. In a world of credentials based in a knowledge economy, independence, and personal agency are paramount.

CONCLUSIONS

In this chapter, we have shown how different models of agency can incur psychological advantage and disadvantage for young people. In our view, these structural factors have received very little attention from social and political psychologists who have left class to sociologists (Ostrove & Cole, 2003), or who may *control for class* (or some variation of economic positioning) while exploring other more "important" variables (Frable, 1997). However, the subjective, lived experience of class is essential to our understanding of politics and psychology. Individual factors such as emotions, thoughts, sense of belonging, and threat to identity as well as social stereotyping and comparative strategies may further endorse a social distinction between "us and them" in which power dynamics lead to advantage for some and disadvantage for others. The invisibility of class remains a pressing concern in twenty-first century politics and it has implications for the way that we study identity, agency, exclusion, and social change. We have highlighted the importance of collective or group approaches to understanding agency, which has been overly "individualized" and "classed."

Individualist and meritocratic discourses and ideologies constructed by the dominant and most privileged in society, implicitly suggest that the class system is open, stable, and legitimate. Even though social mobility has stagnated in recent times (Gillies, 2005), it is flaunted before the public as something desirable, necessary, and possible, and class boundaries are seen as permeable. Most importantly, some individuals may actively disidentify and distance themselves from a "spoilt" or "toxic" working class identity (Skeggs, 1997). Under these conditions, individuals are unlikely to mobilize a challenge to class-based inequality. Consequently, the structural inequalities inherent in the capitalist system are largely hidden from view and the lack of discourse surrounding class leads to the economically advantaged failing to critically evaluate or even acknowledge their privileged position while the economically disadvantaged are silenced (Sanders & Mahalingam, 2012). We suggest that these are pressing issues for political psychology, and that *it is time to develop a social and political psychology of class* with an analysis of agency at its core. Without such, the relationship between social class, inequality, and exclusion will remain concealed and economic disadvantage will continue to be individualized.

SUMMARY

- There is a need to develop a social and political psychology that addresses the connections between social exclusion, social class, and agency.
- Despite prevalent understandings in contemporary Western societies of the self as a free and independent agent with a significant degree of social mobility, individuals within disadvantaged communities experience social exclusion as a result of intersecting structural forces.
- Dominant political ideologies and discourses, including some that dominate social and political psychology itself, such as individualism and meritocracy, tend to construct people as independent agents able and responsible for their own paths, success, and prosperity.
- Because Western capitalist economies have moved from industrialized to "knowledge economies" and the labor market and job opportunities have radically changed, the demand for credentials and qualifications are becoming increasingly important for obtaining secure work, status, and reasonable pay.
- Despite an expanding higher education sector, *access to these credentials is unequal* as economic, social, and cultural forces combined impose significant structural barriers within the education system. Social, cultural, and economic forces, which can be conceptualized as social class, often intersect with other axes of disadvantage such as ethnicity and gender.
- Individuals, families and, often, whole communities experience social exclusion, poverty, and stigmatizing representations, which reproduce their exclusion from the labor market.
- These changes have been accompanied by cultural shifts where social class is rarely considered an important and self-defining identity. This makes classed identities difficult to reconstruct positively or mobilize as a protective resource. Moreover, the weakening of classed identities renders classed social agency and collective action around class less likely.
- Personal agency is "classed", which has associated consequences in terms of social exclusion and (barriers to) social mobility.

GLOSSARY

agency refers to the ability to take action, be effective and have influence in one's life. Agency is a sense of control and a capacity to enact behaviors, thoughts, and feelings.

bonded social capital refers to close connections between similar individuals and homogenous groups, which enables reciprocal helping and community embeddedness, prevalent in working classed contexts.

bridging social capital refers to loose connections and networks existing between diverse individuals and heterogeneous groups that bolster mobility and opportunity, more commonly found in middle classed contexts.

cultural capital is a resource gained through education; it refers to knowledge, vocabulary, values, and tastes that are esteemed and passed from one generation to the next through the family.

meritocracy is a social system, society, or organization that gives power and opportunity to people based on their abilities and not because of money or position.

precariat refers to a social group that is the poorest class economically; they have little social capital and low scores on cultural capital and engagement.

self-efficacy is a psychological construct that represents an individual's belief in their abilities and capacities to deal with the conditions that life puts before them.

social capital refers to a set of horizontal associations between people consisting of social networks and associated norms, which have an effect on the productivity of those involved.

FURTHER READING

Fiske S. T., & Markus H. R. (Eds.) (2012). *Facing social class: How societal rank influences interaction.* New York: Russell Sage Foundation.

Jones O. (2012). *Chavs: The demonization of the working class.* London: Verso Books.

Kraus M. W., & Stephens N. (2012). A road map for an emerging psychology of social class. *Social and Personality Psychology Compass*, 6, 642–656.

Mack J., & Landsey S. (2015). *Breadline Britain: The rise of mass poverty.* London: Oneworld Books.

Savage M. (2015). *Social class in the 21st century (Pelican introduction).* London: Pelican Books.

QUESTIONS FOR GROUP DISCUSSION

- What is the difference between bonding social capital and bridging social capital? How might the availability of either reproduce social inequality?

- How might "agency" be implicitly or explicitly nurtured within the family?

- Schools and colleges tend to promote an independent model of agency in their students. Discuss how this happens and how might these institutions might also support an interdependent model of agency.

- How important is class in your lives? Discuss how class compares with other social identities; for instance, gender or ethnicity?

- Positive discrimination programs are designed to alleviate disadvantage and help working classed or first generation students to gain places in universities and colleges. Discuss the fairness of this approach.

8   Migration

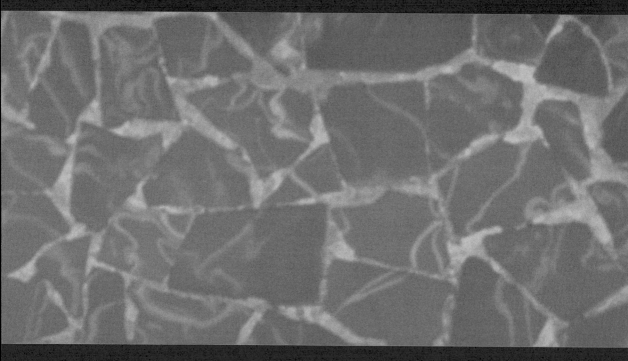

**SPYRIDOULA NTANI, ARTEMIS M. GRIVA, AND
XENIA CHRYSSOCHOOU**

CHAPTER OUTLINE

Migration is not a recent phenomenon: people have always moved in search of a better life. Indeed, countries such as the USA, Canada, and Australia have been founded on migration, and in Europe there has been a constant movement of people between state borders. After WWII, migrants from the south of Europe moved northward to find work, which contributed to the social and economic development of Northern Europe. Other migrant groups in Europe originate from former colonies of nation states, while others from Eastern Europe migrated westwards after the end of the Cold War. There are many reasons why people migrate and there is a long history of relations between newcomers and receiving communities. Thus, we should approach the question of migration without thinking that it is a new phenomenon or that it will not last, or that all migrant groups and their relations with the receiving communities are the same. Having established that, there are common issues at stake that require social psychological analysis.

Although many aspects of migration are worthy of political and psychological investigation, we address here two main issues: (a) the way that receiving societies perceive migrants and the migration process, and (b) the migrant experience of integration into a new society. Migration brings people from different origins, with different cultural practices and understandings of the world (and their own position in it) into the same political entity. This process reshuffles the content of identities, which can be threatening to people in all communities. What is more, migration changes the social stratification of the receiving society since newcomers usually occupy the lower social positions, and their introduction into the workforce allows members of the majority group to move upward. Thus, we face a phenomenon with asymmetric relationships between groups that involve the distribution of material and symbolic resources. More importantly, migration raises the question of entitlement: who may legitimately receive these resources? (Chryssochoou, 2016). Here, the social issue of distribution is transformed into a cultural issue of recognition; what becomes salient, is no longer social class, but culture and ethnicity. New conflicts then emerge regarding how both the cultural majority and minority groups view the incorporation of migrants into that society. A first approach, very familiar to social psychological research in the context of immigration, concerns issues of prejudice, stereotypes, and discrimination.

Political Psychology: A Social Psychological Approach, First Edition.
Edited by Christopher J. Hewer and Evanthia Lyons.

PREJUDICE, STEREOTYPES, AND DISCRIMINATION AGAINST IMMIGRANTS

Traditionally, the notion of prejudice is considered to include negative beliefs, stereotypes, and feelings of a majority ingroup against an immigrant or ethnic minority outgroup, as well as intentions to act in a discriminatory way against the outgroup (Allport, 1954). Relevant research has mainly focused on anti-black prejudice in the US and prejudice against ethnic minorities and new immigrant groups in Western Europe. It is important to note, however, that the societal context of immigration in multicultural societies, such as the US, differs from European states, which have strong national identities (Chryssochoou, 2004, 2016; Zick, Pettigrew, & Wagner, 2008).

STEREOTYPING, RACISM, AND FORMS OF DISCRIMINATION AGAINST IMMIGRANT GROUPS

For the members of the majority group, immigrant groups are often considered to have characteristics that violate majority norms (e.g., criminal, lazy, or incompetent), although the actual content of the stereotype depends on the nationality and socioeconomic status of the immigrant group (Lee & Fiske, 2006). Stereotypes are a way of understanding the social world, and a means by which the ideologies and values of the ingroup are protected (Tajfel, 1981a). More recent approaches have emphasized that representations of immigrant groups are closely linked to intergroup relations of power and dominance, and that stereotypes of immigrants tend to serve the goals and interests of the majority group by legitimizing existing social relations (Leyens & Demoulin, 2009).

Prejudice on the basis of race or ethnicity can take many, and often subtle, forms, both at an individual and societal level. Research on racism in the US has focused on modern, covert forms of racial prejudice. These newer forms—aversive (Gaertner & Dovidio, 1986), symbolic (Sears, 1988), and ambivalent racism (Hass, Katz, Rizzo, Bailey, & Eisenstadt, 1991), are the result of a conflict between negative emotions toward the outgroup and prevailing social norms of equality. What is more, at a societal level, prejudice against migrant groups can be concealed by tokenism, a practice that restricts social mobility for the low-status migrant group by allowing only a small number of its members to access high-status positions in the new country (Wright, 2001; Wright & Boese, 2015). In a European context, this might be relevant for second or third generation migrant groups who may have been collectively denied the right to upward socioeconomic mobility (Heath, Rothon, & Kilpi, 2008). In contrast, in multicultural societies such as Canada and the USA, efforts have been made to "correct" such collective disadvantage through "positive action" policies that encourage more members of culturally disadvantaged groups to access employment or education (Chryssochoou, 2004).

EXPLANATIONS OF PREJUDICE

Possible explanations of prejudice have been sought within (a) the characteristics of individuals, (b) realistic intergroup conflict, and (c) symbolic identity threats experienced by members of the majority group. Individuals with traits such as right-wing authoritarianism (Altemeyer, 1998), or social dominance orientation (Pratto, Sidanius, Stallworth, & Malle, 1994), have been found to value conformity and moral values. They also tend to legitimize hierarchical relations, which provide a basis for the expression of negative attitudes toward migrants.

Individual characteristics notwithstanding, identity, ideological, and structural factors are also important in order to understand prejudice. At the heart of prejudice toward immigrants lies the notion of threat, which has both a material and symbolic aspect (Stephan, Renfro, Esses, Stephan, & Martin, 2005). Realistic conflict theory (Sherif, 1966) posits that competition over limited resources leads to **ethnocentrism** and intergroup conflict. Prejudice arises when migrants are viewed as competing with the majority for limited resources (e.g., jobs or housing), that is, when one group gains, the other loses (Esses, Jackson, & Armstrong, 1998).

Social identity theory (Tajfel & Turner, 1986), on the other hand, focuses more on the symbolic motives to protect the ingroup's positive social identity. Positive identity is achieved through intergroup comparisons, and in this regard, prejudice would be the result of an attempt by members of the majority group to maintain positive distinctiveness. Identity threats are particularly relevant where migrant groups hold religious and cultural practices that are seen as "mutually exclusive" by the majority group, for example Muslim minorities in Europe (Chryssochoou & Lyons, 2011; Fleischmann, Phalet, & Swyngedouw, 2013). This is especially true when an ethnic definition of national identity based on the idea of a shared tradition, ancestry, and culture prevails (Green, Sarrasin, & Fasel, 2015). Indeed, an endorsement of an *ethnic* (rather than civic) definition of "the nation" along with a strong identification with national identity, have been associated with anti-immigrant prejudice (Licata, Sanchez-Mazas, & Green, 2011).

In recent years, social psychology has paid closer attention to the structural factors that promote prejudiced attitudes toward migrants, including state policies and media representations. Following recent international attacks, Muslim minorities, in particular, have been targeted by the media through "threat representations," which have led to restrictive **acculturation** expectations among members of the majority group (Phalet, Baysu, & Van Acker, 2015). Societal factors (historical, societal, and political developments) represented in the media, can influence psychological factors (e.g., realistic and symbolic threat, national ingroup identification), which can lead to the rejection of migrants (Wagner, Christ, & Heitmeyer, 2010). Indeed, political discourse in the media gives rise to different perceptions of the social system, which divide people into dominant or non-dominant categories (Staerklé, Clémence, & Spini, 2011). Thus, there is close interplay between individual prejudice and societal practices toward migrant groups. Perceptions of migrants are closely linked both to policies toward migration, and attitudes toward these policies. For example, where multiculturalism is promoted through prodiversity policies, prejudice toward migrant groups is reduced (Guimond et al., 2013).

INDIVIDUAL AND COLLECTIVE REACTIONS TO PREJUDICE

Perceived discrimination may have serious implications for both individual psychological well-being and collective identification and action. International data show that having immigrant status impacts on psychological well-being and adjustment (Motti-Stefanidi et al., 2008; Liebkind & Jasinskaja-Lahti, 2000). Migrant groups often experience stigmatization and stereotype threat. For example, research in the US has shown that negative stereotypes of "low academic ability" have had a debilitating effect on the academic performance of African American students (Steele, Spencer, & Aronson, 2002).

In view of their threatened identity and material disadvantage, migrant groups may engage in collective action to improve their circumstances. However, a collective strategy of action may only be chosen when the boundaries of the majority group are considered impermeable and illegitimate and when status differences are seen as unstable. Otherwise, deep-rooted meritocratic beliefs, as well as tokenist practices, may lead migrant groups to choose "exit" strategies, that is, a move toward individual mobility (Tajfel & Turner, 1986).

REDUCING PREJUDICE?
THE CONTACT HYPOTHESIS

The classic "intergroup contact" hypothesis proposes that prejudice is based on ignorance, and that it can be reduced through intergroup contact when certain conditions are fulfilled. These conditions include regularity, the closeness, and cooperative nature of contact, equal group status, and institutional support (Allport, 1954). More recent research has pointed out that positive intergroup contact should involve decategorization (seeing the migrant as an individual) recategorization (seeing the migrant as member of a shared superordinate group, or as a member of a crossed-category group), that is, being a member of the ingroup on one dimension and a member of the outgroup on another (Deschamps & Doise, 1978; Hewstone & Swart, 2011).

The contact hypothesis has been criticized on several grounds, such as its utopian perspective regarding intergroup relations, as well as its theoretical individualism, that is, its neglect of the structural and institutionalized bases of prejudice (Dixon, Durrheim, & Tredoux, 2005). Prejudice occurs in unequal intergroup conditions where the dominant group is advantaged both on a material and symbolic level; thus, the content of a superordinate, national identity imposed upon migrant groups reflects the values and practices of the dominant group, and defines those who deserve resources (Chryssochoou, 2004). A common, superordinate identity, however, may not fit the interests of disadvantaged migrant groups. Recent research points out that "dual identity" strategies may not benefit ethnic minority students under conditions of discrimination whereby they are denied the right to be viewed as fellow citizens by the national group (Baysu, Phalet, & Brown, 2011), and when the two identities are viewed as incompatible, migrant or other ethnic groups may resort to political radicalization (Simon, Reichert, & Grabow, 2013).

Dixon, Levine, Reicher, and Durrheim (2012) question the model of prejudice reduction altogether, in the sense that it might have the effect of perpetuating unequal group relations. While the goal of stereotype reduction is to reduce individual discrimination and intergroup conflict, an alternative model of collective action aims to empower migrant groups to change the status quo. However, in the US, positive contact with white, majority students (prejudice reduction) *reduced* support for collective action toward racial equality among African and Latino Americans (Wright & Lubensky, 2009), and a study of Arab and Jewish Israelis showed that intergroup friendship *reduced* a perception of inequality and engagement for social change (Saguy, Tausch, Dovidio, & Pratto, 2009). Therefore, as long as superordinate identities are defined by a powerful national majority, prejudice reduction strategies appear to discourage collective action, which might lead immigrant groups to accept and justify the system (Jost & Major, 2001).

On the other hand, positive intergroup contact may lead members of the majority group to show more willingness to support social change through policies for equality (Pettigrew, 2010). As shown by these recent approaches, issues of power and unequal group status are central to understanding prejudice. The content of core group beliefs about ingroup identity, what constitutes "cultural difference" and what resources immigrant groups deserve may be subject to elite political and media discourse, and these will likely shape representations of identity, difference, and legitimacy. Rather than being the source of the problem, prejudice could simply be the *outcome* of a failed attempt to incorporate minorities within the host society. The question is: what is expected from migrants and ethnic minorities for them to be successfully incorporated into the new environment? This issue was studied through the concept of acculturation.

CHANGING SOCIETIES: THE ISSUE OF ACCULTURATION

According to Redfield, Linton, and Herskovits (1936) acculturation concerns all the phenomena resulting from continuous and sustained contact between individuals and groups from different cultures. Special emphasis is placed on the idea that change concerns both groups and that there is a mutuality of influence (Horenczyk, Jasinskaja-Lahti, Sam, & Vedder, 2013; Sam, 2015). Thus, acculturative processes are considered to be intergroup phenomena (Bourhis, Moise, Perreault, & Senecal, 1997; Brown & Zagefka, 2011). This differentiates acculturation from **adaptation**, which implies a one-way process of influence and a concrete reality to which people have to adapt (Chryssochoou, 2004). Although a mutual influence between the different groups is assumed, power differences at different levels (i.e., economic, political, social, numeric, etc.) mean that one group is in a better position to influence the situation. Thus, most of the time, this involves relations where one group dominates the other (Bourhis et al., 1997). The extensive research carried out on "contact" as a means of improving intergroup relations shows that it is a vital element of the acculturation process. Issues of power, status, similarity, and compatibility of values, norms, and attitudes as well as the emotional consequences of contact are all important determinants of acculturation outcomes.

Berry and his associates (Berry, 1976, 1990, 1997, 2006; Berry, Phinney, Sam, & Vedder, 2006; Sommerland & Berry, 1970) have developed a theoretical framework that has informed acculturation research. According to this framework, two dimensions of acculturation should be taken into account: the degree to which people wish to maintain their heritage cultures and identities (a desire for culture maintenance) and the degree to which people wish to participate in the receiving society and interact with its members (a desire for contact). Whereas there is general consensus as far as the first dimension is concerned, the second dimension has been conceptualized and operationalized in different ways. For example, Bourhis et al. (1997) proposed that the second dimension should be "culture adoption," which should reflect the attitudes toward the cultural practices of the out-group. Others have suggested that acculturation should be conceptualized as a matter of identification and not in terms of behavioral intentions and practices. They therefore suggest that two dimensions shape the acculturation process: identification with the heritage culture and identification with the majority culture (Benet-Martinez & Haritatos, 2005; Nguyen & Benet-Martinez, 2007, 2010; Phinney, Horenczyk, Liebkind, & Vedder, 2001). However, the use of these different conceptions, although valid, does not produce significant differences when applied in research (Brown & Zagefka, 2011).

A preference for the two dimensions leads to four different acculturation strategies: integration, assimilation, separation, and marginalization.

- An integration strategy is where there is an interest in maintaining one's original cultural identity while placing high value on daily interactions with other groups.

- An assimilation strategy refers to a lack of interest in maintaining one's original cultural identity, a desire to seek close interaction with other cultures and, in some cases, an interest in adopting the cultural values, norms, and traditions of the new society.

- A separation strategy places high value on holding onto one's cultural identity and original culture while avoiding interaction with members of the new society.

- A marginalization strategy characterizes situations where there is little interest in cultural maintenance or having relations with others.

These preferences, however, are not static. The strategy adopted reflects the societal climate or the domain of social life (Berry et al., 2006). They also apply to both minority and majority group members. Members of the receiving society form their own acculturation preferences for minority groups (Bourhis et al., 1997; Sam & Berry, 2006). Moreover, there is evidence that integrationist attitudes may be endorsed only for certain, positively evaluated, migrant groups. Assimilationist ideologies, on the other hand, may be preferred for negatively evaluated out-groups (Montreuil & Bourhis, 2001). In any case, the strategy of the majority group may not correspond or fit with the strategy that minority group members wish or endorse.

Other researchers have proposed extensions and changes to the model. The Interactive Acculturation Model (Bourhis et al., 1997) includes the acculturation expectations of members of the receiving society toward specific migrant groups. The model also includes individualism as an alternative strategy to marginalization. This denotes an orientation that stresses personal characteristics rather than group membership in both migrant and majority group acculturation orientations. The Concordance Model of Acculturation (Piontkowski, Rohmann, & Florack, 2002) emphasizes the discrepancies between the acculturation strategies that minority and majority group members are perceived to hold and suggests that the fit between the two preferences, rather than the preferences of each group in isolation, is the best predictor of intergroup attitudes. The model suggests that dominant group members have more control in the acculturation process since they have more power to determine or impose their expectations on migrant groups. According to the model, the two dimensions of acculturation should be considered separately and there is some disagreement over whether the "maintenance of one's own culture" has the strongest influence in intergroup relations (Florack & Piontkowski, 2000).

The Relative Acculturation Extended Model (Navas et al., 2005; Navas, Rojas, Garcia, & Pumares, 2007) distinguishes between real and ideal acculturation. Real acculturation refers to the actual acculturation options that immigrants have put into practice and the strategies that members of the national majority attribute to the immigrants. The ideal acculturation refers to the options that immigrants would like to adopt and those that the majority members would prefer for them. The model also distinguishes between different domains of acculturation (political, economic, work, social, family, religious, and way of life). It has to be noted, however, that at times when majorities talk about integration, they confuse it with assimilation (Bowskill, Lyons, & Coyle, 2007), which sends mixed messages to immigrants.

Acculturation is a process with outcomes at different levels (individual, group, intergroup, and societal). Early research has focused primarily on individual changes of minority group members. At the level of the individual, Ward (2001) proposes an organization into three areas: affective, behavioral, and cognitive, widely recognized as the ABC of acculturation (see also Sam (2015) for a summary of these outcomes). As children and young people from immigrant families in western societies grow up, it becomes apparent that research needs to focus on developmental issues since they simultaneously undergo acculturation and development (Mansten, Liebkind, & Hernandez, 2012). Issues that are relevant here include cultural identity, the development of self, family values, peer relations, school achievements, and civic participation (Motti-Stefanidi, Berry, Chryssochoou, Sam, & Phinney, 2012).

CHANGING INDIVIDUALS: THE ISSUE OF ADAPTATION

Acculturation is closely linked to the question of immigrant adaptation and their incorporation in the new society. Adaptation refers to both individuals and groups and it does not imply a necessary fit. On the contrary, it may involve resistance, an attempt to change the environment or movement away altogether. Adaptation is expected to have both psychological and sociocultural aspects (Berry, 2006; Ward, 2001).

Indicators of successful adaptation at a psychological level are: the absence of psychological problems (e.g., depression or anxiety), high self-esteem, or satisfaction with life. At the sociocultural level, adaptation is related to individual competence: the ability to function in new social and cultural contexts, for example, school, work, and within the wider society. There are mixed results concerning their ability to adapt when compared with members of the majority. Some acculturating groups seem to do better in comparison with their national peers (Berry et al., 2006) whereas other studies have found poor adaptation outcomes (Young, Fang, & Zisook, 2010). In some instances, there is an immigration paradox (Garcia et al., 2012), where immigrants show better adaptation outcomes than their national peers, or where first generation immigrants show a greater ability to adapt than their second-generation peers.

Some research has considered whether certain acculturation strategies result in better adaptation. The most common finding is that an integration strategy is the most adaptive both psychologically and socioculturally—it is also the one most valued by immigrants (Berry et al., 2006). On the other hand, marginalization involves a lack of support from both groups, so it is more likely to produce less positive adaptation outcomes. There is, however, a lack of coherent theory to explain a positive relationship between integration and adaptation. In addition, Brown and Zagefka (2011) point out that the correlations between integration and adaptation are not always strong, which suggests the influence of moderating factors. Berry (1997, 2006) also maintains that acculturation strategies adopted by minorities depend on the societal context in which these strategies are being pursued.

When immigrants experience a high level of discrimination, they are more likely to prefer a separation strategy. Discrimination not only influences acculturation strategies, it is also a powerful predictor of poor psychological and sociocultural adaptation (Berry et al., 2006). A longitudinal study in British schools (Nigbur et al., 2008) tested acculturation attitudes of children belonging to majority and ethnic minority groups at three points in time and found that integration was the preferred strategy of all children. What is more, minority members endorsed this strategy more as they grew older.

This orientation was linked to greater social competence and peer acceptance but also to increasing emotional problems at a later time. Similar results were found by Brown et al. (2013).

Acculturation strategies, adaptive outcomes, and discrimination are closely linked. Integration may be preferred as the best acculturation strategy for minority group members, but only when perceived discrimination is low. Moreover, in a context where multiculturalism is valued, "integration" may be the most socially desirable response for both migrants and the national majority. What happens though when there are asymmetric intergroup relations? What then are the consequences of integration?

CALLING FOR A NEW SOCIAL ORGANIZATION: THE PARADOX OF INTEGRATION

Immigration changes the nature of representations within receiving societies because of the need to accommodate newcomers and their diverse cultures. Nonetheless, social organizations such as European nation states have produced cohesive societies based on a common national identity. These societies, while endorsing the coexistence of different social classes, have sought to avoid class conflict that would undermine the social structure. In a class-based society, individuals are allocated resources on the basis of their citizenship, but these resources are never intended to be distributed equally. According to the meritocratic ideology of modern liberal societies, people are rewarded for their contributions and achievements. Therefore, those on the lower social strata can expect to be socially mobile once they meet the criteria for higher status memberships, which is usually through educational attainment. However, while the opportunity to progress appears open to everyone, relatively few in the low-status group will succeed. The success of the few, nonetheless, serves as a token to confirm the belief that boundaries between social groups are open (Wright, 2001; Wright & Boese, 2015). This alone encourages individuals to strive to improve their condition, and thus class conflicts are avoided. But what happens in the case of immigrants?

Newcomers start at the bottom strata occupying low paid jobs and often working in poor conditions. Do they have the same opportunity for social mobility given that their advancement might threaten members of the majority population who also occupy low positions and who also wish to improve their situation? Either way, the ruling classes benefit from the low pay and poor working conditions of migrants and nationals alike, and so they have every reason to keep this competition alive. For migrant groups, however, a hierarchy based on cultural membership can further restrict their mobility. When someone is designated as a cultural "other," they do not have the cultural assets to succeed (Chryssochoou, 2016) and they may be perceived as having inherent and immutable features that prevent them from becoming members of higher status groups (e.g., class or nation) (Yzerbyt, Rocher, & Schadron, 1997). Indeed, **essentialist beliefs** about people have been found to correlate with a rejection of multiculturalism (Verkuyten & Brug, 2004). Such beliefs also amplify the relationship between national identification and anti-immigrant sentiment (Pehrson, Brown, & Zagefka, 2009; Staerklé, Sidanius, Green, & Molina, 2010).

Members of the majority group with low socioeconomic status may, however, readily accept and endorse the representation of cultural hierarchies because it offers them the possibility of being considered better than immigrants. This representation also helps them to maintain a belief that individual mobility is largely restricted to nationals, which works against any notion of solidarity with migrants—a development that might threaten the position of the ruling classes.

This hierarchical representation, fortified by arguments about "a clash of civilizations" (Huntington, 1996), often impedes the success of second-generation immigrants born and raised in the receiving society. They expect to benefit from the same social mobility as their peers, but their progress is hindered by a cultural hierarchy that keeps them in the same social position as their parents. In the main, these are people for whom the integration strategy was proposed, giving them the opportunity to keep contact with their culture of origin and the new society. However, the two identities may be seen as "incompatible," which not only obstructs their full participation in the new society (Chryssochoou & Lyons, 2011), but also prevents them from becoming legitimate recipients when resources are required.

What is more, dual identity for second-generation migrants may be no asset since it reminds them and others that they belong to a low-status group. Baysu et al. (2011) showed that Turkish-Belgian children with separated or assimilated identity strategies were less likely to disengage from school and had better performance when perceived identity threat was high. Those with dual identity, however, were more successful when perceived threat to identity was low. Indeed, multicultural education only has positive effects when it is linked to the establishment of antiracist norms within the classroom (Verkuyten & Thijs, 2013). This is the paradox of integration: although the policy respects and recognizes the right to claim one's culture of origin, at the same time, in conditions where asymmetric intergroup relations persist, it may hinder the progress of those who claim dual identity (Chryssochoou, 2015).

Would this hegemonic representation where one group dominates the other help to maintain cohesion in culturally diverse societies? Recent attacks in western societies performed by people who are citizens born and raised in that country provide evidence to the contrary. Instead of feeling that they belong to the society into which they were born, young Muslims facing widespread prejudice and discrimination (Heath et al., 2008), may develop a strong sense of belonging to an alternative **supraordinate identity**; one that is also subject to discrimination, and one that they therefore wish to defend. Such individuals who lay claim to an alternative identity are often educated and could have pursued their own social mobility, but perhaps for the third generation, the mask has finally fallen. They have understood that individual mobility is restricted because of their origins (Chryssochoou, 2009).

In times of economic crisis, mobility is also restricted for nationals who may feel particularly threatened by the presence of those whom they consider to be non-legitimate claimants. And instead of calling into question the inequalities of the system, many remain attached to the representation of cultural hierarchies, which is further endorsed by the "threat of terrorism." In these conditions, the more minority members value maintaining their own culture, the more the majority group feels threatened and the less they endorse multiculturalism (Matera, Stefanile, & Brown, 2011; Tip et al., 2012; Zagefka, Tip, Gonzalez, Brown, & Cinnirella, 2012).

What should we conclude? Should we agree with political leaders who claim that multiculturalism has failed?[1] Their claim could also be seen as a failure to convince others that a new social order could be constructed on the basis of cultural difference. It is perhaps not that multiculturalism has failed, but that societies have not improved the situation of their most disadvantaged members. As Berry and Sam (2013) observe, multiculturalism is not only about recognition, respect, and celebration of difference, it also represents social equality.

In times of economic crisis, where the means to support those in need through the welfare system are significantly reduced, the insecurity increases. Political elites are responsible for sustaining this cultural representation of the social order (Chryssochoou, 2016). Indeed, the widespread insecurity produced by the economic instability, political violence, wars, and the large numbers of refugees they produce, erode public trust in political elites and feeds populist discourse that claims to uphold security through violence or social exclusion. In these difficult times, migration will likely increase and societies will need to summon considerable resolve to counter political discourse that seeks to undermine democratic values and human rights.

---

[1] https://www.theguardian.com/world/2010/oct/17/angela-merkel-german-multiculturalism-failed
http://www.bbc.co.uk/news/uk-politics-12371994.

SUMMARY

- Migration is not a new phenomenon and relations between migrant groups and receiving communities vary considerably.

- Migration changes the nature of society because both migrant and receiving communities groups engage in an acculturation process. Social psychologists have developed different approaches to acculturation strategies.

- Migration reconfigures (even threatens) existing identities for migrant groups and receiving communities.

- Migration affects social stratification. Because migrants usually find employment in lower social positions, this allows members of the receiving community to move upwards.

- Migration can transform socioeconomic issues of class into issues of ethnicity, which changes the nature of conflict in society.

- Prejudice and discrimination affects the adaptation of migrant groups. Reducing prejudice and discrimination requires social and societal strategies.

- The ruling classes that benefit economically from migration have every reason to maintain competition between migrants and low-status social groups.

- A strategy of integration can have a paradoxical effect. An ideology about a hierarchy of cultures may impede the success of second-generation migrants by creating incompatibility between the identity of origin and national identity. In addition, it brings to the fore membership of a category with inferior social status.

GLOSSARY

acculturation refers to phenomena that result from direct and continuous contact between groups of individuals from different cultures, and the subsequent changes in the original culture patterns of either or both groups.

adaptation takes place when migrants adjust psychologically to the new sociocultural environment and then participate in it.

essentialist beliefs are based on the classical Aristotelian view that every concept has a set of necessary "essential" features. Psychological essentialism is the lay belief that categories, for example, Caucasian, French, Muslim, and so on, have essences. Moreover, people adopt their own implicit theories about categories and their necessary characteristics or essences. Such theories may concern religion, nationhood, race, or ethnicity.

ethnocentrism refers to a view of the world in which one's own group is the center of everything and that all others are judged with reference to it.

supraordinate identity refers to an overarching identity that embraces people with other affiliations, belongings, and origins. An example would be national identity, which includes people from different social, cultural, racial, ethnic, and regional origins. Another would be European identity, which encompasses people of different nations and religious identities.

FURTHER READING

Berry J. W., & Sam D. L. (2013). Accommodating cultural diversity and achieving equity: an introduction to psychological dimensions of multiculturalism. *European Psychologist, 18* (special issue), 151–157.

Chryssochoou X. (2004). *Cultural diversity: Its social psychology.* Oxford: Blackwell.

Chryssochoou X. (2016). Social justice in multicultural Europe: A social psychological perspective. In P. Hammack (Ed.), *The Oxford handbook of social psychology and social justice.* New York: Oxford University Press.

Mansten A. S., Liebkind K., & Hernandez D. J. (Eds.) (2012). *Realizing the potential of immigrant youth.* Cambridge, UK: Cambridge University Press.

QUESTIONS FOR GROUP DISCUSSION

- Discuss the following terms: foreigner, immigrant, migrant, economic migrant, asylum seeker, and refugee? What is implied about the individual in each of these cases? How are these terms used in (a) the media and (b) everyday conversation? Is there a term in your language to describe migrants that is both welcoming and inclusive?

- How does immigration pose a threat to communities? What are the perceived threats within migrant and receiving communities?

- In what way is the "societal context" of immigration to the United States different to immigration to European nation states?

- How may having a dual identity (origin and receiving society) become an obstacle to social mobility? How might the social and ideological context affect the outcome?

- Does seeing people primarily in terms of their ethnicity, race, or religion make us (and them) "blind" to issues of social class? To what extent could the tendency to see people in this way hide the real reasons for their disadvantaged state?

- What might be the consequences of such division for individuals belonging to these categories? How might this affect intergroup relations and social cohesion? Can you think of any current examples?

9 Political Decision-Making

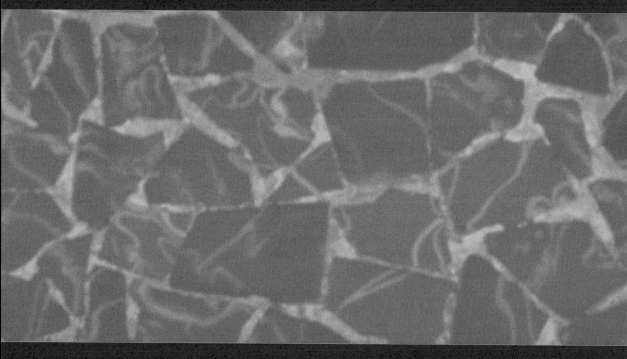

JACK S. LEVY

CHAPTER OUTLINE

How do political leaders make foreign policy decisions? What are the primary influences on those decisions? Do political leaders simply respond to threats and opportunities in the external environment in order to advance the national interests of the state? Or are they influenced by factors internal to the state? How important is public opinion? Do leaders formulate foreign policy with an eye on how that policy will affect his or her domestic political support? To what extent do internal bureaucratic interests and rivalries influence political leaders' decisions or the information upon which they base their decisions? How important is a state's political culture or national identity in shaping its foreign policy decisions? Finally, does it matter who those decision-makers are? How important are political leaders' belief systems, personalities, emotional make-up, political socialization, information-processing tendencies, leadership styles, willingness to take risks, time horizons, and other individual characteristics?

We can ask these questions about any political decision, but in this chapter we focus primarily on decision-making in foreign policy. Scholars generally agree that in most political systems, and certainly democratic political systems, political leaders have more freedom of action in the conduct of foreign policy—and especially in foreign policy dealing with national security issues—than in the conduct of domestic policy. For this reason, we should expect to find political psychology playing a greater role in decision-making on foreign policy than on domestic policy. We begin by putting our discussion of the psychology of foreign policy decision-making into the broader context of foreign policy analysis. We briefly summarize the **"levels-of-analysis framework,"** which is commonly used by international relations scholars to categorize the large number of different causal factors influencing the foreign policy decisions of states. Focusing on the individual level of analysis, we then turn to how leaders perceive the world and make their decisions. After outlining the "**rational actor**" **model of judgment and decision-making**, we turn to systematic deviations from rational decision-making. We examine common biases in the processing of information and departures from rational cost-benefit calculations in decision-making, with illustrations from historical examples.

Political Psychology: A Social Psychological Approach, First Edition.
Edited by Christopher J. Hewer and Evanthia Lyons.
© 2018 John Wiley & Sons Ltd. Published 2018 by John Wiley & Sons Ltd.

THE LEVELS-OF-ANALYSIS FRAMEWORK

The levels-of-analysis framework (Waltz, 1959) aimed to categorize different causes of war, but has subsequently been used as a general framework for categorizing the various causal factors influencing the making of state foreign policies. Scholars offer different conceptions of the number and nature of the levels, but the following characterization is fairly standard. The *system level* refers to the international system. It includes the "anarchic" structure of the international system (defined as the absence of a central authority to regulate disputes and enforce agreements); the number of major powers in the system and distribution of military and economic power among them; patterns of alliances; the structure of the global economy; and other factors common to the external environments of all states, including the nature of international institutions, international norms, and transnational ideologies or cultures.

The *nation-state level* of analysis includes causal variables internal to the state and associated with the government and with society—which leads some analysts to suggest distinct governmental and societal levels of analysis. The governmental level includes variables like regime type, reflecting the hypotheses that democracies behave differently compared to autocracies, and that parliamentary democracies and presidential democracies also behave in different ways. The governmental level also includes internal conflicts between rival bureaucratic agencies (interservice rivalries, for example) and the standard operating procedures of organizations. The societal level includes the structure of a state's economic system, the influence of private groups (economic, ethnic, environmental, etc.), the role of public opinion, and political culture, ideology, and religion.

The *individual level* of analysis consists of two sets of factors relating to elite decision-makers. One includes characteristics shared by all people, such as "human nature" and common tendencies and psychological biases. The second includes individual traits that vary across individuals. The latter include belief systems and world views, personalities, emotions, political socialization experiences, lessons learned from history, leadership style, patterns of information processing, gender differences, willingness to take risks, time horizons, and related variables.

The levels-of-analysis framework raises the key question of the relative causal impact of variables from different levels of analysis on foreign policy, and also on the interaction effects between variables at different levels. It is relevant for explaining particular historical outcomes and more general patterns of decision-making by most states at most times. The questions asked in the opening paragraph of this chapter were basically driven by an implicit levels-of-analysis framework. It is important to note that many prominent theories of international relations give relatively little causal weight to individual-level psychological variables. Individuals play no significant causal role in realist balance of power theory, which posits that state foreign policies and international outcomes are determined primarily by the distribution of power between states; in democratic peace theory, which posits that democracies rarely if ever go to war with each other; in Marxist–Leninist theories, which focus on the economic structure of capitalist states and the role of private economic interests; or in national-level theories that suggest that political leaders subordinate everything to the maximization of their ability to gain and maintain positions of political power. Each of these general theoretical arguments suggest that given the national, class, or individual political interests at stake, most political leaders basically behave the same way.

When we look at a number of specific historical events, however, it appears that political leaders played an important causal role. How could we explain Russian foreign (or domestic) policy in the early twenty-first century without giving attention to the beliefs and idiosyncrasies of Vladimir Putin, Soviet policy in the 1930s and 1940s without Joseph Stalin, the outbreak of the Second World War and the Holocaust without Adolf Hitler, or the communist revolution in China without Mao Zedong? Individual beliefs and psychology may have less of a causal impact in more decentralized democratic states, but they cannot be ignored. British policy in the 1930s probably would have been different had Winston Churchill rather than Neville Chamberlain been Prime Minister; and the United States probably would not have gone to war with Iraq in 2003 if George W. Bush had not been US President. Many individual-level arguments take this form: if another leader had been in power, the outcome would have been different.

It is not often easy to assess the causal weight of individual political leaders in a particular historical episode, much less make a more general theoretical evaluation of their role in most states at most times. If structural pressures from the environment or domestic political pressures are strong, then most leaders might very well make the same decision. When those pressures are weaker or uncertain, however, the belief systems, personalities, and biases of individual political leaders might make more of a difference. When there was uncertainty about Hitler's intentions in 1937 and 1938, the fact that Chamberlain was prime minister made a difference in the British foreign policy response. As the German threat became clear after the "Prague coup" of March 1939 and especially after the German invasion of Poland that September, any British leader probably would have decided to intervene to stop German military expansion, in which case we could not attribute much causal weight to individual leaders. During the July 1914 crisis, British Foreign Secretary Edward Grey wanted to give a clear warning to German leaders that Britain would intervene against Germany if it invaded France. The Cabinet and the public were divided, however, and Grey could not implement his preferred policy until after the war had started. This was consequential. Some argue that a timely warning from Britain would have deterred Germany, and the First World War might have been avoided (Fischer, 1967), though others dissent from this view (Copeland, 2014).

The fact that Grey was politically constrained from implementing his preferred policies in 1914 illustrates something else: psychological explanations of state foreign policies are logically incomplete. The impact of a leader's preferences, and of the beliefs and individual characteristics that generate those preferences are a function of the political context and decision-making process. As the social psychologist Herbert Kelman (1965, pp. 5–7) argued,

> ... it makes little sense to speak of *a* psychological theory of war or of international relations. There cannot be a psychological theory that is complete and self-contained .... There can only be a general theory of international relations in which psychological factors play a part.

This does not mean that individual-level factors are of secondary importance in any particular historical episode, only that it is necessary to include other factors to make the explanation complete.

With these preliminary conceptual considerations in place, we turn to more substantive theories of decision-making. Given that psychological models of decision-making are often viewed as deviations from a rational benchmark, we begin with the rational model of judgment and decision-making, which is regarded as a normative standard for good decision-making.

THE RATIONAL MODEL OF JUDGMENT AND DECISION-MAKING

Rationality is defined in different ways, but most social scientists conceive of rationality as instrumental rationality, in terms of means-ends calculations. Given an actor's goals, do they act to maximize those goals given existing constraints? Scholars disagree on exactly what a rational decision-making process looks like, but the following characterization is representative (March, 1994, Chapter 1; Levy & Thompson, 2010, pp. 130–133). If rationality involves maximization of goals given constraints, the first step is to identify one's goals. Actors usually have more than one goal, these goals often come into conflict, and actors often need to make tradeoffs between these goals (for example, between preserving the state's vital interests in a crisis while simultaneously avoiding a costly war). This requires that actors prioritize among their goals, so that they know how much of one to risk or sacrifice in order to achieve the other.

A second component of a rational decision-making process is to specify the set of available strategies (policies), or combination of strategies, to advance those goals. Integrally related is a third component, the estimation of the consequences of each of the alternatives, to enable decision-makers to weigh the costs and benefits of each strategy. This is a complex and difficult task, because the consequences of each strategy are shaped not only by one's own actions but also by the responses of the adversary, ones allies, and other actors. Those responses are highly uncertain, given the well-known difficulties of assessing the intentions of the adversary (Jervis, 1976). Thus the estimation of the consequences of one's actions has to be strategic and probabilistic— strategic in the sense that it incorporates the likely responses of others, and probabilistic in that it incorporates uncertainty.

The information to make these calculations with complete confidence is rarely available, even after an information search, which is another necessary sub-component of rational decision-making. Uncertainty is pervasive, especially in international relations, where there is no higher authority to enforce agreements and where states have incentives to conceal information and to bluff about their resolve. The existence of uncertainty, or incomplete information, does not preclude rationality, as there are more and less rational ways of responding to uncertainty. One key component of the rational evaluation of information involves learning—using information about another's past behavior to estimate its likely future behavior. We usually have some sense of what kind of actor the adversary is (hawk or dove, for example) and what his intentions probably are, and we can observe how an actor behaves. The question is how much weight to give to prior estimates ("priors") and how much weight to give to new information in the process of "updating" our beliefs about the adversary. The proper balance is specified by a mathematical formula developed by the statistician Thomas Bayes. **Bayesian updating** of one's beliefs based on this formula provides a model of rational learning, another key element of a rational decision process.

After decision-makers have defined their goals and prioritized among them, identified possible strategies for achieving those goals, assessed the consequences of each of those strategies, they need to reach a decision. Rational decision-making under conditions of uncertainty follows an **expected utility** decision rule. For each of their possible strategies, the decision-maker needs to assess the "expected utility" of that strategy, defined as the weighted sum of the utility (net benefits minus costs) of each possible outcome and its probability of occurrence. (There is also a risk component, but I leave that aside). The actor then selects the strategy with the greatest expected utility. It is important to note that rationality is linked to a particular actor or decision-maker. *What is rational for an individual decision-maker is not necessarily rational for her organization* *or state.* If a political leader puts her political interests of getting re-elected before the national interests of the state—and remember that rationality refers to the selection of a strategy to maximize one's goals, not to the goals themselves—then a foreign policy that maximizes the leader's domestic interests may be rational for the leader but not for the state. The "**diversionary theory of war**," for example, suggests that under some conditions a leader may go to war for the primary purpose of bolstering her domestic political support, even though the national interest might not call for war (Levy & Thompson, 2010). Many regard Argentina's 1982 invasion of the Falklands Islands, which led to war with Britain, as motivated by the diversionary ambitions of its political leaders. In the rest of this chapter we focus primarily on psychological models of departures from individual-level rationality.

PSYCHOLOGICAL MODELS OF INFORMATION PROCESSING

Psychological models of judgment and decision-making emerged in a response to dissatisfaction with the concept of a "rational economic man" who perceives the world accurately and who carefully makes the calculations necessary to maximize his utility. One of the most systematic critics of economic rationality was Herbert Simon, whose work won him a Nobel Prize in economics. Simon (1955) argued that *people are limited in their cognitive capacities to process information and attain full economic rationality in a complex and uncertain world.* People try to behave rationally and maximize their interests, but they do so with simplified mental representations of reality. Their behavior is best described as "**bounded rationality**." In an attempt to impose some degree of conceptual order on the world, people tend to adopt a number of **cognitive shortcuts or "heuristics."** These heuristics help people cope effectively with a wide variety of situations, but they also generate some significant cognitive distortions and departures from a value-maximizing rationality.

These mentioned biases in information processing are generally referred to as "cognitive biases," which are unconscious and "hardwired" into the brain. They exist independently of the human emotions and motivations, and for that reason are often described as "unmotivated." A different set of biases emerges from peoples' motivations and emotions. They are driven by an unconscious tendency to process information in a way that advances a goal or interest (state, organizational, or individual) or that fulfills emotional needs and desires, such as avoiding guilt and enhancing self-esteem (Janis & Mann, 1977; Kunda, 1990). Cognitive biases and motivated biases often lead to some of the same behavioral patterns, and are sometimes difficult to distinguish empirically. Moreover, psychologists have demonstrated that people cannot behave rationally in the absence of emotions altogether (Damasio, 1994). Nevertheless, it is still useful to analyze these biases separately. We first examine cognitive biases in information processing, and then turn to motivated biases. These biases can be quite consequential in a wide range of foreign policy judgments and decisions. By generating misperceptions of both the intentions and capabilities of adversaries, and of potential enemies and allies as well, they can contribute in important ways to unwanted wars and other negative foreign policy outcomes (Jervis, 1976; Levy, 1983).

COGNITIVE BIASES

One of the most basic cognitive biases is the tendency for preexisting cognitive mind sets or worldviews to have a disproportionate impact on the way people perceive the world. Although one could not make sense of the world and the enormous amount of information to which one is constantly exposed in the absence of some elemental world view, the problem is that those preconceptions tend to serve as cognitive blinders, leaving people more sensitive to some kinds of information rather than to other kinds of information. This cognitive tendency is reinforced by the human need for **cognitive consistency** among the different elements of a belief system. The result is the **selective attention** to information. Instead of giving equal weight to all information, people tend to focus on the information that is consistent with their prior beliefs, and to dismiss information deviating from their prior beliefs. They tend to see what they expect to see.

One consequence is the "**perseverance of beliefs**," past the point at which the evidence might dictate abandoning or modifying those beliefs. This pattern is reinforced by a tendency to engage in "**premature cognitive closure**." Instead of following the rational ideal of engaging in a complete search for information, people tend to stop their information search after their selective attention to information generates enough information to reinforce their existing views. These tendencies are nicely captured by a particular cognitive heuristic, the "**anchoring and adjustment**" heuristic, in which one's preexisting mind sets or "priors" serve as a cognitive anchor and in which updating is slow and inefficient (Tversky & Kahneman, 1974). Instead of engaging in rational Bayesian updating when processing information, people give their prior probability assessments too much weight and new information too little weight.

A good example of the impact of preexisting beliefs on the perception of threat in international relations is the Israeli intelligence failure that culminated in the 1973 Arab–Israeli War. Israeli intelligence analysts and political leaders had developed an implicit theory that predicted the conditions under which

Egypt and other Arab states might launch a war against Israel. This theory, known as the "Conception," predicted that a necessary condition for an Egypt attack was the ability of the Egyptian air force to acquire a capability for control of the air, which would enable deep strikes into Israel and permit destruction of Israeli air fields. Although Israeli intelligence observed high levels of Egyptian military activity prior to the war, the belief that Egypt had not achieved either control of the air or a capability for crossing the Suez Canal led Israeli analysts to interpret Egyptian military actions as routine military maneuvers. A leading interpretation of Israel's intelligence failure emphasizes the blinders imposed by the cognitive mind sets associated with the "Conception" (Agranat Commission, 1974).

Many analysts make a similar argument about the role of cognitive rigidity in the US failure to anticipate the September 11 2001 terrorist attacks. Although institutional factors such as poor coordination between different intelligence agencies played an important role, many analysts argue that the US intelligence failure was primarily a conceptual failure, driven by the cognitive straitjacket imposed by preexisting mindsets. As the National Commission on Terrorist Attacks Upon the United States (2004, p. 9) stated, "The most important failure was one of imagination."

In these cases of intelligence failure, intelligence officials and political leaders were insufficiently attentive to new information that might have alerted them to an impending attack. Under different conditions, the same selective attention to information can lead to the opposite perceptual error. In a longstanding rivalry between states, it is common for each to develop an image of the other as implacably hostile. If one side makes conciliatory gestures in an attempt to signal its willingness to de-escalate tensions and reach some cooperative agreement, the first reaction of the other is often to misinterpret or discount those conciliatory gestures because they are not consistent with their hardline image of the adversary. This does not mean that beliefs do not change in response to incoming information, only that beliefs change more slowly than warranted by the evidence.

If prior beliefs serve as a perceptual lens through which new information is perceived and evaluated, the question that naturally arises is what determines these prior beliefs. This is hard to answer, given the multiple sources of beliefs, beginning with political socialization, political culture, and other factors. In international relations, to some extent beliefs are induced by the nature of the international system. The combination of anarchy and a fundamental uncertainty about the intentions of others generates a tendency toward "worst-case analysis." This tendency is not universal, but it is common, especially among the leading states in most historical systems, including regional systems, though the European Union serves as a clear exception. The structurally induced tendency toward worst-case analysis is reinforced by a common psychological tendency emphasized by attribution theory (Kelley, 1967), which deals with the question of how people explain the behavior of others. The theory distinguishes between dispositional factors relating to the other's intentions or character, and situational factors relating to outside influences. (It is worth noting that this distinction parallels the levels-of-analysis framework described earlier.) There is overwhelming evidence that individuals tend to interpret others' behavior, particularly behavior that they regard as undesirable, as the result of dispositional factors rather than situational factors. If an adversary state adopts a hardline foreign policy, we tend to assume that the policy reflects the adversary's hostile intentions or evil nature, rather than interpreting it as a defensive response to a hostile environment or perhaps to our own threats. We explain away our own hardline policies, however, by arguing that we had no choice, given the threats that we face. The tendency to interpret others' behavior in dispositional terms is known as the "**fundamental attribution theorem**." The tendency to interpret our own behavior differently, in situational terms, is known as the "actor-observer discrepancy." The combination of the two contributes to the escalation of international conflicts. Each perceives that the other's behavior reflects hostile intentions, not defensive precautions. In addition, the fact that each sees its own actions as defensively motivated, and assumes that the adversary understands those motivations, further reinforces beliefs about the adversary's hostility. The assumption is that only someone with hostile intentions could respond aggressively when they know that we pose no threat. These tendencies increase the likelihood of mutually reinforcing negative feedback and of an escalating conflict spiral. Examples include the US–Soviet rivalry during the Cold War and the ongoing Israeli–Palestinian relationship.

Another source of political leaders' prior beliefs—both about the adversary's intentions and about causal relationships in international politics—is history, and more particularly the lessons political leaders learn from history. In part due to the absence of good theories that provide reliable predictions as to how the adversary is likely to behave and what the consequences of certain policies are likely to be, political leaders often rely on historical analogies or "lessons of the past." The "Munich analogy," and its assumed lesson that appeasement never works, has been extremely influential in US foreign policy for over a half century. It influenced US decision-making in the Korean War, the Vietnam War, and the 1990–1991 Persian Gulf War (Khong, 1992). A competing analogy, for the United States since the 1970s, is the "Vietnam analogy," which suggests that US interventions abroad entail a significant risk of ending in a quagmire.

The analogical reasoning upon which learning from history is based is related to another cognitive heuristic, the "availability" heuristic (Tversky & Kahneman, 1974). Evidence suggests that judgments of probability are disproportionately shaped by events that are *familiar*, *salient*, and that *come easily to mind*, not by more general patterns validated by statistical evidence. People have a tendency to learn from events that have a major impact on themselves or their country, that have occurred fairly recently, and that people observe firsthand and at a formative period in their lives. This suggests that, on average, US political leaders who experienced the Second World War directly (the first President Bush, for example) were likely to be influenced by the Munich analogy, while those who came to age during the Vietnam War (Bill Clinton, for example) were more likely to be influenced by the Vietnam analogy. Within these general tendencies, of course, are many individual variations.

The problem is that relying on such politically and personally salient events generates quite misleading lessons from history. Among other things, people tend to ignore the context within which those events occurred, and to draw universal lessons rather than conditional lessons. As Jervis (1976, p. 228) argued,

> People pay more attention to what has happened than to why it has happened. Thus learning is superficial, overgeneralized ... Lessons learned will be applied to a wide variety of situations without a careful effort to determine whether the cases are similar on crucial dimensions.

In addition, the most salient events do not necessarily provide the best predictor of the future, as implied by the saying that "generals are always fighting the last war." In the period leading up to 1914 generals developed offensive war plans, based in part on the lessons they learned from the last big war in Europe, the Franco–Prussian War of 1870–1871, which was a war of movement. They ignored the lessons of a distant war in Asia that concerned others, not themselves—the Russo-Japanese War of 1904–1905, which demonstrated the contribution of trenches and machine guns to the power of the defensive. The generals of 1914 got it wrong, as the expected war of movement in 1914 soon turned out to be static trench warfare, at least on the western front.

One also needs to be careful when interpreting behavior in which lessons from history are invoked. US President George H. W. Bush (with strong encouragement from British Prime Minister Margaret Thatcher) responded to the Iraqi invasion in 1990 by sending large numbers of American troops to Saudi Arabia, at first to contain Iraq and then to forcefully expel Iraqi troops from Kuwait. He explained his policy in part by arguing that the situation was just like Munich in 1938, and that it was necessary to confront aggressive dictators when they stepped over the line. Did this represent genuine learning from history, in which historical lessons causally influence current policy? Or did Bush invoke the Munich analogy to rationalize and justify a war that he had already decided was necessary on other grounds? In this rhetorical or strategic use of history, the causal arrow is reversed, with policy preferences influencing the selection of historical lessons, not the other way around (Levy, 1994). It is worth noting that critics of American intervention in 1990–1991 invoked the Vietnam analogy about the dangers of getting sucked into a quagmire.

Did they really believe that the desert sands of the Middle East were like the jungles of Vietnam, or was the Vietnam analogy a convenient rationalization to support their opposition to the Bush Administration's policies?

MOTIVATED BIASES

In contrast to cognitive biases, which are hardwired into the way the brain works and which exist independently of emotions and interests, motivated biases are influenced by peoples' psychological needs, fears, guilt, and desires, and also by their interests or policy goals (Janis & Mann, 1977; Kunda, 1990). Information that runs contrary to peoples' goals makes them feel emotionally uncomfortable. This generates the same selective attention to information that is generated by cognitive biases, though the psychological mechanism is different. Instead of seeing what they expect to see based on their implicit theories of the world, people see what they *want* to see—information that provides a convenient rationalization for their underlying political interests and that minimizes their emotional discomfort. Motivated reasoning and the resulting wishful thinking is particularly likely to emerge in decisions that involve high stakes and important value tradeoffs. Rather than recognize that two prized values are in conflict in a particular situation, people tend to deny the need to make tradeoffs between values (George, 1980). The emotional stress present in acute international crises, in which circumstances present substantial threats to vital national interests and which create difficult life and death decisions, also cloud the judgments of political leaders (Holsti & George, 1975).

It is important to emphasize that one consequence of motivated reasoning is that people's assessments of the desirability of various outcomes unconsciously influence their perceptions of the probabilities of those outcomes. They perceive desirable outcomes as more likely to occur and undesirable outcomes as less likely, relative to an objective assessment based on the evidence. If the success of a particular strategy is seen as necessary for highly valued goals to be attained, wishful thinking can lead to an exaggeration of the probability of success of that strategy. This tendency for the desirability of outcomes to influence the subjective probabilities people attach to those outcomes directly violates a fundamental assumption of rational decision theory—that assessments of the probability of an outcome are independent of the utility of that outcome.

In retrospect, we know that British Prime Minister Neville Chamberlain and many of his key advisors significantly underestimated the hostile intentions of German Chancellor Adolf Hitler. A standard interpretation of Chamberlain's judgments about Hitler holds that Chamberlain engaged in wishful thinking. He unconsciously allowed his abhorrence of war and fear of the devastating consequences of war—influenced in part by his images of the horrors of the First World War—to distort his judgment of the likelihood that appeasement would work to satisfy Hitler and avoid a Second World War. Chamberlain's motivated reasoning reinforced his existing policy preferences and distorted British policy. This argument is criticized by some, who argue that Chamberlain was well aware of the risks of war but concluded that he had no choice. Given temporary German military advantages and the expected reversal of the balance of power within a few years, Chamberlain pursued appeasement as a strategy for buying time until Britain was militarily capable of confronting Nazi Germany (Ripsman & Levy, 2008).

Motivated biases, just like cognitive biases, can have the opposite effect on perceptions of adversary intentions, and induce leaders to exaggerate external threats (Stein, 2013). Consider the 2003 Iraq War. Both US President George W. Bush and British Prime Minister Tony Blair defended their policy of an invasion of Iraq by emphasizing the dangers posed by Iraq's nuclear weapons program. We know in retrospect that the Iraqi nuclear program had been discontinued several years before. How do we explain the misguided assumption of an ongoing Iraqi WMD (Weapons of Mass Destruction) program? Part of the explanation derives from the inherent uncertainty of international politics, along with the deliberate strategic deception of Iraqi President Saddam Hussein. In order to deter Iranian adventurism, and concerned about leaks of information, Saddam deceived even his own generals into believing that Iraq had a nuclear weapons program.

In addition to this strategic deception argument, scholars have offered psychological explanations for the erroneous American assumption that Iraq had an ongoing nuclear weapons program. One interpretation focuses on the cognitive biases of US intelligence analysts (Jervis, 2010, Chapter 3). It argues that evidence emerging after the 1990–1991 Iraq War demonstrating that Iraq had been much closer to achieving a nuclear capability than US intelligence had anticipated led analysts to lean over backward not to make the same mistake again. As a result, they were predisposed to make the opposite erroneous judgment. Another interpretation focuses on motivated rather than cognitive biases. It suggests that after the September 11 terrorist attacks on the United States, US President George W. Bush wanted to go to war with Iraq. The existence of an Iraqi nuclear weapons program would make it easier to justify the war, both to himself and to the American public and for foreign audiences as well. Given these goals, unconscious motivated reasoning led him to assume the existence of that program, to facilitate his policy objectives.

Closely related to the motivated bias explanation are two others, each of which is fundamentally rationalist in orientation. One is that Bush understood that Iraq did not have a nuclear program but deliberately deceived the American public by invoking that program. A related argument is that in addition, the Bush White House put pressure on US intelligence agencies to produce intelligence that would support his argument about an Iraqi nuclear capability. That is, the **"politicization of intelligence"** was designed in order to help win public support for the war that the president wanted (Rovner, 2011). Each of these scenarios deviates from a rational state actor model, in which the best intelligence available shapes policy. Here, the causal arrow is reversed, with policy shaping intelligence, either through the psychological mechanism of motivated biases, or through the political mechanism of the politicization of intelligence.

PSYCHOLOGICAL MODELS OF CHOICE

The last section focused on psychological sources of errors in judgment. These errors distort the information that serves as key parameters entering into the calculations of decision-makers when they make choices in foreign policy and other issue areas. Even in the absence of such distortions, however, decision-making can deviate from the normative ideal for a rational decision-making process. As noted earlier, that ideal is defined by the expected utility decision rule, in which an actor selects the strategy with the highest expected utility, where the sum of the utility of each possible outcome is weighted by its expected probability.

One way in which decision-making sometimes departs from the rational ideal was emphasized by Simon (1957) in his early critique of rational choice models. Simon argued that people do not actually go through the complex and time-consuming calculations required by the expected utility rule. Instead of considering all possible options and selecting the one that maximized their expected utility, they implicitly adopt a simpler decision rule. They define a "target" or "aspiration" level of value that must be satisfied. They then examine alternative strategies or options sequentially, beginning with relatively simple ones, and estimate if each option is likely to generate consequences that exceed their aspiration level. If it does not, they move on to the next option. When they reach an option that satisfies their aspiration level, they end their search and select that option. They are willing to accept the first option that is good enough, as defined by their aspiration level, rather than to extend their consideration of additional options in an attempt to maximize their expected utility. This is known as a **satisficing decision rule**.

The concept of a target level has been incorporated into the **"poliheuristic" theory of decision-making** (Mintz, 2004). The theory is based on a two-stage decision-making process. First, the decision-maker eliminates all strategies that are expected to lead to unacceptable outcomes on a particular dimension, as defined by the target level. In the next stage the decision-maker picks the strategy with the highest expected utility. In decision-making in foreign policy, the key dimension is domestic support for the leader. The argument is that political leaders reject any foreign policy strategy that might significantly undermine their domestic political support. This is quite plausible. Note that in contrast to expected utility theory, in which an outcome that is highly beneficial for one policy dimension (military security, for example) can compensate for a bad outcome on another dimension (domestic support, for example), in poliheuristic theory no amount of benefits on another dimension can compensate for sub-target-level outcomes along the critical domestic political dimension. For this reasons, poliheuristic theory is a "noncompensatory" theory of decision-making.

During the last half century or so, social psychologists have identified a number of other ways in which individual decision-making deviates from the predictions of expected utility theory. Many of these have been incorporated into **prospect theory** (Kahneman & Tversky, 1979), which is now regarded as the leading alternative to expected utility as a theory of choice under conditions of risk (where the probabilities of various options are known).

PROSPECT THEORY

The influence of prospect theory has extended beyond its origins in social psychology to many social science disciplines, including **behavioral economics,** behavioral finance, cognitive science, and consumer economics. In political science, prospect theory has been particularly influential in international relations (Levy, 1997; McDermott, 1998). In this section, I summarize the theory and the behavioral patterns on which it is based, and suggest some of its implications for foreign policy and international relations.

The most fundamental assumption of prospect theory is that people define value in terms of *changes in assets*, not in terms of net assets or wealth. The theory posits that people *frame* choice problems around a *reference point*, which is absent in expected utility theory, which focuses on net assets. The reference point is important because losses and gains from the reference point are not treated symmetrically. First, people overweight losses relative to comparable gains, a tendency known as **loss aversion**. For that reason they rarely accept symmetric gambles involving a 50% probability of winning x and a 50% probability of losing x, because losing x brings more pain than gaining x brings pleasure. As the former tennis player Jimmy Connors once said, "I hate to lose more than I like to win."

A second aspect of asymmetry is that people overvalue the things they have relative to the things they do not have, which is known as the **endowment effect**. After people acquire an item, they hesitate to sell it for anything close to the price they paid for it. That is the disutility of giving up a possession exceeds the utility of acquiring it. Acquiring something and then losing it does necessarily leave you back where you started. As Daryl Hannah's character in the movie *Wall Street* said, "… when you've had money and lost it, it's much worse than never having had it at all."

A third dimension of asymmetry with respect to the reference point is that people respond differently to risk in the "domain of losses" than they do in the "domain of gains." If people are faced with choices among gambles that lead to positive outcomes (relative to their reference point), they tend to be risk averse, or cautious. When they are faced with choices among gambles that lead to negative outcomes, they tend to take more risks. In one experimental choice problem, subjects given a choice between a $40 gain for certain and a 50/50 chance of getting nothing or $100 generally chose the sure thing of $40. However, given a choice between a certain $40 loss and a 50/50 chance of no losses and a $100 loss, most subjects prefer the gamble. Note that in each of these scenarios, subjects chose the option with the lower expected value, violating expected utility theory. Losses, particularly "dead" (certain) losses, are so painful that people take substantial risks to avoid them, even at the risk of incurring greater losses.

With value being defined in terms of gains and losses relative to a reference point, the location of the reference point is critical. So is the process through which people identify their reference points, though this may not be a conscious process. In terms of traditional utility theory, it makes no difference whether the glass is half full or half empty. In terms of prospect theory, however, it can make a significant difference. Studies of people facing decisions over medical treatments respond differently if they are told that a particular treatment has a 90% survival rate than if they are told it has a 10% mortality rate. Depending on the precise values and probabilities, changing the reference point can induce a "preference reversal" and a change in choice, even if the two scenarios are mathematically equivalent.

In most applications of prospect theory within political science, scholars focus on the effects of reference points and framing on peoples' choices rather than on how people identify their reference points in the first place. In most situations, especially static situations, people adopt the status quo as their reference point, though social comparisons may also affect reference points. (If I get a salary increase, but everybody else gets a more substantial salary increase, do I treat this as a gain or a loss?) In more dynamic situations, however, when the status quo is changing, people often adopt the previous status quo or perhaps an expectation level or aspiration level as their reference point. There is substantial evidence, for example, that people "renormalize" their reference points after making gains faster than they do after incurring losses. This tendency helps to explain why people go to such lengths to recover "sunk costs." Whereas standard microeconomic theory suggests that people should move beyond losses and think on the margin, prospect theory predicts that people have trouble ignoring losses. Instead, they tend to be willing to take substantial risks to recover those losses.

The basic principles of prospect theory have some interesting and perhaps quite plausible implications for state foreign policies and international interactions.

Different risk orientations in the domains of gains and losses lead to the prediction that political leaders will take more risks to maintain their international positions, territory, and reputations against potential losses than they will to improve their positions. For the same reason, domestic publics punish political leaders more for incurring losses than they reward them for making gains. In dynamic situations involving power shifts, leaders of declining states tend to frame their reference point around their current position. They see inaction as leading to certain losses, and consequently engage in risky behavior, such as preventive war, in an attempt to avoid those losses and maintain their current position. They do so despite the realization that their policies might generate even greater losses. A good example here is the decision by Japan, faced with a conflict of strategic interests and an unwinnable economic competition with the United States, to gamble on a preventive attack against the United States at Pearl Harbor in 1941. In addition, losses can generate a multiplier effect, as gamblers often learn. The tendency not to renormalize reference points after suffering losses makes sunk costs important, generates greater risk-taking, and contributes to gradual entrapment in escalating conflicts (Brockner & Rubin, 1985). Good illustrations include France in Algeria, the United States in Vietnam, and the Soviet Union in Afghanistan (Taliaferro, 2004).

Prospect theory also makes a number of predictions about patterns of strategic interaction between states in the international system. It predicts that coerced territorial conquest is potentially destabilizing because the winner will quickly renormalize its reference point around its new acquisition and take disproportionate risks to defend the new status quo against subsequent losses. The loser will not renormalize its reference point after suffering losses, but instead engage in risky behavior in an attempt to recover its losses. The risky behavior by both sides increases the probability of a subsequent conflict. Another line of argument relates to deterrence. It is often said that it is easier to deter an adversary from engaging in aggressive behavior than it is to compel the adversary to stop doing what it is doing or undo what it has already done (Schelling, 1966). Prospect theory offers an explanation of this phenomenon based on the asymmetry of losses and gains, but at the same time introduces a modification: deterring someone from making gains is easier than either deterring it from recovering losses or compelling it to accept losses.

CONCLUSION

Social-psychological studies have generated substantial evidence that people depart from rational models of information processing and decision-making. Mainstream economists remain highly skeptical, but a small and growing group of economists has initiated a new academic field of "behavioral economics" (Thaler, 2015). They aim to validate (or not) hypothesized deviations from rational choice, and incorporate their findings into new mathematical models of decision-making that relax some of the more stringent assumptions of expected utility theory. An overlapping but more interdisciplinary field of "judgment and decision-making" also emerged (Gilovich & Griffin, 2010). This line of research has had a tremendous impact on political science and other fields (Redlawsk & Lau, 2013). Rational models still dominate the academic study of international relations, but a growing number of scholars have begun to recognize that a complete understanding of foreign policy decision-making and international interactions requires incorporating common biases in information processing and distortions in cost-benefit calculations into their theories and historical interpretations.

SUMMARY

- In analyzing the foreign policy decision-making process of states, it is useful to distinguish among causal factors at the international system, nation-state, and individual levels.

- Social-psychological studies have generated substantial evidence to show that people depart from rational models of information processing and decision-making.

- Rational decision-making entails an analysis of competing goals, strategies to achieve those goals and the cost/benefits of each strategy.

- Cognitive biases such as selective attention, the perseverance of beliefs and premature cognitive closure can distort judgment.

- Motivated biases arising from interests, needs, fears, and desires may also distort the way people process information and make decisions.

- Prospect theory emphasizes that people give more weight to possible losses that to possible gains in their decision-making calculations, and that they often adopt highly risky policies in an attempt to avoid certain losses.

GLOSSARY

anchoring and adjustment is a heuristic or judgmental short-cut for intuitively assessing probabilities. People start with a familiar starting point (anchor) and then adjust or update their estimates and new information.

Bayesian updating reflects a rational model of belief updating involving an optimal balance between "prior" estimates and new information.

behavioral economics explores hypothesized deviations from rational choice, and incorporates findings into mathematical models of decision-making that relax some of the more stringent assumptions of rational expected utility theory.

bounded rationality suggests that individuals cannot be fully rational because of their own cognitive limitations, the complexity of decision problems, the limited information at their disposal, and time constraints.

cognitive consistency refers to the tendency for people to strive for consistency in the different elements of their belief system, to avoid the psychological discomfort of holding contradictory beliefs.

cognitive heuristics are simple rules of thumb or shortcuts for assessing probabilities, making decisions, and solving problems, especially for complex problems for which there is incomplete information.

diversionary theory of war posits that political leaders sometimes resort to military force against an external adversary for the primary purpose of bolstering their domestic political support. They normally do this by creating a "rally 'round the flag" effect.

endowment effect refers to the psychological tendency for people to value what they have more than equivalent things they do not have.

expected utility is a statistical calculation. The expected utility of a strategy or option is the sum, over all possible outcomes, of the value or utility of that outcome weighted by its expected probability. Expected utility theory posits decision-makers select the option with the highest expected utility.

fundamental attribution theorem (traditionally known as the fundamental attribution error) refers to the tendency to attribute observable behavior to the disposition of the individual rather than to social circumstances.

judgment and decision-making is an interdisciplinary field of study focusing on descriptive and normative theories of how people form judgments and make decisions.

levels-of-analysis framework is used by many international relations theorists to classify the different causes of foreign policy behavior.

loss aversion is the common tendency to overvalue losses relative to comparable gains.

perseverance of beliefs is the tendency for people to cling to their beliefs even after a substantial amount of incoming information has contradicted those beliefs.

poliheuristic theory posits a two-stage process of decision-making. The decision-maker first eliminates all strategies that can lead to an unacceptable outcome on a particular highly valued dimension, and then selects from remaining strategies the one with the highest expected utility.

politicization of intelligence refers to the significant alteration of intelligence reports in response to pressure from higher political authorities for intelligence that supports their policies.

premature cognitive closure refers to the tendency for people to end their information search and reach conclusions before they have considered a sufficient amount of information.

prospect theory is a theory of decision-making under conditions of risk. It posits that people evaluate possible outcomes with respect to a reference point, over-value losses relative to comparable gains, and engage in risk-averse decision-making when confronted with choices among possible gains, but risk acceptant decision-making when confronted with choices among possible losses.

rational actor model of judgment and decision-making involves specifying goals, identifying alternative strategies to achieve these goals, estimating the net costs and benefits of each strategy, and making a value-maximizing choice.

satisficing decision rule is a cognitive heuristic that involves specifying a threshold for a "good enough" outcome, searching through possible alternatives and then selecting the first alternative that satisfies that threshold.

selective attention refers to the tendency to select pieces of information—and particularly information that is consistent with one's belief system—from the overwhelming amount of available data.

FURTHER READING

George A. L. (1980). *Presidential decision-making in foreign policy: The effective use of information and advice.* Boulder, CO: Westview.

Halperin M. H., Clapp H. P., & Kanter A. (2006). *Bureaucratic politics with foreign policy* (2nd ed.). Washington, DC: Brookings. Halperin et al. address the politics of decision-making.

Janis I. L., & Mann L. (1977). *Decision making: A psychological analysis of conflict, choice and commitment.* New York: Free Press.

Jervis R. (1976). *Perception and misperception in international politics.* Princeton: Princeton University Press.

Kahneman D. (2011). *Thinking, fast and slow.* New York: Farrah, Straus and Giroux.

QUESTIONS FOR GROUP DISCUSSION

- In the making of foreign policy, are political leaders influenced more by constraints and opportunities in states' external environments, by domestic political pressures, or by their own belief systems and world views?

- In what specific ways can the making of foreign policy deviate from a rational decision-making process?

- Are people truly cognitively consistent or are they a set of walking contradictions? Is there a general tendency to think in one way or another?

- How do peoples' policy preferences influence the way they perceive the world?

10 Foreign Policy and Identity

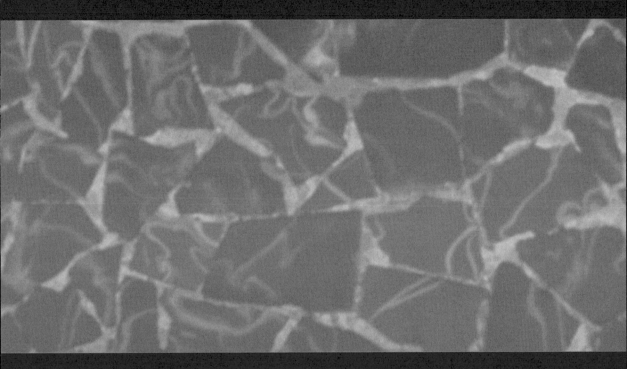

EMMA O'DWYER

CHAPTER OUTLINE

Foreign policy, it may be argued, is some distance away from the daily lives of citizens. Certainly, being perceived as somewhat distant and remote, it can be assumed that people are often less concerned with foreign policy than with policies that relate to domestic matters. However, geopolitical events often bring to the fore issues that can stir a collective conversation on the nature of foreign policy. In certain circumstances, citizens *can* become deeply engaged with foreign policy, despite its remoteness, and can become involved in collective action to try to influence matters. To give a recent example, thousands of British citizens protested their government's decision to engage in military intervention in Syria in November 2015. These thousands of people were not solely driven by self-interested motives such as the fear of a terrorist attack in Britain, but were taking this action because they rejected what such military engagement would say about Britain, their country, and them—its citizens. In sum, they were rejecting the negative implications of this action for British national identity.

Foreign policy is defined here as the *strategy* that a nation state adopts in its interactions with other states. In this sense, it is distinct from state *behavior*, which encompasses the range of unplanned or reactive acts that a state may carry out. It denotes the rules and norms governing the way in which the state deals with its allies and its enemies, its neighbors and far flung countries, in addition to supranational organizations such as the United Nations (UN) and the North Atlantic Treaty Organisations (NATO). In line with its "constructivist turn" (Checkel, 1998, p. 324), international relations (IR) and foreign policy theorists now focus to a greater extent on identity-related concerns in addition to realist (or instrumental) factors in the construction and practice of foreign policy. However, it is argued here that there is relatively little attention given to the participation of citizens in these processes. We should not think that states operate independently of their citizens—foreign policy concerns the thoughts, actions, and representations of citizens. The outcome of IR focus on the behavior of nation states is that this powerful agentic potential—citizen participation—has been underexplored.

In this chapter, we will describe a social psychological approach to these issues, which is well-placed to recognize the central role played by citizens in the construction, practice, and maintenance or resistance of foreign policy. The crux of social psychology's potential contribution stems from its recognition of the nation state as a constellation of identities, representations, and narratives associated with a particular group—the national ingroup. Illustrating such a perspective, this chapter will draw upon empirical work that has explored the case of Irish **neutrality** (O'Dwyer, Lyons, & Cohrs, 2016) using the theoretical

Political Psychology: A Social Psychological Approach, First Edition.
Edited by Christopher J. Hewer and Evanthia Lyons.
© 2018 John Wiley & Sons Ltd. Published 2018 by John Wiley & Sons Ltd.

framework of **social representations theory** (Elcheroth, Doise, & Reicher, 2011; Moscovici, 1961/1976). This research reveals the dynamic relationship between national identity and the Irish state's foreign policy, and considers possibilities for social change in light of this relationship. The chapter closes by outlining possibilities for further social psychological research in this vein.

FOREIGN POLICY AND IDENTITY: CONCEPTUAL AND THEORETICAL ANCHORS

It has been recognized previously (e.g., Kaarbo, 2003) that an understanding of psychological processes would extend and benefit the field of foreign policy analysis. This assertion has been made, in particular, by IR researchers working within the **constructivist** paradigm (e.g., Kubálková, 2001; Wendt, 1992, 1999), who use the concept of identity to understand and explain state behavior and foreign policy. Such a paradigm asserts that state behavior and foreign policy cannot be predicted solely on the basis of material interests or the balance of power, as researchers adopting a realist or neorealist position would propose. Identity, which is informed by the values, beliefs, myth, and histories of nation states and their citizens, can inform our understanding of state behavior to a larger extent than material interests or power asymmetries.

Identity in IR is still a somewhat nebulous concept; it is attributed to the nation state but this necessarily leads to the question of whether nation states can actually *have* identities. The attribution of identities to nation states feeds into the broader process of their **personification**. But if nation states possess personalities, which we would assume would be somewhat stable, how can citizens have any influence? On this, Seed (1966) noted:

> The state is a complex of institutions and yet in international affairs is conceived in personal terms. The state, in reality, may be unco-ordinated (sic) and muddled, and yet built up around it, there is a fantasy of singlemindedness (sic). The state appears at one and the same to be human, non-human and super-human. (p. 11)

We can see that considering the nation state in these terms, granting it superhuman properties, diminishes the capacity and agency of citizens. Two questions remain: to what extent do the identities of nations exist? And do they exist independently of their citizens? I suggest here that, rather than (or in addition to) nation states occupying identity positions and enacting these identities, we should instead consider the collectivities that lend nation states their power and status. This is not to suggest that scholars attempting to understand foreign policy must focus purely on the individual or group level of analysis (clearly broader institutional processes and the balance of power are important). However, any attempt to understand the identities of nation states without considering the identities of their citizens, and the way in which the two interact, would only be partial.

THE INFLUENCE OF CITIZENS ON FOREIGN POLICY

The question may be asked—can citizens influence foreign policy? Much empirical work suggests that they can. According to **the democratic-responsiveness model** (Page & Shapiro, 1983), elite actors are "delegates who respond to the requests of the mass public" (Cunningham & Moore, 1997, p. 643). Proposing this model, Page and Shapiro's (1983) analysis of public opinion and policy data in the USA from 1935–1979, found that there was a good deal of congruence between changes in public opinion and government policy, and this was especially the case when these changes were large, stable, and related to salient issues. Further, in some cases, changes in public opinion actually preceded policy changes.

Foyle (2004) also found support for such claims by showing that public opinion had a major impact on the United States (US) government's decision to invade Iraq in 2003. An analysis of US public opinion and policy decisions (from 9/11 to the invasion of Iraq in 2003) showed that the Bush administration was initially constrained by negative public opinion and as a consequence had to delay the invasion of Iraq until the Al'Qaeda issue had been perceived to have been satisfactorily dealt with, after the invasion of Afghanistan. When this concern had been alleviated, the administration was free to mobilize support for the invasion of Iraq. While the US administration "led" the public to support the invasion of Iraq through the use of persuasion and priming strategies (e.g., linking Iraq to weapons of mass destruction), the government's success in "leading" the American public to war was nevertheless "in large part because, after September 11, the public was inclined to support a war" (p. 288).

Further, Davis (2012) examined the effect of pacifist public opinion on foreign policy in eight Western countries (all US allies) across a 24-year period (1973–1998). Results showed the impact of security threat on the relationship between public opinion and foreign policy. In times of high-threat (during the Cold War), the impact of public opinion on foreign policy lessened, while in the years following the Cold War, when the security threat was lower, governments were more responsive to public opinion.

Taken together, this research suggests that citizens play a part in determining the nature of their nation's foreign policy. Then it follows that the practice of foreign policy should not be seen to be concentrated in the actions and behavior of the nation state. Globalization and new technologies have also changed the parameters and the meaning of foreign policy. As Foyle (2003) noted "to a certain extent, the technology of the Internet is beginning to allow individuals to conduct their own foreign policies and exact costs upon nation states whose policies displease them" (p. 167). Boycotts and "hacktivism" are two examples of what a citizen's foreign policy might look like.

If we accept that (a) an analysis of the identities of nations is incomplete without giving attention to the identities of its citizens; (b) citizens can influence foreign policy under particular conditions; and (c) globalization and new technologies are creating new possibilities for the practice of citizen foreign policy, then it seems clear that a consideration of national identity—the identity of citizens at the individual and group level—is necessary to gain an understanding of foreign policy. This is where social psychological theory becomes particularly useful. Social psychology has developed a well-elaborated conceptualization of identity and different theories, for example, **social identity theory** (Tajfel & Turner, 1979) and **identity process theory** (Breakwell, 1986), have been advanced to specify and define the concept, describe the processes by which it is formed, enacted and changed, and identify the interpersonal and intergroup consequences of identity dynamics. Identity remains a key concern of social psychologists, but there has been no serious attempt to link identity to IR and foreign policy.

If the identities that nation states enact in their dealings with other states are indeed national identities—the identity of citizens at the individual and group level—then we have a substantial body of empirical and theoretical work at our disposal to understand foreign policy. If we consider national identity as a specific type of social identity (group membership), then we are drawn into a series of categorizations in which other individuals, groups, or nations are seen as either ingroup or outgroup members. When a group or nation is seen as an outgroup, then this would explain hostile foreign policy. Moreover, perceptions of similar or shared identity become important because this likely bolsters the probability of cooperative foreign policy. Some empirical work has tested this assertion, primarily using experimental methods.

OUTGROUP PERCEPTIONS AND FOREIGN POLICY ATTITUDES

Rousseau and Garcia-Retamero (2007) conducted a cross-national study on the relative effects of power asymmetries and shared identity on threat perceptions and willingness to cooperate in international affairs. Three experiments were conducted in Spain and the USA in which participants were asked to answer questions about their perceptions of hypothetical countries as well as concrete examples (Russia, in Study 2 conducted in Spain only). When a country was described as relatively more powerful than the home country, participants perceived it as more threatening, while when it was described as similar to the home country, participants perceived it as less threatening. In two of the studies, an interaction was found such that those countries high in power and low in shared identity were seen as the most threatening. In Study 3, framing Russia as an ingroup member had a positive effect on support for a trade agreement, and increasing trade more generally with Spain, while high military power of Russia decreased support for Spanish defense cuts, and shared identity.

Across three studies with US participants using survey and experimental methods, Wetherell, Benson, and Reyna (2015) found that the belief that the citizens of other nations were supportive of US values (value similarity), was linked to more positive views about these countries, in terms of decreased prejudice, increased desire for closeness and support for foreign aid. Interestingly, value similarity was a more consistent predictor of opinion about people in foreign countries than value threat. Value similarity was more important for understanding attitudes toward these people and support for foreign aid while value threat was related to support for aggressive policies (in this case, support for the military overthrow of a country's government).

Similarly, in a series of experimental studies with Swiss students, Falomir-Pichastor, Pereira, Staerklé, and Butera (2011) found support for the **"democracy-as-value" hypothesis**. They measured support for military intervention (which would likely result in civilian deaths) in response to experimental vignettes in which the nature of the political system (democratic or non-democratic) and the level of public support for the government's policy varied. They found that support for military intervention was low when the political system of the target country was democratic. On the other hand, they found that participants perceived military intervention in nondemocratic states as less illegitimate when public opinion in the target country was supportive of its government's policies. Citizens of democratic countries then appear to have differing views on military intervention depending on whether the country involved shares their commitment to democratic values.

Each of the studies outlined above has used experimental methods to investigate the relationship between outgroup perceptions and foreign policy attitudes and all point toward the importance of categorization for the way in which people perceive and respond to international affairs and foreign policy. However, identity is conceptualized solely in relative terms, referring to the similarity or difference of other countries and their citizens to us. Therefore, these studies do not address the issue of the content of national identity, what it means to be a particular member of a national group, and how that affects people's views on foreign policy. The next section comprises a discussion of empirical work conducted on the curious phenomenon of Irish neutrality (O'Dwyer, 2013; O'Dwyer, Lyons, & Cohrs, 2016), which brings these issues to the fore.

A CASE STUDY: IRISH NEUTRALITY

Irish neutrality is an intriguing phenomenon, both from a psychological and lay perspective. Neutrality as a foreign policy orientation denotes "a deliberate, conscious policy of impartial abstention from a war or armed conflict with concomitant rights and duties, together with an intention to resist violations of those rights and duties by armed resistance if necessary" (Salmon, 1989, p. 27). It is a stance that nation states take, during wartime, which places particular obligations on that state while simultaneously conferring specific rights. Neutral states must adhere to particular principles; they should not engage in warfare (nonbelligerence) nor show favor for the warring parties (impartiality). Further, neutrality should not be mistaken for defencelessness; states are entitled and indeed expected to protect their neutral position if it is threatened. Also worth noting is the fact that neutrality, as a specific legal concept codified during the Hague Conventions of 1907, cannot be qualified. It is an all-or-nothing stance; states either sign up to all of the principles that accompany neutrality, or they are not, according to this definition, neutral.

Neutrality is a typically Western European phenomenon, with Austria, Switzerland, Finland, Switzerland, as well as the Republic of Ireland being either officially neutral or having some tradition of the policy. What is essential to note here is that each of these states came to the policy of neutrality for very different reasons. For example, in the aftermath of World War II, Austrian neutrality was stipulated as a condition for independence. Other parties also dictated Finnish neutrality: its nonalignment was set down in the Treaty of Friendship, Co-operation and Mutual Assistance with the USSR in 1948. Switzerland, the archetypal case, adopted and codified its permanent neutrality in 1815. In the present day, Sweden has moved away from its declaration of neutrality in 1834 and, after its accession to the European Union (EU), now uses the term "military nonalignment" to characterize its foreign policy.

IRISH NEUTRALITY IN CONTEXT

The Republic of Ireland's neutrality is different again; it is not shaped by East–West conflict post-World War II, nor is it deeply rooted legally, politically or historically (Binter, 1989). While some theorists (e.g., Fanning, 1982) go back further, Keatinge (1978) points to the introduction of conscription to the British army in Ireland in 1918 and the subsequent withdrawal of the Irish party from Westminster and creation of the Irish parliament, as the time during which "the popular basis of Irish neutrality was enshrined" (p. 47). The Anglo–Irish Treaty signed in 1921 effected the creation of the Irish Free State. However, because key Irish ports were still under British control, it was not possible for the Free State to be neutral. Prior to independence, the Free State asserted itself strongly on the world stage, playing an active role in the League of Nations, for example. Éamon de Valera, the Taoiseach (Prime Minister) at this time and almost certainly the political figure most commonly associated with Irish neutrality, was initially enthusiastic about the League, but after its failures to curb Hitler and Mussolini's forays into the Rhineland and Ethiopia, respectively, came to the view that neutrality was the only credible option available to the Free State. Yet the key Irish ports were still under British control. Negotiations following the Anglo–Irish Trade War (1932–1938) returned these ports to Irish control.

On the outbreak of World War II, de Valera declared Ireland's neutrality—this was met with British opposition, due in part to concerns over their ability to protect the British mainland. De Valera's motives have been a matter of some analysis and speculation—was it a principled objection to war? A strategy to end Irish partition? Or cowardice plain and simple? Fanning (1982) points to his desire to bring about a united Ireland, thus neutrality was a means of buttressing Irish sovereignty. Keatinge (1978) asserts that de Valera wished to underscore Irish independence, the freedom to decide in which wars to participate being one of the key privileges of an independent nation. Salmon (1989) characterizes Irish neutrality instead as nonbelligerence—"piggy-backing" off British defense. Whether Ireland actually observed the particularities of neutrality, or instead, "showed a certain consideration"[1] for Britain has been debated, but it is sufficient to say that Ireland approximated a neutral position during World War II, the perceived success of which laid the foundation for enduring public support for the policy.

Ireland also chose to stay outside NATO in 1949. This was due to the issue of partition (the division of Ireland), but also because of the consensual quality that neutrality had now assumed in Irish public opinion. Ireland joined the UN in 1955, and continues to this day to play an active and valued role in this organization, especially in terms of peace-keeping activities. In 1974, the Republic joined the European Economic Community (EEC, now the EU). While there was debate at the time about neutrality, government officials downplayed this concern and worked with a very minimal definition of neutrality, centered on nonmembership of NATO. While beginning life as a

---

[1] A phrase widely attributed to de Valera (see Fisk, 1983).

trade organization, the EU now encompasses other types of integration between member states, including foreign and security policies (e.g., the development of the Common Security and Defence Policy developed in the 1990s). In Irish referendums seeking to ratify changes to the European Treaty, for example, the Treaty of Lisbon referendum in 2008, the maintenance of neutrality emerged as significant concerns for voters. In particular, the fear that Irish citizens would be conscripted into a European army was a genuine fear and was one of the factors that led to the defeat of the Treaty on its first outing in 2008. The Treaty was only subsequently passed in 2009 when "legally binding guarantees" from the EU on issues including neutrality were received. Devine (2011) has noted that, irrespective of these guarantees, one of the implications of the changes brought about by the Lisbon Treaty is that neutrality "in legal and political terms, is dead" (p. 360).

In spite of the political reality that neutrality is now obsolete in "post-Lisbon" Ireland, a number of surveys indicates that public support for neutrality is high (e.g., Gilland, 2001; Lyons, 2003). It was a factor in voter decision-making in European Treaty referendums (Sinnott & Elkink, 2010; Sinnott, 2003) and is positively linked to support for Irish independence and national identity (Devine, 2008). A central aim of this research was to provide a qualitative investigation of neutrality and its relationship to Irish national identity—an account of this work will be provided in the next section.

THE SOCIAL REPRESENTATION OF IRISH NEUTRALITY

Previous empirical or theoretical work on Irish neutrality either tended to dismiss the concept as a relic of the preglobalized and integrated world system, or else it was partial, failing to acknowledge the meanings that people tied to it. This was a position that often served the authors' self-interests or the groups to which they belonged. It became clear that a theoretical framework was needed that would acknowledge the importance of the everyday sense-making of individuals and communities as well as a consideration of contextual and historical processes. Social representations theory (Moscovici, 1961/1976) offers this framework. To provide a brief overview, the theory characterizes and describes common sense or lay thinking on particular issues. It describes particular processes—**anchoring** and **objectification**—which produce lay knowledge. Social representation (it is thought of as both process and object) is tied to group processes as the creation of social knowledge always functions in the context of that particular group. Social representations may serve individual, intragroup, or intergroup functions, satisfying motives such as continuity or distinctiveness, creating cohesiveness within the group or providing guidance to group members in terms of behavior toward other groups, respectively (Breakwell, 1993). The way in which individuals and groups construct social objects is in line with context-specific demands related to identity.

While social representations theory has been criticized for its alleged **determinism** and tendency toward cognitive **reductionism** (Jahoda, 1988; Potter & Billig, 1992; Potter & Litton, 1985), much current work emphasizes the conflictual and ambivalent nature of these representations (Figueiredo, Valentim, Licata, & Doosje, 2013; Moloney, Williams, & Blair, 2012; Wagner, Duveen, Verma, & Themel, 2000), and the capacity of individuals and groups to resist those that may have stigmatizing consequences or which affect status or group identity (e.g., Howarth, 2002a, 2006). Furthermore, social representations cannot be separated from the political context in which they are embedded; indeed this political dimension "becomes a *condition of intelligibility* for social phenomena" (Elcheroth et al., 2011, p. 733, authors' emphasis).

Social representations theory thus offered a way to approach the puzzle of Irish neutrality. This would be by (a) recognizing and respecting lay thinking on a difficult and possibly obscure concept for Irish citizens: what is more, the representations might be contrary or ambivalent; (b) emphasizing the dynamic relationship between identity and the content and construction of social knowledge; and (c) bringing to the fore the issues of power, resistance, and the political context. The research project adopting this theoretical framework utilized a number of different methodologies in its investigation of Irish neutrality—focus group interviews, secondary survey analysis, and the automated content analysis program, ALCESTE (Reinert, 1990). Although an exhaustive treatment of the methodological and analytic features of the project are beyond the scope of this chapter, the key findings demonstrate the utility of applying social psychological theory and method to the investigation of identity and foreign policy.

CÉAD MILE FÁILTE NEUTRALITY

In the Irish/Gaelic language, the term *céad mile fáilte* is the expression for welcome (literal translation: 100,000 welcomes). Thus, when combined with the word "neutrality," this expression highlights the accommodating and flexible nature of the concept. A **thematic analysis** (Braun & Clarke, 2006) of focus group data with members of proneutrality political parties (the Green Party of Ireland and the nationalist Sinn Féin party) revealed the variable and malleable quality of Irish neutrality. Green Party and Sinn Féin members both supported the stance, but the values and beliefs that they attached to neutrality were very different. For Green Party members, support for neutrality was tied to the recognition of human rights and antipathy toward oppression, while Sinn Féin members consistently linked it to the rejection of imperialism and recognition of national sovereignty and independence in international affairs. More generally, the groups differed in terms of their outlook on war, with Green Party members linking their pacifism to concerns about the protection of the environment and their view of armies as "destructive forces," while Sinn Féin members grounded their antimilitarism in the view that all wars were imperialist conquests in one guise or another. A further study—a secondary analysis using data from the Irish Social and Political Attitudes Survey conducted in 2001/2002 (Garry, Hardiman, & Payne, 2006) explored this point further. The analysis revealed that the meanings that participants attached to neutrality moderated the relationship between basic human values (Schwartz, 1992) and support for neutrality. For those who defined neutrality as independence, support for neutrality was strongly related to high priority of conservation values (tradition, security, and conformity). In contrast, for those who used the definition of peace-keeping, support for neutrality was strongly associated with high priority of openness to change (self-direction, stimulation) values. Taken together, the two studies demonstrate the open and flexible representation of neutrality by the Irish public. People of very different ideological backgrounds can support the same stance. They may possess diverse definitions of neutrality, and anchor it in different values, but its broad appeal and potential for practical use in a number of settings may explain its continued popularity in Ireland.

THE MACROPOLITICAL DIMENSION OF IDENTITY CONSTRUCTION

In a subsequent qualitative focus group study (O'Dwyer et al., 2016), Irish participants of different ages and educational backgrounds were asked to respond to and discuss hypothetical international conflict events (e.g., China had invaded the Philippines), in which the Irish state was being asked to play a part (e.g., allowing US troops to refuel in Shannon). A thematic analysis of the data revealed that participants constructed Irish national identity as being constantly in conversation with the international political system; for example, the idea that national identity and the practice of neutrality were constrained by Ireland's membership of the EU. Participants' talk about the scenarios also revealed the way in which the historical precedents legitimized further similar foreign policy actions. As one participant stated, "And all we're doing is allowing them (the US army) to refuel in Shannon which they're doing all the time anyway, which doesn't affect our military neutrality irrespective of what people say or don't say." We might say then that historical precedents reify current policy and close off possibilities for alternative courses of action and so they become "world-making assumptions" (Elcheroth, Doise, & Reicher et al., 2011). Gaskarth (2006) expresses a similar view:

> Constructing an idea of foreign policy as shaped by historical preconditions, and as a continuous realm of social activity, offers limited scope for new conceptions of its possible practice. It also separates policy from its immediate context – as it is portrayed as functioning within a transcendent reality. (p. 332)

On the other hand, the macropolitical system was also an arena in which Irish national identity could be confidently asserted. This was especially evident in participants' talk about Irish involvement in the UN, which was construed as a means of projecting national identity, underscoring its "moral authority" and status as a "peace-keeping nation." The Irish army specifically was viewed positively due to the specialized military assistance it contributed to UN missions. Participants' talk about the UN more generally belied its positive consequences for the distinctiveness, efficacy, and esteem of Irish national identity.

CONSTRUCTING THE NATIONAL INGROUP IN INTERNATIONAL AFFAIRS

The final theme is related to the issue of **categorization** in foreign policy. How do people decide who is like them, and thus should be defended in the event of conflict? How do people determine which nations should be opposed, militarily or otherwise? Past research suggests that if the country under attack is democratic, and the hostile country is powerful and possesses nuclear weapons, that this motivates support for military action to defend the country being attacked (e.g., Falomir-Pichastor et al., 2011; Herrmann, Tetlock, & Visser, 1999). Value similarity or a sense of shared identity will also motivate cooperative foreign policy (Rousseau & Garcia-Retamero, 2007; Wetherell, Benson, Reyna, & Brandt, 2015). This work was mostly experimental or survey based, whereas the study outlined earlier (O'Dwyer et al., 2016) offered rich qualitative insight into the process through which people decided whether the assistance of the Irish state was warranted. To understand these issues, we chose actors involved in the hypothetical scenarios to reflect differing levels of cultural similarity and power—Germany, the Philippines, China, Guinea, the USA, Great Britain, and Pakistan-based Islamist terrorists.

The analysis plainly showed that categorization in IR is not necessarily a straightforward or predictable process; participants' discussions of the hypothetical conflicts showed the process to be a pragmatic and collaborative endeavor. Participants' discussions of the actors involved were central to the decision over Irish involvement in the conflicts. The assessments of the actors involved were often shaped by perceptions of preexisting, taken-for-granted alliances or links to the Irish diaspora (e.g., in the case of the USA), which tended to underpin support for Irish involvement in the conflict situations.

Two other characteristics of the actors involved were crucial—closeness and threat. Threat was mostly linked to perceptions of terrorism and China, and tended to motivate opposition to Irish involvement. Perceptions of closeness to Ireland worked in the opposite direction. Intriguingly, this closeness was not always geographically determined. One group argued for Irish involvement in a conflict in which the Philippines had been attacked by China on the grounds that the mother of the Rose of Tralee (a famous Irish beauty pageant) and a sizable amount of nurses employed in the Irish health service were from the Philippines. As one participant stated, "They can use Shannon. We have to look after our own!" This creative stretching of the representation and boundaries of the national in-group supports the assertion that identity is a specific social representation (Andreouli & Chryssochoou, 2014, Elcheroth et al., 2011), which is always strategic or action-oriented (Reicher & Hopkins, 1996, 2001a), in this case to justify support for involvement in conflict. Further, this analysis demonstrates that *agency* is an essential part of identity (co-)construction. Our participants, working within the parameters set by the international system (e.g., legacies of past cooperation with other countries, supranational memberships), nevertheless collectively recast Irish national identity as a more inclusive, outward-looking identity to advance particular rhetorical ends.

UNANSWERED QUESTIONS: OPPORTUNITIES FOR FUTURE RESEARCH

The social psychological approach to the investigation of foreign policy brings identity to the fore; both the process of categorization and the content dimension of national identity are important. The research, however, leaves open a number of questions. For example, future research could tackle the issue of resistance and foreign policy. It is clear that public opposition to foreign policy is often insufficient to change it. One need only think of the mass protests that took place globally to oppose the US invasion of Iraq in 2003, to realize that citizens are not always able to influence the direction of foreign policy. Nevertheless, peace activist organizations continue to resist militarist foreign policy. Indeed, it would be interesting to carry out a qualitative analysis of interviews with peace activists to understand the way in which they conceptualize their role and that of other citizens in influencing foreign policy and driving social change. Such an analysis could also provide insight into a process by which people become more efficacious in their engagement with foreign policy as well as their capacity to resist policies with which they disagree.

Moreover, while it is clear that identity plays an important role in the nature of foreign policy, clearly, institutional factors and elite behavior also play a significant part. Research should explore these factors and attempt to provide an account of their relative influence and the way in which they may interact. Such a line of enquiry would necessarily be interdisciplinary and would encompass individual, group/organizational, and national levels of analysis.

Research should also consider historical processes to a much greater extent. In particular, such research may be usefully complemented by a consideration of post-colonial perspectives (e.g., Hook, 2012) and historical work, for example, on collective memory. It is clear that foreign policy decision-making does not take place in a historical vacuum. On the outbreak of war, social representational processes often work to tie the current conflict to past wars (e.g., "the new Iraq")—which functions to make the new war intelligible while simultaneously guiding our reactions and behavior toward it (Cohrs & O'Dwyer, 2016). Other work (Gaskarth, 2006; O'Dwyer et al., 2016) has highlighted the importance of the rhetorical use of historical precedents in foreign policy to legitimize and reify current action. A line of research that prioritizes the analysis of historical events, looking at their discursive use in popular media and political discourse, for example, may provide insight into possibilities for their strategic use to counter hostile foreign policy and foster cooperation between nation states.

Finally, it was noted previously that globalization and new technologies may be creating a context for the practice of new types of citizen engagement with foreign policy (Foyle, 2003). Future research needs to be conducted to determine whether this is indeed the case. Are citizens engaged in collective action which might be construed as foreign policy? And do they see this as effective? How do elites conceptualize this type of "citizen foreign policy," especially in cases where it conflicts with national policy? From a social psychological perspective, a key question would be to what extent involvement in such collective action creates superordinate identities and what might their consequences be? Addressing these questions would enhance our understanding of the future direction and shape of foreign policy in a globalized international system.

SUMMARY

- Much of the previous literature on the relationship between foreign policy and identity has been a consequence of the development of constructivism in IR theory.

- In such a perspective, identities are the properties of nation states, are enacted on the world stage, and can explain state behavior.

- Yet given particular conditions, citizens and public opinion have been shown to influence the nature of foreign policy in a number of different contexts.

- Globalization and new technologies are creating new possibilities for the practice of citizen foreign policy, for example, boycotts or hacktivism.

- Social psychological theory has developed a significant body of theoretical and empirical work that has examined the structure and consequences of identity dynamics.

- Previous experimental work based on social identity theory suggests that perceiving the attacked country as democratic or sharing values with oneself, and the aggressor as powerful and in possession of nuclear weapons, influences the ways in which people respond to international conflicts.

- The case of Irish neutrality shows that we also need to consider the *content* dimension of national identity—what it means to be a member of a particular national group—and the way in which this affects people's assessments of foreign policy.

GLOSSARY

anchoring refers to one of the two interdependent processes that describe the ways in which social representations form and change. It refers to the way in which unfamiliar knowledge is tied to, and understood through existing world-views or knowledge.

categorization refers to the psychological process in which people are assigned to social groups or categories.

constructivism (IR) is a school of thought that emphasizes the role played by non-material factors (ideas, identities, beliefs, culture, and norms) in international affairs and politics.

"democracy-as-value" hypothesis is the claim that democracy bestows value on democratic institutions, groups and citizens, and confers legitimacy to their actions.

democratic-responsiveness model is a theory of the relationship between elite and mass opinion, which asserts that elites are responsive to mass opinion.

determinism is the philosophical position that every event or state of affairs is caused by the inevitable consequences of pre-existing forces or prior events—no other outcome or action was possible.

foreign policy refers to nation state's broad strategy for diplomatic relations with other nation states.

identity (international relations) is a broad term that denotes representations of the state as well as its representations to other states.

identity process theory is a theory that describes the formation and articulation of *personal* identities, and the ways in which people respond to identity threat.

neutrality is a legal position taken by nation states in times of war, which establishes their nonparticipation in the conflict.

objectification refers to one of the two interdependent processes that describe the ways in which social representations form and change. It refers to the way in which unfamiliar knowledge is concretized and takes visual or metaphorical form.

personification refers to the attribution of human-like attributes to nonhuman phenomena.

reductionism is the philosophical position that higher-order phenomena can be explained using lower-level theories.

social identity theory is a theory of intergroup relations, which specifies three key processes in the formation and maintenance of group membership: categorization, comparison, and the drive for positive distinctiveness.

social representations theory is a social psychological theory that outlines the processes involved in generating common sense understanding and social change.

thematic analysis is a method of qualitative analysis based on the identification and analysis of themes.

FURTHER READING

Davis W. (2012). Swords into ploughshares: The effect of pacifist public opinion on foreign policy in western democracies. *Cooperation and Conflict, 47*, 309–330.

Gaskarth J. (2006). Discourses and ethics: The social construction of British foreign policy. *Foreign Policy Analysis, 2*, 325–341.

O'Dwyer E., Lyons E., & Cohrs J. C. (2016). How Irish citizens negotiate foreign policy: A social representations approach to neutrality. *Political Psychology, 37*, 165–181.

QUESTIONS FOR GROUP DISCUSSION

• How are new technologies enabling citizens to have more influence over foreign policy?

• "Ever closer union" is one of the cornerstone principles of the EU. Many policy makers are keen to develop a common foreign policy for member states, with citizens frequently less keen on the idea. How can social representations theory help us to understand the disparity between political elites and the wider public on this issue?

- History is frequently used in political discourse to legitimize foreign policy and to argue for or against militarism. Can you think of some examples?

11 Social Memory and the Collective Past

CHRISTOPHER J. HEWER

CHAPTER OUTLINE

The analysis of social memory and the collective past is an important feature of political psychology. The purpose of this chapter is to review key theoretical and conceptual approaches within the social sciences (including social psychology) and the humanities and to identify common and complementary features that allow us to communicate across disciplines. In this chapter, we explore the dynamics between the individual, the collective, and the wider culture, which inevitably takes the discussion beyond individualized psychological constructs into the realm of history, sociology, politics, and international relations.

To start the discussion, let us consider the connection between the individual and "the social" emerging from the philosophical work of sociologist George Herbert Mead (1863–1931). This is the idea that mind and society are inseparable; that society exists within us, as much as we exist in society (Mead, 1934). If this is so, as we internalize our external world through our own language and culture we develop a very specific worldview, which determines not only *what* we think but also *the way* we think. Because societies are constantly changing over time and vary according to geographical location, we might conclude that thought processes and their content are as diverse as the societies that produce them. Indeed, it is important to acknowledge the broad spectrum of cultural and historic thinking in any analysis of the collective past. What may be universal, however, is the psychological impact of the past on the present, its relation to social structure and its role in the formation of identity.

THE ROLE OF THE PAST IN THE FORMATION OF IDENTITY

Because memory is at the core of human experience, that is, it is involved all aspects of conscious activity, we cannot function properly without it. Those who suffer from debilitating memory deficits such as dementia often seem incomplete, not as they were, lacking a coherent sense of location, time, space, and self. Being human thus incurs a critical relationship with the past since it provides a basis for existential meaning and a life narrative from which we derive and express personal identity. A psychological relationship

Political Psychology: A Social Psychological Approach, First Edition.
Edited by Christopher J. Hewer and Evanthia Lyons.
© 2018 John Wiley & Sons Ltd. Published 2018 by John Wiley & Sons Ltd.

with the past is also forged at birth as we enter a social network and encounter a range of narratives of collective pasts generated from within families, ethnic groups, religions, and nations. Our immersion into these cultural narratives, a process of **mnemonic socialization** (see Zerubavel, 1996), provides an early structure to identity thus creating a reciprocal relationship between social identity (group membership) and historical understanding. In other words, the way we see ourselves and others affects the way we see the past, and the way we see the past affects the way we see ourselves and others.

While social identities arise from group memberships existing at birth, a sense of personal identity also develops over time. According to Identity Process Theory (Breakwell, 1986, 1992), the interplay between self and experience is a universal encounter that involves two psychological processes: assimilation-accommodation and evaluation. The theory posits that new experience is evaluated in relation to guiding principles such as self-esteem, continuity, distinctiveness, efficacy (competence and control), belonging, and coherence (Jaspal & Breakwell, 2014). These guiding principles are weighted and applied uniquely within each individual, and the salience of each guiding principle will vary according to culture and historical epoch. But whatever the emphasis, the orientation is toward self-interest rather than accuracy and once these structures are in place, new knowledge has the potential to reconfigure identity. New knowledge or experience is either assimilated into an existing identity structure, or the identity structure is altered to accommodate the experience. Included in this new knowledge or experience would be accounts of the past related to family, group, or nation; as each relevant account is heard, personal, and political implications start to accrue.

Personal implications arising from the past, benign or otherwise, are an indication that the "past weighs upon the present" (Liu & Hilton, 2005, p. 1). This has a familiar ring within academic psychology. In therapeutic encounters, for example, a client's relationship with the past may be seen as foundational to their psychological state and, largely because of the influence of Freudian psychoanalysis, the importance of childhood experience in the elaboration of adult life has become mainstream thinking in the West among psychologists and laypersons. In these specific areas of psychology enquiry, the content of memory is the main focus; it therefore becomes important to consider what is remembered, the way in which it is renarrated and its emotional effect on self and others. If we extend this principle to larger entities including national groups, we observe that, in many instances, political reality is often deeply affected, influenced, even bound by the past to the point that national and ethnic groups appear unable to free themselves from the consequences of history. The impact of the past on the present has long been acknowledged. When discussing the development of history, German social philosopher, Karl Marx (1818–1883) made an important observation:

> Men make their own history, but they do not make it just as they please; they do not make it under circumstances chosen by themselves, but under circumstances directly found, given and transmitted from the past. The tradition of all dead generations weighs like a nightmare upon the brain of the living. (Marx, 1852/2006, p. 15)

Marx observed that even in the most extreme revolutionary circumstances, people tend to assert, identify with, or align themselves with the past in the form of actions or ideals of significant historical figures. The imposing nature of the past on the political and psychological landscape has been particularly significant since 1914, and perhaps to a greater extent since 1945 (see Liu & Hilton, 2005). The world does not simply receive the past, it is "haunted" by it (Assmann, 1998, p. 9; see also Frosh, 2013) and this continues to play a significant role in contemporary politics. Two world wars, the Holocaust, the formation of the modern state of Israel, the rise and fall of the Soviet Union and the attack on New York in 2001 are just some of the events that continue to reverberate around the world creating diverse waves of volatile memory across generations of people. Although the past no longer exists, it does not simply disappear. It is subject to a dynamic process of re-engagement with the present, transforming itself into a social and psychological experience that shifts and evolves across generations.

THE SOCIAL NATURE OF MEMORY

The faculty of individual memory works consistently with our understanding that each person has a self-contained, neurological system. We know, for example, that any deficiency in our own memory does not extend to other people because biological memory systems are not connected. However, when we consider the *content* of memory, we might draw the opposite conclusion; that despite having independent systems, memories are often shared or are contingent on the presence or existence of others and that the construction, reconstruction, and sharing of memories is a feature of everyday social interaction. For students trained in psychology, the concept of a socialized memory may require a shift of thinking—away from an individualized, biologically based, cognitive system that functions as an archive—toward memory as "lived experience" (see Tileagă, 2013, p. 105). What is more, when we refer to shared, social, or collective memory, it is not always memory in the conventional sense: it is not always the recall of *personal* experience. Rather, events experienced by others may be passed down to us in the form of a narrative because either we were not there or not yet born. In this instance, the memory is socially shared through transmission not through personal experience, for example, our understanding of the First World War. To socialize memory, however, raises some conceptual issues. Historian Geoffrey Cubitt (2014) provides a helpful summary:

> At the one end of the imagined spectrum of approaches, taking a social view of memory may mean simply recognising that much of the content of individual remembering refers to things that are social in character – social occasions, relationships, conversational exchanges, shared endeavors, and so on. At the other end, it might mean positing a "group mind" endowed with a remembering capacity somehow distinct from that of group members. In between are ranged a variety of ways of thinking of memory as socially inflected or conditioned, interactive, culturally mediated, shared or socially distributed. Middling positions along this spectrum may be thought of as being reached either by "socializing" the concept of the remembering individual or by "writing" the individual back into collective memory (p. 16).

TAXONOMIES AND CLASSIFICATIONS

The various conceptions that embrace the idea of a collective past inevitably draw us into a discussion of taxonomies (classifications), descriptions, and definitions (For a detailed discussion of taxonomies, see Cubitt, 2007; also Erll, 2010). We have to be aware that not everyone is enthusiastic about the concept of collective memory (e.g., Assmann, 2010a) and, despite its popularity and wide usage, some see collective memory as a vague and ambiguous construct that is slowly replacing traditional concepts such as myth, tradition, and heritage. What is more, some scholars may refer to social and collective memory interchangeably, while others may be very particular about the way they use these terms. Cubitt (2007), for example, uses **social memory** to refer to *social processes* that sustain knowledge of past events within a group or culture while **collective memory,** he argues, is a very specific *product* of these processes that presents a particular view or representation of the past. Cubitt also reminds us that *memory is not an object with ontological substance* (see also Olick, 2002), therefore researchers need to guard against reifying psychological experience into social or psychological constructs.

Early approaches to the study of collective memory originally found expression within French sociology in the 1920s through Maurice Halbwachs (1877–1945), whose work was influenced by Emile Durkheim (1858–1917), (For a detailed and considered view of these historical developments, see Olick, Vinitsky, & Levy, 2011, also Coser, 1992). Halbwachs (1925) argued that individual memories are acquired and recalled in a social milieu and that group settings provide the context that determines what and how we recall; these **social frameworks** include the family, social class, or nation. This claim was consistent with the findings of laboratory studies of memory in experimental psychology where the content of individual memory reflected patterns of thinking common to the social and cultural groups of the participants (Bartlett, 1932). Halbwachs also made a distinction between **autobiographical memory**—personal events, which have been experienced directly, and **historical memory**—events through which groups construct a continuous identity over time. Halbwachs, however, did not elaborate further: he died in Buchenwald, concentration camp in 1945.

THE RESURGENCE OF INTEREST IN THE COLLECTIVE PAST

In the 1980s, French historian Pierre Nora reinvigorated interest in the collective past with his work *Lieux de mémoire* in which claimed that memory and its values, customarily passed down through family, school, church, and state in France, were in decline. The disappearance of "peasant culture" as a source of collective memory had marked a significant change in French society leading to an erosion of "real memory" among people. Nora cites the "Jews of the diaspora" as an example of a community, which had no need for historians since memory was *lived* through everyday tradition and cultural practice. In the modern age, however, he argued that memory was being replaced by history— the way "our hopelessly forgetful modern societies, propelled by change, organise the past" (Nora, 1989, p. 8). As postwar France became "deeply absorbed in its own transformation and renewal" it valued "the new over the ancient, the young over the old and the future over the past" (Nora, 1989, p. 12). What remained, however, were *lieux de mémoire*—sites of memory— people, places, institutions, museums, works of art, holidays, and events, which endorse and encourage, among other things, the creation of archives and the invention of anniversaries and celebrations. Nora argued that because there was no memory left, the culture had become preoccupied with it and the **"memory boom"** with its tendency toward nostalgia and incessant memorialization had taken up a role in contemporary culture (Nora, 1989, 2002). In response to Nora's critique, French academics traced the public response to specific cultural sites in France over a period of eight years, which brought *lieux de mémoire* to prominence in the field of memory studies.

Since then, scholars across a range of disciplines have considered the complex relationship between history and memory. However, there is little consensus. Some argue that it is more productive to avoid the history–memory dichotomy and simply view both as ways of remembering (e.g., Erll, 2010) while others attach important conceptual and political significance to these distinctions. Wertsch and Roediger (2008), for example, draw a line between history and **collective remembering**. They see history as the study of *what actually happened*: a discipline that employs critical, complex, and reflective thought, while collective remembering, they argue, is an *identity project* that is intolerant of ambiguity or counter-narratives. They also make a distinction between collective memory—a static body of knowledge—and collective remembering—an active reconstruction of the past that takes place in the present. They claim that:

> History is willing to change a narrative in order to be loyal to facts, whereas collective remembering is willing to change information (even facts) in order to be loyal to a narrative. (Wertsch & Roediger, 2008, p. 324).

In contrast to the political and ideological nature of collective remembering, Wertsch & Roediger argue that professional historians continually review evidence-based arguments in order to report events accurately and fairly. Whether history always fits this description or meets the criteria of an objective science is a matter of debate. The formal study of history developed in the nineteenth century to unify people within the nation state; it is therefore not surprising that nations tend to present themselves in a positive light when telling their own national story (Baumeister & Hastings, 1997). Even archaeologists have been known to pursue empirical evidence in support of a particular narrative that is part of a politically charged national identity project (see Vickers, 1998). What is more, in recent years, postmodern critiques within history have called into question a belief in the objectivity of historians and the stability of historical claims (Brown, 2005). Indeed, we have to acknowledge that all historical claims are situated in history—a specific point in linear time, which imposes its own set of assumptions, agendas, and priorities. The claims may be evidence-based, and distance in time may increase objectivity, but the narrative is always situated within a specific cultural and historical location. The boundary between history and memory may therefore be more porous than we imagine (see Hewer & Roberts, 2012).

COMPETING MEMORY NARRATIVES

We might wonder why a study of collective memory had not been at the forefront of our intellectual concerns before the 1980s. In the decades following the Second World War, the Allied narrative of "victory over the evils of Fascism" had become a metanarrative—a definitive moral account of the recent past that lasted throughout the Cold War period and beyond. Brown (2005) describes metanarratives as:

> grand, ideological generalized stories by which societies understand themselves, and which are so normative and all-consuming, that individuals in a society are not aware of them as constantly re-circulated. Metanarratives only work when they become invisible by having no acceptable opposites. (p. 184)

When a metanarrative of the past dominates a culture, the study of collective memory becomes redundant. During the Cold War, little thought was given to the existence of counter-memories in the Soviet Union (see Wertsch, 2002) or other parts of the Eastern bloc (see also Hewer & Kut, 2010) that emerged to challenge particular aspects of the Allied account of World War (WWII). Eventually, the fall of the Berlin wall in 1989, and the Soviet Union shortly after, provided the psychological and political space for the expression of alternative memories from within the Eastern bloc. Even in Germany, after the peaceful unification of East and West in 1990, some aspects of WWII were subject to subtle differences of interpretation (von Benda-Beckmann, 2011).

In some countries, the official state version of the past, endorsed by the school curriculum and ritual commemoration, is at variance with the accounts of ordinary people. A distinction between "official and vernacular memory" (the memory of ordinary people) (Cubitt, 2014, p. 23) usually occurs when an authoritarian state places strict controls on the expression of memory. It may not be possible to express counter-memories because of an impending threat of punishment, or because such views are difficult to voice in the current political climate.[1] Such dissonant memories often occur in the aftermath of conflict. For example, in a study of memory of WWII among families in Germany, Welzer, Moller, and Tschuggnall (2002) identified two competing *modes* of memory—*lexicon*—memory informed by an official account of Germany's role in WWII, and *album*—a more personal and private recollection of loss and suffering among the relatives of German combatants.

In other settings, people have to navigate their way through the complexities, contradictions, and oversimplifications contained within different sources of historical information. Carretero (2011), for example, identifies "three meanings of history – academic, school and everyday history" (p. 1)—each offering a qualitatively different representation of the past. There are also other examples of disparate memory groups. For example, competing and contradictory memory narratives existed among Allied soldiers of WWII: the "righteous" war fought for high democratic ideals was often far removed from

---

[1] For example, the suffering of German civilians during the Allied bombing 1940–1945 only began to be discussed publicly in Germany in the 1980s.

their memory and experience of combat (Curtis, 1995); and memory practices among diasporic peoples may be quite different to those who live in the homeland (Zerubavel, 1995). Indeed, because there are as many versions of the past as there are people or groups, we are drawn into a form of relativism where there is not one single social reality but multiple realities each seeking to gain primacy over the other.

COMMUNICATIVE AND CULTURAL MEMORY

Egyptologist, Jan Assmann offers another perspective on the collective past by identifying two distinct forms of memory: **cultural memory** and **communicative memory.** He also uses the term **mnemohistory** to describe any form of historical investigation that examines the way in which the past is remembered (Assmann, 1992, 2006, 2010b). Cultural memory is based on the idea that "objectivized culture has the structure of memory" (Assmann & Czaplicka, 1995, p. 128). The Greeks, he claims, viewed culture "not only as based on memory, but as a form of memory in itself." (Assmann, 1998, p. 15). This type of culturally embedded memory stands apart from communicative memory, which, he argues, refers to the way in which historical experiences are communicated across the generations over a period of 80–100 years. Assmann's structural model of the collective past may be helpful in some research settings and the characteristics of both forms of memory are shown in Figure 11.1. László (2003, p. 185) provides a translation and summary.

	Communicative Memory	Cultural Memory
Content	Historical experiences life course	Myth of origin, archaic history in the individual and absolute past
Form	Informal, natural, based on communication	Formal, festive, and ceremonial interpersonal
Media	Human memory immediate, dancing, pictures, etc.	Recorded, objectified in writing experiences, oral tradition
Time structure	80–100 years, 3–4 generations	Absolute past to mythical times
Carriers	Contemporaries	Professional carriers of tradition

FIGURE 11.1 *Characteristics of communicative and cultural memory (after Assmann, 1992).*

HOW TO STUDY THE COLLECTIVE PAST

At this point, we might ask, how should we study the collective past? On this question, the sociologist Jeffrey Olick (1999) makes an important distinction between **collected memory**—the collection and aggregation of individual memories, and collective memory—the symbols and deeper structures that are not reducible to individual psychological processes. While the workings of individual memory can be traced back to neural networks in the brain, there appears to be no equivalent and naturally occurring substrate or network for group memory. If we argue that individual group members comprise a substrate, this introduces a particular set of methodological assumptions similar to those that govern attitude research; that is, that we can draw conclusions about collective memory from an aggregation of individual memories taken from within a group. The task of an aggregate approach would be to assemble individual memories into a collage or group mosaic of memory. The focus would be on content, coherence, and its rhetorical stance toward the past, which may tell us something about identity. Most researchers (with the exception of discourse analysts) would assume that such expressions reflect the content of mind.

An aggregate approach, however, may fail to capture more culturally embedded elements of the collective past; for example, it may overlook deeper memory structures existing within objects, institutions, language, and culture. The idea that memory exists beyond the bounds of cognition largely stems from Durkheim's argument that culture is not reducible to what goes on in the minds of individuals. In Durkheim's analysis, collective representations transcend the individual; they are not dependent on any one person for their existence (see Olick, 2010). The study of monuments, museums, street names, flags, media discourse, images, documentary, libraries, archives, and commemorative practices may therefore provide access to more profound and entrenched aspects of the collective past.

LANDSCAPE, SOCIAL SPACE, AND MEMORY

The transformation of memory into objects and images inevitably directs our attention toward the structure of the physical environment. Therein lies a complex relationship between landscape and memory, which may be expressed in a very specific way and within a particular social and historical context. From the study of memory sites in the US, cultural geographer, Kenneth Foote (1993) notes that physical space, which has been the scene of violent and tragic events, may be transformed in four possible ways. The site may be *sanctified*—officially ordained as a place of memory or, over time, it becomes *designated* as a consecrated place of memory. Alternatively, it may be *rectified*—rebuilt and restored to its former use with all evidence of the traumatic event removed or, in the most extreme cases of violence, *obliterated*, completely destroyed with no attempt to restore buildings to their original configuration—and with no public marker of the event.

We might be tempted to think of buildings as static, nonsocial entities, but their construction and demolition are the result of social and historic processes, and their existence or disappearance can affect memory and identity over generations. Buildings, towns, and cities often come to represent the feelings of the community and public buildings, public places, and spaces "speak" to us in the language of signs, symbols, and meanings. These structures, and the physical space they create, generate emotion, ambience, and impressions and the intention, function, and outcome of a space or building may reveal something about the collective past.

For example, in his analysis of the memorial to Nazi book burning in Bebelplatz, Berlin, Brockmeier (2002) deconstructs the narrative of the memorial through an analysis of the *scene* (the historical and political background), the *agent* (the artist or architect), the *action* (e.g., building, rebuilding or restoration), *intentionality* (the intended goal of the installation), the *predicament* (the problem or conundrum that it presents), and the *solution* (a clearer understanding of what the project achieves and the way it achieves it).

In many instances, the construction or destruction of a building creates a predicament that revolves around the issue of remembering and forgetting. For example, the Frauenkirche in Dresden, which was destroyed in the Allied bombing raids in February 1945, was rebuilt and restored between 1992 and 2005. Prior to its restoration, the remains were a stark reminder of war. However, the rebuilding of the church and the main square has transformed the social space. What effect does this have on our apprehension of the past? Does it encourage remembering or forgetting? Did the rebuilding represent forgiveness or healing? Why did it stand in a derelict state for so long? What effect did this scene of destruction have on the postwar generation throughout the Cold War? Why was the church rebuilt and what meaning did it have for the German people and the people of Dresden?

The Frauenkirche, Dresden (April 1991) (above) shortly before the commencement of its rebuilding and restoration now completed (below). Photos: Christopher J. Hewer.

The Ernst-Happel sports stadium in Vienna, Austria presents a different scenario. In this setting, a balance between remembering and forgetting is achieved by the installation of a wall plaque inside the main stand, which acknowledges its darker history—the stadium served as a collection point and detention center for Jews prior to their deportation to concentration camps. As one might expect, however, this memory is overshadowed by the coming and going of large crowds in the pursuit of entertainment: it is not a place for quiet reflection. Indeed, achieving an appropriate balance between remembering and forgetting is difficult and, if not carried out sensitively, tensions may ensue. For example, in a number of German cities (such as Hannover pictured below), German artist Gunter Demnig has installed square brass bricks known as *Stolpersteine* (stumbling blocks) on the public walkway as an act of remembrance for the Jewish families that were arrested and deported during WWII.

Photo: Christopher J. Hewer.

These installations, however—an expression of memory through art—have not pleased all Jewish groups or German nationals, which illustrates the difficulties that beset anyone who ventures into this sensitive terrain.

Because of the events of the Second World War, memory is an issue across the whole of Europe. In Poland, for example, the population have to deal with the memory of tyranny, war, and occupation by the Germans and the Russians, and memory was particularly an issue for Warsaw, the capital. Its complete destruction by the Germans meant that every detail of the old town had to be recreated from drawings hidden away during the war and the paintings of the Italian artist, Canaletto. In each of these cases, the urban landscape expresses a unique, complex, and difficult relationship with the past—a memory of traumatic events expressed or constrained by identity.

NARRATIVES

Although the environment is an important source of memory, the most common way that we acquire an understanding of the past is through storytelling. Indeed, historical accounts disseminated from a variety of sources form a large part of the fabric of our common sense understanding of the past. Narratives allow us to present a morality play to others, clearly identifying those groups or individuals who are "good" and "bad." There is normally a plot, a theme, and an object lesson and we usually assert our authority to speak through knowledge, experience, or association, for example "I studied history at school and it is true that…" or "We were bombed during the war, and it was awful …" or "My uncle was in Vietnam and he says…" However, the stories we tell are often a direct or indirect expression of identity and maybe part of an identity project—especially when they are linked in some way to our own family history.

In psychological terms, narrative thinking may be understood as a complementary alternative to scientific thinking in that it allows the narrator to make assertions about the world, which are seldom subjected to test or scrutiny (Bruner, 1986, 1990). From a research perspective, narrative accounts are useful because they often provide cause and effect explanation from the perspective of the narrator. However, it is a way of thinking that seeks correspondence and coherence with our own established sense of reality rather than truth (László, 2003).

SOCIAL REPRESENTATIONS OF HISTORY

The idea that storytelling creates or constructs a common sense understanding of the past inevitably draws us into a discussion of social representations theory (SRT) (Moscovici, 1961/1976). SRT proposes that social knowledge is constructed, developed—even manufactured—by social processes. Moscovici's original research examined the social and psychological processes through which knowledge of psychoanalysis in France in the 1950s had been transformed into common sense. Moscovici concluded that these processes provide a model for the construction of all forms of social knowledge and further claimed that the age of static collective representations (in the Durkheimian sense) largely transmitted through ritual had come to an end in the postwar period. Where once the past had been transmitted across generations through poetry, dance, and ritual, the social conditions arising from modernity and an emerging age of individualism was now creating dynamic and diffuse representations of social phenomena, which both reflect and create social change (Farr, 1998). These dynamic representations—social representations—filter, reform, and construct all forms of social knowledge and are now arguably "the carriers of collective memory" (Wagoner, 2015, p. 143).

The theory posits that communication, whether interpersonal, media, intergenerational, formal, or informal is the means by which ideas become familiar. When an historical event is discussed in, for example, a documentary, a news broadcast, or a discussion with coworkers, new information is adjusted to fit within existing knowledge structures (anchoring). Once the idea is explained, defined or given a name (objectification), it becomes established, more concrete, to the point that it allows people to discuss the topic without detailed or accurate understanding.

THE NATURE OF REPRESENTATIONS

Messages about the past, transmitted through newspapers, radio, television, film, the Internet, and everyday conversation, converge upon the public to produce a *sketch* of history. The result is seldom a clear, coherent or consistent account; instead, contradictory elements often find expression within cultures, groups, or individuals (**cognitive polyphasia**) (see Jovchelovitch, 2012). There may also be assumptions, distortions, oversimplifications, and gaps in the storyline and such versions of the past have a cyclical and compounding effect since they both *rely upon* and *contribute to* a knowledge deficit within the general population (Baumeister & Hastings, 1997).

People may also make sense of the past by associating historical events with a particular person (personification); for example, Skanderbeg in Kosovo, Guiseppe Garibaldi in Italy, or George Washington in the USA. Another way is to associate historical events with symbols or metaphors (figuration) (see Moscovici & Hewstone, 1983); for example, expressing the need to "turn the page" or "move on" are metaphors that encourage forgetting as though remembering presents a barrier to progress or advancement. Other powerful representations are invoked by symbols. These include images of Adolf Hitler and the Nazi swastika, which are widely recognized as representations of the Second World War: a period of cruelty and intense suffering. Because most people can identify Hitler and the swastika and because they have seen images of concentration camps, they are able to engage with others when the topic comes up in conversation.

This, however, may be the full extent of their knowledge; they may have little or no detailed information about the social, political, and economic context of the rise of National Socialism in Germany before the war. They may not understand the complex internal national politics that led a democratic nation to dictatorship and then global conflict. Political events are complex and because we have limited time, resources, and interest, we rely on image, metaphor, and grand narrative to provide a general outline. The task of uncovering detail, context, analysis, and "truth" is delegated to professional historians who we assume will carry out the task responsibly.

There may also be mythical elements in the storyline, which are there to bolster identity, which include both empirical and ethnographic myths (see Brown, 2005). An **empirical myth** is something that is untrue, an event that never happened, an action of a fictional hero, or the removal from history of someone who once existed. More common perhaps are **ethnographic myths**: cultural beliefs about an event that eventually come to define a people or culture. At the root of ethnographic myths are cultural meanings attributed by, for example, Jews to the Roman siege of Masada in 73 CE or by the British public to the evacuation of British soldiers from the beaches of Dunkirk in 1940. Both events defined a people at a particular place and time and have come to symbolize resistance and defiance in the face of an enemy.

Mythical elements may also appear in the form of societal charters (see Malinowski, 1926). Liu and Hilton (2005) maintain that **charters** serve as "a foundational myth for a society defining rights and obligations for a group and legitimizing its social and political arrangements" (p. 538). After WWII, they argue that charters determined a sense of historical mission and political action for all nations involved. Historical narratives may also contain elements of **presentism** where the past is used to justify the present or we might find that they take a "Whiggish" form (Richards, 2002, p. 5), that is, national history may be presented in "celebratory" or "heroic" terms, as part of "inevitable progress" or within a narrative of "darkness to light" or "enslavement to freedom." Curiously, the history of psychology often succumbs to this type of historiography. Introductory psychology textbooks often assert the discipline's intellectual and scientific credentials by identifying founding fathers and by claiming the discipline's unbroken link to the classic intellectual roots of the Greeks. However, presentism, by necessity, involves forgetting, and for psychology, this includes its more questionable associations with eugenics, phrenology, compulsory sterilization of "mental defectives" and brainwashing, which are generally confined to specialist textbooks on the history of psychology (see Richards, 2002, for a discussion of psychology's histories).

Other representations of history may show signs of **historical determinism** where it is assumed that historical epochs have meaning along "a road to progress." For example, a Marxist–Leninist account of history claims that humans have moved away from a discriminatory, class-based, feudal system, toward other systems, which, they believed, would inevitably lead to a classless, egalitarian society. After the demise of the communist system, we might have assumed that people would be reluctant to invoke historical determinism as a way of thinking about political and economic systems, but soon after, political economist, Fukuyama (1992) pronounced capitalism and western liberal democracy as "the end of history": the endpoint of humanity's sociocultural evolution.

Whatever form social representations of history may take, the theory provides a framework for understanding historical accounts and, in many cases, their disparate nature. Indeed, its constructivist orientation allows researchers to represent, explain and model multiple and multilayered representations existing within and between cultures on a variety of social issues (Sammut, Andreoli, Gaskell, & Valsiner, 2015).

MEMORY AS PERFORMANCE

The collective past is also expressed through performative actions such as ritual commemorations and traditions (see Tilmans, Van Vree, & Winter, 2010) although we might find on closer inspection that traditions that appear to stem from an ancient past may have been invented more recently than we imagine (Hobsbawn & Ranger, 1992). What is more, actors and audiences can be seen regularly performing the past in sport, comedy, art, drama, dance, and film— cultural channels of communication that express the past through ritual, representation, and various forms of reenactment (see Hewer, 2012).

THE COLLECTIVE PASTS OF FAMILIES, GROUPS, AND ORGANIZATIONS

Although the principal way of talking about the collective past is through the history of the nation (Lorenz, 2010), many alternatives are available. History may be gendered—a "her story" rather than "his story" or specific cultural or ethnic groups may choose to recount their collective past in their own voice; for example, Black history. The family also provides a framework for memory and we perhaps know from experience that these dynamics are complex. For example, others family members may have a completely different memory of an event compared to our own and may not even recall events that have caused us concern for decades even though they were present at the time. Such differences in recollection may simply reflect the workings of independent memory systems over many years or they may reflect deeply entrenched issues within the politics of the family. In the 1960s, psychiatrists Laing and Esterson examined the dynamics of communication in families in which one member had been diagnosed with "schizophrenia," and to make sense of what was going on they drew upon psychodynamic theory in the form of defense mechanisms, psychodrama, and cross-generational reenactment. Laing and Esterson (1964) argued that mental distress becomes *comprehensible* when family history and its subtle transmission across generations is understood. Put another way, Laing and Esterson saw the family as a memory system that was able to create and control reality. There was an agenda behind each version of the past and the patient, who was less powerful, had grown to distrust her own perceptions and memory. Even her motives, desires, and behavior were subject to definitive interpretations by other members of the family.

The power dynamics that drive memory games within a dysfunctional family may present a model for understanding political conflict within organizations and between national groups (see Roberts & Hewer, 2015). Given the history of intractable conflict and incessant violence across millennia, we appear to be members of a dysfunctional human family whose behavior only becomes comprehensible when we review what we have done to each other. A history of war, genocide, and slavery has created **historical legacies,** which, when imposed upon a group or nation at birth, compel them to position themselves and act within the framework of the cultural script. Legacies travel across the generations and serious cases of social injustice create a new generation of proxy victims and perpetrators (see Weissmark, 2004).

TIME CONCEPTIONS

When appraising the collective past, it is also important to consider time conceptions. Since the Enlightenment, we have conceived a world governed by linear time largely because of the Christian understanding of God's purpose (**eschatology**) and because of a cultural belief in scientific and technological progress (Lorenz, 2010). Philosopher of history, Chris Lorenz further argues that while we see historical events in linear time, we generally experience them in **chronological time**—the irreversible flow of time in one direction—a conception of time that is constant and normative. In other words, 10 years is the same length of time and passes in the same direction whatever its position in history. However, as we get older, time starts to play tricks, and we start to experience its illusory nature. A day, a year, or a decade no longer seems as long as it used to be. James (1890), citing the work of French author Paul Janet, argues that we experience **psychological time** in relation to the length of the life course. In other words, a decade is half the life of a 20-year old, but for someone aged 60, it is only one-sixth of the life course therefore the duration seems shorter as it passes. Others have claimed that our perception of time is influenced by cultural and economic factors. Literary theorist Svetlana Boym (2007) maintains that the rapid acceleration of time caused by industrialization in late modernity erases the past at the same alarming rate, which inevitably creates a sense of nostalgia—a desire for a different time where one can access "the slower rhythms of our dreams" (p. 8). Nostalgia thus creates a new understanding of time and space, and when such yearnings become part of a political project to resurrect a past that never existed, a "restorative" nostalgia transforms a mythical version of the past into truth and tradition.

Indeed, the passage of time is a subjective experience and therefore we should not be surprised that people experience time in ways other than chronologically. For example, Lorenz (2010) argues that following very specific kinds of events such as physical or sexual assault and injury, natural disasters, wars, and so on people experience **durational time**: a past that is always present. Chronological time and durational time reflect the existence of two very different psychological worlds: two different ways of experiencing a collective past. The difference is well illustrated by a conversation between two women visiting the Holocaust Exhibition at the Imperial War Museum in London in 2006. When considering the images of the Nazi genocide of the Jews, one woman turned to the other and said "You would've thought they'd have got over it by now!" For someone living in chronological time, 60 years was long enough to close the file on this historic event, while survivors, their families, and the families of the deceased likely take a very different view.

THE POLITICS OF REMEMBERING AND FORGETTING

This leads to a key question concerning the politics of memory. How should we deal with a difficult, distressing, and damaging collective past? Is it better to remember or forget historic violence? Cultural theorist, Aleida Assmann (2012) draws our attention to the work of Meier (2010) who argues that the ability of any group or nation to forget is a significant cultural achievement because it prevents the past from disrupting social relations in the present and developing into something worse. Assmann also contends that as the balance between remembering and forgetting shifts, we need to consider "who profits" and "who suffers" and to what degree? (Assmann, 2012, p. 68).

Often, one of the difficulties with our own cultural encounter with the collective past is the pressure to readily embrace a historical narrative of our group's pride or pain while failing to acknowledge the full extent of the harm that our group has done to others (e.g., see Ryan & Hewer, 2016). We might do well to ask, "what has been barely mentioned, minimized, or omitted from our own narrative?" If we cannot answer that question, others may be able to provide an answer for us. Cultural forgetting may be a necessary social and psychological strategy to protect a group or nation from an uncomfortable identity threat (see Connerton, 2008), but it is a precarious position that can evolve into state denial. Cohen (2001) reminds us that denial takes three possible forms: That the event did not happen, that it did not happen to the extent claimed, or that it happened, but is of little consequence. Whatever form denial takes, it has the potential to create problems in the future.

THE INDIVIDUAL AND THE COLLECTIVE PAST

The final question concerns the way the collective past is encountered, processed, and interpreted by individuals: why do people (even members of the same national group or family) interpret the same information about the past in very different ways? We can account for this by understanding the interplay between history, culture, and individual cognition, which not only constructs identity but creates a unique, idiosyncratic worldview (see Hewer & Roberts, 2012). There is also the issue of affiliation.

Consider Niklas Frank, son of Hans Frank, Governor General of Occupied Poland during WWII and Horst von Wächter, son of Otto von Wächter, head of civil administration for the Krakow and Galicia districts in Poland in the same period. The fathers of both men presided over territory in which millions of Poles and Jews were murdered. While Frank acknowledges his father's culpability, Wächter finds it difficult to accuse his father of such crimes and maintains that his father was a "good man" who was simply caught in the chain of command (Hall, 2015). The divergent interpretations of Niklas Frank and Horst von Wächter remind us that our personal involvement with the collective past is no mere academic exercise. Kinship and identity largely direct our understanding of the past (and our response to it) and we have to accept that an overly robust attachment to either can lead us into passive or active involvement in the harm of others. We need to interrogate our beliefs about the past and recognize that our affiliations can distort our understanding and our moral judgment. Ideally, this should be done before we are seduced by a narrative of the past issuing from an authority that seeks to secure its hold over us.

SUMMARY

- The study of the social and the collective past is a complex multidisciplinary project and the way that the collective past is understood may have important political consequences.
- The study of the collective past involves the study of cognition, communication, and culture.
- Memory is to be found within human cognition, between people, and embedded within the culture.
- Achieving an appropriate balance between remembering and forgetting is a sensitive political and cultural issue.
- Social representations theory can explain and model disparate common sense historical representations.

GLOSSARY

autobiographical memory refers to the memory of personal events, which have been experienced directly.

charters are culturally constructed beliefs derived from myths that confer legitimacy, status, rights, norms, and limitations on national or ethnic groups.

chronological time refers to the experience of time as passing in one direction and being of consistent duration.

collected memory refers to the aggregation of individual memories into a coherent and collective form.

collective memory refers to shared representations of the past held by a group or collective.

cognitive polyphasia refers to a state where different kinds of knowledge based on different forms of reasoning and argument exist within the same individual, group or collective.

communicative memory refers to the process by which individual life experiences are communicated informally across three to four generations.

collective remembering refers to the way that groups remember the past in the present.

cultural memory refers to a recorded history that stretches back to an ancient and absolute past—its formal, festive, and ceremonial nature is communicated within the culture by historians, archaeologists, and other professionals.

durational time is a sense of time that occurs after traumatic events where the event is experienced in a permanent present.

ethnographic myths are beliefs or interpretations that are used to define a group or people.

empirical myth is something that is factually untrue; a false belief.

eschatology is the study of the last days or final things in anticipation of divine judgment.

historical determinism is the belief that historical events and epochs are moving along a progressive road to a predetermined outcome.

historical legacies refer to specific histories acquired through national, group, or family ties.

historical memory refers to memory constructed by groups for the purpose of maintaining a continuous and coherent identity.

"memory boom" refers to a post-1980s cultural development whereby people are preoccupied with nostalgia and incessant memorialization.

mnemonic socialization is an immersion into the language, beliefs, and practices of a culture, which includes formal, informal, explicit, and implicit sources of information.

mnemohistory describes any intellectual enquiry concerned with the way in which the past is understood.

presentism is a way of writing of history where the past is used to justify the present.

psychological time refers to time as experienced in relation to the current length of the life course.

social frameworks refer to the structural setting in which we understand an historical past, for example nation, family, or group.

social memory refers to the social processes that create a sense of the collective past.

FURTHER READING

Halbwachs M. (1950/1992). In L. A. Coser (Ed.), Trans. *On collective memory*. Chicago, IL: Chicago University Press.

Liu J. H., & Hilton D. J. (2005). How the past weights on the present: Social representations of history and their role in identity politics. *British Journal of Social Psychology, 44*, 537–556.

Olick J., Vinitsky V., & Levy D. (Eds.) (2011). *The collective memory reader*. Oxford, UK: Oxford University Press.

Reicher S., & Hopkins N. (2001). *Self and nation: Categorisation, contestation and mobilisation*. London: Sage.

A useful resource is *Memory Studies*—a multi-disciplinary journal for the study of memory published by Sage—mss.sagepub.com.

QUESTIONS FOR GROUP DISCUSSION

- In a democracy, who controls public memory and by what means?
- Why is the past so prominent in the construction of identity? Does it have to be this way?

- Are there any narratives that you have accepted uncritically? Does anything prevent you from interrogating these narratives?
- Is it better to remember or forget historical violence?
- When will it be appropriate to stop commemorating the First World War?
- When will it be appropriate to stop commemorating the Second World War?
- At what point in history would it be appropriate to dismantle concentrations camps like Dachau and Auschwitz, and who should decide? Is it appropriate to maintain and restore the wooden barracks or does this constitute a material reconstruction of memory?

12 Crowds, Social Identities, and the Shaping of Everyday Social Relations

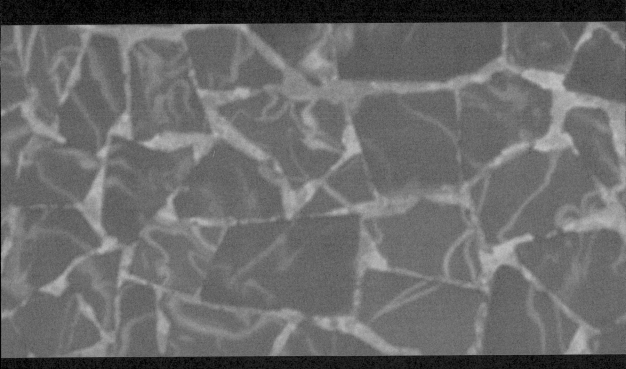

FERGUS G. NEVILLE AND STEPHEN D. REICHER

CHAPTER OUTLINE

In this chapter, we address the relationship between crowd events and the social categories that organize our everyday lives. According to conventional wisdom, crowd events are a pathological disruption of everyday life caused by either a loss of individual identity or a congregation of individuals with pathological identities. We examine and critique this approach before going on to explore the various ways in which crowd events create and endorse social identities (group memberships) within the wider population of nonparticipants in society. In other words, if you want to understand social identities and social relations in society—both what they are and how they are produced—look to the crowd. Crowds constitute the social imaginary: they both reflect and shape the way we think about the groups to which we belong and our relations with others. The idea that crowds play a critical role in the construction of the social imaginary for both those who participate in crowds and those who observe them directly or through the media is controversial because it counters traditional wisdom, and at the root of this argument is a very specific understanding of social identities and their political significance.

THE POLITICAL SIGNIFICANCE OF SOCIAL IDENTITIES

For us, social identities need to be analyzed in relation to the organization of social reality. On the one hand, as stressed by self-categorization theorists (Turner, Hogg, Oakes, Reicher, & Wetherell, 1987), social identities reflect existing social realities. For example, why are national identities so salient in today's world, especially around events such as the Olympics? It is because we live in a world of nations where many specific events, such as the Olympics, are organized along national divides. On the other hand, as we have stressed (Reicher & Hopkins, 2001b), social identities serve to mobilize people to create new social realities. Why do we live in a world of nations, where new nations are still arising? It is because nationalists have mobilized people in the name of country in order to create nationally based state structures.

Insofar as social identities bring people together to act and to apply the power derived from their joint efforts to shape the world (either to consolidate existing arrangements or to change them), they are necessarily political. What is more, insofar as politics involves the exercise of power, it necessarily involves the analysis of social identities that shape how people act with or against each

Political Psychology: A Social Psychological Approach, First Edition.
Edited by Christopher J. Hewer and Evanthia Lyons.
© 2018 John Wiley & Sons Ltd. Published 2018 by John Wiley & Sons Ltd.

other. To make the point more starkly, understanding the dynamics that determine the social identities we live by is at the core of the articulation between politics and psychology. With this in mind, let us now consider what crowds do (or do not) have to do with everyday social identities.

There has always been an interest in crowd psychology and the elites who write history have consistently characterized the masses as less rational, less human, and less deserving. This is particularly true when the masses come together in crowds to challenge these elites (Reiwald, 1949). The more the masses revolt, the less secure the elites feel and the more urgently these concerns are expressed. Thus, as modernity took hold in the nineteenth century and transformed rural landscapes into urban societies, and as peasants who once worked in fields became concentrated in factories, an informal and somewhat negative view of crowds turned into a more systematic crowd psychology.

Many nations were rocked by the rise of the working classes and none felt more fragile than France. The third Republic (1870–1940), which had emerged from the ashes of the Franco–Prussian war and the Paris Commune, was threatened on all sides by the collective activities of the growing Trades Union, syndicalist, anarchist, and socialist movements (Barrows, 1981; Giner, 1976; Nye, 1975). It is no surprise, then, that this new crowd psychology was centered on France and it reflected the fears of the elite. While the goal may have been to understand crowd activity, it was primarily used as a tool for repressing crowd threat. As Rogers (1998, p. 3) puts it, crowd psychology was intended to "discredit both the motives and legitimacy of left-wing movements."

At root, it did this by divorcing the actions of working class crowds from their social context. This new crowd psychology saw crowds as an eruption of the primitive into modern life, an aberration that transforms civilized people into barbarians. In the crowd, we are stripped of our identities; we are turned against ourselves and moved to act against our essential nature and interests. In this analysis, crowds have nothing to do with everyday identities. This classic crowd psychology is a narrative of loss: people are said to lose their minds and their morals and they thereby put both themselves and others at risk. And although there is no loss of power, most crucially, classic crowd psychology claims that people lose their identity in a crowd. But it is a very specific sense of identity that underpins this assumption. In this context, identity is a *unitary* construct that is assumed to be the sole basis of reasoned action.

We challenge this view of identity; we argue that identity is a multidimensional construct that refers both to the way that we, as unique individual subjects differ from other individual subjects (personal identity) and the way that we, as collective subjects, differ from other collective subjects (social identity) (see Tajfel, 1982; Turner et al., 1987). Our contention is that crowds involve a *shift* rather than a loss of identity—a shift from personal identity to social identity. We also argue that mind, morals, and interests are not lost in the crowd, but rather they become tied to collective norms, values, and priorities.

CLASSIC CROWD PSYCHOLOGY: THE LOSS OF INDIVIDUAL IDENTITY IN THE MASS

Among the early work on crowd psychology Gustave Le Bon's book *The Crowd: A Study of the Popular Mind* (1895/2002) is perhaps the most influential. It not only analyzed the mass politics of the twentieth (and the twenty-first) century, but also helped to create it (Moscovici, 1985). Le Bon strongly identified with the social elite; he was a strong nationalist and fervent antisocialist. As Head of Ambulance Services, he had witnessed (and abhorred) the Paris Commune. This experience led him to use his work to advise right-wing leaders about crowd behavior, particularly, the way in which crowds could be turned against the radicals for the defense of the nation (see Nye, 1975). Le Bon saw the crowd as a place in which people are transformed, so that the most rational and mild individual becomes mindless, emotional, and violent. He claimed that the "unconscious action of crowds substituting itself for the conscious activity of individuals is one of the principle characteristics of the present age" (p. iii) and he developed this argument with three core concepts. The first—**submergence**—is where the individual becomes anonymous and loses identity in the crowd (the "conscious personality" in Le Bon's terms). As a result, the crowd member "is no longer himself, but has become an automaton who has ceased to be guided by his will" (p. 8).

The second concept is **contagion**: this is where the individual is no longer able to exert judgment or will, but helplessly goes along with any passing idea or emotion. Indeed, because the capacity to judge and reason is lost in the crowd, ideas play a relatively small role; the crowd is dominated by emotion, which diminishes reason (see McDougall, 1920/1939). The third concept—**suggestion**—attempts to explain the origin of the ideas and emotions that spread contagiously within the crowd. According to Le Bon, some arise by chance like the wind that blows ripples in all directions on the surface of a river. But these are trivial compared to those that originate from the racial unconscious—which, to continue Le Bon's analogy, equate to the flow of the river toward the sea. This racial unconscious is akin to the "atavistic residuum of the instincts of the primitive man" (Le Bon, 1895/2002, p. 22), which gives rise to "primitive" crowd behaviors. For Le Bon, anyone who becomes part of a crowd, even if they are reasonable and benign, is likely to become irrational, brutal, and animalistic.

It is worth noting that, even though Le Bon's book is now over 120 years old, it continues to be cited (over 250 citations in the last year according to Google Scholar) and has given rise to a whole tradition of deindividuation research in contemporary social psychology. There are a number of variants, some of which emphasize the way in which anonymity in groups leads to generically antisocial behavior (e.g., Cannavale, Scar, & Pepitone, 1970; Festinger, Pepitone, & Newcombe, 1952; Zimbardo, 1969), and others that stress that such anonymity leads to loss of control over one's behavior (Diener, 1980; Duval & Wicklund, 1972). But wherever the emphasis is placed, both share the Le Bonian notion that those submerged in the mass are mindless and capable of acts that they would never countenance as individuals (for a review see Reicher, Spears, & Potmes, 1995).

This is remarkable given that the Le Bonian approach presents a distorted view of the phenomenon. Crowds are not generically primitive and violent; indeed violence is the exception rather than the rule (see Barrows, 1981; McPhail, 1991). What is more, even when violence does occur, it is not random and indiscriminate, but rather highly patterned both in terms of what targets are attacked and the forms of violence on display (Davis, 1973; Reicher, 1984; Thompson, 1971). Indeed, crowd behavior in general tends to be highly pattered with those patterns taking a socially meaningful form. That is, crowd behavior—and deindividuated behavior as well—reflects collective beliefs, collective norms, and collective rituals (Postmes & Spears, 1998; Reicher, 2001). It is not at all as Le Bon describes it.

DISPOSITIONAL THEORIES: THE ACCENTUATION OF INDIVIDUAL CHARACTERISTICS IN THE MASS

For all its influence, Le Bonian crowd psychology has not gone unchallenged. Indeed, from the very start it aroused furious opposition, notably from Allport (1924) who rejected the very notion of a group unconscious separate from that of individuals. He lampooned this as an absurdity and famously insisted that: "there is no psychology of groups which is not essentially and entirely a psychology of individuals" (p. 4). This claim was given substance through the notion of social facilitation. That is; each person has a distinctive response profile based on his or her personal learning experiences. In the company of others, this profile is sharpened; dominant responses become more dominant and subordinate responses become further supressed. The implication, then, is that groups accentuate rather than obliterate individuality.

In his own work, Allport (1924) made a distinction between this general group psychology and crowd psychology. He argued that, as the number and density of members grows, so the energy provided by others increases to the extent that our learned responses exceed a peak and we revert to basic instinctual behaviors. *In other words, for all his opposition, Allport's own crowd psychology is not too dissimilar to Le Bon's.* However, all too few people go back to the original sources and, as a result, Allport was used to inspire a dispositionalist tradition of crowd psychology—one in which the character of crowds is said to reveal the character of its members. Or to put it the other way around, particular types of people converge to create particular types of crowd. Hence the term "**convergence theory**" (see Turner & Killian, 1972) has been used to describe this approach.

There are, however, many variants of convergence theory. These differ in the ways that they see the types of individual characteristic that underlie participation in crowds. Many take a Freudian approach. For example, Kornhauser (1959) suggested that crowd members were alienated individuals, while Lasswell (1930), Hoffer (1951), and Klapp (1969) identified political "types" who engaged in collective behavior to fulfill inner needs. As Goodwin, Jasper, and Polletta (2001) noted, these models depict participants as those who "did not choose or enjoy protest, but were compelled to it by their inner demons." (p. 4). Others take a more conventional personality approach, leaving out the psychodynamics, and seeking to find characteristics that lead people to participate in collective action, particularly violent collective action (see Turner & Killian, 1972; US Riot Commission, 1968). But while there are many convergence models, evidence to support them is far harder to find. To date, there is no personality type or personality characteristic that has been definitively linked to crowd participation or crowd violence (e.g., McPhail, 1971; Reicher & Stott, 2011; Rogers, 1998; Rudé, 1959; Stott & Adang, 2004).

Perhaps we are looking in the wrong place for the significance of these theories, which lies less in their empirical validity than in their political efficacy. For all their differences with transformational theories, dispositional approaches retain a view of the crowd as an overwhelmingly negative, destructive, and pathological phenomenon. In effect, they move the locus of pathology from general crowd processes to individual crowd members. In a similar way to Le Bon, this approach has elitist overtones and has shaped policy in right-wing governments. For example, in the aftermath of the 1985 Tottenham and Handsworth riots, Oliver Letwin—advisor to Prime Minister Margaret Thatcher—successfully argued against providing additional social support for unemployed black youth on the grounds that "Riots, criminality, and social disintegration are caused solely by individual characters and attitudes" (Travis, 2015). Equally, following the 2011 English riots, Prime Minister David Cameron blamed the disorder on "thugs … people with a twisted moral code … people with a complete absence of self-restraint" (Cameron, 2011).

The key point about these pathologizing accounts is not so much where they locate the explanation of social disorder, but where they *do not*. That is, whether the focus is on crowd process or on crowd members, the explanatory gaze is firmly turned away from the society, the state, and its agencies. The assumption is that if people protest, it is not because there is something wrong with society; and if they are violent in crowd events, it is not because they are mistreated by the army, national guard, or the police. They riot because rioting is what they do. And so elites and their governments—whose original legitimation lies in their ability to create and maintain social order—cannot be held to account for social disorder.

In the end, what is political about classic crowd psychologies is that they deny that there is anything social or political about crowds. Hence, there is no need to address the social and political structure when crowd conflict occurs. If crowds (or crowd members) are inherently violent, the only effective response is to repress them as quickly and as firmly as possible (Reicher & Potter, 1985). This powerful ideological message is underpinned by a desocialized notion of identity. Idiosyncratic individual identities are seen as the sole basis for judgment and reasoned action. For the Le Bonians, identity is obliterated in the crowd, for the Allportians it is accentuated. But neither has a basis for understanding how identity and action may be shaped by shared social understandings. As a consequence, it is impossible to understand how the individual psychological field can be socially structured or to discern the socially meaningful pattern of crowd action. What is more, it prevents us from drawing any connection between crowds and the social identities that join or divide us from others in everyday social reality.

CROWDS AND THE EXPRESSION OF SOCIAL IDENTITIES

Historians have long recognized what classic crowd psychology denied: that crowd action is firmly rooted in collective systems of belief. Indeed, for the historian, such action provides a solution to a disciplinary dilemma. How can one recover the perspective of those powerless and marginal groups in history that leave few written records? The answer is to look how they act collectively.

A classic example is Thompson's (1971) study of English food riots in the late eighteenth and early nineteenth centuries. Thomson demonstrates how the specific forms taken by these riots reflects what he calls a peasant "moral economy"—a traditional understanding of society based on the locality. In times of scarcity, the emergent mercantile class sought to transport food to distant markets where a higher price could be obtained. At this point, the carts were stopped, the grain seized and sold at the locally accepted price before the money (and sometimes even the grain sacks) were returned to the merchants (Thompson, 1971). Far from representing a chaotic eruption of rage, the "rioting" crowds acted as an "extra-legal enforcer of community norms" (Rogers, 1998, p. 13). The same is true even of the most extreme collective violence—and there are few examples more gruesome than the religious riots that beset Europe, particularly France, in the seventeenth century. Many were tortured and murdered before their bodies were systematically desecrated. And yet even here the forms of action drew upon traditional liturgical forms. Thus, in her analysis of such riots, Natalie Davis contends that, "[collective] violence is intense because it connects intimately with the fundamental values and self-definition of a community" and that "[collective] violence is related here less to the pathological than to the normal" (1973, p. 90).

So what are the psychological mechanisms that allow crowd members to act together in such socially meaningful ways? One obvious answer is that leaders coordinate people who would otherwise be unable to show such coherence. Yet both Thompson and Davis are quite explicit that this was not so in the cases they studied. Crowd members may have invoked authority (the king, the priest) in support of their actions, but authority itself was generally shocked and horrified, and was neither present nor supportive of what went on. The sociality of the crowd appears to have been spontaneous and cannot be explained away as solely a product of leadership.

A SOCIAL IDENTITY MODEL OF CROWDS

The **Social Identity Model of crowds** (SIM: Reicher, 1984, 1987) provides an alternative explanation, one that starts by rethinking the individualistic concept of identity, which, as we have seen, underpins the classic approach. Drawing on the social identity work of Henri Tajfel and John Turner (Tajfel & Turner, 1979; Turner et al., 1987) it is argued that the self it not a unitary construct referring uniquely to the idiosyncrasies of the individual. Rather, it is a system that operates at different levels of abstraction. On one level we may indeed think of ourselves in terms of what renders us unique as an individual compared to other individuals ("I" vs. "you": personal identity). On another level, however, we can think of ourselves in terms of what renders us unique as members of a particular social category compared to members of another social category ("we" vs. "they": social identity).

In psychological crowds, people shift from personal identity to a relevant social identity. By psychological crowds, we mean a set of people who have a sense of themselves as belonging to a social category—for example, football supporters or partisans at a political rally, as opposed to an aggregate of people who happen to be in the same place at the same time but have no sense of commonality, such as shoppers on the High Street. Psychological crowds do not lose control over their behavior; they do not lose standards or the ability to reason. Rather, they think about the world and make decisions about how to act on the basis of collective beliefs, values, and interests.

For instance, Reicher (1984) provides an analysis of the St. Pauls riot (the first of a wave of urban riots that affected many UK cities through the 1980s), which links the pattern of action to the social identity of crowd members. This identity, based in black urban experience, characterized the local community as subject to oppression by the police, and exploitation by a nexus of financial institutions. Hence, where the police or these institutions (the local bank, post office, large shops owned by outsiders) came under attack, others rapidly joined in. However, when other targets were hit (a bus, a locally owned shop), people either shunned or actively stopped such actions.

This analysis makes sense of the pattern of crowd action: people act together in socially meaningful ways because they share a socially defined sense of identity. However, it would be too simple to suggest that what is going on is a simple cognitive process in which people express pregiven understandings of the world. First of all, crowd events are often unprecedented and ambiguous events. The people of St. Pauls did not have clearly defined and pregiven norms as to what they should do (or not do) in a riot, because they had never been in a riot before and did not expect one before it happened. Rather, they had to elaborate a situational set of norms within the broader terms by which St. Pauls identity was defined. More specifically, they inferred norms from the behavior of fellow in-group members as long as these behaviors were not clearly at odds with their higher order understanding of who they were. In short, *norms were created within the broad limits of social identity as they went along.*

Secondly, the roots of crowd action cannot be understood purely in cognitive terms. When people have a shared sense of social identity they have both a common perspective on the world and a sense of intimacy with each other. Fellow crowd members are no longer "other": they are part of an extended self. Their fate becomes our fate; their concerns are our concerns. As a result, we see heightened cooperation, coordination, and support between crowd members (Neville & Reicher, 2011; Reicher, 2011, 2012). This allows people to align their efforts and to gain confidence, knowing that when they act they will have the help of others. Indeed, shared identity empowers people to act on their shared understandings (Drury & Reicher, 1999, 2009).

For example, in the St. Pauls riot, a number of participants acknowledged that they frequently felt antagonism toward the police, but in the power relations of everyday life were unable to act on this because of the consequences. However, when they combined together in the crowd they were able to drive the police from St. Pauls, to attack them and attack police property with impunity. The everyday power relations were reversed. For once, they "called the tune" (Reicher, 1987). This is a critical point for our argument. It is not just that crowds are one of many sites in which people *express* their social identities. Rather, because crowd members have *collective power* as well as a collective perspective, it is uniquely from crowd members that one can see an unconstrained expression of social identity. The great French historian Georges Lefebvre concluded his chapter on the revolutionary crowds of 1789 by observing that it is, perhaps, only in the crowd that people lose their petty day concerns and become true subjects of history (Lefebvre, 1954). This explains why historians—and psychologists—should look to the crowd if they want to understand their own subject.

There is one final point to be made here. When people are able to act on their own terms and fully enact their own identities—what we call collective self-objectification (or realization—see Drury & Reicher, 2009; Reicher & Haslam, 2006), the experience is intense. It leads to great feelings of joy. People describe it with terms such as "sublime." As we have shown, such intense feelings are traditionally taken as a sign that reason has been lost and emotion has taken over. But there is an alternative tradition, deriving from Durkheim's (1912/2001) work on collective "effervescence," which suggests that emotion complements rather than replaces reason. That is what our evidence shows (Hopkins et al., 2016; Neville & Reicher, 2011). We are joyous in crowds because crowds allow us to express our own reason rather than being subject to the reason of others. We love crowds because crowds, literally, make "us" real.

CROWDS AND THE CONSTRUCTION OF SOCIAL IDENTITIES

Before continuing with our argument, we need to look in a little more detail at how we conceptualize social identities (see Reicher & Hopkins, 2001b). For the sake of experimental ease, social identities are often operationalized as sets of traits. For example, to be British can be defined in terms of being hard-working, undemonstrative, proud, ..., and so on. However to say, "I am British," "I am Scottish," or whatever, means far more than this. First of all, it denotes that we look at our world as organized by nationhood. Next, it denotes that we take a particular position within that world of nations. This, is turn, has implications for how we *can* act (if, for instance, we see ourselves as lacking power, we may have to be more indirect in pursuing our goals); and how we *should* act (nationhood in general carries with it certain moral imperatives and particular nations carry certain values). In sum, we describe a social identity as a model of one's position within a set of social relations *along with the actions that are possible and desirable given that position* (e.g., Drury & Reicher, 2009). However, as we already argued, social identities are not just models of how the world is, they are projects for how the world should be. They are statements of intent as to how the world should be organized. In this sense, identity is an inherently prospective and moral construct (Taylor, 1992).

This proposition has two sets of implications when it comes to understanding the way that crowd events involve both the expression and construction of identities. If, on the one hand, identities are projects, the important thing is not whether they are real (an accurate reflection of how the world is) but whether they can be made real. A project that cannot be realized is likely to be discarded. Equally, then, an identity that envisions a world that can never be experienced is unlikely to take hold.

Therefore, one of the core aspects of crowd process is the ability to enact identities in a way that is rarely possible outside of the crowd. Crowds are spaces in which our sense of how the world should be is made real. This of course, takes very different forms in different crowds. In riots, for example, such collective self-realization might be a matter of exerting power and expressing violence against those who normally have the upper hand. Whereas, at a large Hindu festival—for example, the Magh Mela at Allahabad—collective self-realization is achieved by total devotion to spiritual matters, something that is normally impossible given all the distractions of everyday life (Hopkins et al., 2016).

Given that identities depend upon the possibility of realization, and that crowds are spaces where they can be realized, we might predict that crowd participation plays an important role in the consolidation of social identities and that this process continues beyond the event. This is precisely what we find (Khan et al., 2016). A longitudinal analysis of those who participated in the Mela and those who did not shows that Hindu identification increased during and after the event *for those who participated*. The analysis also shows that this increase was dependent upon a sense of shared social identification and collective self-realization, that is living as a Hindu should.

It is important to stress that this is a conditional model: that collective participation may not always strengthen social identification. Such an outcome depends whether one's vision of the world is confirmed and enacted within the collective event. Clearly, this is not always the case. One's understanding of social relations may be contradicted by a collective experience and where this happens, we would expect the experience to bring about a change in the identities of participants. Indeed, an explanation of identity change is the focus of more recent social identity research on crowds, which we distinguish from the initial work through the label of an **Elaborated Social Identity Model of crowds** (ESIM: Drury & Reicher, 2000, 2009; Reicher, 1996, 2001, 2012; Stott & Reicher, 1998).

AN ELABORATED SOCIAL IDENTITY MODEL OF CROWDS

The starting point for ESIM is the recognition that crowd events are characteristically *intergroup encounters* between two different social groups, for instance, the supporters of two football clubs or between a social group and the authorities (usually the police), which is why our understanding of our position within social relations (that is, our social identities) can change. Across a series of studies of different crowd events—an environmental protest (Drury & Reicher, 2000, 2005); a political demonstration (Stott & Drury, 2000); football events (Stott, Hutchison, & Drury, 2001; Stott & Reicher, 1998); student protests (Reicher, 1996)—a characteristic pattern of interaction resulted in far reaching changes in social identity among crowd members.

Initially, there was a heterogeneous crowd in which there was a minority who wanted to confront the police and a majority who simply wanted to assert their liberal-democratic right to assemble and express their views in public. The police, however, viewed these crowds through the lens of classic crowd psychology; they either saw them as sharing illegal/violent intent or having a potential for violent disorder. In other words, they saw the crowd as homogeneously dangerous. More importantly, they acted on this assumption, seeking either to constrain their movements, or disperse them by force. Those participants who previously were well disposed toward the police began to see them as an illegitimate "other" and began to develop a sense of common cause with the more confrontational elements of the crowd.

Having been treated and positioned as a homogeneous "other" by the police, they began to position themselves in the same way by challenging the restrictions imposed upon them. This, in turn, reinforced the initial view of the police that the crowd was uniformly dangerous and so a spiral of escalating conflict arose. In this process, a number of key changes occurred. First and foremost, members of the crowd majority would assume a more radical and "oppositional" identity (Drury & Reicher, 2000); they would begin to see others whom they might previously have rejected for their oppositionalism as part of a common in-group (Drury, Reicher, & Stott, 2003). They would even change the goals of their action, and their understanding of what constituted successful action: for example, standing up to the police and exposing their role as guardians of privilege now counted as a gain (Drury & Reicher, 2000).

To reframe the argument in more analytic and more general terms, ESIM proposes that change occurs in crowds when members who act on the basis of one understanding of their social position cause powerful others to interpret and respond to these actions by repositioning these members. Change is therefore dependent upon three key conditions. First, that there is an asymmetry in the way that crowd members view themselves and the way they are viewed by others (typically, those authorities who seek to control the crowd). Second, that these "others" have the power to impose their understanding on the crowd in practical terms. Third, that crowd members view this imposition as illegitimate and, when united, gain sufficient power to challenge the way that they are treated.

These conditions are quite rare. ESIM does not propose that change occurs in all crowds, or when there is change, it does not claim that it occurs for every member of the crowd. For example, those radicals who see the police as the opposition have their identities confirmed rather than changed when they are kettled or charged by police officers. Nonetheless, even if rare, the potential for being "misrecognized" (that is, seen and treated by others in a way that is at odds with one's own self-perception) is greater in the chaotic and unprecedented context of crowd events than in the routines of everyday life, which revolve around consensual understandings of self and other. Crowd events both reveal the dynamics of identity change and play a critical role in changing the identities that structure our social world.

THE IMPACT OF CROWDS BEYOND THE CROWD

Crowds can be impressively large, but even the largest of crowds only includes a very small proportion of the population. Estimates of those gathered in Cairo's Tahrir Square during the protests of 2011 vary from tens of thousands up to about two million.[1] But even at the upper limit (almost undoubtedly a gross exaggeration) this represents only 2.5 % of the population of Egypt. At the height of the antigovernment protests in Kiev, on 8 December 2013, it is estimated that between 100,000 and 1 million protestors rallied on Independence Square.[2] But again, to be generous and taking the higher figure, this represents little over 2 % of the Ukrainian population. So even if every single person present were radicalized by their participation, this would still not explain how the protests created a momentum that ultimately unseated Mubarak and Yanukovych, the Presidents of the two countries.

The key question then becomes whether crowds influence people outside the crowd—the great majority who are not present, but who see the events through the media? And, if so, how? Since there is precious little direct data that bears upon this issue, we do not really know. However, given the

---

[1] See http://www.wired.com/2011/02/how-many-people-are-in-tahrir-square-heres-how-to-tell/.
[2] See https://www.rt.com/news/ukraine-protest-biggest-kiev-897/.

theoretical and practical importance of these questions, there is some indirect evidence worth considering.

A key concept for our considerations is Benedict Anderson's (1983) "imagined community," which is specifically concerned with nationhood. He argues that nations are far too large for every citizen to gather together in one place, and that we can only imagine ourselves as part of a single community alongside every other nation. There are various historical conditions that make this possible; for instance, the emergence of print media. This allows different people in different places to read the news and have a sense of their fellows reading the same news and reacting in the same way.

Much of Anderson's argument can be applied to other large-scale social categories through which people define themselves. One will never be able to assemble all the Catholics, conservatives, or Manchester United supporters in the world. So, these too are imagined communities. Our contention is that crowds are *the imagined community made manifest*; they are the concrete assembly of an abstract category. Although not every member is assembled, the assembly represents the category as a whole especially when it comes to symbolic events. Citizens who gather on the streets to mourn the death of a President or Monarch tell those reading the next day's newspapers something about who they are as a nation. Believers who congregate to greet the Pope tell other Catholic onlookers something about who they are as Catholics. These assemblies tell us how large and significant (or small and insignificant) we are, what we are like, what we believe in, how we relate to others and hence our standing in the world. Let us consider each of these points.

To start with, let us consider the issue of size and significance. Most systems of power, especially dictatorial systems, maintain stability less through acting on what people think than on what they think others think (metarepresentations). In this way, even those who oppose the system desist from action for fear that others will either shun them or denounce them. In either case, they become easy prey for the authorities. For example, Falasca-Zamponi (1997) analyzed the Italian fascist salute in these terms. While one might give the salute out of convenience, not believing in the system, seeing someone else giving the salute meant that one could never take the risk that they were not true believers. And so, as a public ritual, the salute discouraged dissent. In a similar vein, Kershaw (2011) argues that the fact that Germans kept fighting to the very end of the war in 1945 did not denote individual support for the Nazis. Rather, it reflected the absence of any leadership that could bring people together to show them that they were not alone in opposing the war.

Indeed, crowd events show people that they are not alone but part of a broad movement of opposition. Ghonim (2012), for instance, gives a vivid description of the early days of the anti-Mubarak movement in Egypt. Initially, people were terrified of coming onto the streets for fear of being small in number and easily repressed by the security police. Yet, when the first demonstrations took place and numbers were larger than expected, in part due to social media, this provided a catalyst for Egypt's "Arab Spring." Further use of social media showed the size of the crowd, which influenced turnout at subsequent events. In an analysis of Twitter usage during the revolution, Kharroub and Bas (2015) noted that a large proportion of images depicted crowds and other protest activities. Such tweets, they argued, demonstrated support for the protest movement and increased activist efficacy and participation. This is because the expectation of the number of other people prepared to engage in collective action is one of the best predictors of an individual's willingness to take part (Klandermans, 1984).

In addition to the way that crowds affect the perceptions of non-participants in terms of the size and significance of groups (how many we are), there is now a sizable and relevant literature that concentrates on the content of group identities (who and what we are), especially in relation to festivals and commemorative crowds (e.g., Gillis, 1996; Spillman, 1997). In her seminal study of festivals in the French revolution, Ozouf (1988) shows how these events were restructured in order to reflect social relations within the newly constituted French polity. Under the old regime, festivals were strictly ordered according to a hierarchy of social "estates," whereas, in postrevolutionary France, which was founded on *liberte, egalite, and fraternite*, the only divisions were permeable categories, such as age, through which everyone passes. The clear message was that in France no one comes first: everyone is equally valued. In contrast, Spencer (2000) traces the parades that arose in opposition to the St. Louis, Missouri general strike of 1877 in America. These parades were used by local elites to present a history of St. Louis and the United States in terms of the triumphs of great men (predominantly the ancestors of the parade organizers). Here, the crowds were used to provide a vision of identity that reestablished rather than dismantled hierarchy.

These studies demonstrate that many crowd events should be understood as performances, which are specifically intended to tell a story about who they are to an audience. What is more, they seek to foreground one narrative of identity against others. For example, French revolutionaries performed a narrative of French equality because they needed to counter previous narratives of hierarchy. In St. Louis, there was an opposite state of affairs. Such crowd events can be seen as *embodied arguments* and this becomes clear when different groups contesting the nature of society structure crowd events to communicate their own visions. For example, Gelvin's (1999) analysis of Syria in the aftermath of the First World War shows how those who had a hierarchical vision of the new Syrian nation organized demonstrations composed only of the elite while the masses were consigned to the role of onlookers. However, those who believed in a more egalitarian Syria broke down this division between participant and audience so that all could participate.

If we accept that crowds can function as arguments about identity, we have to ask, do they work? Do they affect how audiences view themselves and their society? Here, the evidence is far sketchier. Consider the 2014 riots that followed the shooting of a young black man, Michael Brown, in Ferguson, Missouri (see Lowery, 2015). Perceptions were highly polarized across racial lines. According to a New York Times/CBS News survey taken shortly after the unrest (Connelly, 2014), 49 % of African Americans believed that the protestors' actions had either "been about right" or "not gone far enough," while only 19 % of white Americans felt the same. Likewise, 50 % of African Americans and 27 % of white Americans felt that the police response to the protests had "gone too far."

More anecdotally, there is evidence that both groups used the riots as a symbolic display of US race relations as a whole. For African Americans, it demonstrated a continual subordination despite official claims of progress while, for many white Americans, the events in Ferguson were evidence of a continual perceived threat from black people. Despite this polarization, both groups seem to agree that race relations remain highly negative. What is more, Ndlovu (2014) endorses this view claiming that, "there is a serious distrust between all races, and the scenes in Ferguson, Missouri, and later in other parts of the US, speak to the same phenomenon." What is particularly telling here is that Ndlovu is writing in the South African *Rand Daily Mail,* and his argument, aimed at a domestic audience, that "the situation between black South Africans and African Americans is indistinguishable," shows that crowd events in one country can affect conceptions of social relations in another.

CONTESTING THE MEANING OF CROWD BEHAVIOR

Before we conclude, there is another form of contestation that is equally important: the way that those with different visions of identity and society contest the very nature of the social categories involved in an event. Who are the crowd, whom do they represent and, equally, who are those who oppose them? This is central to the question of how people relate to the event, and how they read the relevance of the event to their own self-understanding. Crowd struggles are dramas played out in front of a wider audience, designed to win the sympathies of that wider audience (cf. Subašić, Reynolds, & Turner, 2008). Who that audience sees as "us" or "them" will determine who the audience sympathizes with and who might evoke their active support of opposition (cf. Haslam, Reicher, & Platow, 2010). The question of the social identity of the crowd, and hence whether it is an ingroup to the population, is therefore central to the politics of crowd events.

Shortly after the start of the mass protests on Tahrir Square, on January 27 2011, the interior minister Habib-Al-Adli declared: "The millions will decide the future of this nation, not demonstrations even if numbered in the thousands. Our country is stable and not shaken by such actions."[3] In one sense, he was right, but he raised the question, did the thousands represent the millions and therefore did they have the ability to change the nation, or were they separate and insignificant? The fate of the uprising thereby turned on how the Tahrir crowd was represented.

The regime represented the protesting crowd in a number of different ways; all intended to show that Tahrir did not represent the broad Egyptian population and that they stood against most Egyptians. They were represented as hooligans and terrorists under the sway of the Islamists of the Muslim Brotherhood,[4] agents of "foreigners" and "outside forces,"[5] people who lack Egyptian "citizenship values,"[6] or as undefined forces who want to destroy the country. Consider President Mubarak's speech of January 28:[7]

> The country is passing through difficult times and tough experiences, which began with noble youths and citizens who practice their rights to peaceful demonstrations and protests, expressing their concerns and aspirations, but they were quickly exploited by those who sought to spread chaos and violence, confrontation and to violate the constitutional legitimacy and to attack it.

For Mubarak, Tahrir transformed the protests from a noble and civilized phenomenon of practicing freedom of expression to unfortunate clashes, mobilized, and controlled by political forces bent on escalating and worsening the situation. The protestors were alleged to be targeting the nation's security and stability through acts of provocation, theft, and looting, by setting fires, blocking roads, attacking vital installations as well as public and private properties, and storming some diplomatic missions. These arguments not only sought to isolate the protestors from the population, they were also successful in mobilizing the army to repress the crowds. This was because the army had sworn an oath to defend the country, not the President. In contrast, the protestors consistently sought to represent the Tahrir crowd as the voice of Egypt rather than a subsection of Egyptians acting in their own interests.

Ghonim (2012), for instance, describes a key moment from the first day of the protest, January 25th: "one central, overarching, radical demand had captured the attention of every member of that critical mass in Tahrir: to rid our nation of Hosni Mubarak. We all yelled, 'EL SHA'AB YUREED ISQAAT AN-NIZAAM!' (The people want to topple the regime)" (p. 184). "The people"

---

[3] See http://www.theguardian.com/world/blog/2011/jan/27/egypt-protests.

[4] See http://nvdatabase.swarthmore.edu/content/egyptians-bring-down-dictatorship-hosni-mubarak-2011.

[5] See http://www.theguardian.com/news/blog/2011/feb/03/egypt-protests-live-updates.

[6] See http://www.theguardian.com/news/blog/2011/jan/31/egypt-protests-live-updates.

[7] For the full text, see http://www.theguardian.com/world/2011/feb/02/president-hosni-mubarak-egypt-speech.

here serve as the quintessential inclusive national category. Tahrir is the nation against the dictator. In case this was in any doubt, the inclusiveness of Tahrir was spelled out in a statement issued by "the youth of Tahrir Square" on February 3rd. The first thing they sought to make clear was that:

> ...we are a group of young Muslim and Christian Egyptians; the overwhelming majority of us does not belong to political parties and have no previous political activism. Our movement involves elderly and children, peasants, workers, professionals, students and pensioners. Our movement cannot be classified as "paid for" or "directed by" a limited few because it attracted millions who responded to its emblem of removing the regime.[8]

The protestors were clear about representing themselves as the Egyptian people and they used this to include others and to mobilize their support—or at least demobilize their opposition. The key question, however, centered on the position of the armed forces massed with tanks in and around Tahrir. Would they move against the protestors? Would they support them? Would they remain neutral? Steavenson (2015) describes how two fighter planes swooped low over the Square and crowd members yelled back, "We won't leave! We won't leave!" The jets flew away: "the crowd, tested now and feeling a little braver, began to sing to the tanks. *'The army and the people are one hand! The army and the people are one hand!'*" (Steavenson, 2015, p. 16, emphasis in the original). Later, Steavenson describes the moment when the people asked the lead tank commander, "Will you shoot at us? [...] because it was still unclear: were the tanks Egyptians or the army or Mubarak?" (p. 17). In other words, from the perspective of the protestors, it was self-evident that they represented Egypt; the only question was whether the same could be said of the armed forces. Moreover, from the perspective of those observing events: they knew who they were, what was in question was whether the protestors were Egyptians, foreigners, or troublemakers.

To conclude then, the evidence suggests that crowd events do indeed shape identities and that this effect extends far beyond those who take part. For participants, crowd events reflect the categorical understandings of self and other; they can (re)constitute, consolidate, or change social identities (even beyond the event) depending on whether the crowd dynamics confirm or alter their social position. The same can be said for observers. Indeed, the nature of crowds and how they may be understood can be of great societal and historical importance. Crowds need to be brought back from that class of striking but ultimately trivial phenomena existing on the periphery of "serious" investigation (Reicher, 2011); they belong at the very core of the social sciences.

---

[8]For the full statement see http://www.counterfire.org/news/9860-statement-from-the-youth-of-tahrir-square-sit-in.

SUMMARY

- Traditional crowd psychology serves to protect the status quo by pathologizing those who gather together to challenge injustices and inequalities. This pathology is either located in the individuals who join crowds or, more usually, in the crowd process itself. The argument is that people become "submerged," lose identity and hence lose their ability to reason in the crowd.

- Recent crowd psychology argues that identity is not lost in the crowd. Rather people shift from individual identity to social identities and then act in terms of the perspectives, norms, and interests associated with those identities.

- Crowds do not just express preexisting social identities; social identities can change in crowd events through the interactions between crowd members and others, notably the police.

- Participation in crowds can have effects on social identities that endure well beyond the event itself. This is not only true for those present in the crowd but also for those who witness the crowd either directly or indirectly through the media.

- Overall, crowds have an important impact on the social identities of everyday life, which affect how we behave and how we relate to others.

ACKNOWLEDGMENTS

The authors were partially supported during the writing of this chapter by a research grant from the Economic and Social Research Council (ES/N01068X/1).

GLOSSARY

contagion is Le Bon's notion that, since we have lost the capacity for judgment, we automatically go along with any idea or emotion we witness in others.

convergence theory refers to the notion that crowds are made up of individuals who share common dispositions (e.g., a violent crowd can be explained by the fact that it is composed of violent people).

elaborated social identity model of crowds is the argument that social identities are not just expressed in crowds but also that they can change in crowds, specifically as a function of the developing intergroup dynamics between the crowd and external agencies such as the police.

social identity model of crowds is the argument that instead of a loss of identity in crowds, there is a shift from personal to social identification. As a consequence, people do not lose the ability to reason, but rather they reason on the basis of the perspectives, norms, and interests associated with the relevant social identity.

submergence is Le Bon's notion that anonymity in the mass leads to a loss of identity and hence a loss of reason and judgment.

suggestion is Le Bon's notion that the ideas and emotions that circulate in crowds derive from a primitive racial unconscious—leading behavior to be likewise primitive and destructive.

FURTHER READING

Barrows S. (1981). *Distorting mirrors: Visions of the crowd in late nineteenth-century France.* Yale: Yale University Press.

Davis N. Z. (1973). The rites of violence: Religious riot in sixteenth-century France. *Past and Present, 59*, 51–91.

Drury J., & Reicher S. D. (2000). Collective action and psychological change: The emergence of new social identities. *British Journal of Social Psychology, 39*, 579–604.

Neville F. G., & Reicher S. D. (2011). The experience of collective participation: Shared identity, relatedness and emotionality. *Contemporary Social Science, 6*, 377–396.

Reicher S. D. (1984). The St. Pauls riot: An explanation of the limits of crowd action in terms of a social identity model. *European Journal of Social Psychology, 14*, 1–21.

Reicher S. D. (2001). The psychology of crowd dynamics. In M. A. Hogg & S. Tindale (Eds.), *Blackwell handbook of social psychology: Group processes* (pp. 182–208). Oxford: Blackwell.

Reicher S. D., & Stott C. (2011). *Mad mobs and Englishmen? Myths and realities of the 2011 riots.* London: Hachette.

Stott C. J., Hutchison P., & Drury J. (2001). 'Hooligans' abroad? Inter-group dynamics, social identity and participation in collective 'disorder' at the 1998 world cup finals. *British Journal of Social Psychology, 40*, 359–384.

Thompson E. P. (1971). The moral economy of the English crowd in the eighteenth century. *Past and Present, 50*, 76–136.

QUESTIONS FOR GROUP DISCUSSION

- Why do you think Le Bon's work on crowd psychology has endured for so long? To what extent are his views "convenient?"

- Why is the concept of social identity so important for an alternative way of looking at crowd behavior?
- Do crowds truly represent the masses?
- Why might watching a crowd through the media encourage further collective action?

13 State Militarism and International Conflict

STEPHEN GIBSON

CHAPTER OUTLINE

The 20 years or so following the Second World War saw the beginnings of a focus on international[1] conflict within social psychology. In the opening chapter of his landmark edited volume *International Behaviour: A Social-Psychological Analysis*, Kelman (1965, p. 3) was able to speak tentatively of "the beginnings of what seems to be a new and rather vigorous area of specialization … [that] might loosely be called the 'social psychology of international relations'." Similarly, there were other volumes, such as Klineberg's (1964) *The Human Dimension in International Relations* and Janis's (1972) influential *Victims of Groupthink*, which sought to demonstrate the utility of social-psychological analysis for matters of international conflict.

In recent years, however, the trend is toward less, rather than more, research on international conflict. Major social psychology journals such as *Journal of Social and Personality Psychology, Journal of Experimental Social Psychology,* or *Personality and Social Psychology Bulletin* feature very little on international conflict, despite the fact that the USA (where these leading journals are based), and its allies have been engaged in major military action almost constantly in Afghanistan, Iraq, and Syria over the last 15 years. Similarly, scan the contents pages of any introductory social psychology text and one finds chapters on prejudice, attitudes, social influence, attribution, group dynamics, and intergroup behavior, but not on **state militarism** and international conflict. Such matters are generally left to political scientists, historians, and sociologists—disciplines that do not aspire so fervently to the general theories and universal laws so prized by psychologists.

When social psychologists *do* consider state warfare, it is typically as an example of general processes, which tend to be illustrated more readily in relation to *intra*state conflicts. This is where cultural, ethnic, or religious tensions arise between different groups within a state, or where there is conflict over which definition of the state is to be enshrined as the official version. This restricted focus has meant that the role of institutionalized violence in the established states of the West—and beyond—has largely escaped social-psychological attention, and the implications of such an analysis are absent from the discipline's theoretical models. This is particularly problematic in light of the observation that, in the modern world, established states are the only entities allowed to possess and exercise military force (Giddens, 1985), although this requires some qualification given the rise of private military

---

[1] For much of the present chapter, I will follow convention and use the term "international" to denote conflicts between established states. However, the idea of the nation-state is highly problematic, with few existing states corresponding to the classic idea of statehood for a "national" people (Walby, 2003).

Political Psychology: A Social Psychological Approach, First Edition.
Edited by Christopher J. Hewer and Evanthia Lyons.
© 2018 John Wiley & Sons Ltd. Published 2018 by John Wiley & Sons Ltd.

companies in recent years (Kinsey, 2006). Nonetheless, Giddens' (1985, p. 121) argument that "the very existence of 'civil war' presumes a norm of a monopolistic state authority" highlights an assumption that might also be said to apply to social-psychological work on conflict.

A POLITICAL PSYCHOLOGY OF INTERNATIONAL RELATIONS

In some respects the current state of political psychology is moving closer to Kelman's original vision for a social psychology of international relations. For example, the most recent edition of the *Oxford Handbook of Political Psychology* (Huddy, Sears, & Levy, 2013b) includes a whole section (seven chapters) on international relations, which focuses on such topics as foreign policy decision-making (Levy, 2013), conflict resolution (Fisher, Kelman, & Allen Nan, 2013), and crisis management (Dyson & Hart, 2013). This compares favorably with the most recent edition of the *Handbook of Social Psychology* (Fiske, Gilbert, & Lindzey, 2010), which does not include a single chapter on international relations or conflict. It may be that the disciplinary division of labor between "pure" and "applied" branches of psychology is relevant here, with social psychologists increasingly focusing on "core" concepts such as aggression, intergroup relations, and social conflict (all chapters in Fiske et al.'s handbook), while political psychologists apply these to specific topics in the political domain such as international conflict. However, this can lead to conceptual confusion as conflict between complex institutions and polities is understood primarily in terms of conflict between *groups*.

It is possible that the fragmentation of the discipline into differing subspecialities has facilitated this neglect within social psychology. The development of peace psychology, political psychology, and military psychology has arguably taken researchers who might otherwise have remained at the heart of social psychology into more specialist pursuits. This has meant that, since the 1960s, social psychology has developed without significant consideration of matters of international conflict. In recent years, however, some have argued for greater cross-pollination between social psychology and peace psychology (Gibson, 2011; Vollhardt & Bilali, 2008), and the present chapter will suggest that— despite moves in the right direction—state militarism, and international conflict are important areas where further integration between social and *political* psychology needs to take place. In particular, it will be suggested that, although political psychologists have addressed areas of international conflict that have been neglected in social psychology, developments in discursive, and rhetorical social psychology have the potential to enrich political psychological conceptualizations of this subject matter. To begin to sketch this argument, we first need to address a longstanding problem in both social and political psychology: the dichotomy between the individual and the social.

THE INDIVIDUAL-SOCIAL DICHOTOMY IN SOCIAL AND POLITICAL PSYCHOLOGY

A classic statement of the primacy of the individual as the appropriate level for analysis in social psychology can be found in a seminal work of one of social psychology's early architects, Floyd Allport. In his volume *Institutional Behaviour* is an essay entitled "The nationalistic fallacy and war," in which Allport (1933) writes that it is a mistake to conceive of nations, or indeed any groups, as having a reality over and above the individuals within the group:

> The "Nation" cannot, to human knowledge, sign a treaty, establish a foreign policy, contract indebtedness, declare war, conscript citizens for military duty, or conclude peace. ... It is only *individuals* whom we can experience as doing these things. They do them, to be sure, in certain accepted capacities; for example, as representatives of large numbers of other individuals. They do them also "in the name of" the entity called the "Nation." But still it is individuals, and only individuals, whom we see performing political acts. (Allport, 1933, pp. 139–140, italics in original)

Danziger (1992, p. 316) notes that Allport "was a man with a distinctly ideological mission ... he saw himself as defending the truth of individualism against the dangerous illusion of collectivism." However, as social-psychological analyses of international conflict developed, the inadequacy of seeing groups as necessarily bad for us and focusing solely on individual processes was recognized:

> Any attempt ... to conceptualize the causes of war and the conditions for peace that starts from individual psychology rather than from an analysis of the relations between nation-states is of questionable relevance. (Kelman, 1965, p. 5)

This was an important acknowledgment, and the limitations of a purely individual level of analysis were eventually built into the framework of political psychology as a distinct subdiscipline. Indeed, in their introduction to the field, the editors of the *Oxford Handbook of Political Psychology* express caution against any tendency for psychological explanations to over-reach themselves:

> At its core, political psychology concerns the behavior of individuals within a specific political system. Psychology alone cannot explain the Holocaust, intractable

conflicts, war, or most other behavior of states or collective political actors in complex political environments. Individuals do not act within a vacuum. Their behavior varies with, and responds to, differences in political institutions, political cultures, leadership styles, and social norms. (Huddy, Sears, & Levy, 2013a, p. 3)

However, in rejecting explicit **individualism**, an individualism of another form remains. The individual–social dichotomy continues to be taken for granted in much social and political psychological work as the individual is assumed to exist *separately* from the social. Despite the challenge to this binary distinction originating from postmodernist, poststructuralist, and social constructionist thinkers from the 1980s onwards, the issue remains unexamined at the heart of much psychological work (Wetherell, 1996). The main challenge to individualism within psychology has come from critical social psychologists who have argued that the very idea of the individual is a product of particular socio-cultural systems (e.g., Henriques, Hollway, Urwin, Venn, & Walkerdine, 1998; Rose, 1999; Sampson, 1993). The implications of this argument for psychological research have been developed most fully by researchers informed by discursive and rhetorical psychologies (Billig, 1996a; Edwards & Potter, 1992; Potter & Wetherell, 1987). Although there are important differences in emphasis between such scholars, they all nonetheless share a focus on the respecification of psychological research at the level of discourse, which involves the study of language and the way it is used to construct reality. Importantly, the individual is not left to stand outside of this constructive process; the individual is also treated as a construction. Indeed, the discursive psychological approach of Edwards and Potter (1992) recasts many of psychology's individualized concepts, such as identity, representations, attitudes, scripts, and memories, as *socially* produced.

This style of work has begun to influence political psychology (e.g., Abell, Condor, & Stevenson, 2006; Abell & Stevenson, 2011; Di Masso, 2012; Dixon, Levine, & McAuley, 2006; Gray & Durrheim, 2013; Sapountzis & Condor, 2013; Stevenson, Condor, & Abell, 2007), and it is significant that chapters on political rhetoric have been included in both the first and second editions of the *Oxford Handbook of Political Psychology* (Billig, 2003; Condor, Tileagă, & Billig, 2013). One recent and notable development of this work is Tileagă's (2013) *interpretive* perspective on political psychology, which aims "to expand political psychology's traditional focus on political behaviour, narrowly understood in an individualistic theoretical and methodological framework," and to "foster a debate about the meaning of 'scientific knowledge' that crosses beyond the experimental or survey canon that dominates contemporary political psychology" (2013, p. 3). Ultimately, this way of understanding political psychology presents a challenge to any approach where "political behaviour is mostly conceived of as the result of universal, habitual and automatic processes rather than as a product of human social practices" (p. 5).

The value of an approach informed by discursive and rhetorical psychology can be illustrated with examples from two social-psychological studies of state militarism and international conflict. The first study looks at the way that members of the armed forces in England account for their military service. The main contention is that models of social identity and intergroup relations, which were developed to explain intrastate conflict, may not be well suited to matters of interstate conflict. It may therefore be more productive to look at the ways in which people use language to construct their relationship with state institutions. The second study explores "attitudes" to the Iraq War using data from a televised political debate, and rather than taking the traditional view that attitudes are measurable internal mental constructs that guide action, the study adopts an alternative stance that people construct evaluations in particular social contexts, which allows them to perform specific social actions. This moves us away from the individual–social binary that is prevalent in political psychology, toward a more interpretive perspective grounded in human social practices (Tileagă, 2013).

BEYOND SOCIAL IDENTITY: ACCOUNTS OF MILITARY SERVICE

There is a well-developed social-psychological literature on intergroup conflict, which has made an important contribution to our understanding of political issues. However, the extent to which its findings can be applied to interstate conflict may be limited. In focusing on intergroup conflict, social psychologists have tended to make contributions only in those situations where the conflict is clearly between two groups. However, states are much more than social groups, and interstate conflict is about much more than intergroup conflict.

What follows is an alternative approach to interstate conflict that treats states as hybrid categories—combinations of people, places and institutions, and which prioritizes social actors' own accounts of their relationship to these states. This approach was developed by Condor (2006) in relation to national categories but, in principle, it can be applied more broadly. Condor has argued that the tendency to treat national categories as prime examples of social identities (group memberships) formed on the basis of self-categorization, ignores the extent to which nations may be understood as *more* than or *other* than social categories. For example, the state may be understood in geographical terms, as a set of constitutional arrangements, or as an embodiment of its government or leader. Gibson and Condor (2009) explored these possibilities in relation to military service in England, and found that participants emphasized different versions of the polity in order to perform particular rhetorical actions in particular contexts. Consider the following account from a 19-year-old student, Tim (a pseudonym) who was interviewed in March 2004, about a year after the beginning of the Iraq War:

Extract 1

1	Interviewer:	Yeah. Do you think there's any sense in which it's
2		patriotism if you like, that people join up for, that
3		might have an effect?
4	Tim:	Pr- I don't know er, probably yeah. I mean a lot of
5		people, j- I think if, if Britain itself had a problem,
6		then people would be very patriotic and join up.
7		And you know, and like—I mean although it's not
8		joining the army, if you look at the massive
9		marches against the war in Iraq, people thought
10		that was going to be a bad thing for Britain because
11		it was going to waste time, money, people's lives,
12		danger, you know every-, of the army. So that was
13		people standing up, for, for what they believed in
14		within Britain, about Britain. But you know, it's
15		almost like, like Britain is being pushed around by
16		Tony Blair, so they stood up against—obviously it
17		didn't work.
18	Interviewer:	Yeah.
19	Tim:	But then once they actually went to war, more
20		people started supporting it. Opposing the fact that
21		we were at war but supporting the people who were
22		there.
23	Interviewer:	Okay.
24	Tim:	So they support the British people, th- the Britain
25		that we see as our Britain.
26	Interviewer:	Right.
27	Tim:	Which is not always the government.
28	Interviewer:	Yeah.
29	Tim:	Which is slightly different.
30	Interviewer:	Okay.
31	Tim:	So.
32	Interviewer:	Yeah.
33	Tim:	I mean I- I'll stick up for Britain as a country
34		as an island, but I might not stick up for the
35		government, at all ((laughs)).

Tim constructs "Britain" as a populated category (line 24: "the British people") and a place (lines 33–34: "Britain as a country as an island") in order to distinguish "Britain" from the government, and in particular the then-Prime Minister Tony Blair. Indeed, he constructs Britain as "being pushed around by Tony

Blair" (lines 15–16) and argues that antiwar protestors were "standing up ... for what they believed in within Britain" (lines 13–14) in a way that is equivalent to being "patriotic" and joining the military in the event that "Britain itself had a problem" (line 5). Thus, while Tim would "stick up for Britain as a country," he is careful to dissociate himself from the implication that "Britain" might indicate *government*, or that patriotism might be taken as an indication of support for the government and its policies. The fact that Tim has to go to such lengths to point out that "the Britain that we see as our Britain ... isn't always the government" (lines 24–27) suggests that, ordinarily, the two may be assumed to be equivalent.

However, the constitutional arrangements within the UK provide for another institutional understanding of the state. Unlike countries, such as the USA, where the head of state and the head of the government are the same (the President), the system in the UK ensures that the head of state (the monarch), and the head of the government (the Prime Minister) remain separate. In contrast to civilians, the soldiers interviewed for Gibson and Condor's (2009) study were able draw on monarchy (typically in the commonplace cliché of "Queen and country") in order to construct a relatively benign and politically disinterested version of military service. The nature of the institutional relationships underpinning military service were discussed by one participant, Harold, who distanced himself from the monarchy:

Extract 2

1	Harold:	You know like (2) it's not for Queen and country and all
2		that sort of crap. It is—and you might have heard this
3		before and it's—it's stereotypical and it's sort of stayed.
4		It's a sense of letting down your mates.
5	Interviewer:	Yeah, yeah. So when you say it's not about Queen and
6		country, is that, an impression that's created, is it? That
7		it's maybe er—
8	Harold:	Supposed to be.
9	Interviewer:	Yeah.
10	Harold:	But, I—me personally, the bottom line—I think the
11		bottom line, you know, how c- this sounds very
12		mercenary. If they privatised the army and Tesco's were
13		paying my wage I wouldn't really give a shite.
14	Interviewer:	Right. Is that the same with a lot of people do you think
15		or—or are there people that's er, attached to—
16	Harold:	Er, no there—there are people who are very patriotic.
17	Interviewer:	Yeah.
18	Harold:	There are people but, I'm slightly—I'm slightly
19		bordering republican myself but—
20	Interviewer:	Okay.
21	Harold:	Er, I wouldn't get into—I don't think we'd be better off

22		—we wouldn't be better off with a president because
23		that's all political and stuff like that.
24	Interviewer:	Yeah.
25	Harold:	But all this Queen—the Queen's all right, no drama with
26		the Queen.
27	Interviewer:	Yeah.
28	Harold:	And her immediates. It's all the other hangers on.
29	Interviewer:	Right.
30	Harold:	Tossers.
31	Interviewer:	Sure. ((laughs)) Because I noticed that the oath of
32		allegiance[2] is—is all about the—
33	Harold:	Well it is, yeah.
34	Interviewer:	Monarchy isn't it?
35	Harold:	You do. You take an oath of allegiance, but (2) her
36		majesty Queen Elizabeth the Second, her heirs and stuff,
37		you know, the other bit is her heirs and successors and
38		it is—it's an oath of allegiance to the state more than—
39	Interviewer:	Yeah.
40	Harold:	The person.

In the first part of this extract, Harold denies the role of "Queen and country" as a motivating force in military service, and instead prioritizes "your mates"— a common accounting strategy that involves basing motivation for military service on interpersonal ties (Gibson & Abell, 2004). When asked to explain this remark in more detail from line 5 onwards, Harold adopts an individual footing (line 10: "I—me personally"), and positions himself as an employee who would happily do the job regardless of who was "paying my wage" (line 13). He thus constructs military service as equivalent to any other job, thereby downplaying the idea that he may be motivated by ideology or an attachment to monarchy. He then anticipates—and thereby inoculates against—the possibility that this "sounds very mercenary" (lines 11–12). When asked by the interviewer on lines 14–15 whether this is a view that is more widely held, he acknowledges that "there are people who are very patriotic" (line 16) but that he is "slightly bordering republican" (lines 18–19).

This is notable in that he equates patriotic sentiment with monarchist sentiment, and therefore because he is "slightly bordering republican," he cannot also be "patriotic." Harold then makes an indirect reference to the apolitical nature of the monarchy by dismissing the possibility of replacing it with a president because it would be "all political and stuff like that" (line 23). When the interviewer points out that the oath of allegiance sworn by all military recruits is explicitly to the crown, Harold explains that it is symbolically "an oath of

---

[2] The oath of allegiance was reproduced on a board that was hanging on the wall in the room where the interview took place.

allegiance to the state more than … the person" (lines 34–35). From this, we can see the complexities of the ideological resources at his disposal, which are afforded by the UK's constitutional arrangements. Harold has sworn an allegiance to the Queen, but he is "slightly bordering republican," so this exposes him to an accusation of hypocrisy. However, by treating the oath of allegiance as an oath to the state rather than the monarchy, he is able to manage this inconsistency.

By trying to understand "national" identity solely as a group identity, we miss these important institutional constructions, which involve a relationship between the individual, the military, and the state. What is more, the historical alignment of the British military with monarchy rather than government provides an ideological resource—a set of ready-made devices—for constructing military service as apolitical and therefore unaccountable. This involves a shift of focus away from individual motivations theorized as internal psychological processes toward a consideration of the way that cultural resources can be used to perform specific actions (such as managing accountability) in specific contexts (in a research interview, for example). In the next example, these ideas are set out more formally in terms of the classic discourse analytic concepts of construction, function, and situation.

BEYOND ATTITUDES: CONSTRUCTING EVALUATIONS OF THE IRAQ WAR

Despite social psychology's general neglect of international conflict, some social psychologists have been active in the study of attitudes to war, peace, and related constructs. Many studies have addressed the general properties of such attitudes (e.g., Anderson, Benjamin, Wood, & Bonacci, 2006), as well as their manifestation in relation to specific wars (e.g., Cohrs & Moschner, 2002; McFarland, 2005; Roccato & Fedi, 2007; Sherman, 1973). One finding from this work is that general attitudes to war tend to predict attitudes on specific wars—so if someone is inclined to favor military action as a way of dealing with international problems, they are likely to approve of the use of force in relation to specific conflicts (Cohrs & Moschner, 2002; Cohrs, Moschner, Maes, & Kielmann, 2005). However, much of this work has proceeded without engagement with the wider re-specification of the attitude construct, which has been undertaken in discursive-rhetorical psychology in the last 30 years (Billig, 1996a; Potter, 1998a; Potter & Wetherell, 1987; Wiggins, 2016). In particular, discursive critics have emphasized three features neglected by traditional attitude research: construction, function, and situatedness.

Construction: The discourse analytic position challenges the traditional separation between object and evaluation in attitude research (Potter & Wetherell, 1987). In the standard approach to attitude measurement, the separation between object and evaluation is built into the scaling techniques. An object is constructed by the researchers in the form of a statement. For example, Anderson et al. (2006, p. 125) measure attitudes to "violence in war" through several items, one of which is "War is often necessary." Participants respond to this item (the evaluation) using a standard Likert-type response scale, ranging from 1 (strongly disagree) to 7 (strongly agree). Although this procedure might appear quite reasonable, discourse analysts argue that when we analyse the ways in which evaluative statements are formulated in discourse, the object and evaluation are typically inseparable. Therefore, analytic attention is more fruitfully directed at the ways in which evaluative statements are constructed within discourse since even relatively banal turns of phrase can carry evaluative connotations.

Function: Potter and Wetherell (1987) argued that not only are evaluative statements constructed, they also perform functions. In other words, speakers do not make evaluative statements at random; they do so for particular purposes. For example, Billig (1996a) discusses US President Ronald Reagan's construction of the deployment of US forces in Grenada in 1983 as a "rescue mission" rather than an "invasion." This serves an important function: it presents the US action (and ultimately Reagan himself) as motivated by humanitarian concerns, rather than by a desire for conquest. To ask whether this genuinely reflects Reagan's underlying "attitude" misses the point—the important thing about this statement is the function it performs in political discourse.

Situatedness: Discourse analysts also argue that evaluations are always situated in a particular context (Potter & Edwards, 2001). Statements will be tailored to the demands of a particular audience, and to the requirements of a particular function that is to be performed. Thus, construction, function, and situatedness work together; a speaker will construct an evaluation in order to perform a particular function situated in a specific context.

To illustrate these ideas, we will consider an example from a political debate program, broadcast on BBC television in the UK, in the run-up to the invasion of Iraq (for a fuller analysis, see Gibson, 2012). The program, *Question Time*, was shown in the UK on February 13 2003, and featured a panel of politicians and political commentators responding to questions posed by a studio audience. The extract begins with the host, David Dimbleby (DD), inviting an audience member (A7) to ask a new question, and then inviting one of the panelists—the newspaper columnist Simon Heffer (SH)—to respond. Extract 3 uses a simplified form of Jeffersonian transcription conventions. The symbols used in the extract are as follows (adapted from Hutchby & Wooffitt, 1998, pp. vi–vii):

(1.0)   A number in parentheses indicates a time gap to the nearest tenth of a second.

(.)   A dot enclosed in parentheses indicates a pause in the talk of less than two-tenths of a second.

.hh   A dot before an "h" indicates speaker in-breath. The more "h"s, the longer the in-breath.

hh   An "h" indicates an out-breath. The more "h"s, the longer the breath.

(( ))   Double parentheses enclose the transcriber's comments on contextual or other features.

–   A dash indicates the sharp cut-off of the prior word or sound.

> <   "More than" and "less than" signs indicate that the talk they encompass was produced noticeably quicker than the surrounding talk.

Extract 3

1	DD	le-t let's move on let's move on to that
2		subject a question from ((name deleted))
3		please
4		(.)
5	A7	er if Hans Blix says tomorrow that er (.)
6		Iraq is in material breach of Resolution
7		one four four one (.hh) would the panel
8		support a US led invasion (.h) or the
9		Franco-German inspection plan
10	DD	Simon Heffer
11		(1.0)
12	SH	well I'm not a war monger (.) but we have
13		to accept that for (.h) twelve years(.)
14		Saddam Hussein has been taking the mickey
15		(.) out of (.) the western (.) alliance
16		that defeated him in 1991 (.hh) there was a
17		specific (.) peace treaty at that stage we
18		(.) the alliance stopped (.) um fighting in
19		Iraq (.) in return in part for him
20		disarming (.) and he has refused to do
21		that and there have been sporadic bombings
22		of Iraq in (.h) retaliation for his refusal
23		to do it (.hh) if the (h) western powers
24		are to have any (.h) moral authority >an'
25		that is a very< tall order (.h) that
26		authority has to consist in part (.) of
27		the alliance being able to enforce (.h)
28		that peace treaty (.) it has to be able to
29		say look you cannot go on indefinitely (.h)
30		taking the mickey out of us you can't go on
31		concealing weapons refusing to (.) ah

32	cooperate with our inspectors (.) ah you
33	can't go on terrorising your own people er
34	against cooperating with these inspectors
35	(.h) and (.) reluctantly I think that if
36	he is going to (.hh) er refuse to do that
37	and Doctor Blix tomorrow is going to say
38	that they're in breach of Resolution one
39	four four one (.) then (.) after twelve
40	years (.) and no one can accuse us of doing
41	this hastily or impatiently (.) after
42	twelve years and I think (.) reluctantly we
43	have to take (.hh) force (.) against him
44	(.) ah I hope concentrating purely on
45	military targets and er (.h) not civilian
46	targets at all (.) but we have to go in
47	and make our will known that that treaty
48	will be enforced

In general terms, Heffer is carefully setting out his case for military action in Iraq, and in so doing, is seeking to present himself as a reluctant advocate of the use of force. In particular, it is notable that whereas traditional attitude research has claimed that general attitudes to war tend to predict attitudes to specific wars, Heffer positions himself as *not* generally inclined to favor war (line 12: "I'm not a war monger"), but as nevertheless advocating military action in this specific instance. To understand how this perspective differs from traditional approaches that treat attitudes as enduring and measurable mental entities, it is worth setting out how each of the key concepts discussed here—construction, function, and situatedness—can be used to make sense of Heffer's argument.

Construction: Before Heffer begins his answer, it is apparent that the terms of A7's question already carry notable evaluative connotations. The distinction drawn on lines 8–9 between a "Franco-German inspection plan" and a "US led invasion" comes with built-in evaluations. Consider, for example, the different connotations had the options been labeled as a "Franco-German *appeasement* plan" and a "US led *liberation*." Similarly, although we might be tempted to see Heffer's account as indicative of his attitude to war, or his attitude to the possibility of war in Iraq, it is notable that following his initial disclaimer on line 12, he does not use the word "war" again. Instead, he refers on several occasions to a "peace treaty" (lines 17, 28, 47–48), and argues for its enforcement. In his own terms, Heffer is not arguing for *war*, but for the *enforcement of a peace treaty*. Most work on attitudes to war would miss this subtle but important point since attitude constructs in questionnaires are defined *in advance* by the researcher. This approach also highlights the wider benefits of qualitative approaches in general, which explore how people speak about things in their own words (e.g., O'Dwyer, Lyons, & Cohrs, 2016).

Function: Heffer's use of the disclaimer, "I'm not a war monger (.) but," illustrates the way he sets out to manage his own identity and to position himself as not being the sort of person who habitually argues in favor of military action. The construction of the object that he is in favor of as *the enforcement of a peace treaty*, rather than a *war* or an *invasion*, also performs this function. Heffer thus presents himself as a rational and principled moral actor who is not motivated by an unseemly thirst for conquest and bloodshed. Rather like the example of Ronald Reagan and Grenada, constructing military action as the enforcement of a peace treaty allows it to be presented as a reasonable and a morally just course of action. This not only works through the use of the term "peace" rather than "war" or "invasion," but also through the specific obligations invoked through the use of the treaty. In the first few lines of his argument, Heffer constructs the recent history of Iraq by noting that, following the Gulf War of 1991, which saw Saddam Hussein's regime defeated but remain in power, "a specific (.) peace treaty" was signed in which "the alliance stopped … fighting in Iraq (.) in return in part for him disarming" (lines 16–20). Therefore, because Saddam Hussein "has refused to do that" (lines 20–21), he has failed to uphold his obligations under the treaty, and as such can be held responsible for the ensuing military action. The enforcement of the peace treaty therefore arises not from any irrational desire for warfare, but rather as a reluctant and regrettable response to the failure of Iraq's President to meet his obligations under the terms of a peace treaty.

Situatedness: Discourse analysts also propose that talk is shaped by the demands of the context—it is *situated* within a specific social setting. It is therefore important to build into our analysis of Extract 3 the institutional context of the televised political debate program. There have been many analyses of broadcast media talk (e.g., Hutchby, 2005, 2006; Ilie, 2001), and it is worth emphasizing that there are some very specific institutional features of this medium, and of this particular program, *Question Time*. For example, unlike in everyday conversation where there are general norms for managing the transition from one speaker to the next (Sacks, Schegloff, & Jefferson, 1974), in institutional settings there are institution-specific norms concerning who can speak. On *Question Time*, the host, David Dimbleby, has the authority to allocate speaking turns, which he does quite straightforwardly on lines 1–3 and 10 of Extract 3. Similarly, the different lengths of A7's and Simon Heffer's contributions highlight norms governing how long different categories of speaker (audience members; panelists) can speak, as well as what sort of contributions they can make (questions; answers). The explicit purpose of *Question Time* is to provide a platform for the debate of topical political issues, and Heffer's talk is oriented toward the possibility that others on the panel, as well as members of the studio audience and—perhaps most crucially—those watching on their television sets, may require some persuading. The measured, reasonable way in which he articulates the case for war (or in his terms, the enforcement of a peace treaty) should therefore be understood as being shaped by the context in which his talk is situated. An early concern for discourse analysts in social psychology was how the situatedness of discourse could be demonstrated in the variability of speaker's evaluative statements across different contexts (Potter & Wetherell, 1987). Although we only have one extract here, a fuller analysis of Heffer's discourse could consider, for example, a sample of his newspaper columns written for those who share his broad political outlook. This line of argument is important as it further cautions us against reading any accounts of one's position as a literal report of some underlying psychological entity called an attitude. However tempted we might be to seize on some statement or other as being indicative of someone's *real* attitude, we should always attend to the context in which it is situated.

CONCLUDING REMARKS

The field of international conflict is vast and the sketch presented here addresses only a small selection of the potential issues that might be explored. The cautions of Huddy et al. (2013a) and Kelman (1965) apply here as much as they do to more traditional approaches to international conflict within social and political psychology. The discursive-rhetorical approach is not the only way to study these matters, but it has much to offer and has some significant advantages over the more traditional frameworks currently used in political psychology. In particular, whereas more traditional psychological frameworks provide an individual level of analysis, discursive-rhetorical psychology makes no such separation between the individual and the social, and instead takes a broadly social constructionist view of psychological objects.

This approach also points us to the ideological nature of the categories used in relation to international conflict. The "nation" is a good example. Rather than seeing national categories as instances of a more general phenomenon—social identity, for instance—we should consider their specific nature (Billig, 1996b; cf. Tajfel, 1960). Indeed, there are specificities associated with particular "national" categories. For example, the ideological coupling of military service and the monarchy in the UK allows for forms of accounting that would not be available in, for example, the USA. Any attempt to reduce British and US identity to the same basic processes misses this important feature of ideology; and if we treat "nations" or states as just another social category, we fail to recognize the ideological assumption that states alone possess the means to exercise legitimate violence (Giddens, 1985). Therefore, any study of state militarism has to begin by recognizing that, in many states, it is a quiet, banal process (Billig, 1995), and that it is only possible because the existence of a military force and the right to use it is taken for granted and unquestioned.

The emphasis on discourse also highlights the virtues of Tileagă's (2013) approach to political psychology, focusing as it does on social practices rather than processes that are assumed to be universal and automatic. For example, we can see that when we explore evaluative statements in social context, they do not resemble the decontextualized statements of survey-based attitude research (e.g., *war is often necessary*), but rather they are shaped by and for a specific function in a particular social context (e.g., *I'm not a war monger but…*). This may be a radical departure from the social-psychological approach to international conflict advocated by Kelman (1965), but it nonetheless signals a return to a fully *social* psychology. Indeed, Kelman's (1965, p. 22) own position on the scope of social psychology is instructive: "the primary focus for social-psychological analysis is social interaction." While the individual–social dichotomy may have prevented a full appreciation of the possibilities afforded by the study of social interaction, a focus on discourse, rhetoric, and processes of social construction overcomes this (Wetherell, 1996) and provides a basis for a more *social* political psychological perspective on state militarism and international conflict.

SUMMARY

- Despite the appearance of a "social psychology of international relations" in the period after World War Two, recent work in social psychology has tended not to focus on state militarism and international conflict.

- The neglect of state militarism and international conflict can be traced to the distinction between "pure" and "applied" psychology, with social psychology—a form of "pure" psychology—seeking general laws of human social behavior, and political psychology seeking to apply these to political behavior. For this reason, political psychology has considered international relations to a greater extent than social psychology.

- Social psychology and political psychology have tended to make a distinction between the individual and the social, and have thus neglected the extent to which our ideas about the nature of the individual are themselves socially produced. Social psychologists interested in discourse analysis have developed and applied this approach to political psychology.

- When applying discourse analysis to accounts of military service, the idea that social identity is central to understanding the relationship between individuals and nation-states may only be telling part of the story. States can be understood as social identities (i.e., as groups of people), places, and institutions.

- Discourse analysis challenges traditional theories of attitudes. People describe their viewpoints in particular ways in particular contexts and for specific purposes.

GLOSSARY

individualism refers to approaches that prioritize the individual, or in theoretical terms that focuses solely on the individual level of explanation. For example, an explanation that considers only individual factors to the neglect of social factors could be said to be individualistic.

state militarism refers to the taken-for-granted assumption that existing nation-states have the right to possess and exercise military force.

FURTHER READING

Gibson S. (2011). Social psychology, war and peace: Towards a critical discursive peace psychology. *Social and Personality Psychology Compass*, 5, 239–250.

Levy, J. S. (2013). Psychology and foreign policy decision making. In L. Huddy, D. O. Sears, & J. S. Levy (Eds.), *The Oxford handbook of political psychology* (2nd ed.) (pp. 301–333). Oxford: Oxford University Press.

Tileagă C. (2013). *Political psychology: Critical perspectives*. Cambridge: Cambridge University Press.

QUESTIONS FOR GROUP DISCUSSION

- What is the relation between language and social reality? Are there any words or phrases in current political discourse that particularly shape public perception?

- Social psychology has mostly focused on conflict within states; what is then left unexplored? Who does that involve? And what questions might this lead us to ask?

- How does discourse analysis highlight the inadequacies of the concept of the "attitude?" What additional contextual considerations does discourse analysis offer?

14 Social Influence and Malevolent Authority: Obedience Revisited

RON ROBERTS

CHAPTER OUTLINE

MILGRAM'S STUDIES OF OBEDIENCE

Stanley Milgram's studies of obedience in the US in the 1960s sought to uncover the social psychological factors that cause people to carry out malevolent acts toward others. Milgram had worked with Solomon Asch whose work on social conformity (Asch, 1951, 1952) had demonstrated the way in which social forces can influence behavior. During the same period, Theodore Adorno, and his colleagues (Adorno, Frenkel-Brunswik, Levinson, and Sanford, 1950) had argued that the widespread development of an authoritarian personality—the product of an overly strict parenting style was one of the factors that had made the Holocaust possible. Milgram, however, sought a more convincing explanation of the atrocities committed against Jews in World War II and his findings have created discussion, debate, and controversy ever since.

In a series of trials, participants were told that they were taking part in a learning experiment that involved a word-pair test and a shock generator. A paid volunteer (the teacher) was encouraged by an experimenter wearing a white coat to inflict an electric shock on another volunteer (the learner) located in another room every time a wrong answer was given. Shocks were administered in 15 V increments ranging from 15 V "Slight Shock" to 450 V "Danger: Severe Shock". To demonstrate to the participants that the experimenter was authentic, an uncomfortable shock of 45 V was given to the teacher before the study began (Milgram, 1965). At 75 V, the learner voiced his discomfort, and at 150 V, he demanded to be freed from the experiment. At 180 V, he cried out that he could not stand the pain and at 300 V he failed to respond further. The teacher was told to continue to the end of the shock generator and use the switch with the maximum voltage until instructed to stop. The purpose of the study was to see how far along the shock generator the teacher would go before refusing to go any further. The experiment was controversial and the results disturbing. Despite knowing that the learner had a heart condition, 65 % of the participants obeyed the experimenter and inflicted shocks to the maximum level. Eventually, it was revealed to the teacher that no shocks had been administered—the learner in the other room had been an actor whose voice had been recorded.

In the original study (Milgram, 1963), 40 participants had been involved but this was not a small-scale study; Milgram had employed meticulous experimental controls to ascertain the influence of a range of variables on the level of obedience. Eighteen variants of the basic paradigm were employed,

Political Psychology: A Social Psychological Approach, First Edition.
Edited by Christopher J. Hewer and Evanthia Lyons.
© 2018 John Wiley & Sons Ltd. Published 2018 by John Wiley & Sons Ltd.

which included varying the venue, that is, the institutional context of the experiment, the gender of the participants, the physical proximity of the teacher to the authority figure, the presence of conflicting authorities, and a scenario in which the participant was free to choose the level of shock to be administered (Milgram, 1974).

HOW DID MILGRAM INTERPRET HIS FINDINGS?

Milgram's objective had been to explore the nature of human nature, but what took place in the experiments was a lesson in the ethics of personal responsibility. The personalities of the participants, their motivations, their talk, their sense of gratification, and their psychological discomfort as they carried out the task had not been the focus of the experiments. Milgram was primarily interested in what people *did* in these situations. He observed that participants tend to give lower shocks when the experimenter left the room, from which he concluded that the "gratification of sadistic impulses" was not a contributory factor (La Fontaine, 1974). Given that personality factors were not responsible, how might these actions be explained? Milgram argued that the participants had entered into a *coercive relationship* from which they could not easily escape (La Fontaine, 1974). This, however, was no excuse for the behavior. Milgram concluded that, "If there is a moral to be learned from the obedience study it is that every man must be responsible for his own actions" (Milgram, 1964, p. 852).

ETHICS AND ECOLOGICAL VALIDITY

The study was not well received by the scientific community. In a short critique, Baumrind (1964) cites among her many concerns, the emotional state of Milgram's participants following their participation, which may include a change in self-perception, a loss of dignity, a loss of trust in rational authority as well as exposure to stress—a point of caution featured in the *APA Ethical Standards for Psychologists* at the time. She also questioned any parallel with Nazi Germany.

Orne and Holland (1968) also raised important questions about the studies. While they acknowledge that methodological deception was commonplace during this period (e.g., Solomon Asch had performed a similar ruse in his studies of conformity), the real question for the obedience studies is whether the deception technique worked. What did the participants believe about the experimenter? They argue that most would have assumed that an experimental scientist working in a prestigious university was rational and reasonable. Therefore, if the participants believed that the experiment was legitimate and that they were being asked to inflict high levels of electric shocks for a trivial purpose, they may have reasonably but *secretly* concluded that no suffering was taking place at all:

> In an experiment, when it is clearly communicated to the S (the participant) that he is to carry out an action which appears very destructive and dangerous, it is thereby concurrently communicated that it will be safe to do so. (p. 289)

They further argue that many have been reluctant to admit that they knew all along that the experiment was a sham because admission would discredit their performance, their data, and their contribution to science. They may have colluded with the experimenter who also wanted to retain their data. We might then ask: who was being deceived—the participant or the experimenter? Orne and Holland maintain that plausible experimental deceptions are not easy to achieve and that we cannot assume that the procedures were carried out flawlessly every time. As one would expect, Milgram (1970, 1974) rejected these claims and referred to the observable physical stress that many of his participants had exhibited as well as the estimates made by the participants of the subjective levels of pain felt by the victims. Details of the observable stress had been given in the original study (Milgram, 1963), which provided the basis for Baumrind's criticisms.

Orne and Holland's critique was based on the argument that people behave according to what they believe is demanded by the situation, and in experimental laboratories, the principal demand (whatever the experiment) is to obey the experimenter.

> ... the agreement to participate in an experiment gives the E (Experimenter) *carte blanche* about what may be legitimately requested. In asking the S to participate in an experiment, the E implicitly says, "Will you do whatever I ask for a specified period of time? By doing so you may earn a fee, contribute to science, and perhaps even learn something of value to yourself. In return I promise that no harm will befall you. At the completion of the experiment you will be no better or worse off than you are now and though you may experience temporary inconvenience, this is justified by the importance of the undertaking." A corollary to this agreement is that the S may not ask why certain things are required of him. He must assume that these actions are legitimate and appropriate for the needs of the experiment. (p. 291)

The claim that demand characteristics are a feature of all experimental situations (Orne, 1962), means that no broader inference beyond the experimental laboratory may be drawn from obedient behavior within the laboratory. Orne and Holland further argue that a debriefing of participants from another series of studies by Orne and Evans (1965), indicates that there are reality constraints in the psychological laboratory:

> Without having to be told, *Ss* were quite aware of the reality constraints governing research in our society and, correctly, we might add, assumed that as long as we really intended them to carry out these behaviours, we would have made certain no serious injury would befall anyone – neither them nor our research assistants. (p. 289)

To illustrate the point, Orne and Holland draw upon the analogy of the decapitating magician and the obedient volunteer. The volunteer, although nervous and uncertain about the situation, obeys every command based on an understanding of the world that all will end well—that no one will really lose their head in the guillotine. If indeed, this was the overriding belief of the participants in the obedience experiment, it would explain why so many went to the end of the shock generator. However, Milgram (1970) refuted these claims arguing that Orne and Holland's criticisms were based on analogy and inference rather than hard evidence,[1] and in his defense, he drew attention to the postexperimental screening of the beliefs and perceptions of his participants.

In their critique, Orne and Holland conclude from the Orne and Evans (1965) studies that *the participant–experimenter relationship* is central to compliant behavior because it legitimizes all dubious or dangerous behavior. This is the point at which Orne, Holland, and Milgram agree. The difference, however, is that Orne and Holland maintain that this relationship is context-dependent and does not extend beyond the laboratory, whereas Milgram argues that the relationship observable in the laboratory is a model for all hierarchical authority structures.

WAS THERE A LEGITIMATE PARALLEL BETWEEN MILGRAM'S LABORATORY AND NAZI GERMANY?

This is a very important question. Many critics, including Baumrind (1964) and Orne and Holland (1968), dismissed the idea of a legitimate parallel between Milgram's laboratory and the power structures of Nazi Germany. When

---

[1] Interestingly, in an experiment in which live puppies were given real electric shocks, Sheridan and King (1972) found similar levels of obedience to Milgram's studies.

Milgram asked himself the question, he acknowledged a number of differences: for example, that parallel events occur at different times in history and that, while the laboratory experiment took 1 hour, crimes against humanity may develop over years and decades. He goes on to say that despite differences in parallel circumstances, the psychological processes underlying obedient behavior in any coercive context are similar.

> Is the obedience observed in the laboratory in any way comparable to that seen in Nazi Germany? (Is a match flame comparable to the Chicago fire of 1898?) The answer must be that while there are enormous differences of circumstance and scope, a common psychological process is involved in both events. (Milgram, 1974, p. 175)

We might conclude that our acceptance of Milgram's work depends on whether we believe that the events that took place in the laboratory accurately reflected the dynamics of the authoritarian power structures existing within Nazi Germany. The first problem with this parallel is that *we assume* that we already know the nature of these dynamics. We assume that people were ordered to inflict harm on others and that, because of the ruthless nature of Nazism, everything was done through a process of blind obedience to a militarized top-down authority structure. However, we are beginning to learn that historical evidence paints a less structured picture of the internal organization of Nazi Germany (see Haslam & Reicher, 2008). We therefore need to be cautious in our assumption that power always flowed from the top-down rather than individuals on occasion seizing opportunities to acquire power over others simply because they could. Secondly, the research question asks: how was it possible for people to carry out inhumane acts against others? To answer the question, Milgram devised a top-down hierarchical laboratory setting with an authority figure, strict procedures, and orders to follow. Critics might argue that Milgram, by setting up the coercive situation, is presupposing the answer to the question before he has collected the data. The inherent circularity is not immediately apparent because we have all seen Nazi Germany depicted in this manner in films and documentaries. But such presumptions may be misleading. Nonetheless, Milgram set up an experimental drama with an empirical question and it *was* possible to disobey. Had very few obeyed[2] the experimenter, we might today have a very different view of the human

---

[2] Using a discourse analytic framework, Gibson (2013) argues that Milgram's studies demonstrate persuasion and argumentation rather than obedience. This approach also maintains that the defence, "I was only following orders" should not be taken as evidence of an "agentic shift" (Milgram, 1974)—a movement away from being autonomous to becoming an agent of an authority. Rather, it should be seen as a rhetorical strategy used to maintain self-presentation in the face of uncomfortable questioning (see Gibson, Blenkinsopp, Johnstone, & Marshall, 2018).

propensity to do harm. But whether the study provides a legitimate parallel to Nazi Germany or not, Milgram (1974) explicitly warned that:

> To focus only on the Nazis, however despicable their deeds, and to view only highly publicised atrocities as being relevant to these studies is to miss the point entirely. For the studies are principally concerned with the ordinary and routine destruction carried out by everyday people following orders. (p. 177 and 178)

Indeed, the Nazi state apparatus is only one of many instances where human welfare has taken second place to the day-to-day running of officialdom (e.g., see Goldhagen, 1997, ch. 5; Rees, 2005).

THE POLITICAL AND HISTORICAL CONTEXT OF MILGRAM'S STUDIES

The political and historical context of Milgram's studies is also worthy of consideration. After World War II, a metanarrative of good versus evil dominated Cold War rhetoric. By playing a major role in the defeat of Nazi Germany and Imperial Japan, the US had promoted democracy to a free world. The idea that ordinary Americans were not as good as we thought, or were as bad as the Nazis, would likely have sparked discomfort, disbelief, and anger in some quarters. To suggest that Americans could behave like the Nazis may have been difficult for some to accept. Some may even have interpreted Milgram's findings as unpatriotic, or as a threat to national identity. Milgram was asking Americans to stand outside their own beliefs and assumptions and to look at themselves in a different light. This would not only require a reevaluation of their identity but also a reinterpretation of recent global history and particularly the moral superiority of the Allies during World War II.

These findings would likely arouse cognitive dissonance (Festinger, 1957). When two mutually exclusive cognitions, "we are good" and "we are bad," are set against each other, there is a drive to suppress one so that the other dominates. In such circumstances, cognitive dissonance may drive the authorities to "shoot the messenger," which may explain why many sought to discredit Milgram and his work.

What is more, the 1960s were a turbulent time in the U.S. Civil unrest and protest became part of daily life and maintaining order was a priority. Young men were being drafted to fight in Vietnam, which so many opposed and younger people were embracing a counter culture that involved drug use and sexual freedom. This was not the best time for academics to dissect or undermine the dynamics of authority structures. Milgram received no accolades from the psychological community for his work and he failed to get tenure at Yale University. The studies made him famous, but they did not advance his career.

THE CONTEMPORARY RELEVANCE OF MILGRAM'S WORK

It is also important to discuss the studies as a form of social knowledge existing within a larger matrix of political and ethical relationships. This means that we need to look at the values embedded within the obedience experiments and the messages that are disseminated to the psychological community. Should Milgram's work simply be understood within the historical context of the 1960s, or does it have contemporary relevance?

When discussing the obedience studies, most psychology textbooks rely on historical examples in foreign lands to illustrate contemporary relevance. Most popular are the Holocaust and the My Lai massacre in Vietnam. This implies that there are no current examples of obedience through coercion or discomforting adherence to inhumane policies closer to home when our experience may tell us otherwise. The capacity for people to abuse power and inflict harm on others at the command of a punitive authority can be found in most organizations. Indeed, one of the myths to emerge from Nazi Germany is that such inhumane treatment could not happen in the free and liberal western world. Recent events suggest that we need to be more skeptical and more vigilant.

Consider the recent government welfare reforms that have significantly affected the lives of disabled people in the UK. Since 2008, chronically sick and disabled people have been required to undergo a new form of assessment to determine their fitness for work. Work Capability Assessments (WCA) have been conducted in official premises throughout the country and paid employees, after having ignored evidence from medical practitioners have taken decisions that have affected the day-to-day survival of vulnerable people. Some have welcomed this policy since it proposes to expose and punish all forms of perceived state dependent malingering.

However, in 2012 the DWP (Department of Work and Pensions, 2012) published data which indicated that, in the first 11 months of 2011, 1,300 people deemed fit for work at their WCA subsequently died along with a further 7,100 who had been allocated to a support group following their assessment. Given the controversial nature of the report, the UK government decided to withhold publication of further data, after which there followed a lengthy battle with the

Information Commissioner who forced the government to comply with a Freedom of Information request. It was then revealed that between December 2011 and February 2014, 2,380 people had died after having their claim for employment and support allowance terminated because they had been deemed fit to work (Butler, 2015). It would appear that numerous people with lifelong serious illnesses and impairments had been driven to suicide as they were simultaneously deemed fit to work by officials, and no longer eligible for incapacity benefit, yet denied Job Seekers Allowance because they were unfit for work. In 2015, Scottish MP Angus Robertson noted that the DWP had carried out up to 60 investigations into suicides that occurred after benefits were withdrawn or reduced, but has yet failed to publish its findings ("Prime Minister questioned over suicide reports," 2015).

We might ask: why did officials put so many disabled people through the stresses of an unnecessary assessment? And why were they able to find so many demonstrably ill people fit for work? Why did they not refuse to carry out these assessments? We might anticipate the explanation that "there is a job to do;" "our families have to be fed;" and "management must be obeyed," particularly when one is pursuing a chosen career. We may have heard these words in one form or another at our place of employment as individuals justify various forms of questionable practice.[3] The question is: who is responsible for the outcome in these situations?

In 2014, the UK was investigated by the United Nations to ascertain whether these reforms have caused "grave or systematic violations" of disabled people's human rights (Fenton, 2015), which are enshrined in the UN Convention on the Rights of Persons with Disabilities. *Disability News Service* reported in the summer of 2014 that this is the first time a signatory country has faced such an enquiry.[4] The issues under investigation by the UN rapporteur include:

> The government's decision to close the Independent Living Fund; cuts to legal aid; benefit cuts and sanctions, including the impact of the work capability assessment (WCA); the severe shortage of accessible, affordable housing; the impact of the bedroom tax on disabled people; cuts to social care; and the rise in disability hate crime. (Pring, 2015)

---

[3] A similar issue arose after the election of US President Donald Trump. In February 2017, an executive order was given to restrict entry to the United States to people from some countries in East Africa and the Middle East in the interests of national security. It was alleged that "ordinary Americans carried out inhumane acts" to comply with the order. http://www.baltimoresun.com/news/opinion/oped/bs-airport-inhumanity-20170206-story.html.

[4] See http://www.disabilitynewsservice.com/uk-is-first-country-to-face-un-inquiry-into-disability-rights-violations/.

In June, 2016, a UN ruling confirmed that the UK's austerity policies were indeed in breach of its international human rights obligations.[5]

Those with mental health problems have also figured prominently in the DWP's crusade. A report from the charity MIND revealed that in the previous year, 19,259 people with mental health issues lost their Employment and Support Allowance (Stone, 2015), and Cross (2013, p. 719) observes that we are in the midst of a series of:

> ...unprecedented attacks on every source of support and help for disabled people...by 2018, disabled people are set to lose an astonishing £28.3 billion worth of financial support. These changes are going to affect up to 3.7 million disabled people in total.

THE ROLE OF SCIENCE AND BUREAUCRACY

How does a "civilized and caring" society get to this position? Such treatment is dependent on the coercion of the state and the compliance of individuals who fail to consider their moral responsibility to others. What is more, it is a policy endorsed by a private sector bureaucracy that seeks to profit from the common objective to reduce benefits and save public funds. In 2012, *The Guardian* newspaper[6] carried a letter from over 400 signatories, complaining about the role of the private insurance company UNUM, which has been advising the UK government on welfare reform. Since sponsoring the Centre for Psychosocial and Disability Research at Cardiff University over a 6-year period, the company states that the biopsychosocial model of disability has taken pride of place in "its approach to medical underwriting," (the same approach informs the WCA). Despite critics who argue that this model is deeply flawed (e.g., Read, 2005) and that it represents a "colonization of the psychological and social by the biological" (see also Read, Mosher, & Bentall, 2004, p. 4), it nonetheless remains the cornerstone of health psychology and retains a prominent place within clinical psychology. Appropriately, the British Medical Association and the British Psychological Society,[7] condemned these assessments and a number of important lessons for psychological practitioners and researchers come

---

[5]http://www.centreforwelfarereform.org/news/uk-in-breachhuman-rights/00287.html.
http://www.just-fair.co.uk/#!United-Nations-Austerity-policies-breach-the-UK's-international-human-rights-obligations/qbw0c/577384fa0cf231749dc9f955.
http://www.ohchr.org/EN/HRBodies/CRPD/Pages/InquiryProcedure.aspx.
[6]See http://www.guardian.co.uk/society/2012/sep/12/private-firms-disability-assessment-regime.
[7]http://www.bps.org.uk/news/psychologists-call-fundamental-reform-work-capability-assessment.

to the fore. Firstly, we need to discern the way that ideology operates within psychology under a banner of value free, scientific enterprise. We also need to recognize that politicians and corporations may use ideologically inflected psychological research to further their own policy objectives. Thirdly, there is an obligation on the academic community to avoid becoming passive bystanders in the suffering of vulnerable people.

Those affected by these assessments have also drawn attention to the disparaging treatment of disabled people in the media (see Crow, 2015). Disabled people have been regularly described as scroungers, welfare cheats, and an economic burden. Briant, Watson, and Philo (2011), for example, report that in the 5 years to 2010/2011, coverage of disability benefits "cheats" by the British *Daily Mail* increased fivefold. For those who do not have absolute faith in human institutions, it is difficult to avoid comparisons between these developments and the state action against disabled people during the Nazi era. In the Action T4 euthanasia program, which was the forerunner of the Holocaust, over 200,000 disabled people were murdered by the state. Hitler's propaganda regime dismissed disabled people as "life unworthy of life" (Lebensunwertes Leben), or "useless eaters." There are also other disturbing parallels. On the gates of concentration camps in Nazi Germany and Poland, the words "Arbeit Macht Frei"—work sets you free—obscured an impending reality that new arrivals, if they were to survive at all, were to be nothing more than "slave labor." A similar rhetorical technique has been employed in the current political climate. According to the UK government, UNUM, and its psychologist advisers who advocate the biopsychosocial model, work is "good for physical and mental health and well-being" (Waddell & Burton, 2006, p. ix), and "sick and disabled people…should be encouraged and supported to remain in or to (re)-enter work as soon as possible" (Waddell & Burton, 2006, p. viii). However, hidden behind this encouragement to work is a punitive regime of social and economic sanctions for those for whom work is no longer feasible. For many, it has been a case of "work or die."

THE HOLOCAUST AND THE EICHMANN TRIAL

Milgram's obedience studies should also be understood in relation to the trial of Adolf Eichmann in Jerusalem in 1961. Indeed, so strong is the parallel that even the late Gordon. W. Allport referred to Milgram's study as "the Eichmann experiment" (Milgram, 1974, p. 177). *Obersturmbanführer* Eichmann had been the senior Nazi official to have dealings with Jewish organizations. They therefore looked upon him as "one of the two Adolfs who perpetrated the

Holocaust" (Stangneth, 2014, p. 9). Eichmann's everyday tasks were seemingly removed from any direct acts of killing, but they were critical to the Nazi project. They involved the coordinated expulsion of Jews from the Reich, Western Europe, and the Balkans, the forced confiscation of property and ultimately arranging transport to the extermination camps. Writer and philosopher, Hannah Arendt's analysis of the trial influenced Milgram's interpretation of his participants" behavior. Her account *Eichmann in Jersualem: A Report on the Banality of Evil* (1963/2006) (a phrase she later came to regret) examined the relationship between the human cruelty of the Holocaust and the benign bureaucratic processes that made it possible.

Even after the final solution had been put into practice, Arendt remarked (1963/2006, p. 151) that Eichmann was "troubled by no pangs of conscience." The "Adviser for Jewish Affairs" was unrepentant and believed that history would vindicate him and his role in the Holocaust. However, Stangneth's (2014) meticulous research into Eichmann's life between his escape from postwar Germany and his arrest by Mossad (the Israeli Secret Service) make it apparent that he was far from the low key hapless functionary that his self-presentation at the trial made him out to be. Instead, Arendt's original depiction of him as the "desk-murderer" who "lubricates the wheels of destruction" (Goldhagen, 1997, p. 164) is particularly pertinent. Let us consider her argument:

> It is important to the political and social sciences that the essence of totalitarian government, and perhaps the nature of every bureaucracy, is to make functionaries and mere cogs in the administrative machinery out of men, and thus to dehumanise them. And one can debate long and profitably on the rule of Nobody, which is what the political form known as bureaucracy truly is...True we have become very much accustomed by modern psychology and sociology, not to speak of modern bureaucracy, to explaining away the responsibility of the doer for his deed in terms of this or that determinism. Whether such deeper explanations of human actions are right or wrong is debatable. But what is not debateable is that no judicial procedure would be possible without them, and that the administration of justice, measured by such theories, is an extremely unmodern, not to say outmoded institution. When Hitler said that a day would come in Germany when it would be considered a "disgrace" to be a jurist, he was speaking with utter consistency of his dream of a perfect bureaucracy. (Arendt, 1963/2006, p. 290)

Arendt is here signaling a number of concerns. Principally, that our systems of justice in the Western world depend upon an assumption that someone is culpable, and must be held to account, when the law is transgressed. At the same time the administration of justice depends upon the workings of a **bureaucracy** whose own functional requirements often run counter to the values that underpin it.

The Nazi project to subordinate any sense of individual freedom (and thereby morality) to the functioning of the state was seen as serving "the greater good." Arendt's concerns thus revolve around the problematic relationship between the individual and the social system, and more significantly, she questions the relationship between systems of knowledge (within psychology) and the administration of justice. She suggests that psychology's institutional mode of theorizing—notably the downplaying of agency and free will or its complete removal from the analysis—allows us to exonerate perpetrators of evil (see also Arendt, 1978). The diminishing nature of free will within psychological theory in favor of deterministic biological and social theories inevitably leads us to conclude in critical circumstances that no one was responsible: it was simply the workings of bureaucracy.

In her philosophical treatment of mind (Arendt, 1978), the faculty of judgment is accorded a prominent place, and finding Eichmann ethically deficient is consistent with her entire body of work. Reviews and reflections on the behavior of Milgram's participants, that is, that many made an *active* choice to inflict harm is seldom discussed; indeed, there has been a tendency to ignore it or explain it away. Instead, the harsh criticism has been directed at Milgram for organizing the experiment (Baumrind, 1964).

Arendt was struck by Eichmann's apparent ordinariness. Milgram's participants too were ordinary. That later analysis has proved Eichmann to be not so ordinary does not discredit the force of Arendt's argument. Those who commit a great deal of the wrongs in the world are not obvious "monsters" and the critical decisions of many major war criminals have been made from behind a desk or at the end of a phone. As some have pointed out (e.g., Haslam & Reicher, 2008), obedience to authority is more than merely following orders. The desk job perpetrator may actually exhibit creativity and initiative in the way they carry out their duties. Whatever the case, the question of responsibility remains and no amount of reinterpretation of the obedience studies will remove it from the shoulders of the participants. What is more, Milgram's claim that people can be pressured to act against their conscience may not explain all inhumane acts: some may simply have their conscience on a different setting, which allows them to justify an action for a greater good. This was the essence of Hermann Göering's defense at the Nuremburg trials in 1946 and, as we shall see, some offer the same defense for Milgram's participants.

When we demonstrate a reluctance to pursue the issue of responsibility to its final conclusion, we leave open a dangerous space. It is important to consider Arendt's view that evil arises not just from malice aforethought—from an intention to do harm—but from the spaces opened up by people's failure to think. This deserves our continuing attention—all the more so when political interference has seen the withering of free thinking in higher education as financial considerations and corporate goals are elevated above the pursuit of ideas (Giroux, 2014).

A REINTERPRETATION OF MILGRAM'S STUDIES

In recent years, there has been a move to reinterpret Milgram's original findings, which has revolved around two issues. Firstly, whether it is appropriate to condemn the participants in the study for their behavior, an issue linked to our understanding of crimes against humanity and other forms of cruel treatment. The second area of interest, and a more recent development, has been the question of resistance. We should remember that 35 % did not obey the instruction that "the experiment must continue."

In her book, *Behind the Shock Machine*, Gina Perry (2013) provides a compelling and thought provoking account of the Milgram experiments. Perry interviewed several participants in the obedience studies, their relatives and some of Milgram's colleagues. The work also included a thorough analysis of Milgram's private papers. The conclusions are unsettling and the judgment is harsh. Perry judges Milgram guilty of promoting torture with "a dramatic and sinister performance perhaps worthy of Hitchcock" (p. 347), but exonerates those who implemented the shocks—"few people appreciated how difficult it was for subjects to call a halt once the experiment had started" (p. 341). Milgram, for her, is to be judged by the choices he made, but his participants are not. Perhaps there is a cautionary point here: that we hold people in authority (in this case Milgram) to different ethical standards to those over whom they have authority (the participants)—the familiar but flawed philosophy of the superior virtues of the oppressed.

Perry claims that innumerable personal pathways had led people to flick the switches on the shock machine, and each is a human-interest story. However, the same could be said for Eichmann or any other concentration camp guard, torturer, or human rights abuser. If we exonerate Milgram's participants, presumably, we have to do the same for those who carry out any mass crime or inhuman action. Perry also challenges Milgram's interpretation of his results by asserting that his participants often sought to do what *they believed* was good, for example in supporting scientific endeavor. Is this an adequate defense? History is full of examples where evil is carried out in the name of good! In this analysis of individual action versus social pressure there is a risk of rationalizing the behavior to the point of excusing it.

Baumrind's (1964) critique also described the participants as having been "entrapped" (p. 422) while Burger (2011) identifies a series of features that were built into the procedures that made it difficult for "participants to do anything but go along with the experimenter's instructions" (p. 655). (see also Burger, Girgis & Manning, 2011). Even Milgram acknowledged that the

15 V intervals between each punishment made it difficult to disobey because the shock level was not much greater than the previous one—the action (in relation to previous actions) thus provided no moral basis for refusal (La Fontaine, 1974). However, the claim that it was difficult for the participants to do otherwise is no moral defense and curiously supports the ecological validity of Milgram's studies. Social dynamics clearly played a part but the participants still acted in a malevolent fashion.

FREE WILL AND PERSONAL RESPONSIBILITY

Perhaps the attempts to exonerate Milgram's participants can be situated within the discipline's own highly contentious stance toward free will. If individual personal responsibility is to be explained away—rather than expected, promoted, or held up as an ideal then ultimately ethical behavior will become meaningless, and the moral climate will be compromised. Conceptualizing human behavior as the outcome of a solely deterministic system of interacting variables is a dangerous position to take. The more deterministic factors are used to explain human behavior, the less people are deemed responsible for their actions. This has been already been noted in connection with those designated as suffering from biologically caused "mental illnesses" (Cromby, Harper, & Reavey, 2013) and such attributions often go hand in hand with generating fear and distrust.

In a quite different analysis, Haslam, Reicher, Millard, and McDonald (2015) turn to the historical record to form a new position on the participants' behavior in Milgram's experiment. They contend that the most salient feature of Milgram's results in need of explanation is the "happiness" expressed by participants as a result of their involvement in the study. Haslam et al. acknowledge that the participants' behavior followed from the choices they made, which they attribute to "the experimenter's ability to convince participants that they were contributing to a progressive enterprise" (p. 55). They invoke the concept of the "engaged follower"—someone who willingly accedes to what is expected of them because they identify and share the same goals as those in positions of power and authority—which in the case of the obedience studies refers to the presumed "moral, worthy and progressive" (p. 60) nature of science. Put simply, the participants obeyed because they construed their actions as contributing to the greater good and related positively to those whom they saw as pursuing this goal. Their actions were freely chosen, embedded within a system of shared social understanding of the goodness and worthiness of science.

With issues of relationship and choice to the fore, those who were so "engaged" with the (scientific) ethos cannot evade responsibility for their engagement nor for their unquestioned faith in its validity. We should not forget that the Nazi doctors (Lifton, 2000) made similar choices—which did not absolve them from moral responsibility. Many previous objections to Milgram's experiments have made much of the issue of whether the participants were distressed by what they were doing (e.g., Baumrind, 1964). Perhaps of greater interest to us is to understand why they were "glad" to participate. What were they glad about? In a telling aside to her critique, Baumrind (1964) expresses dismay that Milgram's experiments might alter participants' propensity to "trust adult authorities in the future" (p. 422). Some, however, might see this as a good thing.

WHAT DO WE LEARN FROM MILGRAM'S STUDIES?

Milgram's obedience studies bring to our attention the way in which malevolent power structures can get ordinary people to act against their conscience. The studies also ask uncomfortable questions about the issue of free will and moral responsibility, which is seldom discussed within psychology. These issues warrant a permanent place in the curriculum. Indeed, we might ask: is a sense of ethical personal responsibility encouraged within school curricula, higher education, the family, or the workplace? Milgram's work also points to the necessity for vigilance in our stance toward those whose power shapes the world and his findings reveal that the collective social power and prestige accorded to scientific research was part of the problem. In the same way that Haslam and colleagues have asked questions about our blind faith in science and its institutions, (which includes psychological science), we need to move beyond the assumption that the state always acts in our personal interests or in ways that promote our personal freedoms. In response to government moves to increase its powers of surveillance in the UK, Conservative MP David Davis (2015) warned:

> Because for the past 200 years we haven't had a Stasi or a Gestapo, we are intellectually lazy about it, so it's an uphill battle. Even people who are broadly on my side of the political spectrum in believing in privacy and liberty tend to take the state at its word too often.

Such faith in our institutions is grounded in the social representations of despotic powers (see Roberts, 2007), which are depicted as invariably foreign, absolute, and undemocratic[8] and located at the political extremes of left and right (a tyranny of the center seems unimaginable). To the German people of the day, Hitler, was the national, political center of gravity and was initially elected to a position of power through the ballot box. Perhaps one of the unfortunate consequences of the Milgram experiments has been a narrow focus on one specific manner in which people cooperate with regimes of terror, as if there must be a single psychological model to explain the immensity of the Holocaust. Mass crimes are typically a product of both the perpetrators of horrific actions and the popular support of those whose dutiful complicity stands behind it (Dimitrijevic, 2011). Soviet history provides additional examples of the immersion of a population into the everyday administrative "logic" of state terror (see e.g., Figes, 2008, for discussion of daily life in the Stalinist period, and Boym's (1995) discussion of the communal apartment in late Soviet life). China provides other examples (e.g., Chang, 2012). In each case, the banality of cooperation was woven into the fabric of everyday life. One's potential tormentors were everywhere going about their daily business. The narrow focus that we have assumed in the West (the top-down model of despotic power) may be one of the consequences of a very different historical remembrance of the Nazi and Stalinist regimes (Boym, 2006).

A SOCIAL PSYCHOLOGY OF RESISTANCE

For many years, the Milgram experiments were largely interpreted as a depressing commentary on the human propensity to do harm. Attention focused on the two-thirds of participants who were willing to inflict lethal levels of shock on innocent people. It has been routine for students to consider the moral shortcomings of human beings, which means that they come away with the idea that resistance in the face of coercive authority is futile. However, a third of participants—a substantial minority—managed to resist in the baseline experiments.

What factors enabled so many people to resist the experimenter's exhortation—"the experiment must continue"? To provide an explanation, do we have to resort to personality factors or could it be that their behavior was the product of education or experience: a form of life training that prepares people for important forms of resistance in difficult situations? In this vein,

---

[8] In her *Origins of Totalitarianism* written just after the Second World war, Arendt (1976, xxiii) commented that scholars had a disquieting habit of refusing to recognise the mass support extended to totalitarian governments.

Hollander (2015) reexamined the original transcripts of the obedience experiment for signs of defiance and attempted "resistance" in the non-verbal behavior of participants regardless of whether they completed the experiment. He identified several implicit and explicit forms of resistance and showed how these varied between those who continued with the experiments and those who refused. The implications are clear—understand the "interpersonal dynamics of 'authority' relations and resistance to such authority" (p. 16) and then seek to disseminate this knowledge where needed.

Here is an opportunity to teach people to think for themselves, to challenge the imperatives of authority. This would require a change in direction—to go from teaching "value free" knowledge to teaching "value–led" knowledge—an opportunity to draw attention to the ways in which people may resist the demands of illegitimate authority. An example is provided by Ron Ridenhour, a participant in one of the subsequent successful replications of Milgram's findings (Rosenhan, 1969), in which obedience rates of 85 % were obtained at the maximum shock level. Ridenhour was the only person who refused to administer a single shock. By coincidence, Ridenhour is also the name associated with the exposure of the infamous massacre at My Lai during the Vietnam War in which US soldiers on a "search and destroy" mission massacred innocent civilians. Although this was a different individual,[9] two men with the same name provide fine examples of the kind of resistance we could seek to study and promote.

Hollander (2015) highlights a few areas where people would benefit: plane crashes, rape and sexual harassment, bullying, and torture. Several point to what are unfortunately widespread and common features of everyday social life. Given the widespread abuse and misuse of power and authority, we might conclude that psychology could become more active in promoting and facilitating resistance in the population. To do so, we must be quite clear about what needs to be resisted and why. Perhaps it would be appropriate for psychologists who teach or comment on the obedience studies to state where they stand with respect to abuses of authority. One suspects that there would be considerable variation in beliefs about free will, what it is legitimate to resist as well as what is legitimate and illegitimate authority.

Interestingly, Haslam and Reicher (2012) argue that no matter how extreme the situation, resistance is always possible and they propose a social psychology of resistance along with an invitation for the discipline to engage in social change. The discipline has of course always done this—but usually to *preserve* the status quo and uphold a reverence for authority. If this is about to change, then life in the academy will certainly become more interesting.

---

[9] See message posted by Gordon Bear (2008) to *The Society for Personality and Social Psychology* archived at http://groups.google.com/group/spsp-discuss/msg/b7f9cebb868fd187.

SUMMARY

- The validity of Milgram's work has been questioned. Did all the participants believe that they were inflicting painful shocks? Did the "reality constraints" of the experimental setting affect the participants' beliefs about real danger? Is the participant-experimenter relationship, which is central to obedience, context-dependent—restricted to the laboratory— or does it provide a model for all hierarchical authority structures?

- Whether there is a legitimate parallel between Milgram's laboratory and Nazi Germany to some extent depends on our understanding of Nazi Germany. We might assume that because Nazi Germany was a militarized regime with a top-down authority structure that all behavior resulted from this. However, individuals may have sought power over others simply because they could.

- We need to recognize that the implications of Milgram's work did not end in Nazi Germany or his experimental laboratories. The issue of power relationships in all walks of life remains as well as our personal responsibility to resist malevolent authority. We therefore need to be cautious about investing our complete trust in governments, corporations, or other social institutions.

- We need to be fully aware of the impersonal way that bureaucracies work and to question our own ethical behavior if we work within one.

GLOSSARY

bureaucracy refers to a mechanistic social system in which efficiency, calculability, and predictability are the primary goals. Personal fulfillment or initiative are eliminated.

FURTHER READING

Arendt H. (1963/2006). *Eichmann in Jerusalem. A report on the banality of evil.* London: Penguin.

Blass T. (2004). *The man who shocked the world. The life and legacy of Stanley Milgram.* New York: Basic Books.

Figes O. (2008). *The whisperers. Private life in Stalin's Russia.* London: Penguin.

Haslam S. A., & Reicher S. D. (2012). When prisoners take over the prison: a social psychology of resistance. *Personality and Social Psychology Review, 16,* 154–179.

Perry G. (2013). *Behind the shock machine. The untold story of the notorious Milgram psychology experiments.* London: Scribe.

QUESTIONS FOR GROUP DISCUSSION

- What lessons do *you* draw from Milgram's studies of obedience?
- How might the criticism leveled at Milgram be an example of mystification? What is the real issue?
- Should psychological research encourage resistance to authority? In what scenarios might resistance be important?
- What do *you* consider to be legitimate and nonlegitimate authority?

15 Intergroup Conflict, Peace, and Reconciliation

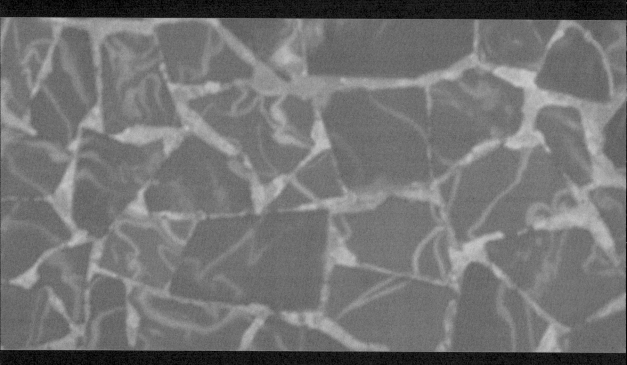

J. CHRISTOPHER COHRS, JOHANNA R. VOLLHARDT, AND SHELLEY MCKEOWN

CHAPTER OUTLINE

Our world has been characterized by numerous armed conflicts between groups. The Conflict Barometer 2014 lists 424 conflicts worldwide (Heidelberg Institute for International Conflict Research/HIIK, 2015). In particular, violent conflicts of medium intensity[1] have been on the rise since the beginning of the 1990s, and most of these conflicts take place *within* states rather than *between* states. Some examples of continuous conflict in (otherwise relatively peaceful) Europe and its surroundings include multiple conflicts in Ukraine, the territorial conflict between Armenia and Azerbaijan, several conflicts in the former Yugoslavia, and the conflicts in Northern Ireland and Cyprus. While scholars, practitioners, and policy makers have analyzed these cases in detail, conflicts that have been transformed and solved constructively as well as contexts where reconciliation attempts have been successful are often less visible and not discussed as widely. From a scientific perspective, it is important to understand both the causes of armed conflicts and violence and the factors that contribute to peace and reconciliation. Alongside other disciplines such as political science, sociology, and economics (Richmond, Pogodda, & Ramovic, 2016), psychology has a lot to say about these issues.

A starting point for our discussion is the framework of conflict and peace suggested by Christie, Tint, Wagner, and Winter (2008), which distinguishes between different phases within a cycle of violence. These are (a) nonviolent intergroup conflict, (b) organized intergroup violence, and (c) postviolence. *Different problem analyses and intervention strategies are required depending on the phase of a conflict.* In the first phase, groups have goals, interests, or views that are perceived to be in conflict, but there has been no violence. Here it is important to find ways to manage nonviolent conflict in order to prevent the emergence of overt violence. If this fails, reactive approaches are required in the second phase, where the goal is conflict deescalation. If **conflict resolution** or **conflict transformation** is successful, it is important in the third phase to achieve reconciliation and strengthen the foundations for sustainable peace that not only includes the absence of overt violence (i.e., **negative peace**) but also the absence of structural violence (i.e., **positive peace**; Galtung, 1969) and cultural violence (i.e., the cultural legitimization of overt and structural violence; Galtung, 1985, 1990).

---

[1] "Violent conflict" and "medium intensity" are terms used in the Conflict Barometer (HIIK, 2015) based on the conflict means (use of weapons and personnel) and conflict consequences (number of casualties, destruction, and refugees/internally displaced persons). Violent conflicts of medium intensity are also referred to as "violent crises."

Political Psychology: A Social Psychological Approach, First Edition.
Edited by Christopher J. Hewer and Evanthia Lyons.
© 2018 John Wiley & Sons Ltd. Published 2018 by John Wiley & Sons Ltd.

In reality, these three phases are not always distinct; they overlap to some degree. Also, conflicts do not always develop in a linear way. For example, it is often unclear when a conflict has moved from the nonviolent phase into the organized violence phase. What is more, in the postviolence phase occasional acts of intergroup violence may still occur. Also, in the third phase new conflicts may emerge or previous conflicts reemerge, taking the situation back to the first phase. And although "conflict" has broadly negative connotations, we should bear in mind that some claim that conflict is an inevitable aspect of human relationships that can have positive functions (e.g., Kriesberg, 2012). For example, the recent move toward greater social equality and inclusion was arguably not possible without conflict. It is *how* we deal with conflict that is crucial.

INTERGROUP CONFLICTS

Intergroup conflicts are characterized by the presence of inconsistent tendencies between groups in terms of their goals, claims, beliefs, values, wishes, feelings, and/or actions (Coleman, 2003). Examples include disagreements about territories, material resources, power relations, self-determination, and values. The ideological projects of different groups can be in conflict with each other when the groups have contradictory beliefs about how they want society to be organized (Cohrs, 2012). An escalation of conflict becomes particularly likely when each group defines the other as an enemy that impedes the fulfillment of the ideal society and has to be fought (i.e., scapegoating; Staub, 1999).

Where violent intergroup conflict has persisted, the societies involved face difficult challenges (see Cohrs, Uluğ, Stahel, & Kıslıoğlu, 2015). The situation creates stress and threatens people's ability to satisfy their basic needs and to withstand the adversary. According to Bar-Tal (2000a), societies adapt to these challenges by developing an "**ethos of conflict**"; that is: a configuration of central, socially shared beliefs about the conflict, which are connected to the dominant narrative and its history. These societal beliefs provide a clear and meaningful view of the conflict and of the parties involved. It allows people to make sense of the conflict and reduce uncertainty regarding its future development (Bar-Tal, 2000a). There are eight features or interrelated themes that become the focus of the group: positive emotional attachment to the group and unity within it, the justness of group goals, concerns about security, positive image, victimization, as well as delegitimization, and dehumanization of the adversary and concerns about peace. When these concerns and beliefs are crystallized in society, the ingroup is seen as a peace-loving victim of the outgroup (adversary), and the adversary is vilified as cruel, inhumane, untrustworthy, and responsible for the violence (e.g., Bar-Tal, Sharvit, Halperin, & Zafran, 2012).

At the individual level of analysis, the endorsement of the dominant ethos of conflict by Jewish Israelis has been shown to correlate with right-wing authoritarianism, dogmatic thinking, a right-wing or "hawkish" political self-definition, and reduced support for compromises with the Palestinians (Zafran, cited in Bar-Tal, Raviv, Raviv, & Dgani-Hirsh, 2009). In addition, in nationally representative samples in Israel and Palestine, endorsement of the ethos of conflict predicted reduced support for compromise and resolution of the conflict (Canetti, Elad-Strenger, Lavi, Guy, & Bar-Tal, 2015). The ethos of conflict also affects perceptual-cognitive processes such as selective attention as well as interpretation and evaluation of information (Bar-Tal, Raviv, Raviv, & Dgani-Hirsh, 2009). For instance, endorsement of the dominant ethos of conflict predicted how Jewish Israeli participants perceived ambiguous photos about encounters between Jews and Palestinians. Specifically, the more participants endorsed the ethos of conflict, the more they perceived Palestinians to be aggressive and the more they attributed Palestinian aggression to internal and stable causes. They were also more likely to engage in positive stereotyping of Jews and negative stereotyping of Palestinians. What we conclude is that the ethos of conflict is a serious obstacle to conflict resolution and compromise.

CONFLICT ANALYSIS

Conflict analysis aims to map systematically the sources of conflict, the actors directly or indirectly involved, mutual relationships between these actors, and dynamic processes in the conflict such as feedback loops. The aim is to identify barriers and opportunities for the resolution and transformation of the conflict (e.g., Shmueli, 2003; Wehr, 2006). In principle, such an analysis can be done in any of the conflict phases defined by Christie, Tint, et al. (2008)—whether or not a conflict has already transitioned into the organized violence phase and whether or not attempts of conflict resolution have already taken place.

Importantly, there is no one true interpretation of a conflict, but conflicts are characterized by perspective divergences due to different positions that individuals and groups occupy (e.g., Dovidio, Saguy, West, & Gaertner, 2012). The same event may be subject to different interpretations. For example, what one group may interpret as an unwarranted and unprovoked act of aggression may be interpreted by the other group as retaliation for a preceding event. Because of this divergence in perspective, conflict analysis has to elicit all perspectives within and between the parties involved in order to obtain a full understanding. To illustrate, Uluğ (2016) explored different understandings of the Kurdish conflict in Turkey, which since 1984 has caused the death of 45,000 people and displaced over a million. The conflict is classified as a conflict of medium intensity in the Conflict Barometer, 2014 (HIIK, 2015), but it has seen renewed escalation recently.[2] Uluğ (2016) sought to identify perspectives on the conflict in Turkey, their differences and commonalities, with an eye toward generating ideas for compromise and constructive conflict resolution. For this purpose, Q methodology was employed—an approach that uncovers distinct socially shared perspectives on the issue at hand. The concept of frames structured the understanding of conflict along the following domains (Entman, 1993):

- Problem definition—how is the conflict defined as a problem?
- Causal interpretation—what are the perceived causes of the conflict?
- Moral evaluation—how are different actors in the conflict evaluated?
- Treatment recommendation—what is suggested to solve the conflict?
- Barriers to solution—what obstacles to a solution of the conflict are identified?

Based on a search of academic publications, journalistic writings, party programs, and political speeches as well as previous qualitative and survey research, a list of 54 statements was generated to represent different views on the conflict along the five domains. Then, three samples of participants were selected, representing different levels of society: 23 politicians (members of parliament, from the four main political parties in parliament at the time of the study), 41 experts (academics from different universities and journalists from newspapers with different political leanings), and 71 members of the general public from different backgrounds. Each participant completed a Q sort, either in person or online—which involves sorting the 54 statements into a quasinormal distribution according to the participant's relative degree of agreement or disagreement. This method forces the participant to think carefully about each statement, compare the statements with one another, and thus create an overall picture that reflects in detail how he or she thinks about the conflict. The analysis yielded five different perspectives on the conflict: (a) a Kurdish rights perspective, (b) a democracy, rights and freedom perspective, (c) an Islamist perspective, (d) an economy-focused perspective, and (e) a terrorism and foreign powers perspective. Uluğ (2016) further provides a detailed analysis of these in terms of similarity and difference, giving an instructive overview of how different sections of society interpret the conflict—an important precondition for developing strategies to address the conflict.

---

[2] See, e.g., http://blog.crisisgroup.org/europe-central-asia/2015/08/11/a-new-cycle-begins-in-turkey-pkk-conflict/

CONFLICT MANAGEMENT, RESOLUTION, AND TRANSFORMATION

Once a conflict is analyzed or assessed, the next step is to decide on the approach that should be taken to help achieve peaceful coexistence. Here, we consider three approaches: **conflict management,** conflict resolution, and conflict transformation. At the most basic level, conflict management can be viewed as an approach that aims to control or manage direct conflict (Spangler, 2003). Unlike other approaches, its goal is not to resolve or transform the conflict. Through conflict management, it is hoped that the negative consequences will be reduced and the beneficial consequences will be maximized. Much of the literature on conflict management focuses on relations between teams, especially within the workplace. Typically, this work draws on conflict management techniques that are underpinned by dual concern theory (Blake & Mouton, 1970), which argues that it is vital to consider both concern for self and others. Depending on whether each of these concerns is high or low, different strategies may result. For example, with low concern for self and low concern for others, avoidance may be the strategy of choice. With high concern for self and low concern for others, people may engage in forcing strategies that result in the views of one side being forced onto the other. Low concern for self and high concern for others may lead to yielding, in which the other side's view is accepted. If concerns for both the self and the other are high, then this is more likely to result in a problem solving approach, which aims to fulfill the needs of both sides. Commentators also suggest that compromise should be considered as a fifth strategy, which is used with average levels of concern for both sides (De Dreu, Evers, Beersma, Kluwer, & Nauta, 2001).

Arguably the best strategies for dealing with intergroup conflict are those akin to problem solving or compromise, as it is through these approaches that the first step toward achieving social justice can be made. If, by contrast, forcing, or yielding are adopted then the consequence will be a unilateral agreement that favors one group over the other. In addition, there is evidence to suggest that individual approaches to conflict management can have political and social consequences for intergroup relations. For example, Schneider, Holman, Diekman, and McAndrew (2015) found that men are more likely to use a forced conflict management strategy than women and that those who prefer a forced conflict management strategy have higher political ambition.

In practice, conflict management can be difficult to achieve and Northern Ireland is one example of a setting in which group dynamics and conflicting political and national ideologies lie at the heart of gross societal divisions. Like the Kurdish conflict in Turkey, the conflict in Northern Ireland is classified as a conflict of medium intensity in the Conflict Barometer 2014 (HIIK, 2015). In a comprehensive review, Wolff (2002) reports on conflict management strategies used in Northern Ireland from the 1960s until the signing of the Peace Agreement in 1998. One clear complication is that when groups and parties cannot agree on the cause of the conflict, it is difficult to agree on one solution. The key solutions appeared to be fourfold: (a) full integration into the United Kingdom, (b) devolution, (c) repartition, or (d) reunification with the Republic of Ireland. Each solution had its proponents and there were many failed attempts toward peace (Wolff, 2002). While relations in Northern Ireland have improved greatly over recent decades, whether the Northern Ireland Peace Agreement is interpreted as forced, compromised or problem solved very much depends on one's group affiliation. Given the complexities of intergroup conflict, we argue that while conflict management may be an important first step in working toward peace, it is particularly important to consider the underlying mechanisms associated with intergroup conflict. Further, it is crucial to work toward—not just ending violence (negative peace), but also putting in place the structures for change and positive peace.

CONFLICT RESOLUTION

Conflict resolution may be viewed as the next step forward from conflict management. Christie and Louis (2012) argue that there are four key conflict management strategies that can facilitate conflict resolution. Firstly, they suggest that peacekeeping (such as the deployment of troops) is an important step, not just to keep groups apart, but to offer protection and facilitate the movement toward building important structures and organizations. Secondly, they argue that confidence-building measures are important in order to build trust between groups. Thirdly, they point to unofficial diplomacy as a tool to promote mutual understanding between the groups involved. Finally, they discuss intergroup contact as a way in which relations between groups can build from the bottom up. Christie and Louis (2012) argue that the combination of these conflict management approaches can help work toward conflict resolution.

In contrast to conflict management, conflict resolution aims to go beyond the interests of the parties involved to addressing the underlying cause of the conflict in a way that respects identities and attitudes on all sides (Spangler, 2003). In a similar vein, Kelman (2010) differentiates political settlement from conflict resolution. He states that:

> a process of conflict resolution goes beyond a realist view of national interests. It explores the causes of the conflict, particularly causes in the form of unmet or threatened needs for identity, security, recognition, autonomy, and justice. It seeks solutions responsive to the needs of both sides through active engagement in joint problem solving. (p. 1)

Sanson and Bretherton (2001) further highlight the role of psychology in conflict resolution by claiming that "the practice of conflict resolution aims to utilize knowledge of psychological processes to maximize the positive potential inherent in a conflict and to prevent its destructive consequences" (p. 1). As such, conflict resolution focuses on establishing a new relationship between the parties involved in the dispute, which encompasses new attitudes. Kelman (2010) argues that conflict resolution is vulnerable to change: change in interests, circumstances, and leadership. Underlying this is the problem of old attitudes that may reemerge and bring about challenges to the new relationship.

PRINCIPLES OF CONFLICT RESOLUTION

Sanson and Bretherton (2001) argue that there are four key principles that underlie conflict resolution: (a) that conflict resolution is a cooperative endeavor, (b) that the solutions sought are integrative, (c) that at the foundation is an understanding of the interests of all parties, and (d) that both the process and its outcome are nonviolent. They argue that conflict resolution not only seeks to minimize the destructive consequences of conflict but also to maximize the positive outcomes. In that sense, conflict resolution aims to work against violence in favor of human security, rights, and equality.

ACHIEVING CONFLICT RESOLUTION

Conflict resolution typically involves mediation, negotiation, and/or problem solving. Part of this process involves the deployment of problem solving workshops that take place between representatives of groups involved in conflict (Maiese, 2003). These have been used in various conflict settings including Cyprus (Broome, 1997) and Israel-Palestine (Kelman, 2005). Problem solving workshops are unstructured, unofficial discussions facilitated by a third party, typically, trained social scientists (Kelman & Cohen, 1976). There are three key phases of the workshop. In phase one, parties (independently) present their understanding of the conflict and their grievances to the facilitators. In phase two, the parties remain separate from one another, but work with the facilitators to analyze the conflict. In phase three, the parties come together and begin to collaborate on establishing a solution to their joint problem. Conflict resolution assumes conflict is negative and undesirable and, as such, aims to address the underlying causes of conflict with the aim of resolving it. In contrast, other models have been put forward that do not necessarily aim to resolve the conflict but instead transform it and work with it, viewing conflict as a natural part of human relationships (Spangler, 2003).

CONFLICT TRANSFORMATION

Conflict transformation is a constructive change orientation to ending violent conflict popularized by Lederach, who was dissatisfied with terms such as conflict resolution and conflict management. According to Lederach (2003),

> Conflict transformation is to envision and respond to the ebb and flow of social conflict as life-giving opportunities for creating constructive change processes that reduce violence, increase justice in direct interaction and social structures, and respond to real-life problems in human relationships. (p. 14)

To fully understand what is meant by conflict transformation, it is important to consider the component parts of the definition. The following summary is based on a shortened online version of Lederach's (2003) book, *The Little Book of Conflict Transformation*.

- *Envision and respond*—refers to seeing conflict as having the potential for positive and constructive change and being directly involved in that process of change through real experience.
- *Ebb and flow*—is related to the nature of human relationships, the good, the bad, and the ugly. Conflict transformation aims to look at the wider picture rather than single episodes of conflict and, as such, considers both individual and broader issues relating to conflict.
- *Life-giving opportunities*—this encourages us to view conflict as a natural part of human life and as something that should be valued as a way of understanding relationships and people. Rather than being a merely negative event, it keeps the world running, enables us to stop and take note, and acts as a catalyst for change.
- *Constructive change processes*—this refers to using experiences borne out of conflict to engender constructive, goal-oriented changes that will improve society and address underlying structural inequalities, as opposed to a quick fix to the problem.
- *Reduce violence and increase justice*—this focuses on addressing both the explicit and underlying causes of the conflict and ensuring that individuals and groups have a political voice to enable social justice.
- *Direct interaction and social structures*—refer to promoting interactions and dialogues across all levels of society from the interpersonal to the

intergroup and the social structural level as a means to promote change. It suggests that dialogue is vital to transforming conflict.

- *Human relationships*—"are at the heart of conflict transformation." Rather than focusing solely on the dispute itself, it is vital to consider the underlying connections that are less visible in these relationships. It is claimed that through understanding these relationships, it is possible to ascertain how and when disputes lead to conflict and violence, as opposed to being quickly resolved.

Through his conflict transformation perspective, Lederach (2003) argues that there are four key dimensions associated with conflict and change: (a) the personal—changes desired by the individual; (b) the relational—changes associated with human relationships; (c) the structural—the underlying structural causes of the conflict; and (d) the cultural—the way in which culture affects how people and groups respond to conflict. As such, conflict is viewed as encompassing multiple levels, and therefore it must be addressed from a multilevel perspective.

CONFLICT TRANSFORMATION IN PRACTICE

According to Lederach (2003), a conflict transformation approach includes three main components:

1. The presenting situation; that is, the conflict situation itself, including what caused the conflict as well as the surrounding context.
2. The horizon of preferred future; that is, what could be built through constructive change. This entails not viewing the direction from the present to the future as linear, but instead as a bidirectional process in which one works with the other and vice versa. Thus, conflict transformation is understood as a circular process.
3. The development of change processes linking the two; taking a multilevel view to conflict transformation involving the individual, group, and social structures in which change is desired beyond the short term.

Unlike conflict resolution, which emphasizes ending conflict, the conflict transformation approach focuses on the importance of change toward building something that is desired—not just ending something that is not desired. This reminds us of Galtung's (1969) conceptualization of positive peace and the need to end structural violence in addition to direct violence in order to promote peace. Conflict transformation is also relationship-focused and goes beyond the immediate conflict to consider the wider issues rather than seek quick solutions.

There are a number of practices that can help us to transform conflict. Lederach argues that we should develop a capacity to (a) see presenting issues as a window, (b) integrate multiple time frames, (c) pose the energies of conflict as dilemmas, (d) make complexity a friend, not a foe, and (e) hear and engage the voice of identity and relationship. Such an understanding of conflict transformation reflects much of the social and political psychology literature on intergroup relations.

For example, there is research that suggests that suffering is sometimes associated with subsequent prosocial behaviors (e.g., Vollhardt, 2009a). Therefore, the altruism that results from suffering could be viewed as a developing capacity to see political issues as a window for change. In a similar way, "to hear and engage the voice of identity" could be understood in relation to research on empathy, which has shown that increased empathy toward outgroup members is associated with a reduction in prejudice, anxiety, and perceived dissimilarity (Stephan & Finlay, 1999). Furthermore, research on common victimhood demonstrates that groups that are primed with a common victim identity are less likely to claim that their group has suffered more during a conflict and are more likely to express forgiveness (e.g., Shnabel, Halabi, & Noor, 2013). Other research also suggests that victim beliefs can promote empathy and prosocial behaviors (Vollhardt, 2009b). As such, there is evidence from the social and political psychology literature to support Lederach's argument that conflict experiences need not always be negative and that they can have transformative powers for social change.

POSTCONFLICT RECONSTRUCTION AND RECONCILIATION

Once direct violence has ceased and so-called negative peace (Galtung, 1969) has been achieved—often through peace agreements at the political level—enormous challenges still remain. First, it is necessary to gain support for the political peace agreements among all segments of society and then the task is to tackle structural violence and achieve positive peace. Finally, in order to prevent the outbreak of renewed violence and build a stable and lasting peace, there is a need to work toward reconciliation—which is an objective and an outcome as well as a process (Bar-Tal & Bennick, 2004).

SOCIAL PSYCHOLOGICAL DEFINITIONS OF RECONCILIATION

Social and political psychologists have defined reconciliation in many different ways. A common feature of these definitions is that reconciliation changes the nature of the relationship between the former opponents, which also involves changes in how one views one's ingroup. For example, Bar-Tal (2000b) states that reconciliation requires the majority to form "new beliefs about the former adversary, their own society, and about the relationship between the two groups" (p. 356). In other words, it requires a change of societal beliefs and, in particular, a change in the ethos that once drove the conflict (Bar-Tal, 2000a). This process, then, should ultimately lead to mutual acknowledgment, acceptance, and trust as well as positive attitudes that consider the other party's needs and interests (Bar-Tal & Bennick, 2004).

INSTRUMENTAL RECONCILIATION

Nadler and colleagues (e.g., Nadler, 2012; Nadler & Shnabel, 2008) further distinguish between instrumental and socioemotional reconciliation. **Instrumental reconciliation** is focused on repairing the working relationship with the former adversary, above all restoring trust in the other conflict party (e.g., Nadler & Liviatan, 2006). It is described as "instrumental" because it lays a foundation for the purpose of achieving common goals. Typical interventions that fall within this type of reconciliation are, for example, those based on intergroup contact (e.g., Wagner & Hewstone, 2012). This type of reconciliation strategy is focused on the present or future. Indeed, Nadler and Shnabel (2008) point out that the goal of such interventions can be merely to restore the relationships and create a conflict-free setting, that is, to achieve instrumental goals and live in separate coexistence. Thus, instrumental reconciliation does not appear to achieve much beyond negative peace and, as such, is closer to definitions of conflict resolution rather than reconciliation.

THE ROLE OF HISTORY AND POWER

However, practitioners and scholars alike have observed that a focus on the present and on "getting along" is not sufficient and can have repercussions over time. It may also reduce the chances for positive peace by creating obstacles to social justice and equality between groups. History matters, and addressing historical victimization, disadvantage, and power imbalance between groups is crucial (e.g., Liu & Hilton, 2005; Vollhardt & Bilewicz, 2013). For example, recent research from postconflict societies such as South Africa and the United States have stressed that intergroup contact interventions work differently for members of high and low status groups (or historically advantaged and disadvantaged groups). Specifically, the interventions seem to have positive effects primarily among the high powered and advantaged groups. Additionally, while one of the goals of instrumental reconciliation is to promote trust and positive relations *between* groups, these interventions can undermine the low-power group's desire for social change (Dixon, Tropp, Durrheim, & Tredoux, 2010). Other studies have come to similar conclusions, showing that intergroup contact that focused on commonalities between high and low-power groups, rather than on differences, increased positive intergroup attitudes but undermined support for social change (Saguy, Tausch, Dovidio, & Pratto, 2009). Such **harmony-focused contact** increased perceptions that the status quo was legitimate but reduced attributions of discrimination among members of disadvantaged groups (Saguy & Chernyak-Hai, 2012).

Another mechanism by which intergroup contact hampers change is by fostering perceptions of a common ingroup identity (Dovidio, Gaertner, & Saguy, 2009; see also Dixon et al., 2010). Single recategorization into one shared identity tends to further advantage the majority or high power group identity by taking it as prototypical for the whole group (Waldzus, Mummendey, Wenzel, & Boettcher, 2004), and it shifts the focus away from difference and inequality. While this common identity tends to be favored by majority or high power groups (Dovidio et al., 2009), minority or low-power groups members often prefer a **dual identity** where both the shared, superordinate identity, and subgroup differences are acknowledged and valued (see Hornsey & Hogg, 2000). Dovidio et al. (2009) argue that a dual identity does not stand in the way of social change because the focus on inequality and difference is still preserved. Thus, this form of identity seems to dissolve the apparent contradiction between instrumental reconciliation and positive peace (see Nadler & Shnabel, 2008).

Qualitative research has also shown how a dual identity in postgenocide Rwanda allows for the recognition of historical victimization and other group-based differences and grievances (Moss & Vollhardt, 2016). This is in contrast to the Rwandan government policy of a state wide, official reconciliation campaign based on "unity" and common goals such as economic development. The policy also outlaws even talking about the distinction between Hutu and Tutsi because this distinction was central to the 1994 Rwandan genocide and several other historical mass atrocities in the country (Straus & Waldorf, 2011). In other words, the Rwandan government has chosen instrumental reconciliation as their favored approach and has turned single recategorization into state policy. Yet, while some Rwandans favor this approach and see some advantages in terms of stabilizing the country and providing security, others criticize it and emphasize the need to acknowledge group differences, historical victimization, and present-day inequality (Moss & Vollhardt, 2016).

We conclude that scholarship in social and political psychology shows the importance of addressing history when tackling the issue of prejudice or working toward reconciliation. Thus, the present and future focus of instrumental reconciliation is problematic, and socioemotional reconciliation—or perhaps, rather, an integration of the two forms of reconciliation—may be more promising.

SOCIOEMOTIONAL RECONCILIATION AND THE NEEDS-BASED MODEL OF RECONCILIATION

Nadler and Shnabel (2008, see also Nadler, 2012) propose that this second form of reconciliation explicitly addresses the past, and does so in ways that alleviates **identity threats** resulting from the past conflict. The focus of **socioemotional reconciliation** is internal in that it aims to change the self-identity and image of each group, rather than merely restoring trust and positive relations between the groups. By reducing identity threats resulting from past conflict, and by encouraging a shift in identity, positive relations between the two groups can be restored.

Nadler and Shnabel (2008, see also Shnabel, Nadler, Ullrich, Dovidio, & Carmi, 2009) further propose that a needs-based model of reconciliation will contribute to socioemotional reconciliation by addressing the frustrated needs of both the victim and the perpetrator group. They demonstrate empirically that while the victim group has the need to be empowered, the perpetrator group wants to be morally accepted and liked. When these needs are mutually satisfied by, for example, messages that communicate these sentiments by members of the other group, or through an apology-forgiveness cycle, people are more likely to express willingness to reconcile. This has been demonstrated among Arab Israelis and Jewish Israelis as well as among Germans and Israeli Jews (Shnabel et al., 2009), and on the interpersonal level (Shnabel & Nadler, 2008). The **needs-based model of reconciliation** has also been applied to and empirically tested in several other conflict settings (e.g., Barlow et al., 2015; Bilewicz & Jaworska, 2013; Kosic & Tauber, 2010) and is arguably one of the most commonly used theoretical frameworks within social and political psychology research on reconciliation.

HISTORY AS A NECESSITY FOR AND AN OBSTACLE TO RECONCILIATION

However, the needs-based model of reconciliation has practical limitations. While the effects have been promising in laboratory-based experimental studies, these studies were based on messages crafted by the researchers, which were given to members of the other group. The messages were not actually formulated and communicated by members of the victim or perpetrator group themselves. Indeed, the likelihood that members of the respective groups will willingly communicate these messages is low. Perpetrator groups are often reluctant to admit guilt and responsibility even for historical crimes (Leach, Bou Zeineddine, & Čehajić-Clancy, 2013), and reminders of such crimes and their consequences can have serious consequences. For example, Imhoff and Banse (2009) found that reminding Germans of the continuing suffering of Jewish people because of the Holocaust increased secondary anti-Semitism. Similarly, contact interventions between Polish Christian and Jewish students from North America or Australia that focused on the past were less productive than those that focused on the present (Bilewicz, 2007). This was presumably because the Jewish group believed that some Poles had been complicit in the Holocaust. From these findings, it would appear that perpetrator groups are unlikely to address the historical harm for which they are responsible, and confrontation will only undermine relationships between the groups.

There is the additional problem that victim groups have a strong desire for their victimization to be acknowledged. Several experimental studies among Armenian and Jewish Americans have shown that such an acknowledgment increased willingness for reconciliation and also increased psychological well-being, whereas denial or lack of explicit acknowledgment had the opposite effect (Vollhardt, Mazur, & Lemahieu, 2014). This creates an obstacle to socioemotional reconciliation: the issue that creates an identity threat for the perpetrator group, namely acknowledgment of the historical crimes, reduces an important identity threat for the victim group and failure to do so has the reverse effect. However, talking about historical victimization is not always good for intergroup relations—indeed, an exclusive focus on an ingroup's historical victimization can legitimize doing harm in present-day conflicts, even when they are appear to be unrelated (Schori-Eyal, Halperin, & Bar-Tal, 2014; Wohl & Branscombe, 2008). Moreover, in conflicts where both sides have been victims and perpetrators, groups often compete over who is the greater victim. Such competitive victimhood, however, is detrimental to trust and reconciliation, as demonstrated in Chile, Northern Ireland, and several other conflict settings (Noor, Brown, Gonzales, Manzi, & Lewis, 2008; Noor, Brown, & Prentice, 2008; Noor, Shnabel, Halabi, & Nadler, 2012). And although experimental studies among Palestinians and Jewish Israelis suggest that reassuring people that their ingroup had "won" the status as the greatest victim, improved willingness for reconciliation (Simantov-Nachnieli, Shnabel, & Halabi, 2015), this acknowledgment is neither realistic, constructive, nor pragmatic because it poses a threat to the identity of the other party. In other words, it addresses the goals of socioemotional reconciliation in an imbalanced way and thereby undermines them.

What, then, can pave the way toward a form of socioemotional reconciliation that faces the past but which removes identity threats for all groups involved? Several intervention strategies have been proposed and tested by social and political psychologists. For example, in a study of Polish Christian and Jewish Israeli students, Bilewicz and Jaworska (2013) demonstrated that intergroup contact interventions that focus on the history of each group improved intergroup attitudes and increased perceived group similarity among Polish participants. The unifying factor was the discussion of Polish nationals recognized by Yad Vashem as "Righteous among the Nations" because they had rescued Jews during the Holocaust.

Čehajić-Clancy, Effron, Halperin, Liberman, and Ross (2011) tested another strategy in a laboratory setting in Bosnia-Herzegovina and Israel. They showed that self-affirmation—being given an opportunity to affirm important personal values—increased willingness to acknowledge ingroup responsibility for inflicting harm during the conflict. It also increased acceptance of collective guilt and support for reparations. Group affirmation, in contrast, did not have any positive effect in these studies. However, in a different context, group affirmation was actually effective in increasing willingness of Canadians to accept collective guilt for the violence and injustice committed against Aboriginals (the indigenous people of North America) (Gunn & Wilson, 2011).

Finally, among members of both victim and perpetrator groups in the aftermath of genocide and mass atrocities in Rwanda and Burundi, an intervention based on *reconciliation radio soap operas* has been somewhat successful in promoting aspects of both instrumental and socioemotional reconciliation. Field experiments conducted in Rwanda after 1 year (Paluck, 2009; Paluck & Green, 2009) and after several years of broadcasting (Bilali & Vollhardt, 2013) showed that listeners (compared to the control group) expressed more intergroup trust, empathy, cooperation, and less social distance from the outgroup. In addition to these indicators of instrumental reconciliation, listeners also expressed greater historical perspective taking, that is, openness toward the historical conflict narrative of the other group. Furthermore, they expressed less competitive victimhood in relation to the historical conflict.

These two findings highlight the intervention's effectiveness in addressing the past and removing related identity-based threats—both indicators of socioemotional reconciliation (for replication of some of these findings in Burundi see Bilali, Vollhardt, & Rarick, 2016). What then accounts for the effectiveness of this intervention? The fictional nature of the soap opera makes it possible for listeners to learn the educational message about reconciliation and the need to confront the past without feeling directly threatened (Bilali & Vollhardt, 2013; Bilali, 2014; Bilali et al., 2016). Thus, fictional interventions may be another useful strategy for addressing identity threats in a process of socioemotional reconciliation.

CONCLUSION

A common feature of the social (and political) psychological research on peace and conflict reviewed here is that scholars are motivated by the ideal of positive peace and an ambition to achieve social justice as they try to understand how conflicts emerge, develop, and change (Vollhardt & Bilali, 2008). To achieve this complex goal, researchers adopt various methodological approaches, ranging from qualitative case studies to large-scale quantitative surveys and experiments. Another common feature is its focus on subjective constructions of the social world and that conflict is viewed as an inevitable human process. Such an approach contributes to our understanding of individuals and groups, and the ways in which they interact with one another in specific contexts. This adds to the body of research found in other disciplines such as international relations or conflict studies, where state level relations are the main focus. Indeed, while social psychological research makes a valuable contribution, to truly understand how to end violent conflict and promote positive peace, we must examine societal, political, and economical structures. The path to positive peace cannot take a one-size-fits-all approach; success depends on understanding the sociocultural context, and recognizing the stage of the conflict—considering the causes, impacts, and outcomes across different levels of analysis including individual differences, processes within and between groups, and societal structures.

SUMMARY

- Conflict and peace can be understood in terms of three different phases of a cycle of violence: (a) nonviolent intergroup conflict, (b) organized intergroup violence, and (c) postviolence.
- Overt violence is not the only form of violence, as structural violence (social inequalities) and cultural violence (use of culture to legitimize violence) also play a role in intergroup conflict.

- The end of overt conflict may go some way to achieving what is known as negative peace, but addressing structural inequalities is important in achieving positive peace.

- Conflict analysis is an important step to understand the sources of conflict and identify barriers and opportunities for peace from multiple perspectives. Some important barriers to peace are of a psychological nature.

- Depending on the context and phase of a conflict, conflict management, conflict resolution, or conflict transformation may be more appropriate strategies toward peace.

- There are many approaches to reconciliation including instrumental (repairing the working relationship and restoring trust between groups) and socioemotional reconciliation (changing the self-identity of the groups). The needs-based model of reconciliation highlights some conditions for the latter form of reconciliation, but may be difficult to implement outside of laboratory settings.

- Understanding the social, political, and historical context, as well as the psychological processes and dynamics involved, is vital to reduce conflict and achieve positive peace.

GLOSSARY

conflict analysis aims to identify barriers and opportunities for the resolution and transformation of conflict through a careful analysis of the sources of conflict, the actors involved, their relationship, and the dynamic processes.

conflict management aims to control or manage conflict (instead of resolving or transforming it) so that its negative consequences are minimized.

conflict resolution aims to address the underlying causes of a conflict in a way that respects the identities and needs of the parties involved.

conflict transformation is a constructive change in orientation to ending conflict that goes beyond conflict management and conflict resolution.

dual identity is where both the shared, superordinate identity and subgroup differences are acknowledged and valued.

ethos of conflict refers to socially shared beliefs about the conflict that are connected to the dominant narrative and history: it is often a barrier to peace.

harmony-focused contact refers to intergroup interactions designed to improve attitudes toward the outgroup, usually without addressing issues that divide the groups, such as power differences.

instrumental reconciliation focuses on repairing the working relationship with a former adversary—above all, restoring trust in the other party.

identity threats are implicit or explicit threats to one's identity, which includes self-esteem and important group values.

needs-based model of reconciliation is a theoretical model that suggests that socioemotional reconciliation can be achieved by addressing the frustrated needs of both the victim and the perpetrator group.

negative peace exists when people are not killed or harmed by war or other forms of direct violence.

positive peace exists when people are not killed or harmed by *indirect* violence, for example hunger or poverty; it is the presence of social justice.

socioemotional reconciliation is a form of reconciliation that focuses on changing the self-identity and image of each group.

FURTHER READING

Bar-Tal D. (2013). *Intractable conflicts: Socio-psychological foundations and dynamics*. New York: Cambridge University Press.

Christie D. J. (Ed.) (2012). *The encyclopedia of peace psychology*. Malden, MA: Wiley-Blackwell.

Tropp L. R. (Ed.) (2012). *The Oxford handbook of intergroup conflict*. Oxford: Oxford University Press.

Social psychological peace research is regularly published in mainstream social psychology journals (see Vollhardt & Bilali, 2008, for a content analysis). There is also a journal specifically dedicated to the psychological study of peace and conflict, *Peace and Conflict: Journal of Peace Psychology* (see http://psycnet.apa.org/journals/pac/). Another journal that regularly includes articles on issues of peace and conflict is the open-access *Journal of Social and Political Psychology* (see http://jspp.psychopen.eu/).

QUESTIONS FOR GROUP DISCUSSION

- What do you think motivates people and groups to engage in conflict?
- In what ways is conflict between groups (intergroup conflict) different from conflict between individuals (interpersonal conflict)?
- Can you think of situations in which conflict has been constructive?
- To what extent is using "peaceful means to a peaceful end" achievable?
- Why do you think members of the historically victimized, disadvantaged group tend to prefer dual identities, whereas members of the advantaged group tend to prefer single, shared identities in the aftermath of conflict and in contexts of structural violence?

- Why is it not sufficient to just have groups "get along" and like each other when trying to achieve peace and reconciliation?
- What do you think about the statement, "Those who cannot remember the past are condemned to repeat it"?
- Will there ever be peace?

Abell J., Condor S., & Stevenson C. (2006). "We are an island": Geographical imagery in accounts of citizenship, civil society, and national identity in Scotland and in England. *Political Psychology, 27*, 207–226.

Abell J., & Stevenson C. (2011). Defending the faith(s)? Democracy and hereditary right in England. *Political Psychology, 32*, 485–504.

Abelson R. P. (1981). The psychological status of the script concept. *American Psychologist, 36*, 715–729.

Abrams D., Hogg M. A., & Marques J. M. (2004). *Social psychology of inclusion and exclusion*. Hove: Psychology Press.

Adler N. E., Boyce T., Chesney M. A., Cohen S., Folkman S., Kahn R. L., & Syme S. L. (1994). Socioeconomic status and health: The challenge of the gradient. *American Psychologist, 49*, 15–24.

Adorno T. W., Frenkel-Brunswik E., Levinson D. J., & Sanford R. M. (1950). *The authoritarian personality*. New York: Harper.

Agranat Commission (1974). *The Agranat report*. Tel Aviv: Am Oved. (Hebrew).

Allport F. (1924). *Social psychology*. Boston: Houghton Mifflin.

Allport F. H. (1933). *Institutional behavior: Essays toward a re-interpreting of contemporary social organization*. Chapel Hill, NC: University of North Carolina Press.

Allport F. H. (1968). The historical background of modern social psychology. In G. Lindzey & E. Aronson (Eds.), *Handbook of social psychology* (2nd ed., Vol. 1)). Reading, MA: Addison-Wesley.

Allport G. W. (1954). *The nature of prejudice*. Cambridge, MA: Addison-Wesley.

Allport G. W. (1962). The general and the unique in psychological science. *Journal of Personality, 30*, 405–422.

Altemeyer B. (1998). The other "authoritarian personality". *Advances in Experimental Social Psychology, 30*, 47–92.

Amato, G., Rizzoli, A. (Producers), & Fellini, F. (Writer/Director). (1960). *La dolce vita* [Motion Picture]. Italy/France: Pathé Consortium Cinema.

Anderson B. (1983). *Imagined communities: Reflections on the origin and spread of nationalism*. London: Verso.

Anderson C. A., Benjamin A. J., Wood P. K., & Bonacci A. M. (2006). Development and testing of the Velicer attitudes toward violence scale: Evidence for a four-factor model. *Aggressive Behavior, 32*, 122–136.

Anderson C., Kraus M. W., Galinsky A. D., & Keltner D. (2012). The local-ladder effect social status and subjective well-being. *Psychological Science, 23*, 764–771.

Andreouli E., & Chryssochoou X. (2014). Social representations of national identity in culturally diverse societies. In G. Sammut, E. Andreouli, G. Gaskell, & J. Valsiner (Eds.), *The Cambridge handbook of social representations* (pp. 309–322). Cambridge: Cambridge University Press.

Andrews M. (2007). *Shaping history: Narratives of political change.* New York: Cambridge University Press.

Arendt H. (1976). *Origins of totalitarianism.* New York: Random House.

Arendt H. (1978). *The life of the mind.* London: Harvest.

Arendt H. (1963/2006). *Eichmann in Jerusalem: A report on the banality of evil.* London: Penguin (Original work published 1963).

Arendt H. (1998). *The human condition* (2nd ed.). Chicago: The University of Chicago Press (Original work published 1958).

Aristotle (1946). *The works of Aristotle translated into English: Volume XI. Rhetorica,* (W. R. Roberts, Trans.). London: Oxford University Press.

Asch S. E. (1951). Effects of group pressure upon the modification and distortion of judgements. In H. Guetzkow (Ed.), *Groups, leadership and men* (pp. 177–190). Pittsburgh: Carnegie Press.

Asch S. E. (1952). *Social psychology.* Englewood Cliffs, NJ: Prentice Hall.

Assmann A. (2010a). Reframing memory. Between individual and collective forms of constructing the past. In K. Tilmans, F. Van Vree, & J. Winter (Eds.), *Performing the past: Memory, history and identity in modern Europe* (pp. 35–50). Amsterdam: Amsterdam University Press.

Assmann A. (2012). To remember or to forget: Which way out of a shared history of violence? In A. Assmann & L. Shortt (Eds.), *Memory and political change* (pp. 53–71). London: Palgrave Macmillan.

Assmann J. (1992). *Das kulturelle Gedaechtnis.* Munich: CH. Beck.

Assmann J. (1998). *Moses the Egyptian: The memory of Egypt in western monotheism.* London: Harvard University Press.

Assmann J. (2006). *Religion and cultural memory: Ten studies* (R. Livingstone, Trans.). Stanford, CA: Stanford University Press.

Assmann J. (2010b). Communicative and cultural memory. In A. Erll & A. Nünning (Eds.), *A companion to cultural memory studies* (pp. 109–118). Berlin: De Gruyter.

Assmann J., & Czaplicka J. (1995). Collective memory and cultural identity. *New German Critique,* 65 CulturalHistory/Cultural Studies (Spring/Summer, 1995), 648–670.

Augoustinos M., Walker I., & Donaghue N. (2006). *Social cognition: An integrated approach.* London: Sage.

Bakouri M., & Staerklé C. (2015). Coping with structural disadvantage: Overcoming negative effects of perceived barriers through bonding identities. *British Journal of Social Psychology,* 54, 648–670.

Ball S. J. (2003). *Class strategies and the education market: The middle classes and social advantage.* London: Routledge.

Bamberg M. (2004). "We are young, responsible and male": Form and functions of "slut bashing" in male identity constructions in 15-year-olds. *Human Development,* 47, 331–353.

Bamberg M., De Fina A., & Schiffrin D. (2011). Discourse and identity construction. In S. J. Schwartz, K. Luyckx, & V. L. Vignoles (Eds.), *Handbook of identity theory and research* (pp. 177–199). New York: Springer.

Bandura A. (2006). Toward a psychology of human agency. *Perspectives on Psychological Science,* 1, 164–180.

Barkun M. (2003). *A culture of conspiracy: Apocalyptic visions in contemporary America.* Berkeley: University of California Press.

Barlow F. K., Thai M., Wohl M. J. A., White S., Wright M.-A., & Hornsey M. J. (2015). Perpetrator groups can enhance their moral self-image by accepting their own intergroup apologies. *Journal of Experimental Social Psychology, 60,* 39–50.

Barrows S. (1981). *Distorting mirrors: Visions of the crowd in late nineteenth-century France.* New Haven: Yale University Press.

Bar-Tal D. (2000a). *Shared beliefs in a society: Social psychological analysis.* Thousand Oaks, CA: Sage.

Bar-Tal D. (2000b). From intractable conflict through conflict resolution to reconciliation: Psychological analysis. *Political Psychology, 21,* 351–365.

Bar-Tal D., & Bennink G. H. (2004). The nature of reconciliation as an outcome and as a process. In Y. Bar-Siman-Tov (Ed.), *From conflict resolution to reconciliation* (pp. 11–38). Oxford: Oxford University Press.

Bar-Tal D., Raviv A., Raviv A., & Dgani-Hirsh A. (2009). The influence of the ethos of conflict on Israeli Jews' interpretation of Jewish-Palestinian encounters. *Journal of Conflict Resolution, 53,* 94–118.

Bar-Tal D., Sharvit K., Halperin E., & Zafran A. (2012). Ethos of conflict: The concept and its measurement. *Peace and Conflict: Journal of Peace Psychology, 18,* 40–61.

Bartlett F. C. (1932). *Remembering: A study in experimental and social psychology.* Cambridge: Cambridge University Press.

Baudrillard J. (1994). *Simulacra and simulation.* (S. F. Glaser, Trans.). Michigan: University of Michigan Press (Original work published 1981).

Bauman S. (2000). *Liquid modernity.* Oxford: Blackwell.

Baumeister R. F., & Hastings S. (1997). Distortions of collective memory: How groups flatter and deceive themselves. In J. W. Pennebaker, D. Paez, & B. Rimé (Eds.), *Collective memory of political events: Social psychological perspectives* (pp. 277–293). Mahwah, NJ: LEA.

Baumrind D. (1964). Some thoughts on the ethics of research: After reading Milgram's "Behavioral Study of Obedience". *American Psychologist, 19,* 421–423.

Baysu G., Phalet K., & Brown R. (2011). Dual identity as a two-edged sword identity threat and minority school performance. *Social Psychology Quarterly, 74,* 121–143.

Beer G., & Martins H. (1990). Introduction. *History of the Human Sciences, 3,* 163–175.

Bem D. J. (2011). Feeling the future: Experimental evidence for anomalous retroactive influences on cognition and affect. *Journal of Personality and Social Psychology, 100,* 407–425.

Benet-Martinez V., & Haritatos J. (2005). Bicultural identity integration (BII): Components and psychological antecedents. *Journal of Personality, 73,* 1015–1105.

Benjamin W. (1999). *Illuminations.* London: Pimlico.

Benzeval, M., Bond, L., Campbell, M., Egan, M., Lorenc, T., Petticrew, M., & Popham, F. (2014). How does money influence health? Retrieved from http://researchonline.lshtm.ac.uk/2167225/1/income-health-poverty-full.pdf (accessed April 2018).

Berger J. (1972). *Ways of seeing.* London: Penguin.

Berry J. W. (1976). *Human ecology and cognitive style: Comparative studies in cultural and psychological adaptation.* New York: John Wiley & Sons, Inc.

Berry J. W. (1990). Acculturation and adaptation: A general framework. In W. H. Holtzman & T. H. Bornemann (Eds.), *Mental health of immigrants and refugees* (pp. 90–102). Austin, TX: Hogg Foundation for Mental Health.

Berry J. W. (1997). Immigration, acculturation and adaptation. *Applied Psychology: An International Review, 46,* 5–68.

Berry J. W. (2006). Design of acculturation studies. In D. L. Sam & J. W. Berry (Eds.), *The Cambridge handbook of acculturation psychology* (pp. 129–336). Cambridge: Cambridge University Press.

Berry J. W., Phinney J. S., Sam D. L., & Vedder P. (2006). *Immigrant youth in cultural transition: Acculturation, identity and adaptation across national contexts*. Mahwah, NJ: Lawrence Erlbaum.

Berry J. W., & Sam D. L. (2013). Accommodating cultural diversity and achieving equity: An introduction to psychological dimensions of multiculturalism. *European Psychologist, 18*, 151–157.

Bilali R. (2014). Between fiction and reality in post-genocide Rwanda: Reflections on a social-psychological media intervention for social change. *Journal of Social and Political Psychology, 2*, 387–400.

Bilali R., & Vollhardt J. R. (2013). Priming effects of a reconciliation radio drama on historical perspective-taking in the aftermath of mass violence in Rwanda. *Journal of Experimental Social Psychology, 49*, 144–151.

Bilali R., Vollhardt J. R., & Rarick J. R. D. (2016). Assessing the impact of a media-based intervention to prevent intergroup violence and promote positive intergroup relations in Burundi. *Journal of Community and Applied Social Psychology, 26*, 221–235.

Bilewicz M. (2007). History as an obstacle: Impact of temporal-based social categorizations on Polish-Jewish intergroup contact. *Group Processes & Intergroup Relations, 10*, 551–563.

Bilewicz M., & Jaworska M. (2013). Reconciliation through the righteous: The narratives of heroic helpers as a fulfillment of emotional needs in Polish-Jewish intergroup contact. *Journal of Social Issues, 69*, 162–179.

Billig M. (1978). *Fascists: A social psychological view of the national front*. London: Academic Press.

Billig M. (1985). Prejudice, categorization and particularization: From a perceptual to a rhetorical approach. *European Journal of Social Psychology, 15*, 79–103.

Billig M. (1987). *Arguing and thinking: A rhetorical approach to social psychology*. Cambridge: Cambridge University Press.

Billig M. (1991). *Ideology and opinions: Studies in rhetorical psychology*. London: Sage.

Billig M. (1995). *Banal nationalism*. London: Sage.

Billig M. (1996a). *Arguing and thinking: A rhetorical approach to social psychology* (2nd ed.). Cambridge: Cambridge University Press.

Billig M. (1996b). Remembering the particular background of social identity theory. In W. P. Robinson (Ed.), *Social groups and identities: Developing the legacy of Henri Tajfel* (pp. 337–357). Oxford: Butterworth-Heinemann.

Billig M. (1997). From codes to utterances: Cultural studies, discourse and psychology. In M. Ferguson & P. Golding (Eds.), *Cultural studies in question* (pp. 205–226). London: Sage.

Billig M. (1999a). Whose terms? Whose ordinariness? Rhetoric and ideology in conversation analysis. *Discourse and Society, 10*, 543–558.

Billig M. (1999b). Conversation analysis and claims of naivety. *Discourse and Society, 10*, 572–576.

Billig M. (2003). Political rhetoric. In D. O. Sears, L. Huddy, & R. Jervis (Eds.), *Oxford handbook of political psychology* (pp. 222–251). Oxford: Oxford University Press.

Billig M. (2009). Discursive psychology, rhetoric and the issue of agency. Semen. Retrieved from http://semen.revues.org/8930 accessed April 2018.

Billig M. (2013). *Learn to write badly: How to succeed in the social sciences*. Cambridge: Cambridge University Press.

Billig M., Condor S., Edwards D., Gane M., Middleton D., & Radley A. (1988). *Ideological dilemmas: A social psychology of everyday thinking*. London: Sage.

Bin Laden, O. (1998). Declaration of the World Islamic Front for jihad against Jews and Crusaders. *Al-Quds al-Arabi* (23 February).

Bin Laden O. (2001). *News broadcast of speech*. Qatar: Al Jazeera.

Binter J. (1989). Neutrality, European community and world peace: The case of Austria. *Journal of Peace Research, 26*, 413–418.

Birchall C. (2006). *Knowledge goes pop: From conspiracy theory to gossip*. Oxford: Berg.

Blake R. R., & Mouton J. S. (1970). The fifth achievement. *Journal of Applied Behavioural Science, 6*, 413–426.

Bourdieu P. (1984). *Distinction: A social critique of the judgement of taste*. Cambridge, MA: Harvard University Press.

Bourdieu P. (1986). The forms of capital. In J. Richardson (Ed.), *Handbook of theory and research for the sociology of education* (pp. 241–258). New York: Greenwood.

Bourhis R. Y., Moise L. C., Perreault S., & Senecal S. (1997). Towards an interactive acculturation model: A social psychological approach. *International Journal of Psychology, 32*, 369–389.

Bowles P. (2012). *Capitalism*. London: Pearson.

Bowskill M., Lyons E., & Coyle A. (2007). The rhetoric of acculturation: When integration means assimilation. *British Journal of Social Psychology, 46*, 793–813.

Boym S. (1995). *Common places: Mythologies of everyday life in Russia*. Cambridge: Harvard University Press.

Boym S. (2001). *The future of nostalgia*. New York: Basic Books.

Boym S. (2005). Poetics and politics of estrangement: Victor Shklovsky and Hannah Arendt. *Poetics Today, 26*, 581–612.

Boym S. (2006). *Territories of terror: Mythologies and memories of the gulag in contemporary Russian-American art*. Seattle: University of Washington Press.

Boym S. (2007). Nostalgia and its discontents. *Hedgehog Review, 9*, 7–18.

Boym S. (2008). *Architecture of the off-modern*. New York: Princeton Architectural Press.

Boym S. (2010). *Another freedom*. London: University of Chicago Press.

Boym S. (2012). Nostalgic technologies: Multitasking with clouds. *Photoworks Spring/Summer*, 6–13.

Bradshaw D., Jay S., McNamara N., Stevenson C., & Muldoon O. T. (2015). Perceived discrimination amongst young people in socioeconomically disadvantaged communities: Parental support and community identity buffer (some) negative impacts of stigma. *Journal of British Developmental Psychology*. Article first published online: 22 October 2015. doi:10.1111/bjdp.12120.

Branscombe N. R., Schmitt M. T., & Harvey R. D. (1999). Perceiving pervasive discrimination among African Americans: Implications for group identification and well-being. *Journal of Personality and Social Psychology, 77*, 135–149.

Braun V., & Clarke V. (2006). Using thematic analysis in psychology. *Qualitative Research in Psychology, 3*, 77–101.

Breakwell G. M. (1986). *Coping with threatened identities*. London: Methuen.

Breakwell G. M. (1992). Processes of self-evaluation: Efficacy and estrangement. In G. M. Breakwell (Ed.), *Social psychology of identity and the self-concept* (pp. 35–55). London: Academic Press.

Breakwell G. (1993). Integrating paradigms, methodological implications. In G. Breakwell & D. Canter (Eds.), *Empirical approaches to social representations* (pp. 180–199). Oxford: Clarendon Press.

Breakwell G. M. (1996). Identity processes and social changes. In G. M. Breakwell & E. Lyons (Eds.), *Changing European identities: Social psychological analyses of social change* (pp. 13–27). Oxford: Butterworth-Heinemann.

Briant E., Watson N., & Philo G. (2011). *Bad news for disabled people: How the newspapers are reporting disability*. Glasgow: Strathclyde Centre for Disability Research and Glasgow Media Unit, University of Glasgow.

Brockmeier J. (2002). Remembering and forgetting: Narrative as cultural memory. *Culture and Psychology, 8*, 15–43.

Brockmeier J., & Meretoja H. (2014). Understanding narrative hermeneutics. *Storyworlds, 6,* 1–27.

Brockner J., & Rubin J. Z. (1985). *Entrapment in escalating conflicts: A social psychological analysis.* New York: Springer-Verlag.

Broome B. J. (1997). Designing a collective approach to peace: Interactive design and problem-solving workshops with Greek-Cypriot and Turkish-Cypriot communities in Cyprus. *International Negotiation, 2,* 381–407.

Brown C. (2005). *Postmodernism for historians.* Oxford: Pearson.

Brown R., & Zagefka H. (2011). The dynamics of acculturation: An intergroup perspective. In J. M. Olson & M. P. Zanna (Eds.), *Advances in experimental social psychology* (Vol. 44, pp. 129–184). Burlington, VT: Academic Press.

Brown R., Baysu G., Cameron L., Nigbur D., Rutland A., Watters C., ... Landau A. (2013). Acculturation attitudes and social adjustment in British South Asian children: A longitudinal study. *Personality and Social Psychology Bulletin, 39,* 1656–1667.

Bruner J. (1986). *Actual minds, possible worlds.* Cambridge, MA: Harvard University Press.

Bruner J. (1990). *Acts of meaning.* Cambridge, MA: Harvard University Press.

Burger J. M. (2011). Alive and well after all these years. *The Psychologist, 24,* 654–657.

Burger J. M., Girgis Z. M., & Manning C. C. (2011). In their own words: Explaining obedience to authority through an examination of participants' comments. *Social Psychological and Personality Science.* Published online January 14. doi:10.1177/1948550610397632.

Burr V. (2003). *Social constructionism* (2nd ed.). Hove: Routledge.

Butler, P. (2015). Thousands have died after being found fit for work, DWP figures show. *The Guardian* (August 27). Retrieved June 6, 2015 from http://www.theguardian.com/society/2015/aug/27/thousands-died-after-fit-for-work-assessment-dwp-figures

Byford J. (2011). *Conspiracy theories: A critical introduction.* Basingstoke: Palgrave Macmillan.

Byrne, D. & Smyth, E. (2010). No way back? The dynamics of early school leaving. Retrieved from http://eprints.nuim.ie/4333

Cameron, D. (2011). PM's speech on the fightback after the riots. *Cabinet Office.* Retrieved from https://www.gov.uk/government/speeches/pms-speech-on-the-fightback-after-the-riots

Campbell C., & Jovchelovitch S. (2000). Health, community and development: Towards a social psychology of participation. *Journal of Community & Applied Social Psychology, 10,* 255–270.

Canetti D., Elad-Strenger J., Lavi I., Guy D., & Bar-Tal D. (2015). Exposure to violence, ethos of conflict, and support for compromise: Surveys in Israel, East Jerusalem, West Bank, and Gaza. *Journal of Conflict Resolution.* Article first published online: 16 February 2015. doi:10.1177/0022002715569771.

Cannavale F., Scarr H., & Pepitone A. (1970). De-individuation in the small group: Further evidence. *Journal of Personality and Social Psychology, 16,* 141–147.

Carretero M. (2011). *Constructing patriotism: Teaching history and memories in global worlds.* Charlotte, NC: IAP.

Carrier R. (2014). *On the historicity of Jesus: Why we might have reason for doubt.* Sheffield: Phoenix Press.

Carver R. P. (1993). The case against statistical significance testing, revisited. *The Journal of Experimental Education, 61*(4) Statistical Significance Testing in Contemporary Practice), 287–292.

Castelvecchi D. (2015). Is string theory science? A debate between physicists and philosophers could redefine the scientific method and our understanding of the universe. *Nature* http://www.scientificamerican.com/article/is-string-theory-science/ (accessed March 2016.

Čehajić-Clancy S., Effron D. A., Halperin E., Liberman V., & Ross L. D. (2011). Affirmation, acknowledgment of in-group responsibility, group-based guilt, and support for reparative measures. *Journal of Personality and Social Psychology, 101,* 256–270.

Chang J. (2012). *Wild swans: Three daughters of China*. London: Harper Press.

Chaplin, C. (Producer/Writer/Director). (1940). The great dictator [Motion picture]. United States: United Artists.

Checkel J. T. (1998). The constructive turn in international relations theory. *World Politics, 50*, 324–348.

Cherry F. (1995). *The stubborn particulars of social psychology: Essays on the research process*. London: Routledge.

Christie D. J., & Louis W. R. (2012). Peace interventions tailored to phases within a cycle of intergroup violence. In L. R. Tropp (Ed.), *The Oxford handbook of intergroup conflict* (pp. 252–272). New York: Oxford University Press.

Christie D. J., Tint B. S., Wagner R. V., & Winter D. D. (2008a). Peace psychology for a peaceful world. *American Psychologist, 63*, 540–552.

Christie H., Tett L., Cree V. E., Hounsell J., & McCune V. (2008b). A real rollercoaster of confidence and emotions: Learning to be a university student. *Studies in Higher Education, 33*, 567–581.

Chryssochoou X. (2004). *Cultural diversity: Its social psychology*. Oxford: Blackwell.

Chryssochoou X. (2009). Identity projects in multicultural nation-states. In I. Jasinskaja-Lahti & T. A. Mahonen (Eds.), *Identities, intergroup relations and acculturation. The cornerstones of intercultural encounters* (pp. 81–93). Helsinki: Gaudeamus Helsinki University Press.

Chryssochoou X. (2015). Le paradoxe de la promotion des identités doubles à l'école. In M.-A. Broyon, N. Changkakoti, & M. Sanchez-Mazas (Eds.), *Education à la diversité: Décalages, impensés, avancées* (pp. 63–79). Paris: L'Harmattan.

Chryssochoou X. (2016). Social justice in multicultural Europe: A social psychological perspective. In P. Hammack (Ed.), *The Oxford handbook of social psychology and social justice*. New York: Oxford University Press.

Chryssochoou X., & Lyons E. (2011). Perceptions of (in)compatibility between identities and articipation in the national polity of people belonging to ethnic minorities. In A. E. Azzi, X. Chryssochoou, B. Klandermans, & B. Simon (Eds.), *Identity and participation in culturally diverse societies. A multidisciplinary perspective* (pp. 69–88). Oxford: Wiley-Blackwell.

Cohen S. (2001). *States of denial: Knowing about atrocities and suffering*. London: Polity Press.

Cohler B. J. (1982). Personal narrative and life course. In P. Baltes & O. G. Brim (Eds.), *Life span development and behavior* (Vol. 4, pp. 205–241). New York: Academic Press.

Cohrs J. C. (2012). Ideological bases of violent conflict. In L. R. Tropp (Ed.), *Oxford handbook of intergroup conflict* (pp. 53–71). New York: Oxford University Press.

Cohrs J. C., & Moschner B. (2002). Antiwar knowledge and generalized political attitudes as determinants of attitude toward the Kosovo war. *Peace and Conflict: Journal of Peace Psychology, 8*, 139–155.

Cohrs J. C., Moschner B., Maes J., & Kielmann S. (2005). Personal values and attitudes toward war. *Peace and Conflict: Journal of Peace Psychology, 11*, 293–312.

Cohrs J. C., & O'Dwyer E. (2016). "In the minds of men…" – social representations of war and military intervention. In P. Hammack (Ed.), *Oxford handbook of social psychology and social justice*. Oxford: Oxford University Press.

Cohrs J. C., Uluğ Ö. M., Stahel L., & Kışlıoğlu R. (2015). Ethos of conflict and beyond: Differentiating social representations of conflict. In E. Halperin & K. Sharvit (Eds.), *The social psychology of intractable conflicts: Celebrating the legacy of Daniel Bar-Tal* (Vol. 1, pp. 33–45). New York, NY: Springer.

Coleman P. T. (2003). Characteristics of protracted, intractable conflict: Towards the development of a metaframework-I. *Peace and Conflict: Journal of Peace Psychology, 9*, 1–37.

Condor S. (2006). Temporality and collectivity: Diversity, history and the rhetorical construction of national entitativity. *British Journal of Social Psychology, 45*, 657–682.

Condor S., Tileagă C., & Billig M. (2013). Political rhetoric. In L. Huddy, D. O. Sears, & J. S. Levy (Eds.), *The Oxford handbook of political psychology* (2nd ed., pp. 262–297). Oxford: Oxford University Press.

Connerton P. (2008). Seven types of forgetting. *Memory Studies, 1,* 59–71.

Connelly, M. (2014). Poll finds racial divide in viewing response to Ferguson unrest. *New York Times.* Retrieved July 6, 2016 from http://www.nytimes.com/2014/08/22/us/politics/racial-divide-seen-in-response-to-ferguson-unrest-poll-finds.html?_r=0

Copeland D. C. (2014). International relations theory and the three great puzzles of the First World War. In J. S. Levy & J. A. Vasquez (Eds.), *Outbreak of the First World War* (pp. 167–198). Cambridge: Cambridge University Press.

Cornish F., Montenegro C., van Reisen K., Zaka F., & Sevitt J. (2014). Trust the process: Community health psychology after Occupy. *Journal of Health Psychology, 19,* 60–71.

Coser L. A. (1992). Introduction. In M. Halbwachs (Ed.), *On collective memory* (L. A. Coser, Trans. (pp. 1–34). Chicago, IL: Chicago University Press.

Cox, B. D. (1987). *Health and lifestyle.* ESRC Data Archive: University of Essex.

Cribb, J., Hood, A., Joyce, R., & Phillips, D. (2013). Living standards, poverty and inequality in the UK: 2013. IFS Reports, Institute for Fiscal Studies. Retrieved from http://www.econstor.eu/handle/10419/83504

Croft, D. J. (Producer). (1982). 'Allo, 'Allo [Television series]. London: BBC.

Croizet J.-C., & Claire T. (1998). Extending the concept of stereotype threat to social class: The intellectual underperformance of students from low socioeconomic backgrounds. *Personality and Social Psychology Bulletin, 24,* 588–594.

Croizet J.-C., Desert M., Dutrevis M., & Leyens J.-P. (2001). Stereotype threat, social class, gender, and academic under-achievement: When our reputation catches up to us and takes over. *Social Psychology of Education, 4,* 295–310.

Cromby J., Harper D., & Reavey P. (2013). *Psychology, mental health and distress.* London: Palgrave.

Cross M. (2013). Demonised, impoverished and now forced into isolation: The fate of disabled people under austerity. *Disability & Society, 28,* 719–723.

Crow L. (2015). Summer of 2012: Paralympic legacy and the welfare benefit scandal. *Review of Disability Studies. An International Journal, 10,* 1–18.

Cubitt G. (2007). *History and memory.* Manchester: Manchester University Press.

Cubitt G. (2014). History, psychology and social memory. In C. Tileagă & J. Byford (Eds.), *Psychology and history: Interdisciplinary explorations* (pp. 15–39). Cambridge: Cambridge University Press.

Cunningham J., & Moore M. (1997). Elite and mass foreign policy opinions: Who is leading this parade? *Social Science Quarterly, 78,* 641–656.

Curtis A. (Writer)(1995). On the desperate edge of now. [Television series episode]. In E. Mirzoeff (Producer), *The Living Dead: Three films about the power of the past.* London: British Broadcasting Corporation.

Damasio A. (1994). *Descartes' error: Emotion, reason, and the human brain.* New York: Putnam.

Danziger K. (1992). The project of an experimental social psychology: Historical perspectives. *Science in Context, 5,* 309–328.

Davies B., & Harré R. (1990). Position and personhood. In R. Harré & L. van Langenhove (Eds.), *Positioning theory* (pp. 32–52). Oxford: Blackwell.

Davis, D. (2015, November 8). British 'intellectually lazy' about defending liberty. *The Guardian.* Retrieved November 15, 2015 from http://www.theguardian.com/politics/2015/nov/08/david-davis-liberty-draft-investigatory-powers-bill-holes?CMP=share_btn_fb.

Davis L. J. (1995). *Enforcing normalcy: Disability, deafness and the body.* New York: Verso.

Davis N. Z. (1973). The rites of violence: Religious riot in sixteenth-century France. *Past and Present, 59,* 51–91.

Davis W. (2012). Swords into ploughshares: The effect of pacifist public opinion on foreign policy in western democracies. *Cooperation and Conflict, 47,* 309–330.

Deaux K. (1992). Personalising identity and socialising self. In G. M. Breakwell (Ed.), *Social psychology of identity and the self-concept* (pp. 9–33). London: Academic Press.

Debord G. (2014). *The society of the spectacle.* (K. Knabb, Trans.). Berkeley, CA: Bureau of Public Secrets. (original work published 1967).

Department of Work and Pensions. (2012, July). *Incapacity Benefits: Deaths of recipients.* Retrieved June 6, 2016 from https://www.gov.uk/government/uploads/system/uploads/attachment_data/file/223050/incap_decd_recips_0712.pdf

Deschamps J. C., & Doise W. (1978). Crossed category memberships in intergroup relations. In H. Tajfel (Ed.), *Differentiation between social groups: Studies in the social psychology of intergroup relations* (pp. 141–158). London: Academic Press.

Devine K. (2008). Stretching the IR theoretical spectrum on Irish neutrality: A critical social constructivist framework. *International Political Science Review, 29,* 461–488.

Devine K. (2011). Neutrality and the development of the European Union's common security and defence policy: Compatible or competing? *Cooperation and Conflict, 46,* 334–369.

De Dreu C. K. W., Evers A., Beersma B., Kluwer E. S., & Nauta A. (2001). A theory-based measure of conflict management strategies in the workplace. *Journal of Organizational Behavior, 22,* 645–668.

Diener E. (1980). Deindividuation: The absence of self-awareness and self-regulation in group members. In P. Paulus (Ed.), *The psychology of group influence* (pp. 209–242). Hillsdale: Erlbaum.

Di Masso A. (2012). Grounding citizenship: Toward a political psychology of public space. *Political Psychology, 33,* 123–143.

Dimitrijevic N. (2011). *Duty to respond. Mass crime, denial and collective responsibility.* Budapest-New York: Central European University.

Dixon J., Durrheim K., & Tredoux C. (2005). Beyond the optimal contact strategy: A reality check for the contact hypothesis. *American Psychologist, 60,* 697.

Dixon J., Levine M., & McAuley R. (2006). Locating impropriety: Street drinking, moral order, and the ideological dilemma of public space. *Political Psychology, 27,* 187–206.

Dixon J., Levine M., Reicher S., & Durrheim K. (2012). Beyond prejudice: Are negative evaluations the problem and is getting us to like one another more the solution? *Behavioral and Brain Sciences, 35,* 411–425.

Dixon J., Tropp L. R., Durrheim K., & Tredoux C. (2010). "Let them eat harmony": Prejudice-reduction strategies and attitudes of historically disadvantaged groups. *Current Directions in Psychological Science, 19,* 76–80.

Donagan A. (1966). The Popper–Hempel theory reconsidered. In W. H. Dray (Ed.), *Philosophical analysis and history* (pp. 127–159). New York: Harper & Row.

Dovidio J. F., Gaertner S. L., & Saguy T. (2009). Commonality and the complexity of "we": Social attitudes and social change. *Personality and Social Psychology Review, 13,* 3–20.

Dovidio J. F., Saguy T., West T. V., & Gaertner S. L. (2012). Divergent intergroup perspectives. In L. A. Tropp (Ed.), *The Oxford handbook of intergroup conflict* (pp. 158–178). New York: Oxford University Press.

Doise W., & Staerklé C. (2002). From social to political psychology: The societal approach. In K. R. Monroe (Ed.), *Political psychology* (pp. 151–172). Hillsdale, NJ: LEA.

Dreifuss, D. M., Larrain, P., & Larrain, J. (Producers), Larrain, P (Director). (2012). *No* [Motion picture]. Chile: Sony Pictures Classics.

Druckman D. (1994). Nationalism, patriotism, and group loyalty: A social psychological perspective. *Mershon International Studies Review, 38,* 43–68.

Drury J., & Reicher S. D. (1999). The intergroup dynamics of collective empowerment: Substantiating the social identity model of crowd behaviour. *Group Processes and Intergroup Relations*, 2, 1–22.

Drury J., & Reicher S. D. (2000). Collective action and psychological change: The emergence of new social identities. *British Journal of Social Psychology*, 39, 579–604.

Drury J., & Reicher S. D. (2005). Explaining enduring empowerment: A comparative study of collective action and psychological outcomes. *European Journal of Social Psychology*, 35, 35–58.

Drury J., & Reicher S. D. (2009). Collective psychological empowerment as a model of social change: Researching crowds and power. *Journal of Social Issues*, 65, 707–725.

Drury J., Reicher S. D., & Stott C. J. (2003). Transforming the boundaries of collective identity: From the "local" anti-road campaign to "global" resistance. *Social Movement Studies: Journal of Social, Cultural and Political Protest*, 2, 191–212.

Durkheim E. (1912/2001). *The elementary forms of religious life*. Oxford: Oxford University Press.

Duval S., & Wicklund R. A. (1972). *A theory of objective self awareness*. Oxford: Academic Press.

Duveen G. (2001). Social representations. In C. Fraser, B. Burchell, D. Hay, & G. Duveen (Eds.), *Introducing social psychology*. Cambridge: Polity.

Dyson S. B., & Hart P. T. (2013). Crisis management. In L. Huddy, D. O. Sears, & J. S. Levy (Eds.), *The Oxford handbook of political psychology* (2nd ed., pp. 395–422). Oxford: Oxford University Press.

Edwards D. (2000). Extreme case formulations: Softeners, investment, and doing nonliteral. *Research on Language and Social Interaction*, 33, 347–373.

Edwards D. (2007). Managing subjectivity in talk. In A. Hepburn & S. Wiggins (Eds.), *Discursive research in practice: New approaches to psychology and interaction* (pp. 31–49). Cambridge: Cambridge University Press.

Edwards D. (2014). Rhetoric, cognition and discursive psychology. In C. Antaki & S. Condor (Eds.), *Rhetoric, ideology and social psychology: Essays in honour of Michael Billig* (pp. 29–42). Hove: Routledge.

Edwards D., & Potter J. (1992). *Discursive psychology*. London: Sage.

Edwards D., Ashmore M. T., & Potter J. (1995). Death and furniture: The rhetoric, politics and theology of bottom line arguments against relativism. *History of the Human Sciences*, 8, 25–49.

Elcheroth G., Doise W., & Reicher S. (2011). On the knowledge of politics and the politics of knowledge: How a social representations approach helps us rethink the subject of political psychology. *Political Psychology*, 32, 729–755.

Entman R. M. (1993). Framing: Toward clarification of a fractured paradigm. *Journal of Communication*, 43, 51–58.

Erll A. (2010). Cultural memory studies: An introduction. In A. Erll & A. Nünning (Eds.), *A companion to cultural memory studies* (pp. 1–15). Berlin: De Gruyter.

Esses V. M., Jackson L. M., & Armstrong T. L. (1998). Intergroup competition and attitudes toward immigrants and immigration: An instrumental model of group conflict. *Journal of Social Issues*, 54, 699–724.

Express Tribune. (2012). *Church hounding of Pussy Riot troubles Russians*. Retrieved from http://tribune.com.pk/story/422105/church-hounding-of-pussy-riot-troubles-russians/

Fairclough N. (2001). *Language and power* (2nd ed.). Harlow: Longman.

Falasca-Zamponi S. (1997). *Fascist spectacle: The aesthetics of power in Mussolini's Italy*. Berkeley: University of California Press.

Falomir-Pichastor J. M., Pereira A., Staerklé C., & Butera F. (2011). Do all lives have the same value? Support for international military interventions as a function of political system and public opinion of target states. *Group Processes and Intergroup Relations*, 15, 347–362.

Fanchner R. E. (1979). *Pioneers of psychology: Studies of the great figures who paved the way for the contemorary science of behaviour*. London: Norton.

Fanchner R. E. (1985). *The intelligence men: Makers of the IQ controversy*. London: Norton.

Fanning R. (1982). Irish neutrality: An historical review. *Irish Studies in International Affairs, 1*, 27–38.

Farr R. M. (1996). *The roots of modern social psychology*. Oxford: Blackwell.

Farr R. M. (1998). From collective to social representations. Aller et Retour. *Culture and Psychology, 4*, 275–296.

Feldman, E. H. (Producer). (1965). *Hogan's Heroes* [Television series] New York: CBS.

Fenton, S. (2015, August 31). UN investigating British Government over human rights abuses caused by IDS welfare reforms. *The Independent*. Retrieved June 6, 2016 from http://www.independent.co.uk/news/uk/politics/un-to-investigate-uk-over-human-rights-abuses-against-disabled-people-caused-by-welfare-reform-10478536.html

Feshbach S. (1987). Individual aggression, national attachment, and the search for peace: Psychological perspectives. *Aggressive Behavior, 13*, 315–325.

Feshbach S. (1990). Psychology, human violence and the search for peace: Issues in science and social values. *Journal of Social Issues, 46*, 183–198.

Festinger L. (1957). *A theory of cognitive dissonance*. Stanford, CA: Stanford University Press.

Festinger L., Pepitone A., & Newcombe T. (1952). Some consequences of deindividuation in a group. *Journal of Abnormal and Social Psychology, 47*, 382–389.

Fienberg S. (1992). A brief history of statistics in three and one-half chapters: A review essay. *Statistical Science, 7*, 208–225.

Figes O. (2008). *The whisperers: Private life in Stalin's Russia*. London: Penguin.

Figueiredo A., Valentim J. P., Licata L., & Doosje B. (2013). The past and the present (re)visited: War veterans' representations of the Portuguese colonial war. In R. Cabecinhas & L. Abadia (Eds.), *Narratives and social memory: Theoretical and methodological approaches* (pp. 76–91). Braga: University of Minho.

Filho D. B. F., Paranhos R., da Rocha E. C., Batista M., da Silva Jr. J. A., Santos M. L. W. D., & Gerais M. (2013). When is statistical significance not significant? *Brazilian Political Science Review, 7*, 31–55.

Fine M., & Ruglis J. (2009). Circuits and consequences of dispossession: The racialized realignment of the public sphere for US youth. *Transforming Anthropology, 17*, 20–33.

Fischer F. (1967). *Germany's aims in the First World War*. New York: W.W. Norton.

Fisher R. A. (1926). The arrangement of field experiments. *Journal of the Ministry of Agriculture of Great Britain, 33*, 503–513.

Fisher R. J., Kelman H. C., & Allen Nan S. (2013). Conflict analysis and resolution. In L. Huddy, D. O. Sears, & J. S. Levy (Eds.), *The Oxford handbook of political psychology* (2nd ed., pp. 489–521). Oxford: Oxford University Press.

Fisk R. (1983). *In time of war: Ireland, Ulster and the price of neutrality, 1939–45*. London: Andre Deutsch.

Fiske S. T., & Taylor S. E. (1984). *Social cognition*. Random House: New York.

Fiske S. T., Gilbert D. T., & Lindzey G. (2010). *Handbook of social psychology* (5th ed.). Oxford: Wiley.

Fleischmann F., Phalet K., & Swyngedouw M. (2013). Dual identity under threat: When and how do Turkish and Moroccan minorities engage in politics? *Zeitschrift Für Psychologie, 221*, 214–222.

Florack A., & Piontkowski U. (2000). Acculturation attitudes of the Dutch and the Germans towards the European Union: The importance of national and European identification. *Journal of Multilingual and Multicultural Development, 21*, 1–13.

Foote K. (1993). *Shadowed ground: America's landscapes of violence and tragedy*. Austin, TX: University of Texas Press.

Forgas J. P. (Ed.) (1981). *Social cognition: Perspectives on everyday understanding*. London: Academic Press.

Foucault M. (2002). *The archaeology of knowledge*. London: Routledge.

Foyle D. (2003). Foreign policy analysis and globalization: Public opinion, world opinion, and the individual. *International Studies Review, 5*, 155–202.

Foyle D. (2004). Leading the public to war? The influence of American public opinion on the Bush administration's decision to go to war in Iraq. *International Journal of Public Opinion Research, 16*, 269–294.

Fowler R. (1991). *Language in the news: Discourse and ideology in the press*. London: Routledge.

Frable D. E. (1997). Gender, racial, ethnic, sexual, and class identities. *Annual Review of Psychology, 48*, 139–162.

Freeman M. (2010). *Hindsight: The promise and peril of looking backward*. New York: Oxford University Press.

French, C. (2012, March 15). Precognition studies and the curse of the failed replications. *The Guardian*. Retrieved March 22, 2016 from http://www.guardian.co.uk/science/2012/mar/15/precognition-studies-curse-failed-replications

Fromm E. (1942). *The fear of freedom*. London: Routledge.

Fromm E. (1957). *The art of loving*. London: Harper Collins.

Fromm E. (1973). *The crisis of psychoanalysis*. Harmondsworth: Penguin.

Fromm E. (1997). *To have or to be?* London: Bloomsbury.

Fromm E. (2011). *Marx's concept of man*. New York: Frederick Ungar.

Frosh S. (2013). *Hauntings: Psychoanalysis and ghostly transmissions*. Basingstoke: Palgrave Macmillan.

Fukuyama F. (1992). *The end of history and the last man*. New York: Free Press.

Gaertner S. L., & Dovidio J. F. (1986). The aversive form of racism. In J. F. Dovidio & S. L. Gaertner (Eds.), *Prejudice, discrimination, and racism: Historical trends and contemporary approaches* (pp. 61–89). San Diego, CA: Academic Press.

Galtung J. (1969). Violence, peace, and peace research. *Journal of Peace Research, 6*, 167–191.

Galtung J. (1985). Twenty five years of peace research: Ten challenges and some responses. *Journal of Peace Research, 22*, 141–158.

Galtung J. (1990). Cultural violence. *Journal of Peace Research, 27*, 291–305.

Garcia C., Paton F., Marks A. K., Dimitrova R., Yang R., Suaraz G. A., & Patrico A. (2012). Understanding the immigrant paradox in immigrant youth: Developmental and contextual considerations. In A. S. Mansten, K. Liebkind, & D. J. Hernandez (Eds.), *Realizing the potential of immigrant youth* (pp. 159–180). Cambridge: Cambridge University Press.

Garfinkel H. (1967). *Studies in ethnomethodology*. Englewood Cliffs: Prentice-Hall.

Garry J., Hardiman N., & Payne D. (Eds.) (2006). *Irish social and political attitudes*. Liverpool: Liverpool University Press.

Gaskarth J. (2006). Discourses and ethics: The social construction of British foreign policy. *Foreign Policy Analysis, 2*, 325–341.

Gelman A. (2008). Objections to Bayesian statistics. *International Society for Bayesian Analysis, 3*, 445–450.

Gelman, A. (2011). What are the open problems in Bayesian statistics. *The Statistics Forum*. Retrieved March 22, 2016 from https://statisticsforum.wordpress.com/2011/04/28/what-are-the-open-problems-in-bayesian-statistics/

Gelvin J. L. (1999). *Divided loyalties: Nationalism and mass politics in Syria at the close of empire*. Berkeley: University of California Press.

George A. L. (1980). *Presidential decision-making in foreign policy: The effective use of information and advice.* Boulder, CO: Westview.

Georgakopoulou A. (2007). *Small stories, interaction and identities. Studies in narrative, 8.* Amsterdam: John Benjamins Publishing Company.

Gergen K. J. (1971). *The concept of self.* New York: Holt, Rinehart and Winston.

Gergen K. J. (1973). Social psychology as history. *Journal of Personality and Social Psychology, 26,* 309–320.

Gergen K. J. (1991). *The saturated self.* New York: Basic books.

Gergen K. J. (1999). *An invitation to social construction.* London: Sage.

Gergen K. J. (2009a). *An invitation to social construction* (2nd ed.). London: Sage.

Gergen K. J. (2009b). *Relational being: Beyond self and community.* New York: Oxford University Press.

Ghonim W. (2012). *Revolution 2.0: The power of the people is greater than the people in power.* Boston: Houghton Mifflin Harcourt.

Gibson S. (2011). Social psychology, war and peace: Towards a critical discursive peace psychology. *Social and Personality Psychology Compass, 5,* 239–250.

Gibson S. (2012). "I'm not a war monger but...": Discourse analysis and social psychological peace research. *Journal of Community & Applied Social Psychology, 22,* 159–173.

Gibson S. (2013). Milgram's obedience experiments: A rhetorical analysis. *British Journal of Social Psychology, 52,* 290–309.

Gibson S., & Abell J. (2004). For queen and country? National frames of reference in the talk of soldiers in England. *Human Relations, 57,* 871–891.

Gibson S., & Condor S. (2009). State institutions and social identity: National representation in soldiers and civilians' interview talk concerning military service. *British Journal of Social Psychology, 48,* 313–336.

Gibson S., Blenkinsopp G., Johnstone E., & Marshall A. (2018). Just following orders? The rhetorical invocation of "obedience" in Stanley Milgram's post-experiment interviews. *European Journal of Social Psychology.* doi:10.1002/ejsp.2351.

Giddens A. (1985). *A contemporary critique of historical materialism, volume 2: The nation-state and violence.* Cambridge: Polity.

Gilbert G. N., & Mulkay M. (1984). *Opening Pandora's box: A sociological analysis of scientists' discourse.* Cambridge: Cambridge University Press.

Gilland K. (2001). Neutrality and the international use of force. In P. Everts & P. Isernia (Eds.), *Public opinion and the international use of force* (pp. 141–162). London: Routledge.

Gillies V. (2005). Raising the "meritocracy" parenting and the individualization of social class. *Sociology, 39,* 835–853.

Gillis J. R. (1996). *Commemorations: The politics of national identity.* Princeton: Princeton University Press.

Gilovich T. D., & Griffin D. W. (2010). Judgment and decision making. In S. T. Fiske, D. T. Gilbert, & G. Lindzey (Eds.), *Handbook of social psychology* (5th ed., pp. 542–588). New York: Wiley.

Giner S. (1976). *Mass society.* New York: Academic Press.

Giroux H. A. (2014). *Neoliberalism's war on higher education.* Chicago: Haymarket.

Gjertsen D. (1992). *Science and philosophy: Past and present.* London: Penguin.

Glazier, S. (Producer) & Brooks, M. (Writer/Director). (1968). *The Producers* [Motion picture]. United States: Embassy Pictures.

Gliner J. A., Leech N. L., & Morgan G. A. (2002). Problems with null hypothesis significance testing (NHST): What do the textbooks say? *The Journal of Experimental Education, 71,* 83–92.

Goldhagen D. J. (1997). *Hitler's willing executioners: Ordinary Germans and the Holocaust.* London: Abacus.

Goldthorpe J. (2003). The myth of education-based meritocracy. *New Economy, 10,* 234–239.

Goodwin J., Jasper J. M., & Polletta F. (2001). Introduction: Why emotions matter. In J. Goodwin, J. Jasper, & F. Polletta (Eds.), *Passionate politics: Emotions and social movements* (pp. 1–24). Chicago: University of Chicago Press.

Graumann C. F. (1986). The individualization of the social and the desocialization of the individual: Floyd H. Allport's contribution to social psychology. In C. F. Grauman & S. Moscovici (Eds.), *Changing conceptions of crowd mind and behavior* (pp. 97–116). New York: Springer-Verlag.

Gray D., & Durrheim K. (2013). Collective rights and personal freedoms: A discursive analysis of participant accounts of authoritarianism. *Political Psychology, 34,* 631–648.

Green E. G. T., Sarrasin O., & Fasel N. (2015). Immigration: Social psychological aspects. In J. D. Wright (Ed.), *The international encyclopedia of the social and behavioral sciences* (2nd ed., pp. 675–681). Oxford: Elsevier.

Greenwald A. G. (2004). The resting parrot, the dessert stomach and other perfectly defensible theories. In J. Jost, M. R. Banaji, & D. A. Prentice (Eds.), *The yin and yang of social cognition: Perspectives on the social psychology of thought systems* (pp. 275–285). Washington, DC: American Psychological Association.

Greenwood J. D. (2004). *The disappearance of the social in American social psychology.* Cambridge: Cambridge University Press.

Guimond S., Crisp R. J., De Oliveira P., Kamiejski R., Kteily N., Kuepper B., … Zick A. (2013). Diversity policy, social dominance, and intergroup relations: Predicting prejudice in changing social and political contexts. *Journal of Personality and Social Psychology, 104,* 941–958.

Gunn G. R., & Wilson A. E. (2011). Acknowledging the skeletons in our closet: The effect of group affirmation on collective guilt, collective shame, and reparatory attitudes. *Personality and Social Psychology Bulletin, 37,* 1474–1487.

Gurr T. R. (1970). *Why men rebel.* Princeton, NJ: Princeton University.

Habermas T., & Hatiboğlu N. (2014). Contextualizing the self: The emergence of a biographical understanding in adolescence. In B. Schiff, Rereading personal narrative and life course. *New Directions for Child and Adolescent Development, 145,* 29–41.

Hagen S. (2012). *Why the world doesn't seem to make sense.* Boulder Colorado: Sentient Publications.

Halbwachs M. (1925). *Les cadres sociaux de la mémoire.* Paris: Alcan.

Hall, A. (2015, November 6). My Nazi Legacy: The son who still worships his Nazi father – and Hitler's godson's desperate attempt to make him accept the truth. *Mail Online.* Retrieved May 18, 2016 from http://www.dailymail.co.uk/news/article-3305489/My-Nazi-legacy-two-sons-Hitler-s-trusted-henchmen-British-lawyer-entire-family-wiped-Holocaust-unlikeliest-friends.html

Haller H., & Kraus S. (2002). Misinterpretations of significance: A problem students share with their teachers? *Methods of Psychological Research Online, 7,* 1–19.

Hammack P. L., & Toolis E. (2014). Narrative and the social construction of adulthood: Narrative and the social construction of adulthood. In B. Schiff. Rereading personal narrative and life course. *New Directions for Child and Adolescent Development, 145,* 43–56.

Hannam J. (2012). *Feminism.* Harlow: Pearson.

Haslam S. A., & Reicher S. D. (2008). Questioning the banality of evil. *The Psychologist, 21,* 16–19.

Haslam S. A., & Reicher S. D. (2012). When prisoners take over the prison: A social psychology of resistance. *Personality and Social Psychology Review, 16,* 154–179.

Haslam S. A., Reicher S. D., & Platow M. J. (2010). *The new psychology of leadership: Identity, influence and power*. Hove: Psychology Press.

Haslam S. A., Reicher S. D., Millard K., & McDonald R. (2015). "Happy to have been of service": The Yale archive as a window into the engaged followership of participants in Milgram's obedience experiments. *British Journal of Social Psychology*, *54*, 55–83.

Hass R. G., Katz I., Rizzo N., Bailey J., & Eisenstadt D. (1991). Cross-racial appraisal as related to attitude ambivalence and cognitive complexity. *Personality and Social Psychology Bulletin*, *17*, 83–92.

Heath A. F., Rothon C., & Kilpi E. (2008). The second generation in Western Europe: Education, unemployment, and occupational attainment. *Annual Review of Sociology*, *34*, 211–235.

Hedin K., Clark E., Lundholm E., & Malmberg G. (2012). Neoliberalization of housing in Sweden: Gentrification, filtering, and social polarization. *Annals of the Association of American Geographers*, *102*, 443–463.

Hegarty P., & Walton Z. (2012). The consequences of predicting scientific impact in psychology using journal impact factors. *Perspectives on Psychological Science*, *7*, 72–78.

Heidelberg Institute for International Conflict Research (HIIK) (2015). *Conflict barometer 2014*. Heidelberg: Heidelberg Institute for International Conflict Research.

Heider F. (1958). *The psychology of interpersonal relations*. New York: John Wiley & Sons, Inc.

Henriques J., Hollway W., Urwin C., Venn C., & Walkerdinde V. (1998). *Changing the subject: Psychology, social regulation and subjectivity* (2nd ed.). London: Routledge.

Hepburn A. (2003). *Critical social psychology*. London: Sage.

Heritage J. (2009). Conversation analysis as social theory. In B. S. Turner (Ed.), *The new Blackwell companion to social theory* (pp. 300–320). Chichester: Wiley-Blackwell.

Hermann M. G. (1986). What is political psychology? In M. G. Hermann (Ed.), *Political psychology* (pp. 1–10). London: Jossey-Bass.

Herrmann R. K., Tetlock P. E., & Visser P. S. (1999). Mass public decisions to go to war: A cognitive-interactionist framework. *American Political Science Review*, *93*, 553–573.

Hewer C. J. (2012). Tracing the social dynamics of peace and conflict. *Papers on Social Representations*, *21*, 12.1–12.22.

Hewer C. J., & Kut M. (2010). Historical legacy, social memory and representations of the past with a Polish community. *Memory Studies*, *3*, 1–15.

Hewer C. J., & Roberts R. (2012). History, culture and cognition: Towards a dynamic model of social memory. *Culture & Psychology*, *18*, 167–183.

Hewer C. J., & Taylor W. (2007). Deconstructing terrorism: Politics, language and social representation. In R. Roberts (Ed.), *Just war: Psychology and terrorism* (pp. 199–212). Ross-on-Wye: PCCS Books.

Hewstone M., & Swart H. (2011). Fifty-odd years of inter-group contact: From hypothesis to integrated theory. *British Journal of Social Psychology*, *50*, 374–386.

Higgins E. T., Klein R. L., & Strauman T. J. (1985). Self-concept discrepancy theory: A psychological model for distinguishing among different aspects of depression and anxiety. *Social Cognition*, *3*, 51–576.

Hill J. (2004). *Faith in the age of reason*. Oxford: Lion Hudson.

Hobsbawn E., & Ranger T. (1992). *The invention of tradition*. New York: Cambridge University Press.

Hodge R., & Kress G. (1993). *Language as ideology* (2nd ed.). London: Routledge.

Hodgetts D., Groot S., Garden E., & Chamberlain K. (2017). The precariat, everyday life and objects of despair. In C. Howarth & E. Andreouli (Eds.), *Everyday politics*. (pp. 173–188) London: Routledge.

Hoffer E. (1951). *The true believer: Thoughts on the nature of mass movements*. New York: Harper and Row.

Hogg M., & Abrams D. (1988). *Social identifications: A social psychology of intergroup relations and group processes*. London: Routledge.

Holland D., Lachicotte Jr. W., Skinner D., & Cain C. (1998). *Identity and agency in cultural worlds*. Cambridge, MA: Harvard University Press.

Hollander M. M. (2015). The repertoire of resistance: Non-compliance with directives in Milgram's "obedience" experiments. *British Journal of Social Psychology, 54*, 425–444.

Holsti O. R., & George A. L. (1975). The effects of stress on the performance of foreign policy-makers. In C. P. Cotter (Ed.), *Political science annual* (pp. 255–319). Indianapolis: BobbsMerrill.

Hook D. (2012). *A critical psychology of the postcolonial: The mind of apartheid*. London: Routledge.

Hopewell S., Loudon K., Clarke M. J., Oxman A. D., & Dickersin K. (2009). Publication bias in clinical trials due to significance of trial results. *Cochrane Database of Systematic Reviews, 2009*(1), MR000006.

Hopkins N., Reicher S. D., Khan S. S., Tewari S., Srinivasan N., & Stevenson C. (2016). Explaining effervescence: Investigating the relationship between shared social identity and positive experience in crowds. *Cognition & Emotion, 30*, 20–32.

Horenczyk G., Jasinskaja-Lahti I., Sam D. L., & Vedder P. (2013). Mutuality in acculturation: Toward an integration. *Zeitschrift für Psychologie, 221*, 205–213.

Hornsey M., & Hogg M. (2000). Assimilation and diversity: An integrative model of subgroup relations. *Personality and Social Psychology Review, 4*, 143–156.

Hothersall D. (2004). *The history of psychology* (4th ed.). New York: McGraw-Hill.

Hourigan N. (2011). *Understanding Limerick: Social exclusion and change*. Cork, Ireland: Cork University Press.

Howarth C. (2002a). Identity in whose eyes? The role of representations in identity construction. *Journal for the Theory of Social Behaviour, 32*, 145–162.

Howarth C. (2002b). "So, you're from Brixton?" The struggle for recognition and esteem in a stigmatized community. *Ethnicities, 2*, 237–260.

Howarth C. (2006). A social representation is not a quiet thing: Exploring the critical potential of social representations theory. *British Journal of Social Psychology, 45*, 65–86.

Huddy L. (2001). From social to political identity: A critical examination of social identity theory. *Political Psychology, 22*, 127–156.

Huddy L., Sears D. O., & Levy J. S. (2013a). Introduction: Theoretical foundations of political psychology. In L. Huddy, D. O. Sears, & J. S. Levy (Eds.), *The Oxford handbook of political psychology* (pp. 1–19). New York: Oxford University Press.

Huddy L., Sears D. O., & Levy J. S. (2013b). *The Oxford handbook of political psychology* (2nd ed.). Oxford: Oxford University Press.

Humphreys E. (2011). Social capital, health and inequality: What's the problem in the neighbourhoods? In N. Hourigan (Ed.), *Understanding Limerick: Social exclusion and change* (pp. 185–210). Cork, Ireland: Cork University Press.

Huntington S. P. (1996). *The clash of civilizations and the remaking of world order*. New York: Simon & Schuster.

Hutchby I. (2005). Conversation analysis and the study of broadcast talk. In K. L. Fitch & R. E. Sanders (Eds.), *Handbook of language and social interaction* (pp. 437–460). Mahwah, NJ: Lawrence Erlbaum.

Hutchby I. (2006). *Media talk: Conversation analysis and the study of broadcasting*. Maidenhead: Open University Press.

Hutchby I., & Wooffitt R. (1998). *Conversation analysis: Principles, practices and applications*. Cambridge: Polity.

Hyvärinen M. (2010). Revisiting the narrative turns. *Life Writing, 7*, 69–82.

Ichheiser G. (1949). Misunderstandings in human relations: A study in false social perception. *American Journal of Sociology, 55*, 1–67.

Ilie C. (2001). Semi-institutional discourse: The case of talk shows. *Journal of Pragmatics, 33,* 209–254.

Imhoff R., & Banse R. (2009). Ongoing victim suffering increases prejudice: The case of secondary anti-semitism. *Psychological Science, 20,* 1443–1447.

Ioannadis J. P. A. (2005). Why most published research findings are false. *PLoS Med.* August, *2*(8), e124. doi:10.1371/journal.pmed.0020124.

Itten T., & Roberts R. (2014). *The new politics of experience and the bitter herbs.* Monmouth: PCCS Books.

Iyengar S. (1993). An overview of the field of political psychology. In S. Iyengar & W. J. McGuire (Eds.), *Explorations in political psychology.* Durham, NC: Duke University Press.

Iyer A., Jetten J., Tsivrikos D., Postmes T., & Haslam S. A. (2009). The more (and the more compatible) the merrier: Multiple group memberships and identity compatibility as predictors of adjustment after life transitions. *British Journal of Social Psychology, 48,* 707–733.

Jackman S. (2004). Bayesian analysis for political research. *Annual Review of Political Science, 7,* 483–505.

Jahoda G. (1988). Critical notes and reflections on "social representations". *European Journal of Social Psychology, 18,* 195–209.

James W. (1890). *Principles of psychology.* New York: Dover Books.

Janis I. L. (1972). *Victims of groupthink: A psychological study of foreign-policy decisions and fiascoes.* Boston, MA: Houghton Mifflin.

Janis I. L., & Mann L. (1977). *Decision making: A psychological analysis of conflict, choice, and commitment.* New York: Free Press.

Jaspal R., & Breakwell G. M. (Eds.) (2014). *Identity process theory: Identity, social action and social change.* Cambridge: Cambridge University Press.

Jay S. (2015). *Classed identities in adolescence.* University of Limerick, Ireland: Unpublished doctoral dissertation.

Jay S., & Muldoon O. T. (in press). A difference denied? The study of social class in social psychology. *Personality and Social Psychology Review.*

Jervis R. (1976). *Perception and misperception in international politics.* Princeton: Princeton University Press.

Jervis R. (2010). *Why intelligence fails: Lessons from the Iranian revolution and the Iraq War.* Ithaca, NY: Cornell University Press.

Jetten J., Iyer A., Tsivrikos D., & Young B. M. (2008). When is individual mobility costly? The role of economic and social identity factors. *European Journal of Social Psychology, 38,* 866–879.

John L. K., Loewenstein G., & Prelec D. (2012). Measuring the prevalence of questionable research practices with incentives for truth telling. *Psychological Science, 23,* 524–532.

Jost J. T., & Major B. (2001). *The psychology of legitimacy: Emerging perspectives on ideology, justice, and inter-group relations.* New York: Cambridge University Press.

Jovchelovitch S. (2012). Narrative, memory and social representations: A conversation between history and social psychology. *Integrated Psychological Behaviour, 46,* 440–456.

Kaarbo J. (2003). Foreign policy analysis in the twenty-first century: Back to comparison, forward to identity and ideas. *International Studies Review, 5,* 155–202.

Kahneman D., & Tversky A. (1979). Prospect theory: An analysis of decision under risk. *Econometrica, 47,* 263–291.

Kansteiner W. (2002). Finding meaning in memory: A methodological critique of collective memory studies. *History and Theory, 41,* 179–197.

Kauffman K., & New C. (2004). *Co-counselling. The theory and practice of re-evaluation co-counselling.* New York: Brunner-Routledge.

Keatinge P. (1978). *A place among the nations: Issues of Irish foreign policy.* Dublin, Ireland: Institute of Public Administration.

Kelley H. H. (1967). Attribution theory in social psychology. *Nebraska Symposium on Motivation, 15*, 192–238.

Kelman H. C. (1965). Social-psychological approaches to the study of international relations: Definition of scope. In H. C. Kelman (Ed.), *International behavior: A social psychological analysis* (pp. 3–39). New York: Holt, Rinehart and Winston.

Kelman H. C. (1969). Patterns of personal involvement in the national system: A socio-psychological analysis of political legitimacy. In J. N. Roseau (Ed.), *International politics and foreign policy* (pp. 276–288). New York: Free Press.

Kelman H. C. (2005). Interactive problem solving in the Israeli-Palestinian case: Past contributions and present challenges. In R. Fisher (Ed.), *Paving the way: Contributions of interactive conflict resolution to peacemaking* (pp. 41–63). Lanham, MD: Lexington Books.

Kelman H. C. (2010). Conflict resolution and reconciliation: A social-psychological perspective on ending violent conflict between identity groups. *Landscapes of Violence, 1*(1)), Article 5. http://scholarworks.umass.edu/lov/vol1/iss1/5.

Kelman H., & Cohen S. (1976). The problem-solving workshop: A social-psychological contribution to the resolution of international conflicts. *Journal of Peace Research, 13*, 79–90.

Kerbo H. R. (1976). The stigma of welfare and a passive poor. *Sociology & Social Research* http://psycnet.apa.org/psycinfo/1977-25219-001.

Kershaw I. (2011). *The end: The defiance and destruction of Hitler's Germany, 1944–1945*. London: Penguin.

Khan S. S., Hopkins N., Reicher S. D., Tewari S., Srinivasan N., & Stevenson C. (2016). How collective participation impacts social identity: A longitudinal study from India. *Political Psychology, 37*, 309–325.

Kharroub T., & Bas O. (2015). Social media and protests: An examination of Twitter images of the 2011 Egyptian revolution. *New Media & Society*, February 23, 1–25.

Khong Y. E. (1992). *Analogies at war*. Princeton: Princeton University Press.

Kim, H. & Lalacette, D. (2013). Literature review on the value-added measurement in higher education. *Ahelo Feasibility Study*. OECD. Retrieved November 22, 2016 from http://www.oecd.org/edu/skills-beyond-school/Litterature%20Review%20VAM.pdf

Kinsey C. (2006). *Corporate soldiers and international security: The rise of private military companies*. London: Routledge.

Kirk R. E. (1996). Practical significance: A concept whose time has come. *Educational and Psychological Measurement, 56*, 746–759.

Kirtsch I. (2009). *The emperor's new drugs. Exploding the antidepressant myth*. London: The Bodley Head.

Kitzinger C. (1989). Liberal humanism as an ideology of social control: The regulation of lesbian identities. In J. Shotter & K. Gergen (Eds.), *Texts of identity* (pp. 82–98). London: Sage.

Klandermans B. (1984). Mobilization and participation: Social-psychological expansisons of resource mobilization theory. *American Sociological Review, 49*, 583–600.

Klapp O. (1969). *Collective search for identity*. New York: Holt, Rinehart.

Klineberg O. (1964). *The human dimension in international relations*. New York: Holt, Rinehart & Winston.

Knight P. (2000). *Conspiracy culture: From Kennedy to the X-Files*. London: Routledge.

Kornhauser W. (1959). *The politics of mass society*. Glencoe: The Free Press.

Kosic A., & Tauber C. D. (2010). Promoting reconciliation through youth: Cross-community initiatives in Vukovar, Croatia. *Peace and Conflict: Journal of Peace Psychology, 16*, 81–95.

Kosterman R., & Feshbach S. (1989). Toward a measure of patriotic and nationalistic attitudes. *Political Psychology, 10*, 257–274.

Kraus M. W., & Keltner D. (2013). Social class rank, essentialism, and punitive judgment. *Journal of Personality and Social Psychology, 105*, 247–261.

Kraus M. W., Piff P. K., & Keltner D. (2009). Social class, sense of control, and social explanation. *Journal of Personality and Social Psychology, 97,* 992–1004.

Kraus M. W., Piff P. K., & Keltner D. (2011). Social class as culture the convergence of resources and rank in the social realm. *Current Directions in Psychological Science, 20,* 246–250.

Kraus M. W., Rheinschmidt M. L., & Piff P. K. (2012). The intersection of resources and rank: Signalling social class in face-to face encounters. In S. T. Fiske & H. R. Markus (Eds.), *Facing social class: How societal rank influences interaction* (pp. 152–172). New York: Russell Sage Foundation.

Kraus M. W., Tan J. J., & Tannenbaum M. B. (2013). The social ladder: A rank-based perspective on social class. *Psychological Inquiry, 24,* 81–96.

Kress G., & Trew A. (1978). Ideological transformation of discourse: Or how The Sunday Times got its message across. *Sociological Review, 26,* 755–776.

Kriesberg L. (2012). Conflicts, constructive. In D. J. Christie (Ed.), *The encyclopedia of peace psychology* (pp. 236–240). Chichester, UK: Wiley-Blackwell.

Kubálková V. (Ed.) (2001). *Foreign policy in a constructed world.* Armonk, NY: M.E. Sharpe.

Kuhn T. S. (1970). *The structure of scientific revolutions* (2nd ed.). Chicago: University of Chicago Press.

Kuklinski J. H. (2002). Introduction: Political psychology and the study of politics. In J. H. Kuklinski (Ed.), *Thinking about political psychology* (pp. 1–22). Cambridge: Cambridge University Press.

Kunda Z. (1990). The case for motivated political reasoning. *Psychological Bulletin, 108,* 480–498.

Kusserow A. (2012). When hard and soft clash: Class-based individualisms in Manhattan and Queens. In S. T. Fiske & H. R. Markus (Eds.), *Facing social class: How societal rank influences interaction* (pp. 195–215). New York: Russell Sage Foundation.

La Fontaine, C. (Executive Producer). (1974, October 28). *Horizon: You do as you are told!* [Television broadcast]. London: British Broadcasting Corporation.

Laing R. D. (1965). Mystification confusion and conflict. In I. Boszormenyinagi & J. L. Framo (Eds.), *Intensive family therapy: Theoretical and practical aspects* (pp. 343–363). New York: Harper & Row.

Laing R. D. (1967). *The politics of experience and the bird of paradise.* Harmondsworth: Penguin.

Laing R. D. (1971). *The politics of the family and other essays.* New York: Vintage Books.

Laing R. D., & Esterson A. (1964). *Sanity, madness and the family: Families of schizophrenics.* London: Tavistock Publications.

Laing R. D., Phillipson H., & Lee A. R. (1966). *Interpersonal perception.* London: Tavistock.

Lareau A., & Weininger E. B. (2003). Cultural capital in educational research: A critical assessment. *Theory and Society, 32,* 567–606.

Lasswell H. D. (1930). *Psychopathology and politics.* Chicago: University of Chicago Press.

László J. (2003). History, identity and narratives. In J. László & W. Wagner (Eds.), *Theories and controversies in societal psychology* (pp. 180–192). Budapest: New Mandate.

László J. (2008). *The science of stories: An introduction to narrative psychology.* New York: Routledge.

Latour B. (2004). Why has critique run out of steam? From matters of fact to matters of concern. *Critical Inquiry, 30,* 225–248.

Le Bon G. (2002). *The crowd: A study of the popular mind* (Anonymous, Trans.). New York: Dover. (Original work published 1895).

Le Grand J. (2006). Equality and choice in public services. *Social Research: An International Quarterly, 73,* 695–710.

Le Roux B., Rouanet H., Savage M., & Warde A. (2008). Class and cultural division in the UK. *Sociology, 42,* 1049–1071.

Leach C. W., Bou Zeinnedine F., & Cehajic-Clancy S. (2013). Moral immemorial: The rarity of self-criticism for previous generations' genocide or mass violence. *Journal of Social Issues, 69*, 34–53.

Leahey T. H. (1980). *A history of psychology: Main currents in psychological thought.* London: Prentice-Hall.

Leahey T. H. (2000). *A history of psychology: Main currents in psychological thought* (5th ed.). London: Prentice-Hall.

Lecoutre B., Lecoutre M.-P., & Poitevineau J. (2001). Uses, abuses and misuses of significance tests in the scientific community: Won't the Bayesian choice be unavoidable? *International Statistical Review, 69*, 399–418.

Lederach J. (2003). *The little book of conflict transformation.* Intercourse, PA: Good Books.

Lee T. L., & Fiske S. T. (2006). Not an outgroup, not yet an ingroup: Immigrants in the stereotype content model. *International Journal of Intercultural Relations, 30*, 751–768.

Lefebvre G. (1954). *Etudes sur la Revolution Francaise.* Paris: Presses Universitaires de France.

Lehmann W. (2009). Becoming middle class: How working-class university students draw and transgress moral class boundaries. *Sociology, 43*, 631–647.

Levy J. S. (1983). Misperception and the causes of war. *World Politics, 36*, 76–99.

Levy J. S. (1994). Learning and foreign policy: Sweeping a conceptual minefield. *International Organization, 48*, 279–312.

Levy J. S. (1997). Prospect theory, rational choice, and international relations. *International Studies Quarterly, 41*, 87–112.

Levy J. S., & Thompson W. R. (2010). *Causes of war.* Chichester, UK: Wiley-Blackwell.

Levy J. S. (2013). Psychology and foreign policy decision making. In L. Huddy, D. O. Sears, & J. S. Levy (Eds.), *The Oxford handbook of political psychology* (2nd ed., pp. 301–333). Oxford: Oxford University Press.

Lewin K. (1951). *Field theory in social science.* New York: Harper.

Lewis D. M. (2010). *The origins of Christian Zionism: Lord Shaftesbury and evangelical support for a Jewish homeland.* Cambridge: Cambridge University Press.

Leyens J. P., & Demoulin S. (2009). Hierarchy-based groups. In S. Otten, K. Sassenberg, & T. Kessler (Eds.), *Intergroup Relations: The Role of Motivation and Emotion* (pp. 199–214). New York: Psychology Press.

Licata L., Sanchez-Mazas M., & Green E. G. (2011). Identity, immigration, and prejudice in Europe: A recognition approach. In S. J. Schwartz, K. Luyckx, & V. L. Vignoles (Eds.), *Handbook of identity theory and research* (pp. 895–916). New York: Springer.

Liebkind K., & Jasinskaja-Lahti I. (2000). The influence of experiences of discrimination on psychological stress: A comparison of seven immigrant groups. *Journal of Community & Applied Social Psychology, 10*, 1–16.

Lieblich A. (1993). Looking at change. Natasha, 21: New immigrant from Russia to Israel. In R. Josselson & A. Lieblich (Eds.), *The narrative study of lives* (Vol. 1, pp. 92–129). Newbury Park, CA: Sage Publications.

Lifton R. J. (2000). *The Nazi doctors.* New York: Basic Books.

Liu J. H., & Hilton D. J. (2005). How the past weighs on the present: Social representations of history and their role in identity politics. *British Journal of Social Psychology, 44*, 537–556.

Locke S. (2011). *Re-crafting rationalization: Enchanted science and mundane mysteries.* Farnham: Ashgate.

Longley, C. (Presenter). (2014, February 3). Thought for the Day. [Radio broadcast]. London: British Broadcasting Corporation.

Lorenz C. (2010). Unstuck in time. Or: The sudden presence of the past. In K. Tilmans, F. Van Vree, & J. Winter (Eds.), *Performing the past: Memory, history and identity in modern Europe* (pp. 67–102). Amsterdam: Amsterdam University Press.

Lott B. (2002). Cognitive and behavioral distancing from the poor. *American Psychologist, 57*, 100–110.

Lott B., & Bullock H. E. (2001). Who are the poor? *Journal of Social Issues, 57*, 189–206.

Lowery W., & The Washington Post (2015). *Ferguson: Three Minutes that Changed America*. New York: Diversion Books.

Lynch K. (2006). Neo-liberalism and marketisation: The implications for higher education. *Symposium Journals* http://researchrepository.ucd.ie/handle/10197/2490.

Lyons P. (2003). Public opinion in the Republic of Ireland – 2001. *Irish Political Studies, 17*(Supplement 001), 4–16.

MacDonald R., Shildrick T., Webster C., & Simpson D. (2005). Growing up in poor neighbourhoods: The significance of class and place in the extended transitions of "socially excluded" young adults. *Sociology, 39*, 873–891.

Maiese M. (2003). Problem-solving workshops. In Beyond Intractability. Retrieved September 30, 2015 from http://www.beyondintractability.org/essay/problem-solving-workshops.

Major B., & O'Brien L. T. (2005). The social psychology of stigma. *Annual Review of Psychology, 56*, 393–421.

Malinowski B. (1926). *Myth in primitive society*. London: Kegan Paul, Trench, Trubner.

Mansten A. S., Liebkind K., & Hernandez D. J. (2012). *Realizing the potential of immigrant youth*. Cambridge: Cambridge University Press.

March J. G. (1994). *A primer on decision-making: How decisions happen*. New York: Free Press.

Markova I. (2012). "Americanisation" of European social psychology. *History of the Human Sciences, 25*, 108–116.

Markus H. R., & Kitayama S. (2010). Cultures and selves: A cycle of mutual constitution. *Perspectives on Psychological Science, 5*, 420–430.

Marmot M. (2004). *The status syndrome: How social standing affects our health and longevity*. New York: Holt Paperbacks.

Marx K. (1852/2006). *The eighteenth brumaire of Louis Bonaparte*. Champaign, IL: Standard Publications Inc.

Marx K. (1888). *Ludwig Feuerbach und der Ausgang der Klassischen deutschen Philosophie - Mit Anhang Karl Marx über Feuerbach von Jahre* (pp. 69–72). (Ludwig Feuerbach and the End of Classical German Philosophy - With Notes on Feuerbach by Karl Marx 1845)). Berlin: Verlag von J.H.W. Dietz.

Mason A. (2016). A brief introduction to using Bayesian statistics in your thesis. *Psychology Postgraduate Affairs Group Quarterly, 98*, 43–46.

Matera C., Stefanile C., & Brown R. (2011). The role of immigrant acculturation preferences and generational status in determining majority intergroup attitudes. *Journal of Experimental Social Psychology, 47*, 776–785.

McAdams D. P. (1985). *Power, intimacy, and the life story: Personological inquiries into identity*. New York: Guilford Press.

McAdams D. P. (2001). The psychology of life stories. *Review of General Psychology, 5*, 100–122.

McAdams D. P. (2011). Narrative identity. In S. J. Schwartz & V. L. Vignoles (Eds.), *Handbook of identity theory and research* (pp. 99–116). New York: Springer.

McCoy S., Smyth E., Watson D., & Darmody M. (2014). *Leaving school in Ireland: A longitudinal study of post-school transitions*. The Economic and Social Research Institute.

McDermott R. (1998). *Risk-taking in international polities: Prospect theory in American foreign policy*. Ann Arbor: University of Michigan Press.

McDougall W. (1920/1939). *The group mind: The principles of collective psychology and their application to the interpretation of national life and character*. Cambridge: Cambridge University Press.

McFarland S. G. (2005). On the eve of war: Authoritarianism, social dominance, and Amercian students' attitudes toward attacking Iraq. *Personality and Social Psychology Bulletin, 31*, 360–367.

McGuire W. J. (1993). The poly-psy relationship: Three phases of a long affair. In S. Iyengar & W. J. McGuire (Eds.), *Explorations in political psychology* (pp. 9–35). Durham, NC: Duke University Press.

McNamara N., Muldoon O. T., Stevenson C., & Slattery E. (2011). Citizenship attributes as the basis for intergroup differentiation: Implicit and explicit intergroup evaluations. *Journal of Community & Applied Social Psychology, 21,* 243–254.

McNamara N., Stevenson C., & Muldoon O. T. (2013). Community identity as resource and context: A mixed method investigation of coping and collective action in a disadvantaged community. *European Journal of Social Psychology, 43,* 393–403.

McPhail C. (1971). Civil disorder participation. *American Sociological Review, 38,* 1058–1073.

McPhail C. (1991). *The myth of the madding crowd.* New York: Aldine de Gruyter.

Mead G. H. (1934). In C. W. Morris (Ed.), *Mind, self and society from the standpoint of a social behaviorist.* Chicago: University of Chicago.

Meier C. (2010). *Das Gebot zu vergessen und die Unabweisbarkeit des Erinnerns* [The imperative to forget and the inescapability of remembering]. Munich: Siedler Verlag.

Merton R. K. (1968). Science and democratic social structure. In *Social theory and social structure* (2nd ed., pp. 604–615). New York: Free Press.

Mickelson K. D., & Williams S. L. (2008). Perceived stigma of poverty and depression: Examination of interpersonal and intrapersonal mediators. *Journal of Social and Clinical Psychology, 27,* 903–930.

Miles J., & Shevlin M. (2003). Navigating spaghetti junction. *The Psychologist, 16,* 639–641.

Milgram S. (1963). Behavioral study of obedience. *Journal of Abnormal and Social Psychology, 67,* 371–378.

Milgram S. (1964). Issues in the study of obedience: A reply to Baumrind. *American Psychologist, 19,* 848–852.

Milgram S. (1965). Some conditions of obedience and disobedience to authority. *Human Relations, 18,* 57–76.

Milgram S. (1970). Interpreting obedience: Error and evidence – a reply to Orne and Holland. In A. G. Miller (Ed.), *The social psychology of psychological research* (pp. 138–154). New York: Free Press.

Milgram S. (1974). *Obedience to authority.* London: Tavistock.

Mintz A. (2004). How do leaders make decisions? A poliheuristic perspective. *Journal of Conflict Resolution, 48,* 3–13.

Moghaddam F. M., Harré R., & Lee N. (2008). Positioning and conflict: An introduction. In F. M. Moghaddam, R. Harré, & N. Lee (Eds.), *Global conflict resolution through positioning analysis* (pp. 3–20). New York: Springer.

Moloney G., Williams J., & Blair D. (2012). Cognitive polyphasia, themata and blood donation: Between or within representation. *Papers on Social Representations, 21,* 4.1–4.12.

Montreuil A., & Bourhis R. Y. (2001). Majority acculturation orientations toward "valued" and "devalued" immigrants. *Journal of Cross-Cultural Psychology, 32,* 698–719.

Monroe K. R. (Ed.) (2002). *Political psychology.* Hillsdale, NJ: LEA.

Morrison D., & Henkel R. (Eds.) (2006). *The significance test controversy.* Chicago: Aldine Publishing Company.

Moscovici, S. (1976). Psychoanalysis: Its image and its public. Paris, France: PUF (Original work published in 1961).

Moscovici S. (1972). Society and theory in social psychology. In J. Israel & H. Tajfel (Eds.), *The context of social psychology: A critical assessment.* London: Academic Press.

Moscovici S. (1985). *The age of the crowd.* Cambridge: Cambridge University Press.

Moscovici S., & Hewstone M. (1983). Social representations and social explanations: From the "naive" to the "amateur" scientist. In M. Hewstone (Ed.), *Attribution theory: Social and functional extensions* (pp. 98–125). Oxford: Basil Blackwell.

Moscovici S., & Markova I. (2006). *The making of modern social psychology: The story of how an international social science was created*. Cambridge: Polity.

Moss S. M., & Vollhardt J. R. (2016). "You can't give a syringe with unity": Rwandan responses to the government's single recategorization policies. *Analyses of Social Issues and Public Policy*, *16*, 325–359.

Motti-Stefanidi F., Berry J., Chryssochoou X., Lackland S., & Phinney J. (2012). Positive immigrant youth adaptation in context: Developmental, acculturation and social psychological perspectives. In A. S. Masten, K. Liebkind, & D. J. Hernandez (Eds.), *Realizing the potential of immigrant youth* (pp. 117–158). Cambridge: Cambridge University Press.

Motti-Stefanidi F., Pavlopoulos V., Obradović J., Dalla M., Takis N., Papathanassiou A., & Masten A. S. (2008). Immigration as a risk factor for adolescent adaptation in Greek urban schools. *European Journal of Developmental Psychology*, *5*, 235–261.

Mulkay M. (1993). *Science and the sociology of knowledge*. Aldershot: Gregg Revivals.

Murad N. (2002). The shortest way out of work. In Biography and social exclusion in Europe (pp. 97–114).

Murphy, D. (April 2012) Where is the value in value-added modeling? White Paper Series. Pearson.

Myers G. (2004). *Matters of opinion: Talking about public issues*. Cambridge: Cambridge University Press.

Nadler A. (2012). Intergroup reconciliation: Definitions, processes, and future directions. In L. R. Tropp & L. R. Tropp (Eds.), *The Oxford handbook of intergroup conflict* (pp. 291–308). New York: Oxford University Press.

Nadler A., & Liviatan I. (2006). Intergroup reconciliation: Effects of adversary's expressions of empathy, responsibility, and recipients' trust. *Personality and Social Psychology Bulletin*, *32*, 459–470.

Nadler A., & Shnabel N. (2008). Instrumental and socioemotional paths to intergroup reconciliation and the needs-based model of socioemotional reconciliation. In A. Nadler, T. E. Malloy, J. D. Fisher, A. Nadler, T. E. Malloy, & J. D. Fisher (Eds.), *The social psychology of intergroup reconciliation* (pp. 37–56). New York: Oxford University Press.

National Commission on Terrorist Attacks upon the United States (2004). *The 9/11 commission report: Final report of the National Commission on terrorist attacks upon the United States*. New York: W.W. Norton.

Navas M., Garcia M. C., Sánchez J., Rojas A. J., Pumares P., & Fernández J. S. (2005). Relative Acculturation Extended Model: New contributions with regard to the study of acculturation. *International Journal of Intercultural Relations*, *29*, 21–37.

Navas M., Rojas A. J., Garcia M. C., & Pumares P. (2007). Acculturation strategies and attitudes according to the Relative Acculturation Extended Model (RAEM): The perspectives of natives versus immigrants. *International Journal of Intercultural Relations*, *31*, 67–86.

Ndlovu, A. (2014). What the Ferguson riots tell us about being black in South Africa. *Rand Daily Mail*. Retrieved July 6, 2016 from http://www.rdm.co.za/incoming/2014/11/27/what-the-ferguson-riots-tell-us-about-being-black-in-south-africa

Nelson J. S., Megill A., & McCloskey D. N. (Eds.) (1987). *The rhetoric of the human sciences: Language and argument in scholarship and public affairs*. Madison, WI: University of Wisconsin Press.

Neville F. G., & Reicher S. D. (2011). The experience of collective participation: Shared identity, relatedness and emotionality. *Contemporary Social Science*, *6*, 377–396.

Neyman J. (1937). Outline of a theory of statistical estimation based on the classical theory of probability. *Philosophical Transactions of the Royal Society A*, *236*, 333–380.

Nguyen A.-M. D., & Benet-Martinez V. (2007). Biculturalism unpacked: Components, individual differences, measurement, and outcomes. *Social and Personality Psychology Compass*, *1*, 101–114.

Nguyen A.-M. D., & Benet-Martinez V. (2010). Multicultural identity: What it is and why it matters. In R. Crisp (Ed.), *The psychology of social and cultural diversity* (pp. 87–114). Hoboken, NJ: Wiley-Blackwell.

Nigbur C., Brown R., Cameron L., Hossain R., Landau A., Le Touze D., et al. (2008). Acculturation, well-being and classroom behavior among white British and British Asian primary-school children in the south-east of England: Validating a child-friendly measure of acculturation attitudes. *International Journal of Intercultural Relations, 32*, 493–504.

Nolan B., & Whelan C. T. (1999). *Loading the dice? A study of cumulative disadvantage.* Dublin: Oak Tree Press for the Combat of Poverty.

Noor M., Brown R. J., & Prentice G. (2008a). Precursors and mediators of intergroup reconciliation in Northern Ireland: A new model. *British Journal of Social Psychology, 47*, 481–495.

Noor M., Brown R., Gonzales R., Manzi J., & Lewis C. A. (2008b). On positive psychological outcomes: What helps groups with a history of conflict to forgive and reconcile with each other? *Personality and Social Psychology Bulletin, 34*, 819–832.

Noor M., Shnabel N., Halabi S., & Nadler A. (2012). When suffering begets suffering the psychology of competitive victimhood between adversarial groups in violent conflicts. *Personality and Social Psychology Review, 16*, 351–374.

Nora P. (1989). Between memory and history: Les Lieux de memoire. *Representations, 26*, 7–24.

Nora P. (2002). Reasons for the current upsurge in memory. *Transit, 22*, 1–8.

Nye R. (1975). *The origins of crowd psychology.* London: Sage.

O'Dwyer, E. (2013). Social representations of Irish neutrality (Unpublished doctoral dissertation). Queen's University, Belfast.

O'Dwyer E., Lyons E., & Cohrs J. C. (2016). How Irish citizens negotiate foreign policy: A social representations approach to neutrality. *Political Psychology, 37*, 165–181.

Olick J. K. (1999). Collective memory: The two cultures. *Sociological Theory, 17*, 333–348.

Olick J. (2002). Introduction. In J. Olick (Ed.), *States of memory: Continuities, conflicts and transformations in national retrospection.* Durham, NC: Duke University Press.

Olick J. (2010). From collective memory to the sociology of mnemonic practices and products. In A. Erll & A. Nünning (Eds.), *A companion to cultural memory studies* (pp. 151–161). Berlin: De Gruyter.

Olick J., Vinitsky V., & Levy D. (Eds.) (2011). *The collective memory reader.* Oxford: Oxford University Press.

Open Science Collaboration (2015). Estimating the reproducibility of psychological science. *Science, 349*(6251). doi:10.1126/science.aac4716.

Orbach S. (1978). *Fat is a feminist issue.* London: Penguin.

Orne M. T. (1962). On the social psychology of the social psychology experiment: With particular reference to demand characteristics and their implications. *American Psychologist, 17*, 776–783.

Orne M. T., & Evans F. J. (1965). Social control in the psychological experiment: Antisocial behaviour and hypnosis. *Journal of Personality and Social Psychology, 1*, 189–200.

Orne M. T., & Holland C. H. (1968). On the ecological validity of laboratory deception. *International Journal of Psychiatry, 6*, 282–293.

Ostrove J. M., & Cole E. R. (2003). Privileging class: Toward a critical psychology of social class in the context of education. *Journal of Social Issues, 59*, 677–692.

Ostrove J. M., & Long S. M. (2007). Social class and belonging: Implications for college adjustment. *The Review of Higher Education, 30*, 363–389.

Ozouf M. (1988). *Festivals and the French revolution.* Cambridge, MA: Harvard University Press.

Page B., & Shapiro R. (1983). Effects of public opinion on policy. *The American Political Science Review, 77*, 175–190.

Pakulski J., & Waters M. (1996). *The death of class*. London: Sage.

Paluck E. L. (2009). Reducing intergroup prejudice and conflict using the media: A field experiment in Rwanda. *Journal of Personality and Social Psychology, 96*, 574–587.

Paluck E. L., & Green D. P. (2009). Deference, dissent and dispute resolution: An experimental intervention using mass media to change norms and behaviour in Rwanda. *The American Political Science Review, 103*, 622–644.

Parish J., & Parker M. (Eds.) (2001). *The age of anxiety: Conspiracy theory and the human sciences*. Oxford: Blackwell.

Parker I. (2007). *Revolution in psychology: Alienation to emancipation*. London: Pluto Press.

Pehrson S., Brown R., & Zagefka H. (2009). When does national identification lead to the rejection of immigrants? Cross-sectional and longitudinal evidence for the role of essentialist in-group definitions. *British Journal of Social Psychology, 48*, 61–76.

Penrose R. (1999). *The emperor's new mind: Concerning computers, minds, and the laws of physics*. Oxford: Oxford University Press.

Penrose R. (2013). Foreword. In H. Zenil (Ed.), *A computable universe: Understanding and exploring nature as computation* (pp. i–xxiv). Singapore: World Scientific Publishing.

Pepitone A. (1981). Lessons from the history of social psychology. *American Psychologist, 36*, 972–985.

Perry G. (2013). *Behind the shock machine. The untold story of the notorious Milgram psychology experiments*. London: Scribe.

Pettigrew T. F. (2010). Commentary: South African contributions to the study of intergroup relations. *Journal of Social Issues, 66*, 417–430.

Phalet K., Baysu G., & Van Acker K. (2015). Ethnicity and migration in Europe. In J. D. Wright (Ed.), *International encyclopedia of the social and behavioral sciences* (2nd ed., pp. 675–681). Oxford: Elsevier.

Phinney J. S., Horenczyk G., Liebkind K., & Vedder P. (2001). Ethnic identity, immigration, and well-being: An interactional perspective. *Journal of Social Issues, 57*, 493–510.

Pickerill J., & Krinsky J. (2012). Why does occupy matter? *Social Movement Studies, 11*, 279–287.

Piff P. K., Kraus M. W., Côté S., Cheng B. H., & Keltner D. (2010). Having less, giving more: The influence of social class on prosocial behavior. *Journal of Personality and Social Psychology, 99*, 771–784.

Piff P. K., Stancato D. M., Côté S., Mendoza-Denton R., & Keltner D. (2012). Higher social class predicts increased unethical behavior. *Proceedings of the National Academy of Sciences, 109*, 4086–4091.

Piketty T., & Goldhammer A. (2014). *Capital in the twenty-first century*. Cambridge, MA: Harvard University Press.

Piontkowski U., Rohmann A., & Florack A. (2002). Concordance of acculturation attitudes and perceived threat. *Group Processes and Intergroup Relations, 5*, 221–232.

Poincaré H. (1952). *Science and hypotheses*. New York: Dover.

Pollner M. (1987). *Mundane reason: Reality in everyday and sociological discourse*. Cambridge: Cambridge University Press.

Popper K. (2002). *The logic of scientific discovery*. London: Routledge.

Postmes T., & Spears R. (1998). Deindividuation and anti-normative behavior: A meta-analysis. *Psychological Bulletin, 123*, 238–259.

Potter J. (1996). *Representing reality: Discourse, rhetoric and social construction*. London: Sage.

Potter J. (1998a). Discursive social psychology: From attitudes to evaluative practices. *European Review of Social Psychology, 9*, 233–266.

Potter J. (1998b). Fragments in the realization of relativism. In I. Parker (Ed.), *Social construction-ism, discourse and realism* (pp. 27–45). London: Sage.

Potter J. (2012). Discourse analysis and discursive psychology. In H. Cooper (Ed.), *APA handbook of research methods in psychology, Quantitative, qualitative, neuropsychological and biological* (Vol. 2), pp. 111–130). Washington: American Psychological Association Press.

Potter J., & Billig M. (1992). Re-representing representations. *Ongoing Production on Social Representations, 1,* 15–20.

Potter J., & Edwards D. (2001). Discursive social psychology. In W. P. Robinson & H. Giles (Eds.), *The new handbook of language and social psychology* (pp. 103–118). Chichester, UK: John Wiley & Sons, Ltd.

Potter J., & Linton I. (1985). Some problems underlying the theory of social representations. *British Journal of Social Psychology, 24,* 81–90.

Potter J., & Wetherell M. (1987). Discourse and social psychology: Beyond attitudes and behaviour. In London: Sage.

Pratto F., Sidanius J., Stallworth L. M., & Malle B. F. (1994). Social dominance orientation: A personality variable predicting social and political attitudes. *Journal of Personality and Social Psychology, 67,* 741.

Prime minister questioned over suicide reports. (2015, October 21) [Video file]. Retrieved from https://www.facebook.com/Channel4News/videos/10153291785181939/

Pring, J. (2015). *Cameron challenged twice in a minute over disability rights.* Retrieved from http://www.disabilitynewsservice.com/cameron-challenged-twice-in-a-minute-over-disability-rights/

The Psychologist (2012). Replication: Where do we go from here? *The Psychologist, 25,* 349.

Putnam R. (1995). *Bowling alone: The collapse and revival of American community* (New edition). New York, NY: Simon & Schuster Ltd.

Rahn W. M., Sullivan J. L., & Rudolph T. J. (2002). Political psychology and political science. In J. H. Kuklinski (Ed.), *Thinking about political psychology* (pp. 155–186). Cambridge: Cambridge University Press.

Read J. (2005). The bio-bio-bio model of madness. *The Psychologist, 18,* 596–597.

Read J., Mosher L., & Bentall R. (2004). *Models of madness.* London: Routledge.

Reay D. (1996). Contextualising choice: Social power and parental involvement. *British Educational Research Journal, 22,* 581–596.

Reay D. (2005). Beyond consciousness? The psychic landscape of social class. *Sociology, 39,* 911–928.

Reay D. (2006). The zombie stalking English schools: Social class and educational inequality. *British Journal of Educational Studies, 54,* 288–307.

Reay D., Crozier G., & Clayton J. (2009). Strangers in paradise? Working-class students in elite universities. *Sociology, 43,* 1103–1121.

Reay D., Davies J., David M., & Ball S. J. (2001). Choices of degree or degrees of choice? Class, race and the higher education choice process. *Sociology, 35,* 855–874.

Redfield R., Linton R., & Herskovits M. (1936). Memorandum on the study of acculturation. *American Anthropologist, 38,* 149–152.

Redlawsk D. P., & Lau R. R. (2013). Behavioral decision-making. In L. Huddy, D. O. Sears, & J. S. Levy (Eds.), *The Oxford handbook of political psychology* (2nd ed., pp. 130–164). Oxford: Oxford University Press.

Rees L. (2005). *The Nazis: A warning from history.* London: BBC Books.

Reicher S. D. (1984). The St. Paul's "riot": An explanation of the limits of crowd action in terms of a social identity model. *European Journal of Social Psychology, 14,* 1–21.

Reicher S. D. (1987). Crowd behaviour as social action. In J. Turner, M. Hogg, P. Oakes, S. D. Reicher, & M. Wetherell (Eds.), *Rediscovering the social group: A self-categorization theory* (pp. 171–202). Oxford: Blackwell.

Reicher S. D. (1996). The Battle of Westminster: Developing the social identity model of crowd behaviour in order to deal with the initiation and development of collective conflict. *European Journal of Social Psychology, 26*, 115–134.

Reicher S. D. (2001). The psychology of crowd dynamics. In M. A. Hogg & S. Tindale (Eds.), *Blackwell handbook of social psychology: Group processes* (pp. 182–208). Oxford: Blackwell.

Reicher S. D. (2011). Mass action and mundane reality: An argument for putting crowd analysis at the centre of the social sciences. *Contemporary Social Science, 6*, 433–449.

Reicher S. D. (2012). Crowds, agency and passion: Reconsidering the roots of the social bond. In R. Parkin-Gounelas (Ed.), *The psychology and politics of the collective: Groups, crowds and mass identifications* (pp. 67–85). London: Routledge.

Reicher S. D. (2014). In praise of activism: Rethinking the psychology of obedience and conformity. In C. Antaki & S. Condor (Eds.), *Rhetoric, ideology and social psychology: Essays in honour of Michael Billig* (pp. 94–108). Hove: Routledge.

Reicher S. D., & Haslam S. A. (2006). Rethinking the psychology of tyranny: The BBC prison study. *British Journal of Social Psychology, 45*, 1–40.

Reicher S. D., & Hopkins N. (1996). Seeking influence through characterizing self-categories: An analysis of antiabortionist rhetoric. *British Journal of Social Psychology, 35*, 297–311.

Reicher S. D., & Hopkins N. (2001a). Psychology and the end of history: A critique and a proposal for the psychology of social categorization. *Political Psychology, 22*, 383–408.

Reicher S. D., & Hopkins N. (2001b). *Self and nation: Categorization, contestation and mobilisation.* London: Sage.

Reicher S. D., & Potter J. (1985). Psychological theory as intergroup perspective: A comparative analysis of "scientific" and "lay" accounts of crowd events. *Human Relations, 38*, 167–189.

Reicher S. D., & Stott C. J. (2011). *Mad mobs and Englishmen?: Myths and realities of the 2011 riots.* London: Constable & Robinson.

Reicher S. D., Spears R., & Postmes T. (1995). A social identity model of deindividuation phenomena. *European Review of Social Psychology, 6*, 161–198.

Reinert M. (1990). ALCESTE: Une methode de classification descendante hierarchique: Application à l'analyse lexicale par contexte. *Les Cahiers de l'Analyse des Donnees, 8*, 187–198.

Reiwald P. (1949). *L'Esprit des Masses.* Neuchatel: Delachaux & Niestle.

Richards G. (2002). *Putting psychology in its place: A critical historical overview* (2nd ed.). Hove: Routledge.

Richmond O. P., Pogodda S., & Ramovic J. (Eds.) (2016). *The Palgrave handbook of disciplinary and regional approaches to peace.* London: Palgrave-Macmillan.

Ripsman N. M., & Levy J. S. (2008). Wishful thinking or buying time? The logic of British appeasement in the 1930s. *International Security, 33*, 148–181.

Ritchie S. J., Wiseman R., & French C. C. (2012). Replication, replication, replication. *The Psychologist, 25*, 346–347.

Roberts R. (2005). Problems in replicating multivariate models in quantitative research. *Health Psychology Update, 14*, 10–16.

Roberts R. (2007). Sleepwalking into totalitarianism: Democracy centre politics and terror. In R. Roberts (Ed.), *Just war: Psychology and terrorism* (pp. 181–198). Ross-On-Wye: PCCS Books.

Roberts R. (2015). *Psychology and capitalism.* Winchester: Zero Books.

Roberts R., & Hewer C. J. (2015). Memory, "madness" and conflict: A Laingian perspective. *Memory Studies, 8*, 169–182.

Roccato M., & Fedi A. (2007). "Not in my name"? The Italians and the war in Iraq. *Journal of Community and Applied Social Psychology, 17*, 229–236.

Rogers N. (1998). *Crowds, culture, and politics in Georgian Britain.* Oxford: Clarendon Press.

Rose N. (1999). *Governing the soul: The shaping of the private self* (2nd ed.). London: Free Association.

Rosenhan D. (1969). Some origins of concern for others. In P. Mussen, J. Langer, & M. Covington (Eds.), *Trends and Issues in developmental psychology* (pp. 134–153). New York: Holt, Rinehart and Winston.

Rosenthal R. (1979). The file drawer problem and tolerance for null results. *Psychological Bulletin*, *86*, 638–641.

Ross L. (1977). The intuitive psychologist and his shortcomings. In L. Berkowitz (Ed.), *Advances in experimental social psychology* (pp. 174–220). New York: Academic Press.

Rousseau D. L., & Garcia-Retamero R. (2007). Identity, power, and threat perception: A cross-national experimental study. *Journal of Conflict Resolution*, *51*(5), 744–771.

Rovner J. (2011). *Fixing the facts: National security and the politics of intelligence*. Ithaca, NY: Cornell University Press.

Rudé G. (1959). *The crowd in the French revolution*. London: Oxford University Press.

Runciman W. (1966). *Relative deprivation and social justice*. London: Routledge.

Ryan J., & Hewer C. J. (2016). What did we do to Germany during the Second World War? A British perspective on the Allied strategic bombing campaign 1940–45. *Papers on Social Representations*, *25*, 10.1–10.28.

Sacks H. (1995). *Lectures on conversation*. Oxford: Blackwell.

Sacks H., Schegloff E. A., & Jefferson G. (1974). A simplest systematics for the organization of turn-taking in conversation. *Language*, *50*, 696–735.

Saegert S. C., Adler N. E., Bullock H. E., Cauce A. M., Liu W. M., & Wyche K. F. (2007). *Report of the APA task force on socioeconomic status*. Washington, DC: American Psychological Association.

Saguy T., & Chernyak-Hai L. (2012). Intergroup contact can undermine disadvantaged group members' attributions to discrimination. *Journal of Experimental Social Psychology*, *48*, 714–720.

Saguy T., Tausch N., Dovidio J. F., & Pratto F. (2009). The irony of harmony: Intergroup contact can produce false expectations for equality. *Psychological Science*, *20*, 114–112.

Salmon T. C. (1989). *Unneutral Ireland: An ambivalent and unique security policy*. Oxford: Clarendon.

Sam D. L. (2015). Acculturation. In J. D. Wright (Ed.), *The international encyclopedia of the social and behavioral sciences* (2nd ed., pp. 68–74). Oxford: Elsevier.

Sam D. L., & Berry J. W. (2006). *Cambridge handbook of acculturation psychology*. Cambridge: Cambridge University Press.

Sammut G., Andreouli E., Gaskell G., & Valsiner J. (Eds.) (2015). *The Cambridge handbook of social representations*. Cambridge: Cambridge University Press.

Sampson E. E. (1993). *Celebrating the other: A dialogic account of human nature*. New York: Harvester Wheatsheaf.

Sanders M. R., & Mahalingam R. (2012). Under the radar: The role of invisible discourse in understanding class-based privilege. *Journal of Social Issues*, *68*, 112–127.

Sanson A., & Bretherton D. (2001). Conflict resolution: Theoretical and practical issues. In D. J. Christie, R. V. Wagner, & D. D. Winter (Eds.), *Peace, conflict, and violence: Peace psychology for the 21st century* (pp. 193–209). Englewood Cliffs, New Jersey: Prentice-Hall.

Sapountzis A., & Condor S. (2013). Conspiracy accounts as intergroup theories: Challenging dominant understandings of social power and political legitimacy. *Political Psychology*, *34*, 731–752.

Sarbin T. R. (1986). The narrative as a root metaphor for psychology. In T. R. Sarbin (Ed.), *Narrative psychology: The storied nature of human conduct* (pp. 3–21). New York: Praeger.

Savage M. (2003). Review essay: A new class paradigm? *British Journal of Sociology of Education*, *24*, 535–541.

Savage M., Devine F., Cunningham N., Taylor M., Li Y., Hjellbrekke J., ... Miles A. (2013). A new model of social class? Findings from the BBC's Great British Class Survey experiment. *Sociology*, *47*, 219–250.

Savage M., Warde A., & Devine F. (2005). Capitals, assets, and resources: Some critical issues. *The British Journal of Sociology, 56*, 31–47.

Sayer A. (2005). Class, moral worth and recognition. *Sociology, 39*, 947–963.

Schank R. C., & Abelson R. P. (1977). *Scripts, plans, goals, and understanding an enquiry into human knowledge structures.* Hillsdale, NJ: Erlbaum.

Schegloff E. A. (1997). Whose text? Whose context? *Discourse and Society, 8*, 165–187.

Schegloff E. A. (1998). Reply to Wetherell. *Discourse and Society, 9*, 457–460.

Schegloff E. A. (1999a). "Schegloff's texts" as "Billig's data": A critical reply. *Discourse and Society, 10*, 558–572.

Schegloff E. A. (1999b). Naivete vs. sophistication or discipline vs. self indulgence. *Discourse and Society, 10*, 577–582.

Schelling T. C. (1966). *Arms and influence.* New Haven, CT: Yale University Press.

Scherger S., & Savage M. (2010). Cultural transmission, educational attainment and social mobility. *The Sociological Review, 58*, 406–428.

Schiff B. (2002). Talking about identity: Arab students at the Hebrew University. *Ethos, 30*, 273–304.

Schiff B. (2012). The function of narrative: Toward a narrative psychology of meaning. *Narrative Works: Issues, Investigations & Interventions, 2*, 34–47.

Schiff B. (2017). *A new narrative for psychology.* Oxford: Oxford University Press.

Schmidhuber J. (2013). The fastest way of computing all universes. In H. Zenil (Ed.), *A computable universe: Understanding and exploring nature as computation* (pp. 383–400). Singapore: World Scientific Publishing.

Schneider M. C., Holman M. R., Diekman A. B., & McAndrew T. (2015). Power, conflict, and community: How gendered views of political power influence women's political ambition. *Political Psychology.* Article first published online: 17 June 2015. doi:10.1111/pops.12268.

Schori-Eyal N., Halperin E., & Bar-Tal D. (2014). Three layers of collective victimhood: Effects of multileveled victimhood on intergroup conflicts in the Israeli–Arab context. *Journal of Applied Social Psychology, 44*, 778–794.

Schwartz S. (1992). Universals in the content and structure of values: Theory and empirical tests in 20 countries. In M. Zanna (Ed.), *Advances in experimental social psychology* (pp. 1–65). New York: Academic Press.

Scruton R. (2001). *Kant: A very short introduction.* Oxford: Oxford University Press.

Searle J. (1980). Minds, brains and programs. *Behavioural and Brain Sciences, 3*, 417–457.

Sears D. O. (1988). Symbolic racism. In P. A. Katz & D. A. Taylor (Eds.), *Eliminating racism: Profiles in controversy* (pp. 53–84). New York: Plenum.

Sears D. O., Huddy L., & Jervis R. (Eds.) (2003). *Oxford handbook of political psychology.* New York: Oxford University Press.

Seed P. (1966). *The psychological problem of disarmament.* London: Housmans.

Shakespeare W. (2004). *The tempest.* Ware, Herts: Wordsworth.

Shapin S., & Schaffer S. (1985). *Leviathan and the air pump: Hobbes, Boyle, and the experimental life.* Princeton, NJ: Princeton University Press.

Sheldrake R. (2012). *The science delusion.* London: Coronet.

Sheridan, C. L. & King, R.G. (1972). Obedience to authority with an authentic victim. *Proceedings of the 80th Annual Convention, APA.*

Sherif M. (1966). *In common predicament: Social psychology of inter-group conflict and cooperation.* Boston, MA: Houghton Mifflin.

Sherman R. C. (1973). Dimensional salience in the perception of nations as a function of attitudes toward war and anticipated social interaction. *Journal of Personality and Social Psychology, 27*, 65–73.

Shirer W. L. (1960). *The rise and fall of the Third Reich.* London: Pan.

Shklovsky V. (2005). *Knight's move.* London: Dalkey Archive Press. (Original work published 1923).

Shmueli, D. (2003) "Conflict Assessment". Beyond intractability. Retrieved March 9, 2016 from <http://www.beyondintractability.org/essay/conflict-assessment>.

Shnabel N., & Nadler A. (2008). A needs-based model of reconciliation: Satisfying the differential emotional needs of victim and perpetrator as a key to promoting reconciliation. *Journal of Personality and Social Psychology, 94*, 116–132.

Shnabel N., Halabi S., & Noor M. (2013). Overcoming competitive victimhood and facilitating forgiveness through re-categorization into a common victim or perpetrator identity. *Journal of Experimental Social Psychology, 49*, 867–877.

Shnabel N., Nadler A., Ullrich J., Dovidio J. F., & Carmi D. (2009). Promoting reconciliation through the satisfaction of the emotional needs of victimized and perpetrating group members: The needs-based model of reconciliation. *Personality and Social Psychology Bulletin, 35*, 1021–1030.

Simantov-Nachlieli I., Shnabel N., & Halabi S. (2015). Winning the victim status can open conflicting groups to reconciliation: Evidence from the Israeli-Palestinian Conflict. *European Journal of Social Psychology, 45*, 139–145.

Simon B., & Klandermans B. (2001). Politicized collective identity: A social psychological analysis. *American Psychologist, 56*, 319–331.

Simon B., Reichert F., & Grabow O. (2013). When dual identity becomes a liability: Identity and political radicalism among migrants. *Psychological Science, 24*, 251–257.

Simon H. A. (1955). A behavioral model of rational choice. *Quarterly Journal of Economics, 69*, 99–118.

Simon H. A. (1957). *Models of man: Social and rational.* New York: John Wiley & Sons, Inc.

Simons H. W. (Ed.) (1989). *Rhetoric in the human sciences.* London: Sage.

Sinnott, R. (2003). Attitudes and Behaviour of the Irish Electorate in the Second Referendum on the Treaty of Nice. Institute for the Study of Social Change Discussion Paper Series, University College Dublin.

Sinnott, R. & Elkink, J. (2010). Attitudes and behaviour in the second referendum on the Treaty of Lisbon. Retrieved April 30, 2018 from https://www.ucd.ie/t4cms/Attitudes%20and%20Behaviour%20in%20the%20Second%20Referendum%20on%20the%20Treaty%20of%20Lisbon.pdf

Sirin S. R. (2005). Socioeconomic status and academic achievement: A meta-analytic review of research. *Review of Educational Research, 75*, 417–453.

Skeggs B. (1997). *Formations of class and gender: Becoming respectable* (Vol. 51). London: Sage.

Smith B., & Sparkes A. (2008). Contrasting perspectives on narrating selves and identities: An invitation to dialogue. *Qualitative Research, 8*, 5–35.

Smoliarova T. (2006). Distortion and theatricality: Estrangement in Diderot and Shklovsky. *Poetics Today, 27*, 3–34.

Smyth E., & McCoy S. (2011). The dynamics of credentialism: Ireland from bust to boom (and back again). *Research in Social Stratification and Mobility, 29*, 91–106.

Snibbe A. C., & Markus H. R. (2005). You can't always get what you want: Educational attainment, agency, and choice. *Journal of Personality and Social Psychology, 88*, 703–720.

Sommerland E., & Berry J. W. (1970). The role of ethnic identification in distinguishing between attitudes towards assimilation and between integration of a minority racial group. *Human Relations, 23*, 23–29.

Spangler, B. (September 2003) "Settlement, Resolution, Management and Transformation. Beyond Intractability". Retrieved March 9, 2016 from <http://www.beyondintractability.org/essay/meaning-resolution>.

Spencer T. M. (2000). *The St. Louis veiled prophet celebration: Power on parade, 1877–1995.* Columbia: University of Missouri Press.

Spencer B., & Castano E. (2007). Social class is dead: Long live social class! Stereotype threat among low socioeconomic status individuals. *Social Justice Research, 20*, 418–432.

Spillman L. (1997). *Nation and commemoration: Creating national identities in the United States and Australia*. Cambridge: Cambridge University Press.

Stangneth B. (2014). *Eichmann before Jerusalem*. New York: Alfred A. Knopf.

Staerklé C., Clémence A., & Spini D. (2011). Social representations: A normative and dynamic intergroup approach. *Political Psychology, 32*, 759–768.

Staerklé C., Sidanius J., Green E. G. T., & Molina L. (2010). Ethnic minority-majority asymmetry in national attitudes around the world: A multilevel analysis. *Political Psychology, 31*, 491–519.

Staub E. (1999). The origins and prevention of genocide, mass killing, and other collective violence. *Peace and Conflict: Journal of Peace Psychology, 5*, 303–336.

Steavenson W. (2015). *Circling the square: Stories from the Egyptian revolution*. New York: Ecco Press.

Steele C. M., Spencer S. J., & Aronson J. (2002). Contending with group image: The psychology of stereotype and social identity threat. *Advances in Experimental Social Psychology, 34*, 379–440.

Stein J. G. (2013). Threat perception in international relations. In L. Huddy, D. O. Sears, & J. S. Levy (Eds.), *The Oxford handbook of political psychology* (2nd ed., pp. 364–394). Oxford: Oxford University Press.

Stephan W. G., & Finlay K. (1999). The role of empathy in improving intergroup relations. *Journal of Social Issues, 55*, 729–743.

Stephan W. G., & Stephan C. W. (2000). An integrated threat theory of prejudice. In S. Oskamp (Ed.), *Reducing prejudice and discrimination* (pp. 23–45). Mahwah, NJ: Psychology Press.

Stephan W. G., Renfro C. L., Esses V. M., Stephan C. W., & Martin T. (2005). The effects of feeling threatened on attitudes toward immigrants. *International Journal of Intercultural Relations, 29*, 1–19.

Stephens N. M., Fryberg S. A., & Markus H. R. (2012a). It's your choice: How the middle-class model of independence disadvantages working-class Americans. In S. T. Fiske & H. R. Markus (Eds.), *Facing social class: How societal rank influences interaction* (pp. 87–106). New York: Russell Sage Foundation.

Stephens N. M., Hamedani M. G., & Destin M. (2014). Closing the social-class achievement gap a difference-education intervention improves first-generation students' academic performance and all students' college transition. *Psychological Science, 25*, 943–953.

Stephens N. M., Markus H. R., & Fryberg S. A. (2012b). Social class disparities in health and education: Reducing inequality by applying a sociocultural self model of behavior. *Psychological Review, 119*, 723–744.

Stephens N. M., Markus H. R., & Townsend S. S. (2007). Choice as an act of meaning: The case of social class. *Journal of Personality and Social Psychology, 93*, 814–830.

Sterling T. D., Rosenbaum W. L., & Weinkam J. J. (1995). Publication decisions revisited: The effect of the outcome of statistical tests on the decision to publish and vice versa. *The American Statistician, 49*, 108–112.

Stevenson C., Condor S., & Abell J. (2007). The minority-majority conundrum in Northern Ireland: An orange order perspective. *Political Psychology, 28*, 105–125.

Stevenson C., McNamara N., & Muldoon O. T. (2014). Stigmatised identity and service usage in disadvantaged communities: Residents', community workers' and service providers' perspectives. *Journal of Community & Applied Social Psychology, 24*, 453–466.

Stone, J. (2015, November 12). Benefit sanctions against people with mental health problems up by 600 per cent. *The Independent*. Retrieved June 6, 2015, from http://www.independent.co.uk/news/uk/politics/benefit-sanctions-against-people-with-mental-health-problems-up-by-600-per-cent-a6731971.html

Stone W. F., & Schaffner P. E. (1988). *The psychology of politics* (2nd ed.). New York: Springer.

Stone J. V. (2013). *Bayes' rule. An introduction to Bayesian analysis*. Sheffield: Sebtel Press.

Stott C. J., & Adang O. M. J. (2004). "Disorderly" conduct: Social psychology and the control of football "hooliganism" at "Euro2004". *The Psychologist, 17*, 318–319.

Stott C. J., & Drury J. (2000). Crowds, context and identity: Dynamic categorization processes in the "poll tax riot". *Human Relations, 53*, 247–273.

Stott C. J., Hutchison P., & Drury J. (2001). "Hooligans" abroad? Inter-group dynamics, social identity and participation in collective 'disorder' at the 1998 World Cup Finals. *British Journal of Social Psychology, 40*, 359–384.

Stott C. J., & Reicher S. D. (1998). How conflict escalates: The inter-group dynamics of collective football crowd violence. *Sociology, 32*, 353–377.

Stouffer S. A., Suchman E. A., De Vinney L. C., Star S. A., & Williams Jr. R. B. (1949). *The American soldier: Adjustment during army life.* (Studies in social psychology in World War II, Vol 1). Princeton, NJ: Princeton University Press.

Straus S., & Waldorf L. (Eds.) (2011). *Remaking Rwanda. Statebuilding and human rights after mass violence.* Madison, WI: University of Wisconsin Press.

Stryker S. (1987). Identity theory: Development and extensions. In K. Yardley & T. Honess (Eds.), *Self and identity: Psychosocial perspectives* (pp. 89–103). Chichester: John Wiley & Sons Ltd.

Subašić E., Reynolds K., & Turner J. C. (2008). The political solidarity model of social change: Dynamics of self-categorization in intergroup power relations. *Personality and Social Psychology Review, 12*, 350–352.

Sullivan J. L., Rahn W. M., & Rudolph T. J. (2002). The contours of political psychology: Situating research on political information processing. In J. H. Kuklinski (Ed.), *Thinking about political psychology* (pp. 23–47). Cambridge: Cambridge University Press.

Tajfel H. (1959). Quantitative judgment in social perception. *British Journal of Psychology, 50*, 16–29.

Tajfel H. (1960). Nationalism in the modern world: The nation and the individual. *The Listener, 63*, 846–847.

Tajfel H. (1974). Social identity and intergroup behaviour. *Social Science Information, 13*, 65–93.

Tajfel H. (1977). The achievement of group differentiation. In H. Tajfel (Ed.), *Differentiation between social groups: Studies in the social psychology of intergroup relations* (pp. 77–98). European Monographs in Social Psychology Number 14). London: Academic Press.

Tajfel H. (Ed.) (1978). *Differentiation between social groups: Studies in the social psychology of intergroup relations.* London: Academic Press.

Tajfel H. (1981a). Social stereotypes and social groups. In J. C. Turner & H. Giles (Eds.), *Intergroup behaviour* (pp. 144–167). Oxford: Blackwell.

Tajfel H. (1981b). *Human groups and social categories: Studies in social psychology.* Cambridge: Cambridge University Press.

Tajfel H. (1982). Experiments in a vacuum. In J. Israel & H. Tajfel (Eds.), *The context of social psychology: A critical assessment.* Oxford: Academic Press.

Tajfel H., Billig M., Bundy R. P., & Flament C. (1971). Social categorisation and intergroup behaviour. *European Journal of Social Psychology, 1*, 149–177.

Tajfel H., & Turner J. C. (1979). An integrative theory of intergroup conflict. In W. G. Austin & S. Worchel (Eds.), *The social psychology of intergroup relations* (pp. 33–47). Monterey, CA: Brooks/Cole.

Tajfel H., & Turner J. (1986). The social identity theory of intergroup behavior. In S. Worchel & W. Austin (Eds.), *The psychology of intergroup relations* (pp. 7–24). Chicago: Nelson-Hall.

Tajfel H., & Wilkes A. (1963). Classification and quantitative judgment. *British Journal of Psychology, 54*, 101–114.

Taliaferro J. W. (2004). *Balancing risks: Great power intervention in the periphery.* Ithaca, NY: Cornell University Press.

Tate W. F. (2008). Geography of opportunity: Poverty, place, and educational outcomes. *Educational Researcher, 37*, 397–411.

Taylor C. (2007). *A secular age*. Cambridge, MA: Harvard University Press.

Taylor C. (1992). *Sources of the self*. Cambridge: Cambridge University Press.

Thaler R. H. (2015). *Misbehaving: The making of behavioral economics*. New York: W.W. Norton.

Thompson E. P. (1971). The moral economy of the English crowd in the eighteenth century. *Past and Present, 50*, 76–136.

Thompson R., Russell L., & Simmons R. (2014). Space, place and social exclusion: An ethnographic study of young people outside education and employment. *Journal of Youth Studies, 17*, 63–78.

Thomson R., Henderson S., & Holland J. (2003). Making the most of what you've got? Resources, values and inequalities in young women's transitions to adulthood. *Educational Review, 55*, 33–46.

Tileagă C. (2013). *Political psychology: Critical perspectives*. Cambridge: Cambridge University Press.

Tilmans K., Van Vree F., & Winter J. (Eds.) (2010). *Performing the past: Memory, history and identity in modern Europe*. Amsterdam: Amsterdam University Press.

Tip L. K., Zagefka H., Gonzalez R., Brown R., Cinirella M., & Na X. (2012). Is support for multiculturalism threatened by…threat itself? *International Journal of Intercultural Relations, 36*, 22–30.

Travis, A. (2015). Oliver Letwin blocked help for black youth after 1985 riots. *The Guardian*. Retrieved July 6, 2016 from http://www.theguardian.com/politics/2015/dec/30/oliver-letwin-blocked-help-for-black-youth-after-1985-riots

Turner J. C. (1982). Towards a cognitive redefinition of the social group. In H. Tajfel (Ed.), *Social identity and intergroup relations* (pp. 15–40). Cambridge: Cambridge University Press.

Turner J. C., Hogg M. A., Oakes P. J., Reicher S. D., & Wetherell M. S. (1987). *Rediscovering the social group: A self-categorization theory*. Oxford & New York: Blackwell.

Turner R. H., & Killian L. M. (1972). *Collective behaviour*. Englewood Cliffs: Prentice-Hall.

Tversky A., & Kahneman D. (1974). Judgment under uncertainty: Heuristics and biases. *Science, 185*, 1124–1131.

Uluğ, Ö. M. (2016). *Subjective understandings of the Kurdish conflict: A Q methodological investigation among parliamentarians, experts and lay people in Turkey* (Unpublished doctoral dissertation). Jacobs University, Bremen, Germany.

US Riot Commission (1968). *Report of the National Advisory Commission on Civil Disorders*. New York: Bantam.

Vickers M. (1998). *Between Serb and Albanian: A history of Kosovo*. London: Hurst.

Vignoles V. (2011). Identity motives. In S. J. Schwartz & V. L. Vignoles (Eds.), *Handbook of identity theory and research* (pp. 403–430). New York: Springer.

Vincent A. (1992). *Modern political ideologies*. Oxford: Blackwell.

Verkuyten M., & Brug P. (2004). Everyday ways of thinking about multiculturalism. *Ethnicities, 4*, 53–74.

Verkuyten M., & Thijs J. (2013). Multicultural education and inter-ethnic attitudes: An intergroup perspective. *European Psychologist, 18*, 179–190.

Vollhardt J. R. (2009a). Altruism born of suffering and prosocial behavior following adverse life events: A review and conceptualization. *Social Justice Research, 22*, 53–97.

Vollhardt J. R. (2009b). The role of victim beliefs in the Israeli-Palestinian conflict: Risk or potential for peace? *Peace and Conflict: Journal of Peace Psychology, 15*, 135–159.

Vollhardt J. R., & Bilali R. (2008). Social psychology's contribution to the psychological study of peace: A review. *Social Psychology, 39*, 12–25.

Vollhardt J. R., & Bilewicz M. (2013). After the genocide: Psychological perspectives on victim, bystander, and perpetrator groups. *Journal of Social Issues, 69*, 1–15.

Vollhardt J. R., Mazur L. B., & Lemahieu M. (2014). Acknowledgment after mass violence: Effects on psychological well-being and intergroup relations. *Group Processes and Intergroup Relations, 17,* 306–323.

Von Benda-Beckmann B. (2011). Imperialist air war: East German academic research and memory politics reflected in the work of Olaf Groehler. In H. Schmidt & A. Seidel-Arpaci (Eds.), *Narratives of trauma: Discourses of German wartime suffering in national and international perspective* (pp. 33–58). New York: Rodopi.

Waddell G., & Burton A. K. (2006). *Is work good for your health and well being?* London: The Stationery Office.

Wagner U., Christ O., & Heitmeyer W. (2010). Anti-immigration bias. In J. F. Dovidio, M. Hewstone, P. Glick, & V. M. Esses (Eds.), *Handbook of prejudice, stereotyping, and discrimination* (pp. 361–376). Los Angeles, CA: Sage.

Wagner W., Duveen G., Verma J., & Themel M. (2000). "I have some faith and at the same time I don't believe"–cognitive polyphasia and cultural change in India. *Journal of Community and Applied Psychology, 10,* 301–314.

Wagner U., & Hewstone M. (2012). Intergroup contact. In L. R. Tropp (Ed.), *The Oxford handbook of intergroup conflict* (pp. 193–209). New York: Oxford University Press.

Wagoner B. (2015). Collective remembering as a process of social representation. In G. Sammut, E. Andreouli, G. Gaskell, & J. Valsiner (Eds.), *The Cambridge handbook of social representations* (pp. 143–162). Cambridge: Cambridge University Press.

Walby S. (2003). The myth of the nation-state: Theorizing society and polities in a global era. *Sociology, 37,* 529–546.

Waldzus S., Mummendey A., Wenzel M., & Boettcher F. (2004). Of bikers, teachers and Germans: Groups' diverging views about their prototypicality. *British Journal of Social Psychology, 4,* 385–400.

Walkerdine V. (2003). Reclassifying upward mobility: Femininity and the neo-liberal subject. *Gender and Education, 15,* 237–248.

Walkerdine V., & Bansel P. (2010). Neoliberalism, work and subjectivity: Towards a more complex account. In *The Sage handbook of identities* (pp. 492–507). Thousand Oaks, CA: Sage.

Waltz K. N. (1959). *Man, the state, and war.* New York: Columbia University Press.

Ward C. (2001). The ABC's of acculturation. In D. Matsumoto (Ed.), *The Handbook of culture and psychology* (pp. 411–445). Oxford: Oxford University Press.

Warr D. (2005a). Social networks in a "discredited" neighbourhood. *Journal of Sociology, 41,* 285–308.

Warr D. (2005b). There goes the neighbourhood: The malign effects of stigma. *Social City, 19,* 1–11.

Watson J. B. (1913). Psychology as the behaviorist views it. *Psychological Review, 20,* 158–177.

Wehr, P. (September 2006). Conflict Mapping. Beyond intractability. Retrieved March 9, 2016 from <http://www.beyondintractability.org/essay/conflict-mapping>.

Weis L. (2013). *Working class without work: High school students in a de-industrializing economy.* New York: Routledge.

Weissmark M. S. (2004). *Justice matters: Legacies of the Holocaust and World War II.* Oxford: Oxford University Press.

Welzer H., Moller S., & Tschuggnall K. (2002). *Opa war kein Nazi: National sozialismus und Holocaust im Familiengedächtnis.* Frankfurt: Fischer.

Wendt A. (1992). Anarchy is what states make of it: The social construction of power politics. *International Organization, 46,* 391–425.

Wendt A. (1999). *Social theory of international politics.* New York: Cambridge University Press.

Wertsch J. V. (2002). *Voices of collective remembering.* Cambridge: Cambridge University Press.

Wertsch J. V., & Roediger H. L. (2008). Collective memory: Conceptual foundations and theoretical approaches. *Memory, 3,* 318–326.

Wetherell G., Benson O. S., Reyna C., & Brandt M. J. (2015). Perceived value congruence and attitudes toward international relations and foreign policies. *Basic and Applied Social Psychology*, *37*, 3–18.

Wetherell M. (1996). Constructing social identities: The individual/social binary in Henri Tajfel's social psychology. In W. P. Robinson (Ed.), *Social groups and identities: Developing the legacy of Henri Tajfel* (pp. 269–284). Oxford: Butterworth Heinemann.

Wetherell M. (1998). Positioning and interpretative repertoires: Conversation analysis and post-structuralism in dialogue. *Discourse and Society*, *9*, 387–412.

Wexler P. (1983). *Critical social psychology*. Boston, MA: Routledge & Kegan Paul.

Whiston W. (1895). *Whiston's Josephus: The excelsior edition*. London: W. P. Nimmo.

White R. W. (1952/1966). *Lives in progress* (2nd ed.). New York: Holt, Rinehart & Winston.

Whitty G. (2001). Education, social class and social exclusion. *Journal of Education Policy*, *16*, 287–295.

Wiggins S. (2016). From Loughborough with love: How discursive psychology rocked the heart of social psychology's love affair with attitudes. In C. Tileagă & E. Stokoe (Eds.), *Discursive psychology: Classic and contemporary issues* (pp. 101–113). Abingdon: Routledge.

Wilkinson R., & Pickett K. (2009). *The spirit level: Why greater equality makes societies stronger*. Bloomsbury Publishing USA.

Williams, J., Greene, S., Doyle, E., Harris, E., Layte, R., McCoy, S., … O'Dowd, T. (2011). *Growing up in Ireland national longitudinal study of children. The lives of 9 year olds*. The Stationery Office. Retrieved from http://www.lenus.ie/hse/handle/10147/143172

Williams W. R. (2009). Struggling with poverty: Implications for theory and policy of increasing research on social class-based stigma. *Analyses of Social Issues and Public Policy*, *9*, 37–56.

Willig C. (2011). Cancer diagnosis as discursive capture: Phenomenological repercussions of being positioned within dominant constructions of cancer. *Social Science and Medicine*, *73*, 897–903.

Wohl M. J. A., & Branscombe N. (2008). Remembering historical victimization: Collective guilt for current ingroup transgressions. *Journal of Personality and Social Psychology*, *94*, 988–1006.

Wolchover, N. (2015). A fight for the soul of science. *Quanta Magazine*. Retrieved January 20, 2016 from https://www.quantamagazine.org/20151216-physicists-and-philosophers-debate-the-boundaries-of-science/

Wolff S. (2002). Conflict management in Northern Ireland. *International Journal on Multicultural Societies*, *4*, 1–30.

Wolpert L. (1992). *The unnatural nature of science*. London: Faber & Faber.

Wood M. J., Douglas K. M., & Sutton R. M. (2012). Dead and alive: Beliefs in contradictory conspiracy theories. *Social Psychological and Personality Science*, *3*, 767–773.

Wright S. C. (2001). Restricted intergroup boundaries: Tokenism, ambiguity, and the tolerance of injustice. In J. T. Jost & B. Major (Eds.), *The psychology of legitimacy: Emerging perspectives on ideology, justice, and intergroup relations* (pp. 223–254). New York: Cambridge University Press.

Wright S. C., & Boese G. (2015). Meritocracy and tokenism. In J. D. Wright (Ed.), *The international encyclopedia of the social and behavioral sciences* (2nd ed., pp. 239–245). Oxford: Elsevier.

Wright S. C., & Lubensky M. (2009). The struggle for social equality: Collective action vs. prejudice reduction. In S. Demoulin, J. P. Leyens, & J. F. Dovidio (Eds.), *Intergroup misunderstandings: Impact of divergent social realities* (pp. 291–310). New York: Psychology Press.

Young C. B., Fang D. Z., & Zisook S. (2010). Depression in Asian-American and Caucasian undergraduate students. *Journal of Affective Disorders*, *125*, 379–382.

Yzerbyt V. Y., Rocher S. J., & Schadron G. (1997). Stereotypes as explanations: A subjective essentialist view of group perception. In R. Spears, P. Oakes, N. Ellemers, & A. Haslam (Eds.), *The psychology of stereotyping and group life* (pp. 20–50). Oxford: Basil Blackwell.

Zagefka H., Tip L. K., Gonzalez R., Brown R., & Cinnirella M. (2012). Predictors of majority members' acculturation preferences: Experimental evidence. *Journal of Experimental Social Psychology, 48,* 654–659.

Zerubavel E. (1996). Social memories: Steps towards a sociology of the past. *Qualitative Sociology, 19,* 283–299.

Zerubavel E. (2004). *Time maps: Collective memory and the social shape of the past.* Chicago: The University of Chicago Press.

Zerubavel Y. (1995). *Recovered roots: Collective memory and the making of Israeli national tradition.* Chicago: University of Chicago.

Zick A., Pettigrew T. F., & Wagner U. (2008). Ethnic prejudice and discrimination in Europe. *Journal of Social Issues, 64,* 233–251.

Ziliak S. T., & McCloskey D. N. (2011). *The cult of statistical significance: How the standard error costs us jobs.* Michigan: University of Michigan Press.

Zimbardo P. G. (1969). The human choice: Individuation, reason, and order versus deindividuation, impulse, and chaos. *Nebraska Symposium on Motivation, 17,* 237–307.

Political Psychology: A Social Psychological Approach, First Edition.
Edited by Christopher J. Hewer and Evanthia Lyons.
© 2018 John Wiley & Sons Ltd. Published 2018 by John Wiley & Sons Ltd.